# FOR ALL THE SAINTS

"After reading *For All the Saints*, I felt as if I had walked and talked with some of the finest disciples who have lived and worked on the earth. In our day of drifting ideologies, apathy, discontent, and entitlement, our faith is strengthened by reading about exemplary people who have made and kept covenants. This thoughtful and well-written book is a spiritual record that is relevant and of great value today. It confirms the divine nature of mankind, reveals the hand of the Lord in individual lives, and establishes the direction of righteous and happy living."

—JULIE B. BECK, former Relief Society general president

"When John Winthrop settled Boston in 1630, he poetically envisioned a righteous colony that would rise up and become a 'city upon a hill.' The tale of that hardy band of settlers and the wide-ranging influence of their example and legacy has been told many times. Here, for the first time, Dayley provides a truly inspiring account of the rise of Boston's Latter-day Saint community—a narrative that in its own way proves Winthrop right again. Aided by the artistry of Dayley's style, this story indeed provides an exemplary light 'for all the saints,' if not all the world."

—MATTHEW S. HOLLAND, president of Utah Valley University

"With vivid anecdotes and flowing narrative, *For All the Saints* gives a fascinating view into how the gospel was restored to the ancestral lands of its founding prophets. The LDS Church began in New England, the cradle of religious liberty in the New World, and then moved westward. This book brings that compelling history full circle, home to its roots. And it evokes my profound gratitude to the Mormon pioneers of the 'reverse migration' back East, who built the foundation of faith upon which my family and so many others now stand."

—JANE CLAYSON JOHNSON, Award-winning journalist and author

"Kristen Smith Dayley's book *For All the Saints* is a wonderful read. It not only is an interesting history of the Church in New England as Boston as its hub, but its pages also capture inspiring and faith-building stories of members of the Church and how they built the Church in New England. No matter where you live, this book teaches us how to build the kingdom of God in any geographical area and how we should live our daily lives in serving others. I could not put the book down."

—NOLAN D. ARCHIBALD, Executive Chairman
of The Stanley Black & Decker Corporation

"Even if New England were not familiar to you as it is to me, the gathering and building will resonate in the heart of anyone committed to building the Kingdom of God anywhere in this world. It is aptly written For All The Saints. Because of lessons learned from living, its pages provide a pattern for any one of us who prays to be a builder. Thank you for the polishing and honing that gives us this joyous journey."

—ANN N. MADSEN, Senior Lecturer
in Ancient Scripture at Brigham Young University

"*For All the Saints* is an intimate, faith-promoting story of the growth of the Church in New England. The story is told through the inspiring experiences of some well-known Church leaders, including Joseph Smith, Brigham Young, John Taylor, and current General Authorities who studied and served in the Greater Boston area. *For All the Saints* also introduces us to many less recognizable yet equally admirable women and men whose sacrifices have helped fulfill the prophecies of strong stakes and beautiful temples in New England. Getting to know these Saints will stir fond memories for readers who have lived in that region and inspire those who haven't with the desire to visit soon and feel the spirit of the land of Joseph and Brigham."

—HENRY J. EYRING, administrator,
Brigham Young University–Idaho

"A deeply touching and inspiring book, *For All the Saints* illustrates the remarkable conviction and courage of Latter-day Saints in New England. It provides a unique window into the lives of countless unassuming individuals and families, whose steady acts of faith, service, and perseverance have created an extraordinary heritage and a miraculous harvest."

—RYAN MURPHY, associate director, Mormon Tabernacle Choir
(born and raised in New England)

"For those whose sojourns in the Boston area have cast a pebble on the lake of time, *For All the Saints* is an opportunity to see how the ripples have spread over the years . . . familiar names, familiar places, shared experiences across what is now generations. For those who haven't had a Boston experience, this is a fascinating microcosm of the growth of the Church and the myriad miracles associated with that growth in one corner of the vineyard."

—SCOTT BARRICK, general manager, Mormon Tabernacle Choir.

"This remarkable history is a wonderful tribute to the Lord's plan for His children in New England, and to the work of those whose hearts were not only receptive to the gospel message but who were willing to put the kingdom of God first above all else. It is an inspiring record of their trials and accomplishments and their sacrifices and blessings. This story of faith and service will stand alongside those of so many faithful Saints who have labored unceasingly to prepare the earth for the Savior's Second Coming. I look forward to sharing its messages with my children and grandchildren."

—STEVE WHEELWRIGHT,
president of Brigham Young University–Hawaii

"The story of the implantation and growth of The Church of Jesus Christ of Latter-day Saints in New England is a telling 're-enactment' of the landing of the Pilgrims at Plymouth Rock two centuries earlier. Faith, courage, and imagination have combined with an almost unique merger of the search for 'Faith and Reason' in a corner of the nation that had—and has still—unique roots in both. This book will warm the heart of those who participated. . . . It also provides a template for those today who seek to engage the spiritual in a world grown callused from a preoccupation with materialism."

—CHASE N. PETERSON, MD, President Emeritus
and Professor of Medicine, University of Utah;
previous Dean and Vice President, Harvard

FOREWORD BY
CLAYTON M. CHRISTENSEN

# FOR
## ~⚬~ ALL THE ~⚬~
# SAINTS

## KRISTEN SMITH DAYLEY

CFI
An Imprint of Cedar Fort, Inc.
Springville, Utah

This is not an official publication of The Church of Jesus Christ of Latter-day Saints. The opinions and views expressed herein belong solely to the author and do not necessarily represent the opinions or views of Cedar Fort, Inc. Permission for the use of sources, graphics, and photos is also solely the responsibility of the author.

ISBN 13: 978-1-4621-1064-3

Published by CFI, an imprint of Cedar Fort, Inc.
2373 W. 700 S., Springville, UT 84663
Distributed by Cedar Fort, Inc. www.cedarfort.com

LIBRARY OF CONGRESS CATALOGING-IN-PUBLICATION DATA

Dayley, Kristen Smith, 1971- author.
 For all the saints : lessons learned in building the kingdom / Kristen Smith Dayley.
   pages cm
 Includes bibliographical references and index.
 Summary: True stories that illustrate the great and marvelous things that the Lord can do through faithful, dedicated people.
  ISBN 978-1-4621-1064-3
 1. Mormons--Massachusetts--History. 2. Church of Jesus Christ of Latter-day Saints--Massachusetts--History. 3. Mormon Church--Massachusetts--History. I. Title.

BX8615.M37D39 2012
289.3'744--dc23

2012021822

Cover photography by Steve Porter
Illustrations by Angelina Carini Barlow
Cover design by Erica Dixon
Cover design © 2012 by Lyle Mortimer
Edited and typeset by Melissa J. Caldwell

Printed in the United States of America

10  9  8  7  6  5  4  3  2  1

TO MY PARENTS,

who introduced me to the city where my soul sings.

# CONTENTS

# FOREWORD

SEVERAL YEARS ago I was engaged in consulting for the senior executives for Intel. My research on disruptive innovation had convinced their chairman, Andy Grove, that Intel needed to go to the bottom of the market and launch a low-cost microprocessor that they subsequently named the Celeron.

During a break, Grove cornered me to ask, "Tell me how to do all of this."

I replied, "It's just like I said in my presentation, Andy. You'll need to create a new business unit. And you'll need to build a new sales force."

Grove (who rarely wastes words) retorted, "You are such a naïve academic, Clay. I asked you *how* to do it—and you told me *what* to do. I watched your presentation. I read your book. I know what to do. I just don't know how to do it!"

I stood there, judged by one of the deities of management. Grove was right. I was a naïve academic. I didn't know the difference between *how* and *what*.

In my service in the The Church of Jesus Christ of Latter-day Saints, I have seen the *what* but not *how* vignette played over and over. As a rule, when we do not succeed in the assignments that we have been asked to do, it rarely is because we are not motivated. Most of the time we know *what* we are supposed to do, and we *want* to do it. We just don't always know *how*.

Moses's father-in-law, Jethro, was a great help to Moses as he undertook the charge to lead and build the kingdom of God in Egypt. If you remember, Moses was helping every single person individually. After seeing this, Jethro said that he needed to choose some able men to spread responsibility. "And thou shalt teach them ordinances and laws, and shalt shew them the way wherein they must walk, and the work that they must do" (Exodus 18:20). And then Jethro said Moses needed to train them on *how* to do the work of the Lord.

What we have tried to do in this book is show you *how* the work of the Lord, and the building of His kingdom, came about in our area. The idea for this book emerged in 1995 as I served as high priests group leader in the Belmont Ward of the Boston Stake. I was struck one Sunday as I looked around our room in priesthood meeting that there was more education, achievement, faith, commitment, wisdom, and humility per square foot in that room than anywhere else on earth. That group could have run most corporations—or nations—with aplomb. We needed to harness more of this for the work of the Lord.

As members of this great Church, we often hear the phrase "building the kingdom of God." It is a beautiful image, a powerful vision, and something that we all want to be able to do. But much like Jethro talking to Moses about teaching others to be judges and Andy Grove talking to me, figuring out how to do this and what it looks like in daily life is a bit tricky.

About a month after my initial idea for this book, I stood in front of my fellow high priests. I introduced and proposed that we research and write a history of The Church of Jesus Christ of Latter-day Saints in New England. The goal, we decided, was that we distill from our history the principles and practices of building the kingdom of God. We wanted to find the universal *hows* so that they could be repeated for any time and any place.

We listed scores of people, ultimately numbering over two hundred, who we decided we needed to interview. In the image of J. Reuben Clark's magnificent sermon, "To Them of the Last Wagon" (1947), we resolved to interview the leaders in the front, for sure. But we agreed to interview many of those who toiled in the back of the company, and of those who were in between as well. It sampled the spectrum of the Saints. Every member of our high priests group but one raised their hands to sustain this endeavor. Those whose names are listed inside consecrated thousands upon thousands of hours and tens of thousands of dollars to interview these people where they now live—across the globe—and in person, whenever possible. We thought the project would take us three years, from start to finish. It took seventeen years instead. The reason is that each of us shouldered heavy callings in the Church that, combined with our families and professions, absorbed most of our time and energy.

It was exciting to gather, read, and then apply the stories and principles and have them influence our personal, daily actions. But then our problem was this: using this mass of information, how in the world could we distill from this a book—not just a history book, but a handbook—on how to build the kingdom of God? But more: We needed not just a cogent handbook, but a delightful book that was hard to put down; and not just an engaging book, but one that was so compelling and motivating that it made its readers instinctively stand up with resolve in their hearts and excitement in their feet that they would go and do the things from which the kingdom of God is built.

I spent days in deep prayer and fasting on this question: Where in the world could I find an author who could do this? The answer was Kristen Smith Dayley. I had known her parents, Cheryl and Lonnie. They have been heroes to Christine and me. Some of the adjectives that characterize the home in which they raised Kristen include "how-to," "delightful," and "engaging." When Kristen arrived to study at Harvard Law School, I was stuck from our first conversation that Kristen had questions about the restored gospel, but no doubts—a woman who is truly compelled to build the kingdom of God. I am grateful beyond words that with courage and commitment, she undertook the writing of this book.

Kristen, I pray that God will bless you and your family forever for your thousands of selfless hours to teach and inspire each of us. I feel taught and inspired.

Clayton M. Christensen

# ACKNOWLEDGMENTS

ALTHOUGH IT is impossible individually to thank each person who contributed to the seventeen-year project that has culminated in this book, I thank collectively the high priests and their spouses in the Belmont Ward. These are busy men and women—and yet month after month, year after year, they selflessly tracked down and interviewed the hundreds of people whose personal stories and histories have taught us so much about how to build the kingdom of God. And I thank the wonderful people we interviewed. They served the Lord when they were asked to take their position as the last wagon in their branches and their wards, as well as when they were asked to lead from the front. The perspective that they gave us on how to build the kingdom of God, and how to serve within it, is unmatched.

Not all of their stories and histories could fit into this volume. But nearly all have given us permission to put the transcripts of their interviews in the L. Tom Perry Special Collections in the Harold B. Lee Library at BYU. These are available to all who wish to study them—and I hope that many will, because there is so much more that we can learn from these Saints.

I was forty-three years old when we started this project. I am now sixty. Many of those who were old when we met with and interviewed them have subsequently passed away. We revere them, even as we now stand on their shoulders.

Gael and Laurel Ulrich and Claudia and Richman Bushman helped Karl Haglund define the scope and purpose of the project. Tony Kimball helped us decide who needed to be interviewed. Kori Tueller transcribed most of the recordings of the interviews, even as she cared for her young children and her graduate student husband, Michael. Elizabeth Young Christensen interviewed, with professionalism, people whose perspectives proved to be crucial as we were trying to finish this project. Karl Haglund and my wife, Christine Christensen, edited most of the transcripts.

I thank each of you for your sacrifice and inspiration. I pray that the Lord will bless you, even as you have blessed us.

*—Clayton Christensen*

I NEVER aspired to write a book. As such, there are many people I must thank, since this book would not exist if not for them.

Thank you to Clayton Christensen for his vision as to what this book could and should be, and for having the faith in me to accomplish that.

Thanks to the great editorial skills of Justine Dorton, along with her patience, insight, and direction, which helped me get my manuscript to a point where it was worthy of publication. After having been out of contact for many years, our paths crossed at a time when I needed her talent and skill. That was a direct answer to prayer.

My great appreciation to Professor Christensen's able assistants at the Harvard Business School, specifically JaNeece Thacker, Lisa Stone, and Emily Snyder, who helped me track down countless facts, individuals, and source materials over the course of the last several years. Knowing you were always willing to help was a tremendous comfort during this process. Sincere thanks also to Christine Christensen, who carefully and sensitively reviewed the final manuscript to make sure the accounts it contained were consistent with actual events.

Thanks to Angelina Barlow, who produced the charts and graphs in this book to clarify the places and timeframes referenced. Angelina was unfailingly professional, pleasant, and helpful, even when I asked ridiculous things of her on very short time frames! I am also indebted to

Elin Mcleod, who helped me communicate this book's message in other media, a talent she has generously lent me in past endeavors as well.

The deepest gratitude to my family and friends who encouraged me along the way, particularly Kristy and Dee Ann Ludwig. If it had not been for your insistence that this book needed to be published and your constant cheerleading, I suspect I would have given up the quest three or four roadblocks ago.

Love and appreciation to my husband, Marlowe Dayley, and our children, who have accommodated the countless hours invested in this project. When I started, I thought I could write the book in a year or two. Eight years later, I cannot say enough about their patience.

Thank you to the team at Cedar Fort, who was willing to take a risk on an unknown, first-time author.

Finally, and most of all, thank you to all the men and women who took the time to share their memories, insights, and testimonies through the oral histories on which this book is based. My life has been greatly enriched by your experiences and I am better as a result. It is ultimately because I felt so strongly that your stories needed to be shared with a wider audience that this book now exists. Thank you.

*—Kristen Smith Dayley*

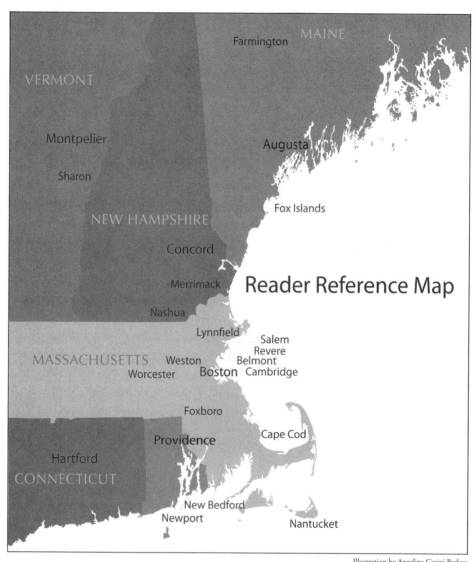

Illustration by Angelina Carini Barlow

New England—Points of Interest

# CONGREGATIONAL GROWTH CHART

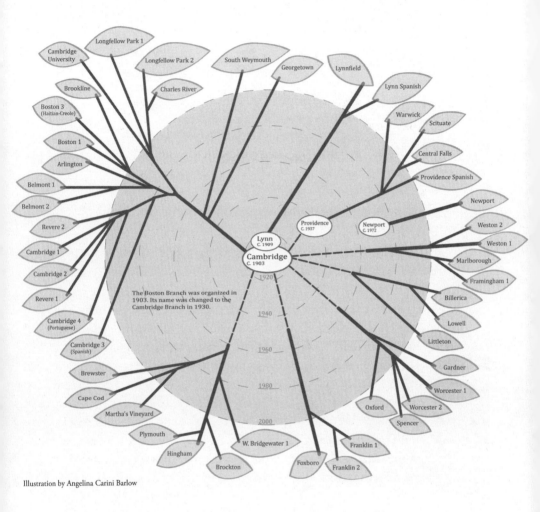

Illustration by Angelina Carini Barlow

This illustration shows those present-day wards and branches that can trace their roots to the original Cambridge Branch and other early branches of the Church within the greater Boston area. Solid lines indicate when these congregations were formed and branches provide a simplified representation of the organizational divisions that have resulted in new Church units.

# INTRODUCTION

WHEN THE Cambridge, Massachusetts, chapel at Longfellow Park was dedicated by President David O. McKay in 1956, it was the first building specifically constructed as a place for Latter-day Saints to meet and worship in New England. As overjoyed members gathered from distances as far away as Halifax, Nova Scotia, to celebrate, they recognized that a "chapel is not an end in itself." A commemorative dedicatory program documenting events that led to the construction of the meetinghouse ended with their bold aspiration for the future: "[T]he saints hope and pray that soon their faith and works will bring a Stake of Zion as prophesied; and that the time will come when a Latter-day Saint Temple will overlook the Charles River as it flows on to the sea, along the course trod by the Patriots who lived and fought and died that this land might fulfill its destiny."[1]

Forty-four years later, on Sunday, October 1, 2000, the foresight of these visionary members of The Church of Jesus Christ of Latter-day Saints was rewarded when President Gordon B. Hinckley dedicated the Boston Temple. The dedication attracted the attention of Church members around the world, as the temple perched atop the granite ledge in Belmont, Massachusetts, became the Church's one hundredth operating temple. An impressive milestone in itself, the temple was completed and dedicated just two and a half years after President Hinckley announced at the conclusion of the April 1998 general conference that the Church had nearly fifty operating temples, but needed twice that number to meet the needs of its members.

Nancy Call, a young, single sister from the Longfellow Park Ward, was asked to direct the youth choir that would sing outside the temple prior to the dedicatory services as well as during the cornerstone ceremony. As she prayerfully selected the songs that the youth from the Boston Massachusetts Stake would sing, she felt keenly impressed to choose the traditional processional hymn, "For All the Saints." Questioned repeatedly about her unconventional selection, Nancy bore fervent testimony of the truth the Spirit had witnessed to her: the dedication of a temple in Boston was the fulfillment of promises made not only to faithful, living members of the Church, but also to America's Founding Fathers, pilgrims, and patriots; pioneers of the Restoration; and generations of Saints long since departed, whose accounts are told in the Book of Mormon.

And so it was that the anthem notes accompanying William How's stirring text pealed through the crisp autumn air as the prophet and others took part in sealing the cornerstone of the Boston Temple, celebrating the ties that connect the faithful of all generations.

*For all the Saints who from their labors rest,*
*Who thee by faith before the world confessed,*
*Thy name, O Jesus, be forever blest.*
*Alleluia, Alleluia.*

*Oh, may thy soldiers, faithful, true, and bold,*
*Fight as the Saints who nobly fought of old,*
*And win with them the victor's crown of gold.*
*Alleluia, Alleluia.*

*Thou art our rock, our fortress, and our might;*
*Thou, Lord, our captain in the well-fought fight;*
*Thou, in the darkness drear, our one true light.*
*Alleluia, Alleluia.*

*And when the strife is fierce, the warfare long,*
*Steals on the ear the distant triumph song,*
*And hearts are brave again, and arms are strong.*
*Alleluia, Alleluia.*

*From earth's wide bounds, from ocean's farthest coast,*
*Through gates of pearl streams in the countless host,*
*Singing to Father, Son, and Holy Ghost.*
*Alleluia, Alleluia.*

Today the Boston Temple stands with over 130 other LDS temples to bless the lives of present and future members of the Church, while the covenants and ordinances made and received within its walls bless countless numbers who have gone before.

The stories recounted in this book are a tribute to the lives of those Saints who made the establishment of many stakes of Zion and the building of a temple in New England a reality today. They are stories of faith, dedication, and a willingness to serve. Out of necessity, these accounts are only the smallest representation of the experiences and contributions shared by faithful men and women who laid the foundation for these blessings. While the details of these stories relate specifically to the Church's growth within Boston and other portions of New England, the principles they illustrate and lessons they teach are not unique to any particular geography. Indeed, the personal reflections and testimonies related herein are the common lot of latter-day pioneers in all parts of the Lord's vineyard and the spiritual legacy and promise of all who faithfully seek to follow the Lord's commands and build up His kingdom.

In other words, these chapters are written not just for those members who call or have called New England home—they are written for all the Saints.

FOR ALL THE SAINTS WHO FROM THEIR LABORS REST,
WHO THEE BY FAITH BEFORE THE WORLD CONFESSED,
THY NAME, O JESUS, BE FOREVER BLEST.

# THE PATHS THY
# SAINTS HAVE TROD

THE ROOM was uncomfortably silent as the question hung in the evening air. The Presbyterian meetinghouse was full of people who had come to hear the curious teachings of the visiting Mormon elder, but none volunteered when the sermon concluded and the stranger asked if anyone present would provide him some food and a night's lodging "in the name of Jesus."[1]

Impatient and bemused, Daniel Spencer finally stood. "I will entertain you, sir, for humanity's sake."[2] The owner and operator of one of the largest stores in West Stockbridge, Massachusetts, Daniel was not affiliated with any church but was recognized for his influence and fairness and had obtained use of the meetinghouse for the missionary. Daniel frequently housed traveling preachers at his hotel, but this evening he changed course and took the lonely elder into his sizable home, presenting him with a new suit of clothing the next morning.

The missionary's preaching attracted a great deal of ridicule and hostility in town. Disgusted by the malevolence to which the visitor was subjected by local preachers and self-professed Christians, Daniel "resolved to investigate the cause of this enmity and unchristianlike manifestation."[3] Closing his establishment and secluding himself in his office, Daniel commenced a two-week study of the Book of Mormon. Pondering in his study during this period, Daniel suddenly burst into tears, exclaiming to his son, "My God, the thing is true, and as an honest man I must embrace it; but it will cost me all I have got on earth."[4]

Aware of the stir it would create, Daniel Spencer informed his townsmen that he had decided to be baptized by way of a public notice. On the appointed day, Daniel walked the town's main street to the banks of the river, followed by hundreds of West Stockbridge residents. As the baptism proceeded, "the profoundest respect and quiet were manifest by the vast concourse of witnesses, but also the profoundest astonishment."[5] Daniel's courageous action opened doors that led to the establishment of a branch within the town, but other residents manifested their feelings through actions that ultimately forced the close of his business.[6]

Orson and Catherine Spencer lived in Middlefield, Massachusetts, where Orson made his living as a Baptist minister. Daniel visited his brother in 1840 to share the account of his conversion, sparking a lengthy debate and discussion on the subject of Mormonism. After several days of this activity, Catherine exclaimed with exasperation, "Orson, you know this is true!" The family was baptized, costing Orson his paid ministry. Catherine's family responded by disowning her and revoking her share of her father's estate. Friends offered financial assistance if Catherine would leave her new faith, but she was undeterred. "I would rather abide with the Church in poverty, even in the wilderness, without their aid," said she, "than go to my unbelieving father's house and have all that he possesses."[7]

With little to keep them in Massachusetts, the brothers moved their families to Nauvoo. After the martyrdom of the Prophet Joseph, Daniel Spencer served as mayor of Nauvoo and later president of the Salt Lake Stake from 1849–68. Orson was the founding president of the University of Utah and his daughter, Aurelia Spencer Rogers, started the Primary organization.[8]

The Prophet Joseph Smith was born in Vermont, the progeny of several generations of New Englanders. He shared these roots with many of the men called to lead the newly restored Church, over two-thirds of whom hailed from Vermont, Massachusetts, Connecticut, and Maine. Yet it was not until 1832, after the Saints had moved to Kirtland, Ohio, to escape mounting prejudice and persecution in New York, that organized efforts to preach the gospel in New England commenced.

Orson Hyde, Samuel H. Smith, Lyman Johnson, and Orson Pratt were the first to heed the revelation, now found in Section 75 of the Doctrine and Covenants, calling for a number of elders to return to the eastern United States to proclaim the word of the Lord (see Doctrine and Covenants 75:13–14; 79:1; 99:1). Traveling on foot without purse or scrip, Orson Pratt and Lyman Johnson traveled over four thousand miles, preaching in Ohio, Pennsylvania, New Jersey, and New York before reaching New England, where they taught and baptized in Vermont, New Hampshire, and Connecticut.[9] Elder Hyde and Elder Smith took a different route and were the first missionaries of record to preach the gospel in Massachusetts. Arriving in Boston on Friday, June 22, 1832, Orson Hyde wrote that the pair "commenced preaching with great success." Four people were baptized within four days, and an additional seven converts joined the Church by July 5. This quick success attracted attention leading to publication of the first anti-Mormon leaflets, one of which read:

> It is well known to some of our fellow citizens that two preachers of the Mormonites, a fanatical sect, which originated a few years since in the western part of New York, have recently come to this city to propagate their strange and marvellous [sic] doctrines. . . .
>
> However, strange to relate, about fifteen persons in this city have been led away by these false doctrines [and] have been baptized and joined the Mormon Church . . .[10]

Interest in the missionaries' message continued and the first Boston branch, comprised of approximately thirty members, was organized before the end of the year.[11]

Jared Carter, a convert from Vermont, was similarly directed to "go again into the eastern countries . . . proclaiming glad tidings of great joy, even the everlasting gospel" (Doctrine and Covenants 79:1). Answering the call, Jared returned to his hometown and, together with his brother Simeon, shared his faith with his family, friends, and former townsmen. Within months, a branch of twenty-seven converts was organized, and by the end of 1832 there were one hundred members in Vermont.[12]

News of the Restored Church had reached Maine soon after its formation, but the first branches in the state were organized in the autumn of 1832 by Samuel Smith and Orson Hyde.[13] The most notable missionary work in the state, however, took place five years later on the Fox Islands, located off the state's coast. Weeks after his marriage to Pheobe Carter in Kirtland, Wilford Woodruff found himself increasingly preoccupied with the impression that he should preach the gospel in his wife's native state— Maine. Wilford relayed his feelings to the Quorum of the Twelve and was firmly advised to heed the prompting.[14] Wilford and his companion,

Jonathan Hale, reached the shores of North Fox Island (known today as North Haven) at 2:00 a.m. on Sunday, August 20, 1837. Despite the unusual hour, a kindly islander opened her door to the men and, after providing a place to rest and a warm breakfast, told her visitors of a Baptist meetinghouse five miles away.

The elders arrived at the chapel just before services and were invited to sit on the stand. After speaking to the pair, the minister told his congregation the men had a message to present at the meetinghouse that evening at 5:00 p.m. In his journal that night, Elder Woodruff wrote:

"Elder Hale and I went to the stand, and I arose with peculiar feelings and addressed the congregation for one hour. . . . I had much liberty in speaking, and informed the people that the Lord had raised up a prophet and organized His Church as in the days of Christ and the ancient apostles, with prophets, apostles, and the gifts as anciently."[15]

The missionaries left a copy of the Doctrine and Covenants with the Baptist minister, Mr. Newton. The minister read its contents and received a witness that the book was of God. Certain that accepting the elders' message would exact too dear a price, Mr. Newton responded by commencing an organized campaign against the Mormons.[16]

Over the course of the next week, Elders Woodruff and Hale delivered several discourses at the island's schoolhouses, and baptisms commenced. Desperate, Mr. Newton petitioned Mr. Douglas, the Methodist minister from South Fox Island with whom he had previously been at odds, to join his cause and "help him put down 'Mormonism.'"[17] Mr. Douglas cooperated, delivering a stirring condemnation against the Prophet Joseph and the Book of Mormon. Elder Woodruff delivered a rebuttal the following Sunday and continued to baptize until he and Elder Hale had baptized "every person who owned an interest in the Baptist meeting-house."[18] Mr. Douglas most likely regretted his participation when the two missionaries followed him back to South Fox Island and proceeded to baptize a large portion of his congregation.

"The excitement became great on both islands,"[19] Elder Woodruff wrote in his journal, and by the end of September the missionaries had baptized over one hundred people and organized branches on both Fox Islands. Pheobe Woodruff joined her husband when Elder Hale had to leave the islands in late autumn, and baptisms continued.[20]

The Woodruffs remained in Maine until autumn 1838, following Wilford's receipt of a letter from Thomas B. Marsh informing Elder Woodruff that he had been appointed to fill a vacancy in the Quorum of the Twelve. The letter instructed Elder Woodruff to leave for Missouri at once, but as he prepared to depart, Wilford felt impressed that he should "take with him those Saints from Maine who wished to gather."[21] Outfitting the new Saints for the journey was difficult and most of the island inhabitants "knew more about handling a shark than a horse,"[22] but eventually the Woodruffs reached Missouri accompanied by fifty-three of the Fox Island Saints.

Missionary work also commenced in Holliston, Massachusetts, during the 1830s with some success. Brigham Young's grandmother lived in nearby Hopkinton and town records indicate that Brigham was a resident of Holliston for a time, laboring as a blacksmith and baptizing new converts in the brook running by his shop.[23] A Holliston Branch was organized by Brigham Young and Willard Richards in the spring of 1837,[24] and Parley Pratt reported continued interest in the Church when he visited the following September:

> I gave a course of lectures in the town house, and [the] building was decently full at first, but the congregation continued to increase insomuch that some put ladders to the windows and listened from without by climbing to the second story. I baptized two persons in Holliston, and I think many more will come forward soon. Indeed, the work must be firmly rooted in the minds of many in that place, judging from the attention of the people who listened with intense interest through a regular course of instruction.[25]

John Haven, a deacon of the local Congregational Church and an uncle, by marriage, to Brigham Young, was dismayed to see several of his children embrace this new faith. His son-in-law, Albert Perry Rockwood, was one of the first Holliston residents to join the Church. Albert traveled to Kirtland in 1837 and was baptized there by Brigham Young. Instructed to return to Holliston to strengthen the Church in that area, Brother Rockwood found sentiment in the town increasingly antagonistic, spurred on in part by clergy who were alarmed to see large portions of their congregations defecting to the Mormons. Wilford Woodruff recounted visiting Brother Rockwood in a Cambridge, Massachusetts, jail where Albert had been incarcerated on questionable charges of a bad debt. After resolving the matter, Brother Rockwood gathered his family and left Holliston.[26]

By this time, John Haven too had found that he could not deny the truthfulness of the Book of Mormon.[27] Deacon Haven's conversion and subsequent move west to join the Saints sent shock waves through the town. Albert Perry Rockwood went on to serve as one of the first seven presidents of the First Quorum of the Seventy, but reaction to his decision to continue with the Mormon "delusion" is recorded in a family history compiled by relatives:

> An event untoward, unlooked for and incomprehensible, came to pass in this family in the spring of 1838. That religious humbug of Joe Smith and others, called Mormonism, was embraced by many in Holliston during that year, and among the number were our relatives, Albert P. and Nancy (Haven) Rockwood.
>
> From that day to this, they have defended the notions, followed the teachings, and endured the toils and hardships of this peculiar and deluded sect. He was with them in their pilgrimage from Missouri to Illinois, from thence back to the frontier settlements of Missouri again, and to Great Salt Lake City. He was one of the small party of pioneers who made a tour of exploration from Council Bluffs, Missouri, to the Utah Territory, in 1847. As one of the two "Captains of 100s," he was also in charge of building bridges and fording rivers. . . . Very few, in these days of progress, ingenuity and thrilling adventure, have lived a more chequered and toilsome life than Albert Perry Rockwood.[28]

Following the departure of the Rockwoods, a number of Latter-day Saint families chose to leave Holliston. The Mormon exodus of the 1840s was so significant that Holliston residents regarded it as a source of shame for decades after. As friends and neighbors packed their homes and cast lots with a strange, frontier-based sect, one resident wrote, "We tried to plead with them to change their minds."[29] Town records show more than one hundred residents "of all ages and conditions in life, from the prosperous man of business to the humblest worker"[30] who migrated west.

## Beginning Again

These migrations were not unique to the Fox Islands or Holliston. The desire to gather with other members and meet the Lord's prophet led many New England converts to leave their homes for Ohio, Missouri, and later Illinois, a trend often reinforced by local suspicion and animosity toward the Church. Due to this gradual migration, missionaries often found themselves re-introducing the message of the restored Church, despite early footholds in these same areas.

Such was the case with Freeman Nickerson, a missionary sent to

Massachusetts. Although a branch had been organized in Boston in 1832 and nearly twenty individuals within the city had been baptized by Brigham and Joseph Young in 1836, there were no members to be found when Elder Nickerson began preaching there on May 30, 1841.[31] Looking for opportunities to deliver his message, Elder Nickerson arranged to present "a public defense of Joseph Smith and the Golden Bible" under the auspices of the Boston Free Discussion Society.[32] A pamphlet advertising the lecture caught the eye of Abijah Tewkesbury, a local businessman who had read newspaper reports of the persecutions against Mormons in Missouri. Known publicly as an "unbeliever" when it came to religion, Mr. Tewkesbury decided to attend out of curiosity.

The rules of the Boston Free Discussion Society called for alternating presentations by persons with different viewpoints, which required Elder Nickerson to yield the floor to anyone who wanted to debate him. Elder Nickerson had no lack of opponents and skeptics, but his response to each challenge was the same: He testified that he had met the Prophet Joseph, had enquired of God to know whether the gospel was true, and had received divine assurance that it was. Despite the simplicity of this defense, one critic reported that "when Elder Nickerson spoke, he imparted a 'magnetizing influence,' which was 'wonderfully apparent.'"[33]

Abijah Tewkesbury sensed something unique in Elder Nickerson's message and began investigating the Church, eventually requesting baptism in the fall of 1841. Over the next six months, another thirty converts joined, and on March 9, 1842, the Boston Branch was reorganized at Brother Tewkesbury's shipping office located at 82 Commercial Street, a brick building off the Boston Harbor that served as the Church's first regular meeting place in the city.[34]

Erastus Snow, a contemporary of Elder Nickerson, was asked to labor in another area of Massachusetts. Elder Snow hailed from Vermont, where he had heard and believed the testimonies of Orson Pratt and Luke Johnson a decade prior in 1832.[35] Erastus had been serving as a missionary in Pennsylvania and New Jersey in the summer of 1841 when Hyrum Smith asked if he would be willing to go to Salem, Massachusetts, "and try to establish the Kingdom in that City."[36]

Five years prior, in August 1836, Hyrum had visited Salem with his brother Joseph, Sidney Rigdon, and Oliver Cowdery. The impetus for the trip was a story told by a convert of a treasure hidden in the cellar of a Salem home. The Kirtland Saints were facing serious financial pressures, aggravated by the destitute condition of new members flocking to Ohio, and the trio hoped to discover funds that would alleviate the Church's burdens.[37] Shortly after their arrival, the Lord chastened the men, describing their motivation as "follies." Nonetheless, the Lord counseled, "I have much treasure in this city for you, for the benefit of Zion, and many people in this city, whom I will gather out in due time for the benefit of Zion" (Doctrine and Covenants 111:1–2). Hyrum, Joseph, Sidney, and Oliver spent a month in Salem preaching publicly and going door to door, but even this treasure proved elusive and they discovered little interest.[38]

Elder Snow found the request troubling, even after Hyrum provided him a copy of the revelation referencing treasures in Salem. Erastus had looked forward to returning to Nauvoo in the autumn and, in a letter addressed to Hyrum Smith and William Law, admitted that he initially found their counsel "somewhat repugnant to [his] feelings."[39] Only after Erastus's wife, Artimesia, assured him that they could delay their return home, did Elder Snow seriously ponder the calling, describing his decision-making process as follows:

> I felt willing to do the will of the Lord; I prayed earnestly to know His will, and His Spirit continually whispered to go to Salem. I also thought of the Apostles who cast lots to see which should take the place of Judas. I, therefore, after writing on one ballot 'Nauvoo' and on the other 'Salem' prayed earnestly that God would show by the ballot which way I should go, and I drawed the ballot that had 'Salem' on it twice in succession; and then I resolved as soon as I filled the appointments I had out I would go to Salem.[40]

Destitute of means to support his family and wary that he was being asked to labor in an unfamiliar and "superstitious place among enemies" to the Church,[41] Elder Snow prayed that the Lord would open a way before him. Joining Benjamin Winchester, Erastus started for Salem on August 20, 1841. The two found lodging in the city for $3.50 a week, the cheapest available, and, after traversing the area to locate a meeting place, secured use of the Masonic Lodge by way of solicited donations. Newspaper advertisements and an eight-page pamphlet summarizing their message led to strong attendance, but few results. "It was a long time before I could get people to take notice of me more than to come and hear and go away again," Elder Snow wrote.[42]

A turning point came when Reverend A. G. Comings, a Baptist preacher, began using his newspaper, the *Genius of Christianity*, to launch a series of bitter accusations against the Church. Reverend Comings refused to let the missionaries use his publication to respond to his charges but agreed to debate Elder Snow in a series of meetings. The debate took place over six nights and attracted several hundred observers. Unwittingly, the minister's fiery opposition to Mormonism sparked interest in many who would not otherwise have investigated the Church. As the discussions wore on, Elder Snow wrote that "the public feeling continued to turn against my opponent, for his arguments were chiefly epithets and insults."[43]

After months of preaching, Elder Snow's efforts were rewarded. Reporting to Hyrum Smith and William Law, Elder Snow wrote:

> I did not baptise [sic] any until the latter part of November, and had I not known that Jesus had many sheep in this city, I think I should have been disheartened and not tarried to reap where I had sown, for this is the only place in which I ever preached so long without baptizing. The first man I baptised [sic] here was one who was an infidel until I came here. The saints now number 36 including five in Lynn who attend meeting here, all strong in faith, and enjoying the Holy Spirit, and scores are believing. I have many calls for preaching and visiting people in all parts of this city and in the neighboring villages. . . . Those baptized are respectable and good livers, but not wealthy.[44]

"Mormonism is advancing with a perfect rush in this city," the *Salem Register* reported,[45] and the Masonic Lodge was no longer adequate for the crowds that gathered to hear Elder Snow. To accommodate the interest, three men in the community took it upon themselves to rent a new building that would seat six hundred. By March 1, 1842, members from Salem and the nearby communities of Lynn and Marblehead comprised a good branch, and by June of that year there were ninety members of record, including one Hyrum K. Bryant, who had previously been an elder in Reverend Comings's congregation and had served as moderator of their debates.[46]

Nearly ten years after the first missionaries were instructed to travel to the "eastern countries," proselyting efforts were yielding strong harvests throughout New England. Elder Eli P. Maginn arrived in Peterborough, New Hampshire—a town where as many as 230 people are reported to have joined the Church during the 1840s—and organized a branch in 1841.[47] Addressing church leaders at a conference in Salem the following year, Elder Maginn declared "he was almost exhausted from excessive labors, having the charge of four or five large branches, all of which he had built up the past year."[48]

A conference held at Boylston Hall in downtown Boston in February 1843, included representatives from thirteen local branches,[*] comprised of 793 members within Massachusetts and southern New Hampshire.[49] A local paper, the *Boston Bee*, reported on the meeting, noting that the participants assembled at an early hour and the event was attended by a "respectable assembly of all sects and denominations, both infidel and Christian." The article went on to state:

> In the short space of about fifteen months, a society that was only known among us by reports, now actually numbers near one thousand in this immediate vicinity, and their preachers seem imbued with a spirit and determination to carry every thing before them; for, in fact, they all seem to have the Bible at the end of their tongue. . . . On Sabbath morning, at nine o'clock, the ice was brushed away, and eight of our citizens were very decently buried in the river, after the ancient order, by Elder Adams, who seems a perfect water fowl.[50]

A non-member who attended the conference recorded his impressions in a letter to the editor, under the pen "A seeker after truth," as follows:

> Dear Sir, I wish through the medium of your valuable paper to make some remarks concerning the Latter-day Saints or Mormons, as people in general appear to be entirely ignorant of their doctrine. I had been led, from out door and newspaper reports, to believe they were people of the worst character—a sect who denied the Bible and substituted another book in its stead; and in short, that they were everything that was bad. Curiosity led me to their meeting at the Boylston Hall, and I can truly say I was astonished and most agreeably disappointed. First a beautiful hymn was read and sung. Then a Prayer, . . . after which a text was chosen from the New Testament

---

* Branches and membership represented at this conference were as follows: Boston Branch (114 members represented by Freeman Nickerson); Petersboro, NH Branch (115 members represented by E.P. Maginn); Gilsum, NH Branch (30 members represented by E.P. Maginn); Lowell, MA (60 members represented by E.P. Maginn); New Salem, MA (45 members represented by E.P. Maginn); Wendell, MA (50 members represented by E.P. Maginn); Northbridge, MA (35 members represented by E.P. Maginn); Leverett, MA (35 members represented by E.P. Maginn); Salem, MA (110 members represented by Erastus Snow); Georgetown, MA (32 members represented by Erastus Snow); New Bedford, MA (96 members represented by Hutchings); Millbury, MA (11 members represented by Benson); Cape Cod, MA (35 members represented by T. Nickerson); 25 members not organized.

from which the speaker descanted at considerable length; and I must say that I never heard a more able sermon. . . . The doctrine certainly appears to be plausible, consistent and in accordance with that laid down in the Scriptures. I have been induced to make these remarks from a conviction that this people have been grossly slandered and defamed. . . . If they are wrong, the world ought to know it; and if they are right, it is of vital importance that their doctrine should be widely disseminated.[51]

Whether "A seeker after truth" ultimately cast his lot with the Saints is not known, but many did and, by so doing, drastically altered the course of their lives. Emmeline B. Wells was fourteen and pursuing a teaching certificate at the New Salem Academy when her mother and three younger siblings were baptized after being taught by Elder Eli Maginn. Emmeline hoped to pursue a teaching and literary career in New England, but she recognized the truth of Elder Maginn's message and was baptized on March 1, 1842, against the backdrop of protests and criticism from friends, associates, and mentors. After her graduation at age fifteen, Emmeline began teaching school and married James Harris (also fifteen), the son of the presiding elder of the New Salem Branch who, like Emmeline's mother, was anxious to see his children marry within their new faith.

In the spring of 1844, Emmeline and James moved to Nauvoo. The Prophet Joseph Smith was murdered within a few weeks of their arrival, following which Emmeline's parents-in-law apostatized. After losing a baby, Emmeline was widowed when her young husband was killed in an accident. Her mother died a year later in New Salem. Despite this quick succession of paralyzing losses, Emmeline began teaching again and joined the trek to Utah. There, Sister Wells served thirty-seven years as editor of *The Women's Exponent*, a semi-monthly publication for LDS women, and at age eighty-two was called as the fifth general president of the Relief Society organization.[52]

## After the Martyrdom

The growth of the Church in New England took a defining course change following the Prophet Joseph's death. In the spring of 1844, many of the apostles had been sent to the eastern states to supervise missionary activities and publicize Joseph Smith's candidacy for the United States presidency. On June 20, 1844, Joseph penned a letter to Brigham Young asking him to return to Nauvoo immediately.[53] A week later, on June 27, 1844, both Joseph and Hyrum Smith were killed by assassins in Carthage, Illinois.

Unaware of these events, Brigham Young presided over a state convention at the Melodeon Hall in Boston on July 1, 1844, where several elders and members of the Quorum of the Twelve campaigned for Joseph Smith's presidential bid. After the convention, Brigham Young traveled to Salem to visit local members and his daughter Vilate, who attended finishing school there. Rumors of the Carthage murders began circulating among the Saints during Brigham's visit,[54] but Brigham's own account indicates that it was not until July 16, when he and Orson Pratt were in Peterboro, New Hampshire, that these rumors were confirmed by a letter from Nauvoo. Devastated, Brigham immediately set off for Boston.[55]

Similarly unaware of Joseph's death, Wilford Woodruff left Boston with the intent of visiting the remaining Saints on the Fox Islands. He was boarding a steamer from Portland, Maine, when a man on the dock approached Wilford's father-in-law, Ezra Carter, waving a newspaper and crying, "Father Carter, Joseph and Hyrum Smith have been martyred—they have been murdered in Carthage Jail!" As soon as Elder Woodruff saw the paper, the Spirit bore witness that the report was true. With the bell of the steamer ringing, Wilford retrieved his trunk, disembarked, and began his return trip to Boston.[56]

Arriving in Boston on July 17, Elder Woodruff reunited with Brigham Young. Unable to speak, they walked to the home of a Sister Voce, located behind the Massachusetts State House. "We each took a seat and veiled our faces," Elder Woodruff wrote. "We were overwhelmed with grief and our faces were soon bathed in a flood of tears."[57] Together with Orson Pratt, Wilford Woodruff, and Heber C. Kimball, Brigham Young began planning their return to Nauvoo and sent out a letter calling all missionaries back to Illinois. After preaching to the Boston Saints on Sunday and ordaining thirty-two elders, Brigham Young left the area on July 24, 1844, joined by other members of the Twelve who had been laboring in New England and New York.[58] The apostles' departure was followed by that of the missionaries, including Erastus Snow, who was serving in Vermont when he got the news.[59]

With the departure of leaders and missionaries, contact between the body of the Saints in Illinois and the eastern branches was sporadic. Wilford Woodruff visited Boston in October 1844 and found the Church doing well.[60] A year later, Jedediah Grant reported that "Boston is blessed with more Saints than any other city in the Eastern States," with a branch comprised of three hundred to four hundred members.[61] This mass of eastern Saints was temporary, however, as the "spirit of gathering" that had always affected New England congregations took on a new urgency. In May 1846, a conference was convened to determine the most expedient means of moving the Saints west.[62] Within the passage of a year, William I. Appleby, then president of the Eastern States Mission, wrote that numbers were down to "about thirty true hearted Saints in the city" of Boston,[63] as the bulk of the New England Saints had already traveled west and those with access to means were preparing to join them.[64]

Efforts to help remaining Saints emigrate to Utah continued through the beginning of the Civil War, but missionary activity effectively ceased in New England following the Martyrdom, and the Eastern States Mission was discontinued in 1850. The mission briefly reorganized in 1854 with John Taylor as president, but closed in 1858 when Brigham Young called outlying settlers and missionaries back to Utah to defend their homes against threats from the federal army in 1857. The mission reopened in 1865, only to be dissolved once more in 1869.[65] Records show a branch organized in Providence, Rhode Island, in 1857 and a Sunday School Jubilee held there in 1876,[66] but Church activity in New England was largely dormant for three decades. Rumors of polygamy circulated as East Coast branches and congregations disappeared. The Church, led largely by former New Englanders, was soon regarded as little more than a Utah Territory curiosity.

## The Reverse Migration

In 1891, eight graduates of Brigham Young College in Logan, Utah, traveled to Cambridge, Massachusetts, in the company of Dr. J. M. Tanner to pursue studies at the educational institutions for which Cambridge is famed. One member of the group was John A. Widtsoe, who began studying at Harvard University when he was 19.[67] A man who went on to preside over the Utah Agricultural College (now Utah State University) and the University of Utah, John worried he was out of his element. Writing of his experience, he recalled:

"Classwork had scarcely begun when I was stricken by a terrific attack of homesickness—my first and last attack. . . . I suspect that the cause of this attack was a hidden fear of my ability to hold my own in

17

this great institution and in competition with students prepared in the famous schools of the land. Such fear, if it existed, vanished after the first examinations."[68]

Academic insecurities were not all the future apostle found himself confronting as an adherent to a religion that was regarded as entirely strange and foreign within his new community of scholars.

"At that time I was having my religious battles. Was Mormonism what it pretended to be? Did Joseph Smith tell the truth? I read, listened, compared, thought, prayed. It was a real search for truth. Out of it in time came the certain knowledge that the restored gospel is true and that Joseph Smith was indeed a Prophet, and a restorer of the simple true gospel of Jesus Christ. There has never been any doubt about it since that time of deep study and prayer."[69]

Dr. Tanner's initial cohort of students was followed by handfuls of LDS students, male and female, anxious to expand their educational opportunities in Cambridge. This trickle of students between Utah and Massachusetts was concurrent with the reopening of the Eastern States Mission in 1893, headquartered in Brooklyn, New York. The mission was comprised of eight conferences, of which the New England Conference was only one, with boundaries extending from Virginia on the south to the Canadian Maritime Provinces on the north. Within this immense geography, President Job Pingree's first task was to locate former members and friends of the Church. Searching for Saints, President Pingree was able to locate the remnants of only one branch, and the statistical report at the close of 1893 listed a meager fifty-five members in the eastern United States and Canada. Hardy missionaries who traveled without purse or scrip and often slept under the stars increased this number to ninety-six the following year.[70]

Proselyting work was slow, and prejudice and misunderstanding were prevalent. Following a meeting of the New England Conference in Providence, Rhode Island, in 1900, discouraged missionaries canceled meetings for the summer, given abysmally poor attendance.[71] Missionaries in Boston were denied permission to hold street meetings for a period of years, after which a group of local ministers began a campaign of organized opposition. With more impediments than opportunities, it took ten years to organize a branch in New England, located in Boston and known as the New England Branch of the Eastern States Mission.[72] President John McQuarrie of the Eastern States Mission saw the 1903 formation as a major victory since "there were no Saints and very few friends in the city of Boston" just eighteen months previous.[73]

With limited occasions to meet with other members, Saints from Boston and New York happily traveled to Sharon, Vermont, to join the prophet, Joseph F. Smith, and a number of prominent Church leaders to celebrate the one hundredth anniversary of Joseph Smith's birth on December 23, 1905. The festivities included a dedication of the 38½-foot-high granite shaft monument, placed into position just ten days prior.[74] Speaking at the event, President Francis M. Lyman of the Quorum of the Twelve referenced the fundamental ties the Church had to the area. "We are intensely interested in Vermont," he stated. "We are descended of stock from New England—from Massachusetts, New Hampshire, Rhode Island, and Vermont."[75]

Yankee pedigree notwithstanding, progress was slow and marked by individual events. Missionaries organized a Mutual Improvement Association in Boston in 1908. A year later, a branch was organized in Lynn, Massachusetts;[76] a small Sunday School began meeting in Providence, Rhode Island; and the first cottage meeting in many years was held in New Haven, Connecticut.[77] Local missionaries reported persistent rumors that elders were trying to "ship women to Utah,"[78] and a missionary writing for the Eastern States Mission in the Church's *Improvement Era* in 1919 opined that Maine and New Hampshire were "the most impregnable, when it comes to teaching the plan of life and salvation, of all the states in our Country."[79]

The Boston-based branch was primarily comprised of students, and it was not until 1915 that the first "resident" was called to lead the group. All Church activities up to that point had been organized and led by the Eastern States Mission. To address the congregation's natural influx and outflow, this foray into local leadership was entrusted to Frank Brown, director of the Joseph Smith farm, in the summer and passed to visiting students in the autumn. This change allowed branch members to take on more responsibility but also led to frequent turnover in leadership.[80]

Claire and Rulon Robison were unusual—Westerners who chose to stay east following Rulon's music studies.[81] When the first Relief Society in New England was organized under the auspices of the Boston Branch in the mid-1920s, Claire was called as its president. Working without manuals and handbooks, branch members later recalled it as a "do-it-yourself" Relief Society.[82] What she did not have access to in terms of programs or curriculum, Sister Robison made up for in her empathy for the young students and wives who comprised the majority of the branch, all of whom were far from home, short on funds, and part of a misunderstood minority religion. Claire organized regular opportunities to gather widely dispersed members so they could mingle and strengthen one another.[83] A counselor of Sister Robison described the Relief Society as the heart of the branch and credited her for holding the small congregation together during those lonely years.[84] Perhaps Claire filled the role too ably. Although branch presidents rotated frequently, Claire was not released until 1951, serving twenty-seven years as Relief Society president![85]

Adelbert Garr (A.G. to friends) and Naomi Cranney settled in Massachusetts not long after the Robisons. The Cranneys had arrived as newlyweds in 1930 for A.G. to attend Harvard Business School. Faced with the Depression's aftermath and a lack of professional opportunities elsewhere following graduation, they decided to stay.[86]

The Boston Branch that the Cranneys first attended was comprised of approximately twenty-five members who met downtown in the Richards Dance Hall in a room filled with garish decorations and stale odors from the prior night's parties. The dance hall was one of a long series of public spaces that had been utilized by the Church. It had been used for fifteen years' worth of Sabbath meetings, despite the fact that it was often filled with noise and smoke from the trains at nearby North Station.[87] There was interest in finding a new meeting place, but a search by men in the branch failed to turn up any viable alternatives. When a number of women complained of the hall's unsuitability for worship during a visit by the mission president, the president's wife quickly retorted, "Why wait for the men? Why don't you find it yourself?"[88]

Re-inspired, it was only a matter of weeks before one of the sisters obtained permission to hold meetings at the Cantabridgia Club at 100 Mount Auburn Street, just off Harvard Square. Under the leadership of Branch President William Knecht, another of the small cluster of resident members, the Boston Branch became the Cambridge Branch with its relocation in 1930.[89]

Over the course of the intervening years, the boundaries of the Eastern States Mission had changed with the creation of the Canadian Mission in 1919 and the North Central States Mission in 1925, which together took in the Maritime Provinces and the states of Maine, New Hampshire, and Vermont.[90] The outbreak of World War I had resulted in a brief interruption of missionary work, following which new missionaries were overwhelmed with the challenges involved in covering an immense geography. In a 1928 *Improvement Era* article, President Henry Rolapp of the Eastern States Mission stated that even with the 120 missionaries then serving under him, "we could use, to advantage, many times the number we now have."[91]

Missionaries serving in Boston and Providence were frequent guests in the Cranney home during the mid-1930s while A.G. was presiding over the Cambridge Branch. Convinced there was work enough for the missionaries in Massachusetts and the surrounding New England states, A.G. and George Albert Smith Jr., a young professor at Harvard Business School, began discussing the feasibility of a new mission, even outlining proposed boundaries on a road map laid over the Cranney's kitchen table. George Albert discussed the idea with his father, then President of the Quorum of the Twelve, who agreed with their recommendation.[92] Still, it was a surprise when the Cranney's doorbell rang at 6:30 a.m. one summer morning in 1937. Glancing at her husband, Naomi stepped out of their walk-up apartment and looked into the lobby two floors below. Smiling up at her were twelve young men. "We're here, Sister Cranney!" the boys exclaimed, rushing up the stairs without waiting for an invitation. Having left Salt Lake City by train before a mission home had been purchased, the missionaries had been given the Cranneys' address, assured that Brother and Sister Cranney would care for them and tell them what to do.

"For three days in a row, sets of twelve missionaries came to our door," said Sister Cranney. "We fed them breakfast and delivered each set to the mission home. For months we got stacks of mail delivered to our address."[93]

Dr. Carl F. Eyring served as the first president of the New England Mission, which had been carved out of the Eastern States and Canadian Missions. It took in the six New England states of Connecticut, Maine, Massachusetts, New Hampshire, Rhode Island, and Vermont, as well as the Canadian Maritime Provinces of New Brunswick, Nova Scotia, Prince Edward Island, Cape Breton Island, and Newfoundland. Organizing the mission was a daunting task, as its boundaries extended 1,500 miles from north to south, within which 1,061 members of record resided, only 40 percent of whom were associated with the eight branches existing within the same geography.* While some members were affiliated with Sunday

---

* Five of the eight branches were located within the Massachusetts District: Cambridge, New Bedford, Fall River, Lynn-Salem, and Providence (R.I.), while the other three—New Haven, Hartford, and Springfield—were branches in the Connecticut Valley.

Schools or other small groups of Saints, over 400 members lacked contact with any local Church organization. Most of these isolated Saints resided in Vermont, New Hampshire, Maine, and the Canadian Provinces, where little missionary work had taken place for several years. One of President Eyring's first objectives was to assign missionaries to areas where they could strengthen these members.[94]

The dedication of a mission headquarters by Elder John A. Widtsoe on September 24, 1937,[95] was followed by the arrival of additional missionaries and more frequent visits by Church leaders. Levi Edgar Young, second president of the mission, appreciated the prevalent sense of history in the area and was anxious to help the Church establish deep roots in the east. When President Young learned in 1941 that a piece of property comprising the Henry Wadsworth Longfellow estate on Cambridge's historic Brattle Street was available for purchase, he took the Cranneys to view it. The home overlooked the Charles River, and its location was ideal. Fearing only that it was too good to be true, A.G. Cranney told President Young that he should by all means buy it![96]

Before the transaction could close, word leaked out that the Mormons were purchasing the famous property. Opposition flared within the neighborhood and community, pressuring the real estate agent to find another buyer. President Young was still making arrangements to procure the home when he received an unexpected telephone call from the individual handling the sale. "If you're not here in an hour with the money," the man on the line informed the president, "the deal is off." Keenly aware that the branch had no funds for a purchase of this magnitude, President Young hastily contacted the few LDS families in the area to no avail. There was no way to come up with the required amount in so short a time.

Unwilling to let the property slip through his fingers, President Young rushed downtown. At the agent's office, he opened his personal checkbook and wrote a check for over twenty thousand dollars, knowing there was nothing in his account to cover such a figure. The agent had not expected the president to meet his demand and eyed the check warily. "How do I know this check is good?" he asked. Breathing a prayer, President Young said simply, "Call my bank."

Before President Young had a chance to warn anyone what he had done, the man picked up the phone and called the Utah State National Bank, where his call was received by bank president, Orvill Adams. "I have a man here named Young," barked the Boston professional. "He has just written a check for $26,000. Will you stand behind it?"

Pausing to process this abrupt interrogatory, Orvill asked, "Who did you say?"

"Levi Edgar Young," replied the man in Boston.

The response held no hesitation: "Mr. Young's check is good for any amount he wants to write."[97]

With a confirmation of liquidity, the agent acknowledged President Young's right to purchase the property. President Young transferred ownership to the Church, leaving bank accounts to be reckoned with later.[98] With the purchase complete at the end of 1941, 100 Brattle Street became the mission home and meeting place for the MIA and Relief Society. Despite his love for the property, President Young never lived in the home, as Judge William H. Reeder and Bertha Stone Reeder were called to head the New England Mission in January 1942.

President Reeder believed that establishing permanent places of worship for the Saints built community recognition and provided a foothold for growth. As such, the Reeders were instrumental in helping the Church acquire properties in Rhode Island, Connecticut, Vermont, and Massachusetts. One of these Massachusetts properties was the house adjacent to the mission home—96 Brattle Street. While not as stately or well-appointed as the mission home (and widely remembered for the pervasive smell of the prior owners' cats), 96 Brattle was quickly transformed into the most spacious meetinghouse in New England, thanks to the hours of renovation work contributed by members, many of whom were stationed in the area with the military.[99]

With the outbreak of World War II, servicemen replaced the students who, together with the five resident families, traditionally comprised the Cambridge Branch. Local members assumed the branch would shrink at war's end, but the G.I. Bill's government-sponsored education program brought increasing numbers of families to nearby universities. As sacrament meeting attendance outgrew the large room at 96 Brattle, members began seating themselves along the stairway, the foyer, and all adjacent rooms. The meetinghouse had been dedicated by David O. McKay in 1943, but by 1948 it was already clear a new chapel was needed.[100]

The two lots comprising the Longfellow property provided an ideal site for a chapel. The house used for Sunday meetings at 96 Brattle was quickly torn down, but there was a strong desire to preserve the majestic mission home. A piece of land was obtained around the corner from the mission home's original site and the residence was cut in half, jacked from its foundation and placed on rollers to make its slow and arduous journey to its new lot.*

With the cut-away sides of the home draped in dirty canvas to protect against the elements, the mission family and a number of missionaries continued to live at the residence until the last of the utilities were disconnected, at which point, a few hardy elders were asked to stay on and to watch over things. The house was already in transition when two hurricanes hit Boston, ripping off a section of the roof and flooding a large portion of the building. One evening, following another large storm, a cab driver ignored the traffic barricades along Brattle Street and nearly skidded into the house, which was then sitting in the middle of the road. Getting out of his car, the man walked around the home and climbed into the kitchen through a hole from the basement. This was something to talk about—a house completely displaced by a hurricane! Making his way through the main floor into the living room, the cabbie was shocked to encounter a young man playing the piano while a small group of missionaries read their scriptures using flashlights. Turning quickly around, he left while muttering, "They're nuts—or I'm nuts. Nuts!"[101]

With the land cleared, the Cambridge Branch laid the cornerstone for a new chapel on October 22, 1955. The branch now had more than five hundred members, but it was still a shock when the construction budget of $72,000 had to be increased to almost $300,000. Students and young families with scant financial reserves comprised the bulk of the congregation, so fund-raising efforts already underway increased with a new urgency. Every third Sunday of the month was set aside as a day of fasting and prayer for the chapel's construction, and letters enlisting monetary contributions from former members of the branch were sent across the country.[102]

By April 1956, the chapel could begin accommodating branch meetings. In accordance with Church policy, however, it was not until after construction costs were completely paid that the building serving as the Cambridge chapel and New England Mission offices was dedicated by President David O. McKay on September 23, 1956. In an era when converted homes typically served as meetinghouses, the dedication of a chapel constructed specifically for that purpose was momentous. Having the dedication performed by a president of the Church was a

---

* The mission home was moved to 15 Hawthorne Street in Cambridge, Massachusetts.

once-in-a-lifetime opportunity for the majority of area Saints. Over 1,200 members from all regions of New England and many of the Canadian Provinces attended the dedication of the building that quickly became the hub of the mission and Atlantic District, of which the Cambridge Branch was a part.[103]

## Expanding Outward

Outside of Cambridge, the Church increased in strength as existing Sunday School groups grew into small branches. Georgetown, Massachusetts, is located a short distance from Topsfield, home of five generations of Joseph Smith's paternal ancestors. In the 1830s and '40s, Georgetown was the site of an early branch of the Church and was frequently visited by Joseph and Hyrum Smith, John Taylor, Wilford Woodruff, and Brigham Young. A century later, Hilda Lindgren Tidd came across copies of the Pearl of Great Price, Doctrine and Covenants, and the Book of Mormon and joined the Church. Following her baptism, missionaries were frequent guests in her home. One of these elders invited Hilda's grandson, Elsworth, to attend a cottage meeting at his grandmother's home. Elsworth and his wife, Mabel, attended for almost a year until Mabel finally asked her husband, "Well, what are you waiting for?" Challenged in this manner, Elsworth was baptized with Mabel and her sister in an indoor swimming pool. "From that date our lives, and others after us, were forever changed," Brother Tidd reflected.

By 1949, there were enough members in the area to form a Sunday School at Sister Hilda Tidd's home. S. Dilworth Young, president of the New England Mission, ordained Elsworth as an elder and set him apart as Sunday School president. When the missionaries left the area, Brother Tidd found himself on his own, relying occasionally on assistance from his Aunt Clara, who had joined the Church earlier in 1945 and thus "knew how things were supposed to work."

Within two years, the mission presidency determined it was time for a Georgetown Branch, and Brother Tidd was called as branch president. "Having been Sunday School president wasn't much help," President Tidd rued, noting he had only been to two or three branch meetings in Cambridge. "I would have paid more attention if I had known what was coming," he admitted.

Before the district leaders returned to Cambridge, Elsworth thought to ask if there was a handbook or some other resource that would tell him what to do in his new role.

"Do?" one of the leaders repeated quizzically.

"Uh, yeah," President Tidd stammered. "How to run a branch."

A look of recognition passed over the district leader's face. "Oh yes," he replied. "Well, you have a Bible, don't you? And a Doctrine of Covenants and a Book of Mormon?"

"Oh yes," President Tidd assured him.

"Well then, that's all you need," the district leader replied matter-of-factly. "It's all in there." And handing the new branch president a pad of forms for financial records and membership reports, the district presidency was gone.

"I had no counselors. I was alone," said Brother Tidd. "I had Aunt Clara. Maybe I was the only branch president of record who had his aunt as a counselor. She was one smart woman and never hesitated to set me straight. This was serious business, and it had to be done just right."

The fledgling branch returned to the Sunday School's prior location in the front room of Granny Tidd's farmhouse. The room could accommodate twenty-five people, although comfort was an issue when the wood-burning stove got going during the winter. A large Philco console radio served as the pulpit, and Aunt Clara played the hymns on an old reed organ with a number of missing keys. "Thinking back on it," Elsworth remarked, "I guess it was all kind of primitive, and I suppose we were, in a way, pioneers, although we didn't feel like it then."

One Sunday, as President Tidd stood at the "pulpit" to begin services, a Jeep pulled in front of the house and a large family poured out of it. Putting the meeting on hold, President Tidd met the family at the door. "Is this where the Mormons have meetings?" the father enquired. Assuring them that it was, President Tidd welcomed the visitors in, urging them to find seats where they could. After services, the newcomers introduced themselves as the Ralph Noyes family from Kensington, New Hampshire. They'd read about Mormons in the newspaper and had been looking for them ever since. "How do we go about getting baptized?" Mr. Noyes asked.

Following the baptism of both Ralph's family and that of his brother George, the little branch could no longer fit in Granny's front room. After a brief stay in rented halls, the branch received permission to build a meetinghouse, which was designed to look like a house minus interior walls. This typical plan provided financial protection by allowing the Church to resell buildings to residential buyers if a branch grew too large for the space or failed and had to be dissolved. Mixing mortar, laying bricks, raising the walls and framing the roof, the Georgetown members built one of the earliest Church-owned meetinghouses within the mission.[104*]

Beginning in the late 1940s, under President S. Dilworth Young, missionaries in the New England Mission were asked to travel without purse or scrip during the summer, just as their forbearers had. Chandler and Edith Abbott of Foxboro, Massachusetts, encountered a bedraggled pair of missionaries involved in this effort and allowed the young men to spend a night in their home. The elders were grateful for the shelter and did some needed washing, but ultimately continued on their way without saying a word about their purpose. Mr. Abbott returned home the next evening, and he told his wife that he had worried about the young men all day. When Edith echoed his concern, the Abbotts got into their car and headed out to look for the missionaries. They found the elders walking along the road approximately fifteen miles from the Abbotts' home. Stopping the car, Chandler and Edith asked the pair why they were traveling this way and what they were teaching. They returned home with the missionaries and ultimately joined the Church with their children[105]—the first members of what became the Foxboro Branch in 1950.

Traveling without purse and scrip was discontinued after a few years, but produced one hundred baptisms for the New England Mission in 1948, the first year of the program. Baptisms within the mission had ranged from only eighteen to thirty-eight over the three preceding years.[106] Much like the Abbotts, Isabelle and John Jacobson of Upton, Massachusetts, were introduced to the Church when they opened their home to two missionaries in 1950. Isabelle was immediately intrigued by the two men who knocked on her door. They had answers to questions she'd had about religion from childhood. Because her husband was not home, Isabelle asked the pair to return the next day. The elders returned but came late, having attempted to wash in a nearby brook, inadvertently submerging their scriptures in the process. Turned away repeatedly, the missionaries had not had a meal or a place to sleep for three days. The Jacobsons had never heard of The Church of Jesus Christ of Latter-day Saints, but due to Isabelle's initial impressions and the pair's sad story, the Jacobsons' house became a home base for that set of elders and several sets thereafter.

---

* President Elsworth Tidd served as the primary architect on several branch buildings and supervised construction of the Cambridge chapel.

Mr. Jacobson found himself as intrigued by the new doctrine as his wife and kept the missionaries talking until 3:00 a.m. that first evening. As the elders came and went, word got out about the guests the Jacobsons were keeping. Suspicion grew, and former friends and neighbors forbade their children to visit the Jacobson home. Undeterred, the Jacobsons invited everyone they knew to meet with the missionaries. After visiting the branch in Cambridge to attend services, the Jacobsons were baptized with their six children in June 1951. Brother Jacobson was set apart as a Sunday School leader and they began meeting with three other families and local missionaries in Worcester, Massachusetts, a group that became a branch three years later in 1954.[107]

## Stakes in Zion

A few months before the Prophet Joseph's death, he announced a revelation at a general conference meeting held in Nauvoo on April 8, 1844:

"I have received instructions from the Lord that from henceforth whenever the Elders of Israel shall build up churches and branches unto the Lord throughout the States there shall be a stake of Zion. In the great cities, as Boston, New York, etc., there shall be stakes. It is a glorious proclamation and I reserved it to the last."[108]

This revelation was finally fulfilled with respect to the first-named city, Boston, after 118 years.

On the evening of May 20, 1962, President John E. Carr of the New England Mission convened a meeting in the Cambridge chapel. It was necessary to use the recreation hall and the stage to accommodate everyone in attendance. Elder Henry D. Moyle, first counselor in the First Presidency, presided while Elders Harold B. Lee, Gordon B. Hinckley, and Franklin D. Richards conducted the business of the meeting, held to establish the first stake of Zion in New England. Wilbur W. Cox, then president of the Atlantic District, was sustained as the first stake president, members of a high council and a patriarch were called, and at 8:08 p.m., Elder Harold B. Lee of the Quorum of the Twelve declared the 354th stake of the Church, the Boston Stake, to be in existence. Created from eight branches of the New England Mission, five of which were reorganized as wards in conjunction with the formation of the stake, the new unit accounted for 1,714 members in Boston and its surrounding communities.* Four years later, on May 29, 1966, membership doubled when four branches comprising the Providence District were annexed to the Boston Stake, encompassing Saints in Cape Cod and New Bedford, Massachusetts, and Newport and Providence, Rhode Island.[109]

Missionary work was rapid during the 1960s, with over two thousand convert baptisms in the New England Mission during 1963 and 1964 alone.[110] Many of these baptisms took place in Maine, and in 1968 a stake was organized in the northernmost state of New England. The Merrimack Stake at Portsmouth, New Hampshire, was organized in 1970,[†] and a stake was organized in Providence, Rhode Island, in 1977. This growth impacted the mission, which was divided in 1973 to create the Canada-Maritimes Mission, following which the New England Mission was renamed the Massachusetts Boston Mission. The mission was further split to create the Connecticut Hartford Mission in 1979 and the New Hampshire Manchester Mission in 1987.[‡]

The Boston Massachusetts Stake has since been joined by the Cambridge Massachusetts Stake, organized in 1998. Those two stakes,

---

* The eight branches originally comprising the Boston Stake, the size of the respective congregations, and the individual sustained as bishop or branch president, as applicable, for each such body of Saints on May 20, 1962, were as follows:

*Cambridge Branch*—became Cambridge Ward: 561 members, Bishop Bert Van Uitert

*Fort Devens Branch*—124 members, President Lee G. Cantwell

*Foxboro Branch*—150 members, President Lawrence A. Haines

*Georgetown Branch*—123 members, President Cyril C. Poulsen

*Lynn Branch*—became Lynn Ward: 155 members, Bishop Nephi E. Berg

*North Middlesex Branch*—became Billerica Ward: 253 members, Bishop Spencer S. Hunn

*South Weymouth Branch*—became South Weymouth Ward: 204 members, Bishop Max W. Nelson

*Wayland Branch*—became Weston Ward: 138 members, Bishop Robert D. Hales

Two months later, in July of 1962, the Worcester Branch was added to the Boston Stake.

† The Billerica Ward, Georgetown Ward, and Fort Devens Branch were taken from the Boston Stake and became original units of the Merrimack Stake upon its organization.

‡ The Connecticut Hartford Mission was folded back into the Massachusetts Boston Mission in 2011 as a result of fewer missionaries and increased missionary activity in other areas of the country.

encompassing the city and towns where the first institutions of the Church were reestablished in New England at the outset of the twentieth century, are two of thirteen stakes of The Church of Jesus Christ of Latter-day Saints operating within the New England states as of 2012.* A beautiful temple, situated on a hill at Belmont, Massachusetts, seven miles outside Boston and adjacent to Cambridge, was dedicated in October 2000; the crowning goal to which New England Saints had aspired since the dedication of the Cambridge Longfellow Park chapel almost fifty years prior.[111]

Among the first twenty-six men to be called as General Authorities of the Restored Church, following its organization in 1830, eight hailed from Vermont, six from Massachusetts, three from Connecticut, and one from Maine.[112] Similar connections continue today. "There is an astonishing number of General Authorities who have been through Boston at one time or another as a mission president, student, or working," observed Elder Bruce Porter of the First Quorum of the Seventy, who obtained his doctorate in Boston. "If you look at the Quorum of the Twelve, about half of them have some kind of tie, if not with Boston, certainly with New England. . . . [New England] was a part of the church legacy early on, but the legacy . . . continues in that sense."[113]

One individual with such ties is President Henry B. Eyring. As a student in the Boston area from 1957 to 1962, President Eyring served in the Atlantic District presidency with presidents John Noble Hinckley and Wilbur W. Cox, giving him a bird's-eye view of the scattered groups of Saints that ultimately grew into wards, stakes, and missions. "I know something about how the Church grows from little branches and districts," President Eyring remarked, noting that while New England has always been a draw for students, the Church's present strength in the northeastern United States is a credit to those families who chose to stay

---

* Four of the thirteen stakes within New England are located in Massachusetts: Boston Massachusetts (20 May 1962), Cambridge Massachusetts (18 October 1998), Hingham Massachusetts (30 August 1981), and Springfield Massachusetts (28 June 1987). The other nine stakes are Nashua New Hampshire (22 March 1970—originally named the Manchester New Hampshire Stake, which was then changed to the Merrimack New Hampshire Stake); Exeter New Hampshire (6 September 1981—originally named the Portland Maine Stake), Concord New Hampshire (6 September 1981), Bangor Maine (20 April 1986), Augusta Maine (23 June 1968—originally named the Maine Stake), Montpelier Vermont (11 April 1976), Providence Rhode Island (20 March 1977), Hartford Connecticut (18 September 1966), and New Haven Connecticut (30 August 1981).

in New England and raise their children when the Church was virtually unknown. "Those were the real heroes," he stated. It would have been easy for those pioneering Saints to give into the pressure to move west where opportunities in the Church were greater, or to draw close and become insular in the interest of self-preservation. Instead, they opened their doors wide, embracing students, investigators, converts, and neighbors, building up stakes of Zion in the process.

"What you learn is that it's not about buildings, it's not huge congregations; it's a few faithful families and then the Lord builds around them." While the particulars vary with local circumstances, the Lord's pattern for the Church's growth is consistent worldwide, whether in New England, Arizona, or Peru. "It's a story of heroes," President Eyring concluded. "It's a story of how the Lord grows the Church."[114]

OH, MAY THY SOLDIERS, FAITHFUL, TRUE, AND BOLD,

FIGHT AS THE SAINTS WHO NOBLY FOUGHT OF OLD,

AND WIN WITH THEM THE VICTOR'S CROWN OF GOLD.

# 2

# THE INFLUENCE
# OF THE ONE

ANDREW BURNHAM* was known to be casual in his Church activity as a youth, but after a handful of years at a university in Boston, he returned home fully committed to the gospel. When a friend asked about the notable changes in his life, Andrew said simply, "I've got to tell you about John and Betty Hinckley." It was the Hinckleys, Andrew explained, who welcomed him when he arrived in Massachusetts, far from family and friends. It was the Hinckleys who included him in their Cambridge Branch family. And it was the Hinckleys who set Andrew on a path that shaped the rest of his life.[1]

John Noble Hinckley and his wife, Elizabeth (Betty to all who knew her), were early stalwarts of the New England church. Raised in the West, Betty Skolfield was a missionary in the Eastern States Mission under B. H. Roberts when she met John Hinckley, a student at Carnegie Tech in Pittsburgh. President Roberts married the two in 1927 following Betty's release[2] and employment took the Hinckleys to Massachusetts in the early 1930s. Given the scarcity of LDS families in the area, John and Betty became part of a tight nucleus of Saints who worshipped together within a church that, at times, seemed tenuously planted on foreign soil.

"Permanent" members were in short supply, but area colleges and universities brought a steady flow of LDS students to the city. Some stayed a semester and others years, just as they do today. Robert Fletcher, an

---

* Name has been changed for purposes of this account.

33

MIT alum who came to Cambridge in 1939, said many families played a role in welcoming students, but "John and Betty were truly loving parents of the ward. They were both very gregarious and welcomed newcomers warmly. John used to say that he lived at 'six bits' (for 75) Orchard Street, and all were welcome there."[3]

With this open invitation, the Hinckleys' Belmont home served as a natural gathering spot where long-time residents mixed with transient academics, some single and others with families in tow, as they passed through the Cambridge Branch. "I soon discovered that probably everybody in the Church in New England knew how to get to 75 Orchard Street because it was . . . the center and heart of everything warm and welcoming about the Church," remarked Mary Finlayson, who attended school in the area as a young woman. "Betty and John had a way of embracing everybody. They made people feel like they were a part of their family and part of the kingdom."[4]

In a city where people are commonly measured by academic achievements or professional distinctions, Betty was singularly unimpressed by such matters. It was not uncommon for Betty to greet newcomers on her porch, where she would ask them about their background, accomplishments, and what brought them to the area. Once introductions concluded, Betty would smile and extend an arm to her new friends, inviting each to leave his or her credentials at the door, and enter her home as a member of the Cambridge Branch, a place where everyone was equally welcome and worthy of love.[5]

Raising four daughters of their own and the son of a friend, John and Betty embraced everyone who walked in the door of the Cambridge meetinghouse, and they did so for the better part of three decades. "I'm not sure that John ever got to sleep in his own bed in that house," Truman Madsen mused.[6] Indeed, family lore has it that in later years John insisted on living in a one-bedroom apartment since anytime they had an extra bed it was being used.[7] It was hard to define where her family began or ended, Brother Madsen noted, observing that "every living thing somehow caught the waft of Betty Hinckley's love."[8]

Russell M. Nelson was one of those temporary members who came to Boston for a medical residency. Arriving before their moving van to a bare apartment with three hungry and tired little children, Elder Nelson later wrote, "We moved to Boston not knowing a single soul there. . . . On the evening of our arrival, two 'angels' appeared at our door, John N. and Elizabeth Hinckley. Those dear folks saw to it that we had sleeping bags and bedrolls, pillows and food, and all that was needed to sustain life until our material goods arrived. We still regard that as a miracle, for we were total strangers to each other."[9]

"Sister Hinckley . . . was a heart as big as all outdoors," President Henry B. Eyring stated of his own experiences with the Hinckleys. "They took in strays."[10]

Betty was renowned for her hospitality, but the wisdom, instruction, and guidance she imparted was of greater consequence. A passionate and devoted student of the gospel, Betty Hinckley loved the scriptures, particularly the Book of Mormon, a volume from which she frequently taught. Former University of Utah president Chase Peterson recalled Sunday afternoon gatherings at the Hinckley home, where branch members would focus on a specific aspect of the gospel and explore its applications in depth.[11] Impatient when discussions grew too philosophical, Betty was the first to reel things in whenever she thought a conversation was veering off course. "Just leave off that philosophical stuff!" she'd exclaim. "Just give us the gospel."[12]

Betty always seemed to know when someone needed a gentle push or a word of encouragement, a friend recalled, noting that in attending to those in need, she often ventured into places and neighborhoods "where the brethren feared to tread." Never one to mince words, Betty could be devastatingly direct, yet because any reprimand was followed by words of loving concern, she could instruct without sparking resentment.[13] Imbued with these traits, Betty was often the catalyst a person needed to change his life. Said another, "She was the difference it takes to make a person change his goals . . . to make something of themselves."[14]

Betty's enthusiasm for the gospel and those around her was mirrored in her appreciation for her New England home. Each autumn, Betty gave a similar lesson in Relief Society, directed to the latest batch of young wives who had come east with their husbands, many reluctantly. "Don't hold your nose and wait until you get home to Utah," Betty admonished. "Don't cook the stuff from Utah and say, 'This Boston clam chowder is no good.' Dip your feet here. Come to the clambake . . . hear the Boston Pops. Take some culture home with you from this place."[15]

Ann Madsen took Betty's admonition to heart, finding a life lesson in this advice that equipped her to embrace new experiences, including the ability to appreciate multiple cultures when she and her husband, Truman, were asked to lead the BYU Jerusalem Center years later. "I've thanked her in person and by way of prayers many times since for what she did for me in that regard," Ann stated.[16]

Visiting a daughter in Boston some years after she had moved from the area, Betty encountered an old friend while running errands. Hugging her tightly, Betty seized the moment and exclaimed, "Helen, I want you to meet with our missionaries and read the Book of Mormon!" Helen was surprised by the sudden invitation, but accepted the offer to begin meeting with the missionaries and was soon baptized.[17]

This impromptu meeting with Helen Rhodes was not extraordinary. "The fact is that even after her release, Mother never left her mission," her daughter explained.[18] Like Paul, Betty Hinckley was "not ashamed of the gospel of Christ," (Romans 1:16) and her actions matched her bold confidence in its teachings. There wasn't anything Betty wouldn't do for the Church or the Lord.[19]

Speaking at her funeral, Truman Madsen described Betty and John as exemplars of compassionate service who served as a literal anchor to hundreds of students (not unlike Andrew Burnham) during a sensitive period in their lives when they faced difficult intellectual, spiritual, and material cross currents.[20]

Mindful of the Hinckleys' impact on her own life, after moving back to California, Mary Finlayson and her husband deliberately adopted a policy of opening their home to anyone in need. "We've tried to follow their policy of always trying to create a safe, peaceful, and happy haven for any and all comers," Mary stated, noting that she knew other couples who had chosen to honor Betty in a similar way. "We have all tried to be in our communities the 'Hinckleys' of Stanford and Davis and Houston and Washington. There just aren't words to express the profound effect that woman has had on all of us, and then through us on so many people who [have been in] our homes. I hope that in some way we've been able to effect the feelings of closeness to Christ and self-worth in the people who have stayed at our home in the same way that Betty shaped those feelings in us."[21]

Elizabeth Hinckley passed away in California in 1979, approximately two decades after she and John left Massachusetts. Today there are still individuals like Ann Madsen and Mary Finlayson who passed through Boston during the 1930s, '40s, and '50s who consciously seek to emulate Betty's qualities, quietly extending the kind of care and concern for which Betty was known. Even more striking is the impact Betty's actions continue to have on the Boston and Cambridge Stakes today, over fifty years after her departure from the area. Although few know Betty's name or recognize the significance of 75 Orchard Street as an early pillar of the Church in New England, Betty and her family fostered a pattern of acceptance and community that continues to characterize aspects of the Boston LDS experience.

Years after Betty left, newcomers to Boston frequently remarked on the egalitarianism they found in wards where the diversity of the membership could, in other settings, lead to pride and division. Indeed, when Institute director Alan Parrish was asked to move his family east, he feared that the university atmosphere could be a breeding ground for speculation and apostasy. Once there, Alan marveled. "I remember being very, very, very touched by how ordinary and humble and extremely confident and accomplished successful people could be," he said. "When people talked with us, I said, 'Hey, one of the great things about living in the Boston Stake is that the distance between the haves and the have-nots is almost minimal.'"[22]

Jamie and Dorothy Lyon were similarly impressed by the spirit of helpfulness and community they encountered when they moved into the Cambridge Ward. "What was it there that made the difference?" Dorothy asked. "There were some key people who made you feel welcome, who took you under their wing, and who just made it a very special place."[23]

Although Dorothy Lyon never knew Betty Hinckley, each of the women Dorothy credited for setting the tone in her ward knew Betty and had been a frequent guest in the Hinckley home. They had experienced Betty's unconditional love and acceptance, her disregard for outward trappings. Is it any wonder that the men and women Betty invited into her inclusive Cambridge Branch would feel a responsibility to extend the same unconditional welcome to others?

Betty's influence was not the single factor in establishing and maintaining this tone, of course. Many early LDS families are remembered for the way they opened themselves to newcomers who found Massachusetts a strange and unfamiliar place, yet Betty's contribution was unique in its breadth and depth. "She had the capacity of dissolving the differences between people," Mary Finlayson explained, "just by her unpretentiousness and her openness toward us and everybody. Everybody felt okay. Everybody felt acceptable. . . . Nobody had a difficulty without somebody coming to their aid. . . . I think a lot of that was Betty. She was like that. She knew everything that was going on and everybody. There was a feeling of helpfulness and we're all in this together."[24] By leaving an indelible imprint in the lives of those she touched even after her name faded from collective memory, Betty Hinckley left a legacy of inclusiveness and acceptance that continues to color interactions within area congregations, carried on unconsciously by members who never met her.

## Setting a Pattern

How many attributes of group culture can be traced back to individuals like Betty Hinckley, whose actions and approach set a standard for others to follow? When Clayton and Christine Christensen moved to the Cambridge area in the late 1970s, they were immediately impressed by the depth of content present in the faith-building Sunday School lessons held each week in their new ward. The Christensens had attended other university-adjacent wards, many of which had been imbued with an intellectual arrogance and a tendency for discussions to take a cynical, skeptical direction. Classes in Cambridge often departed from the manual, Clayton acknowledged, but such departures were motivated by the shared desire of students and teacher to delve into the truths covered by the lesson, rather than a desire to speculate. "The lessons were all deeply spiritual and very thoughtful," Clayton stated. "Every week we would just walk away from church having learned so much from the quality of the speaking and the teaching."[25]

Long-time resident and member Ruth Ray Kelleher listed exceptional teaching as a favorite attribute of her ward in Weston, Massachusetts. Describing classes as inspirational, informative, and exciting, Ruth said, "Most of these teachers, if I were able to mention the hundreds of teachers who have been here, have that same kind of intense spirituality combined with intelligence combined with presentation that has made this an outstanding area to live."[26]

The high concentration of educators in the greater Boston area undoubtedly influences gospel instruction, but the accounts of individuals who attended the Cambridge Branch during the 1930s, '40s, and '50s suggest there is more to the story than simple proximity to universities and colleges. One after another, these members shared profound and vivid memories of the Sunday School lessons taught by George Albert Smith Jr. over the course of more than twenty years.

George Albert Smith Jr., son of the prophet whose name he shared, came to Cambridge as a student in 1932[27] and began his career as a professor in 1934. Shortly after his arrival, Brother Smith was asked to teach the branch Sunday School class. Working without the luxury of a class manual, George Albert prepared his lessons from the standard works, bringing to the task all the intellectual acumen and teaching abilities he possessed. He often taught principles using case studies, the same technique he used at Harvard Business School, presenting New Testament parables against present-day scenarios to which class members were asked to apply Christ's teachings. He delved deeply into the scriptures and challenged his students to accompany him on that journey, exploring and discussing spiritual principles in a way they had not done previously. A favorite topic was the Sermon on the Mount, which provided Brother Smith with enough material for three years' worth of class material. Upon concluding the Savior's sermon, branch membership had changed enough to justify starting over again![28]

By the time standardized manuals from the Deseret Sunday School Union were readily available, George Albert's lessons had developed a curriculum of their own. At times, members expressed dismay that Brother Smith wasn't following the standard lesson plans, but it never took long for them to develop a distinct preference for his classes.[29] "He brought the parables alive with his analytical mind and made them . . . relevant to our modern situation," reported Talmage Nielsen, who attended Brother Smith's lessons during the 1940s. "We were always thrilled to go to his class. . . . I wasn't aware that he was departing from any kind of schedule because we didn't know that there was one. We just came and enjoyed it."[30]

William Knecht was a child when he heard George Albert teach but still describes Brother Smith's lessons as the thing he remembered most from his youth in the Church.[31] Another brother described George Albert as the most stimulating teacher he ever had, while his wife stated she could live from week to week for Brother Smith's lessons.[32] "I loved to follow his reasoning," said a woman who recalled many Sunday afternoons spent lingering outside the meetinghouse with friends, dissecting each segment of the day's lesson. "We took away a lot to think about later."[33]

"There was something he did that set the tone," Norris Finlayson explained. "Everybody remembers his classes, but the thing I remember most distinctly about his class is that whenever he called on you, he acquired a look on his face as you were talking as if, 'Boy, what a great idea you have. Listen to this everybody.' Everybody who spoke in his class came away thinking, 'I really got it. I really got a handle on this.

I'm really getting into it.' I think in retrospect that one thing generated a 'can do' attitude of competence and capability that spread among the members."[34]

Many members knew how to excel academically, but Brother Smith's instruction helped them see that applying the same kind of effort, energy, and intellect to the scriptures could open new doors of spiritual understanding. Class members came away with a new confidence that they could handle gospel questions, one sister stated simply.[35]

"The impact," said Chase Peterson, who served as George Albert's Sunday School assistant for five years, "was that you could be spiritual and you could be thoughtful. The mind and the spirit were not at odds with each other, and that's a terribly important imprint to have early on. There's not a battle going on in heaven between mind and spirit."[36]

Individuals attending Brother Smith's classes learned from his example as well as his material. When congregations split off from the Cambridge Branch, teachers in the new units deliberately sought to apply the teaching methods they'd seen Brother Smith model on a weekly basis. Eventually others who never attended George Albert's classes adopted variations of his approach by assumption, having learned through repeated example a specific approach to gospel teaching. Over time, a culture of thoughtful gospel instruction and discussion emerged where Spirit and intellect are regarded as mutually reinforcing and intellectual capacity is applied to strengthen faith, rather than challenge it.[37]

The outcome of George Albert's approach is perhaps best illustrated by Vance Smith's summary of what he learned attending a ward in Belmont, Massachusetts, many decades after Brother Smith stopped teaching. "So little energy [was] spent on mysteries of the gospel," noted Vance, of a congregation where others might assume people would devote their brain power to divining imponderables. Instead members were focused on how they could be a better ward mission leader, a better Scoutmaster, a better Nursery worker. With that example, Vance said, "You can't leave and help but be better prepared to be a worker in the Church. . . . I know it's flavored the way I look at the gospel. I'll never be one that does anything but try to steer the gospel topics back to the basics. . . . How can we be more like the Savior, rather than how we can show how much we know."[38]

Elizabeth Skolfield Hinckley and George Albert Smith Jr. are compelling examples of individuals who left an enduring legacy. Their actions established expectations and left cultural markers that have impacted generations of Massachusetts Saints who readily identify acceptance, inclusion, and spiritual scholarship as defining traits of their Church experience. These and other attributes of group behavior do not evolve in a vacuum, nor are they static. When diligent and inspired individuals seek improved ways to address tasks and meet challenges, they have a profound impact on practice and tone. The commitment of a few can affect many.

## I'll Serve Where You Want Me to Serve

A simple example of this phenomenon began in the late 1960s within the youth programs of the Cambridge Ward. Latter-day Saint teenagers were sparse and scattered across the ward's large boundaries. Many lacked parental support and access to transportation, making it difficult to attend Church meetings. As a result, they were falling through the cracks. Surveying the needs of her small flock, a new Young Women's president took it upon herself to spend each Tuesday afternoon collecting girls from Boston, Everett, Revere, Medford, and other outlying communities. Packed into one car, the young women traveled to the meetinghouse together to participate in a Mutual lesson and activity, after which Ann Hinckley Romish made the same trip in reverse, returning to her home after 11:00 p.m.

Carpooling was not new among the widely dispersed New England Saints, but Ann systematized it when she determined transportation was a necessary component of a successful MIA program. Ann's simple action served the girls for whom she was responsible and set a pattern of pragmatic service replicated by subsequent leaders in both the Mutual and Primary organizations. When asked why she went to so much effort, Ann always responded, "It's because I want these Young Women to go to the temple." Once Sister Romish demonstrated how effective the youth programs could be when she reached out with this long-term vision, remarked her bishop, it was only natural that leaders who came after would follow Ann's example.[39]

Organized shuttle services eventually became a regular part of area youth programs, involving numerous individuals beyond auxiliary leaders. To ensure that youth could attend early-morning seminary, teams of adults were assembled to carpool young men and women to class each morning in the predawn hours. Wards were divided into geographic routes and anyone who was willing and able was asked to help. "And everybody did that, everybody cooperated," recalled Grethe Peterson, whose husband spent six months picking up youth for seminary while serving as a vice president at Harvard University. There wasn't an alternative, she shrugged in explanation, because so many wouldn't have gotten there any other way.[40] Some forty years later, many area congregations still maintain organized driving pools to make certain their youth can access activities and opportunities the Church provides.

Tom Eagar saw a similar evolution with Scouting in a ward where no one had stepped up to advocate the program. After several years of virtual inactivity, a brave Scoutmaster did what he could by taking the boys camping and providing activities where they could master required skills. His successor in the foreboding assignment wasted no time in approaching the bishopric, stressing the support he expected and needed from the ward leadership. Armed with a promise that the leaders would support his efforts, it was not long before the program was vibrant, attracting boys within the ward as well as their non-member friends. "The principle here," Tom observed, "is it takes one or two people to turn something around from a non-program to a very important program. . . . All of a sudden, you end up with something that was a non-event, brought along to a very strong program, all within three or four years."[41]

Collective efforts such as these underscore and reinforce a culture of dedication and participation that extends beyond an individual's particular calling or connection to the need at hand. Years after leaving their post with the Institute program in Boston, Alan and Marcia Parrish still marveled that ordinary members got up every day to take youth to seminary, whether or not their own children needed driving. People seemed naturally inclined to look for ways to magnify their callings, said Marcia, which they defined broadly. "Everyone would've taken anything they were asked for and would've made it the most wonderful thing they knew how to make out of it . . . even the most minuscule job in the Church. It was such a privilege to serve." Early-morning seminary worked despite distance, Alan observed, because good, devout people decided to make it work.[42] If that meant doing more than was expected or required, so be it.

## I'll Go Where You Want Me to Go

Just as small acts of selflessness can forge a tenor of dedication within a ward, powerful things can result when people are simply willing to serve where they are asked. Justin Lindsey and his fiancée, LeAnn Wimmer, were attending the Cambridge University Ward when they got engaged in 1993. Approaching the bishop of the vibrant family ward that shared the Longfellow Park chapel with the University Ward, Justin and LeAnn asked if the apartment they had chosen to rent fell within its boundaries. The bishop admitted that while many young couples living in that area chose to attend his ward, technically the apartment was in the Boston Branch. Exchanging a quick look, Justin and LeAnn immediately said they would attend the branch.

After taking a subway downtown to locate the building where the branch met, Justin and LeAnn began attending services the Sunday following their wedding. With sixty people in sacrament meeting on a good day, the congregation included just a handful of couples, all passing through the branch as they pursued school or professional training. The rest of the branch was composed of recent converts who spoke a variety of languages, most of whom had joined the Church alone. Justin had spent his mission serving in inner-city wards in the southeastern United States and knew how overwhelming, demanding, and all-encompassing service in such a congregation could be. With a combination of excitement and trepidation, he wondered whether the Boston Branch would be a good fit for his new family, given that all their peers seemed to be attending the more familiar married student ward in Cambridge.

Indeed, as soon as the Lindseys entered the meetinghouse that first Sunday, the branch president pulled LeAnn aside to ask if she would serve in the Primary. When LeAnn agreed, he asked if she could teach a lesson that morning. "That was probably a good introduction to the Boston Branch," said Justin. The congregation was extremely short on people able or willing to fill callings. Cognizant of the fact that they needed to develop capacity and leadership among the members, the branch presidency was desperate for people with long-term Church experience and perspective to help. The Cambridge wards had large pools of capable students and couples, and branch leaders were struggling to find a way to harness some of that talent.

Convinced that many young families were missing opportunities for personal growth and contribution by remaining in wards so large that bishoprics had to create callings, Justin and LeAnn began actively recruiting people to live in the city and attend the branch. Starting with friends and acquaintances, they contacted members of the University Ward who were getting married and individuals out of state who were rumored to be moving to the area. Meeting out-of-towners at the airport, Justin and LeAnn acted as hosts, chauffeurs, and tour guides to newcomers. They organized dinners for prospective branch members where they shared experiences in the Boston Branch and touted the advantages of living downtown. Acting as amateur real estate locators, the Lindseys took couples to areas of the city featuring pleasant and safe apartment units. These orientations always concluded with an invitation to attend the branch on Sunday where the Lindseys focused on the unique opportunities to serve and learn with a dynamic and diverse congregation.[43]

As a result of Justin and LeAnn's efforts and those of similarly motivated individuals, it was not long before a number of young LDS married couples were living in a downtown apartment complex and attending church in Boston. As the number of couples in the branch increased, families already living within the branch's boundaries began attending, no longer afraid that leaving the Cambridge wards would require them to forsake friends. The energy, enthusiasm, ability, and experience these young families brought provided much-needed strength, stability, and support during a critical period when baptisms were doubling the size of the Boston congregation on an annual basis. Today there are two English-speaking wards and a Haitian-speaking ward in downtown Boston, due in part to the service, fellowship, and missionary work rendered by many of these newly married couples. There is no longer a question of which ward young families living downtown will attend—they attend the ward in which they reside.

## I'll Be What You Want Me to Be

Ann Romish and Justin and LeAnn Lindsey each made choices and took actions in the face of a specific task or challenge that ultimately changed the expectations and, subsequently, the practices of those around them. Others, like Betty Hinckley, influence the tone within a congregation simply by the way they live. One such "tone setter" was Robert Tarte.

An active, vigorous, long-time member of the Boston Stake, Robert, or Bob to his friends, was deeply involved in the stake's organization and had taken great joy in its growth. Bob possessed a particularly strong love for family history work and temple ordinances and was serving as president of the Massachusetts Genealogical Society when he was diagnosed with amniotrophic lateral sclerosis (ALS), a debilitating degenerative condition commonly referred to as Lou Gehrig's Disease. The ravages of ALS are so severe that many people die within a few years of diagnosis, but Bob refused to give in easily.

As coordinator for stake temple trips, Bob continued to arrange the Thursday evening buses that took members from Boston to Washington, D.C., where participants would begin sessions at dawn on Friday. The overnight bus trip and accompanying two-day temple marathon were physically demanding for the hardiest members, yet Bob went on every trip. "Bob was too committed to get people to the temple," a stake member grinned. "We called him the temple decathlete. . . . He just didn't have time to die."[44]

Notwithstanding his age or afflictions, in the days when wards were required to record endowments, Bob Tarte stood at the bus door at the end of each trip, holding a notepad in his shaking hands and greeting members as they climbed onto the bus to return home. His illness had robbed his ability to speak clearly, yet Bob asked the same gentle question over and over in his raspy voice: "How many endowment sessions did you do?"

"Sometimes you wanted to just whisper what you did," admitted former stake president Ken Hutchins. If you used all the time you had at the temple, he explained, you could attend fifteen or sixteen sessions. No one wanted to report a number like six or seven, because they knew Bob Tarte would have maxed out. "He would work from the time he got there until the time he left," said President Hutchins. "Bob would set the standard every time you went to the temple with him."[45]

Even when the disease progressed to a point that Bob was no longer able to coordinate buses, Brother Tarte attended the temple whenever someone could help him get there. "He was a faithful home teacher to the end," President Hutchins added. "He would come to every high priest group meeting. He could barely hold his head up, but he would look at you with his eye peering up. He would question you about your home teaching. He was just such a wonderful soul. . . . It was like he gave a hundred and fifty percent of himself the whole time. He was so faithful to the Church and was such a great example. He set the high water marks for a lot of people's lives.

"There is no doubt in my mind that if there [was] a single soul from heaven who [was] present at the dedication of [the Boston] Temple," President Hutchins summed up, it was Bob Tarte. "Bob Tarte was a giant."[46]

Just as Bob Tarte was embedded in the stake, Thelma Wilson was a fixture in the ward where she'd served as ward organist for as long as anyone could remember. It was not until fellow ward member Dave Foster was asked to assist with an elders quorum Christmas project, however, that he appreciated her true impact. In conjunction with the holiday, Dave accepted an assignment to take a plate of cookies to an inactive sister who lived in his town. The woman, Linda Butler, invited Dave in and he had a pleasant visit with her and her eleven-year-old daughter. Within a month, Dave was asked to return and begin home teaching the Butler family.

Dave assumed he was playing a role in a made-for-the-*Ensign* reactivation story but had to reevaluate his part after Linda accompanied him to church for the first time. In the course of introducing Linda to various members, Dave asked her to meet Sister Wilson. Although the two had never met, Linda immediately offered Thelma a sincere thanks for staying in touch. Unbeknownst to Dave, and to probably everyone but a stream of ward Relief Society presidents, Thelma had faithfully written monthly letters to Linda Butler for the better part of twenty years, after being asked to do so by a long-past leader. Nobody knew. It was quiet work, the kind that is done without any fanfare at all. "That's the kind of stuff that builds long-term strength in a stake or a ward," Dave stated, shaking his head. "That's been a real testimony to me of just being faithful."[47]

Neither Robert Tarte nor Thelma Wilson were serving in traditional leadership positions during the period for which they are best remembered. They were not standing at the pulpit or teaching at the front of the class. Their influence stemmed purely from the service they rendered. Reflecting on the influence of countless members like Bob and Thelma, one bishop observed, "It seems to me that what you might call the rank and file in the church are the ones who . . . provided the day-to-day motivating example to actually get out and do things."[48]

## I'll Do Thy Will with a Heart Sincere

Our sphere of responsibility is not limited to our callings, and the righteous influence we wield when pursuing our Father's work is not dependent on years of service. We each play a role in shaping the spirit, tone, and culture of the communities we inhabit and the groups in which we participate. We cannot shirk that responsibility by sitting idly, hoping others will address the needs around us.

Helen Low was asked to visit teach a woman who had joined the Church with her husband a few years prior. The two had attended church meetings regularly for a time, but eventually stopped coming. When Helen called the woman's home to schedule a visit, the sister protested, insisting it was unnecessary as she and her spouse had decided to return to their old faith. Helen was not willing to take no for an answer and said she was coming anyway.

Hurrying into the snow and sleet, Helen was dismayed to find that her car had a flat tire. Undeterred, Helen walked two miles to the sister's home and arrived in such a sorry state that the woman could not turn her away. A long conversation ensued regarding the couple's misgivings toward the Church. Finally the sister admitted that she had stopped attending because she felt the members of her ward weren't friendly and she had little in common with them. Acknowledging her discomfort, Helen asked quietly, "What do you do? Do you hug and greet people?" No, the sister replied, explaining she was too shy. "How do you know there aren't other people in the ward that feel exactly the same way that you do?" Helen posited. The question startled the woman. Asked to examine the role she played in shaping her experience, the sister returned to church with her husband. Some years later, after Helen had left the area, she paid a visit to her old ward and found that same couple actively greeting and welcoming people in the foyer.[49]

We don't have to teach for thirty years like George Albert Smith Jr., spend six hours a night in the car like Ann Romish, or write hundreds of letters like Thelma Wilson. What we are asked to do is use our time, talents, and abilities to build up the kingdom, which is what the Betty Hinckleys, Justin and LeAnn Lindseys, and Bob Tartes of the Church have in common with one another. We can make meaningful contributions simply by making a commitment of self.

Kristy Ludwig came to Massachusetts in 1996 for graduate studies and stayed on to work within the Boston public school system. As a stake service missionary serving in the Boston Ward, Kristy was intrigued by the number of youth filing in and out of the downtown chapel on weekday evenings to play basketball, many of whom were non-members. Channeling her professional training, Kristy wondered if there was a way to design a program within the Church to provide academic support for these urban teenagers, most of whom struggled with school.

Kristy approached the bishop of her singles ward with her query, and he advised her to talk to the stake president, Lloyd Baird. A man of great enthusiasm and big ideas, President Baird was immediately on board, but told Kristy that he felt the youth in Revere needed the program more than those in Boston. Caught off guard, all Kristy could ask was, "Where is Revere?"

With no connection to the teenagers in Revere, Kristy began attending the Revere Second Ward to get to know the youth and their leaders. The ward had more than one hundred young members, many of whom were first-generation Americans who had joined the Church alone, and all of whom were bombarded with challenges of living in communities where gang membership was prevalent and broken families were the norm. The bishop was involved with the youth and deeply concerned about the challenges they faced. He wanted them to develop life skills and prepare for the future, but many weren't making it through high school. The few who went to college often found the transition so difficult that they dropped out within a semester or two.

Brainstorming with ward leaders, Kristy suggested leveraging the ward's gymnasium to draw in youth. Weekly tutoring sessions at the meetinghouse would be followed by time on the basketball court. Kristy's initial solicitation of interest from the youth garnered no takers, but as she continued to meet with them regularly over the course of several months, a few agreed to give it a try. The first "Books and Basketball" activity was held in April 1999 and although the kickoff went well, within weeks it was clear that adjustments were needed. Volunteers solicited from the singles ward came only on the evenings for which they signed up and were not present enough to connect with students. Kristy knew she had to find a way for the tutors to develop real relationships with the youth.

Over the summer, Kristy concluded that Books and Basketball had to incorporate a one-on-one tutoring program where each student was assigned a tutor for the entire school year. Despite her confidence that this was best for the youth and necessary for the program's success, Kristy wondered how she could ask young adults consumed with demanding schedules of their own to devote one night a week to youth they did not know in an unfamiliar community. Suppressing her misgivings, Kristy pushed forward, praying that others would feel the same commitment she did. She visited apartments and homes within the singles wards, letting her peers know how much they were needed, while simultaneously encouraging the youth in Revere to participate in the program.

"The first full year was incredible," Kristy stated. "It was a great combination of people who were committed." Somehow the right people were always there at the right time and although there were more women in the singles wards than men, in its initial year the program attracted more male tutors than female, which was critical since there were more male youth. In other cases, it was clear a youth needed the right tutor to benefit from the program. Each time Kristy despaired of finding anyone prepared to work with a particular student, a new tutor would show up and some-how establish the relationship that ultimately worked.[50]

Even with these positive events, the nature of the program brought constant challenges. "There were many times," Kristy acknowledged, "that I contacted President Baird because I had run into roadblock after roadblock and feared that the program would have to fold if I did not have help. Each time he responded quickly and optimistically, running the interference I needed and obtaining the resources we needed to continue going forward." The reason it worked so well in Revere, Kristy continued, was because the stake president, bishop, and Young Men president were so supportive and committed. "They encouraged the kids to come and enabled the program to grow."[51]

Before long, word of the program spread from the youth of the Revere Second Ward to their friends. Tiffany Coolong showed up one Thursday evening after being invited by her friend Kathryn Ruiz, who attended each week with her three siblings. Even after the Ruiz family moved, Tiffany continued to attend, bringing more and more children and youth from the projects where she lived. Other kids did the same. Four years into the program, non-members made up almost three-quarters of the youth attending Books and Basketball at the Revere meetinghouse.

Throughout this period, Kristy had not forgotten the youth in the Boston Ward, which had since been split into three congregations. Every semester Kristy returned to President Baird to ask if the program could be expanded. Each time President Baird responded, "Not yet." Finally the Revere program reached a point where it was moderately self-sustaining. At a meeting with her bishop in the summer of 2003, Kristy restated her desire to take the Books and Basketball program to Boston. Knowing it was useless to talk Kristy out of her goal, her bishop contacted President Hiers of the newly formed Boston Stake. A few weeks later, Kristy found herself at a meeting with the new stake president and stake youth leaders, presenting a proposal for a Books and Basketball program to be held in the city.

The stake leaders were enthusiastic and agreed to make sure the youth were at the church when the kick-off event began. One Young Men leader felt so strongly about the program's potential that he personally promised to get the youth there. With repeated reminders that threatened to turn into harassment, he succeeded in delivering every youth and all the lead-ers to the building on the chosen night, driving many of them himself.

The first event involved a team-building activity that encouraged interaction, cooperation, and creativity. When the evening ended, it was clear there would be no problem getting the youth back the next week.[52]

Operating in Boston on Tuesdays and Revere on Thursdays, the Books and Basketball program became a powerful way of introducing young people, their parents, and urban neighborhoods to the Church and the gospel. Working with elementary and secondary school–age children, tutors spent the first ninety minutes of each evening working with youth on school assignments and academic goals, followed by refreshments, basketball, and socializing.[53] "Though the homework that is done each week is crucial," a Boston tutor remarked, "I believe it is the relationships that form over the course of the year that lead to the success of Books and Basketball."[54] Kristy Ludwig agreed that the consistency and support were crucial. "Especially in the beginning, the kids were just so surprised that someone would spend the time to help them with their homework and be involved in their lives. Some of the kids had not been particularly active in Church, but they became more involved after they began participating in the program."[55]

Volunteers in the program experienced similar benefits, as expressed by Katie Hart, who tutored in Revere. "One of the best decisions I have made," Katie said, "was to participate in the Books and Basketball program. Through the program I have learned of Heavenly Father's love for His children. I have witnessed troubled teens get their lives back on track because of the encouragement of dedicated tutors. I have seen confidence grow as students set aggressive goals and obtain them with the help of someone who believed in them. It is amazing that such a small sacrifice of time can so greatly enhance someone's life."[56]

Like most young adults who come to Boston for education and professional pursuits, Kristy Ludwig no longer lives in Massachusetts. Since her departure, the Books and Basketball program has continued to evolve. With fewer LDS youth in the Revere area and growing numbers of teens in the Boston units, the tutoring program Kristy felt inspired to start was consolidated in Boston, where it continues to bless the lives of youth and young adult volunteers and has served over four hundred youth since its founding in 1999.[57] A similar program was begun in Washington, D.C., after concerns about poor academic performance among LDS youth living in the heart of the capital led Church leaders to consult with other urban wards, including Boston. As in Boston, participants in the Washington, D.C., program have seen not only improvement with academic issues, but also increased missionary activity within the Church as a result of their efforts.[58]

Actively seeking a way to consecrate the knowledge, skills, and love for youth that she had developed through her profession, Kristy started something that enables other young adults to use their talents to bless others and do great good. The stake and ward leaders and countless volunteers who rallied behind Kristy's efforts made Books and Basketball's successes possible—a program that by its very nature leaves an indelible imprint in the lives of those involved. Bryan Goodliffe, another Boston tutor, summed it up when he said, 'I've been around long enough to know that things have a way of making a difference in someone's life, including my own, when you least expect it. It's all about having a willing mind, ready hands, and a pledged heart."[59]

Individual contributions can seem insignificant when viewed in isolation, but aggregated over a lifetime of faithful service and combined with those of others seeking similar pursuits, it is clear that we are building patterns and standards for others to follow. "Be not weary in well-doing," the Lord counsels, "for ye are laying the foundation of a great work" (Doctrine and Covenants 64:33).

# HOW FIRM
# IS YOUR FOUNDATION?

NAOMI CRANNEY moved to Boston in 1930 in connection with her husband's studies. By the time the Cranneys decided to remain in Massachusetts, Naomi's life was entwined with that of the branch, district, and mission, where the scarcity of members made each individual essential. Years stretched into decades as Naomi traveled the vast distances comprising the Atlantic District and New England Mission, serving as a Relief Society counselor, wife of the Cambridge Branch president, and the mission Primary president.

At that time, Primary administration fell to wives of the mission presidents, who asked sister missionaries to organize and teach Primary classes in the areas where they served. These classes would meet for a while but typically disbanded when the missionaries were transferred. Seeking to break this less-than-successful pattern, Naomi was asked to serve as Primary supervisor for the New England Mission in the early 1950s and charged with establishing Primaries among the scattered membership. Sister Cranney spent hours at the mission home, scouring mission records to locate children of Primary age. Once located, Naomi had to convince local branch leaders and families to organize and support the program. In an area filled with tiny branches and dispersed pockets of Saints, leaders were often skeptical of the program's value and reluctant to ask overstretched members to take on another project.

Naomi was attending a leadership conference in Keene, Vermont, when she was approached by a woman who announced they would no longer hold Primary in her area. "You don't understand the Church," the young sister spluttered. "I came here from Reno, Nevada, and I know all about the Church. . . . They're asking us to do three or four jobs here. We're not going to. We have a Relief Society bazaar coming up, and we don't have the time." Momentarily quiet, Naomi asked curiously, "Do you think the Lord is more interested in your Relief Society bazaar or in having the children taught the gospel? . . . Of course we'll have Primary."[1]

By her own calculation, Naomi spent five or more hours a day working to ensure each LDS child in New England had access to the blessings of Primary. Given immense distances and limited transportation options, most Primaries were held in homes, with instruction provided by mothers. At one point, Sister Cranney was supervising over 125 home Primaries, stretching from Connecticut up into Canada. When she was released after nine years of service, Primary was operating within each branch in the mission. Asked fifty years later which of her many callings she had found most difficult, Sister Cranney hesitated. "Well, I never looked at them that way," she finally said matter-of-factly. "They were there to be done, and I did them."[2]

District President Wilbur Cox set Nephi Edward Berg apart as president of the Lynn Branch in 1960. Immediately after doing so, President Cox informed President Ed Berg and his counselors that the branch needed to build a meetinghouse. "I don't know how you can do it, or even whether you can," President Cox stated. "Just try. Tell me if it works, and don't tell me that it won't work." Given no opportunity to object, President Berg got busy. "My counselors said it was impossible," Ed remembered, "but I and the Relief Society President . . . said it was possible."[3]

Church policy required local congregations to supply the first third of the funds necessary to construct a new building. With only four full tithe payers in the Lynn Branch, it was no surprise when President Berg's application to Church headquarters was rejected. Undeterred, President Berg borrowed a large sum of money from his sole proprietorship and traveled to Salt Lake City. The men with whom President Berg met at the Church Building Department were not encouraging. He persisted nonetheless. If permission was not granted to the branch, President Berg stated, he would mortgage his home and, combining those funds with monies withdrawn from his business, would build a chapel himself. The branch's application was granted.

To meet the remainder of the congregation's construction budget allotment, other members were required to provide labor and donations. Dean Williams was building his own home when construction on the meetinghouse began. Like the early Saints in Kirtland, Ohio, who heeded the Prophet's call to build the temple before tending to their homes, Dean immediately ceased work on his residence and did not resume construction until the chapel was finished. Because the branch could not afford to leave one stone unturned, Leonard Nuttall, an inactive brother, was asked to contribute several thousand dollars to the building fund. After some thought, Leonard agreed. Interested in the fate of his sizable investment, Leonard followed his money into activity, later serving as bishop of the Lynn Branch's descendant, the Lynnfield Ward.

Ed Berg's personal commitment did not insulate his family from trials. Although funds from his business enabled his congregation to act on the district president's admonition, President Berg's company floundered. Ed was quiet about the failure of his business, which he was ultimately compelled to close, as he led the branch in its efforts to complete the building. Taking advantage of his lighter schedule, President Berg spent six months working full-time at the construction site. He secured another job once the meetinghouse was finished and, a natural entrepreneur, went on to organize a number of successful business ventures afterward.[4]

Like the Cranneys, Loren and Sharon Dunn came to Boston with their one-year-old to pursue graduate school. The Dunns were asked to lead the Young Women and Young Men programs for the mission, which oversaw all ecclesiastical activities in the area since there were no stakes in New England. Juggling the demands of Loren's academic program, the Dunns spent their spare time traveling the mission for meetings and conferences.

A change in mission presidency yielded no reprieve, as Loren was called to serve as a counselor to President Truman Madsen. "We were at that time trying to cover a vastly large area as best we could," said Elder Dunn. "[I] and the other counselor would take two or three districts and President Madsen would take Canada and one or two other districts as well. . . . Our responsibility was, in effect, to try and develop the Church."

Sharon continued on as Young Women's president despite Loren's new call. "In the first years, [we didn't] get too well-acquainted in Boston," said Elder Dunn of that period, noting that they were required to be out of the city almost every weekend. "It was quite a challenge, but it was also quite an adventure to be . . . in these wonderful districts and branches throughout New England to help the Church to grow and to get acquainted with the Saints."[5]

Boyd K. Packer presided over the mission following the Madsens. While he released others, President Packer did not release Loren Dunn, although he granted Loren a two-month "leave of absence" to complete a critical portion of his studies. Brother Dunn fulfilled his personal responsibilities as expeditiously as possible and returned to serve until President Packer's release, at which point Elder Dunn was called as a Seventy and moved to Utah. Asked what he thought of the responsibilities he'd been asked to shoulder as a young student and father, Elder Dunn simply replied, "If that's what was required, that's what we did. It was never a matter of how we felt about it, it was just a matter of let's figure out how we're going to get it done. That was the approach. That's how we all were. . . . You're young and you're energetic. The challenge is not, 'Gee, I've got too much to do'; the challenge is, 'Let's figure out how we're going to do it.' That's how we all got through those years, wasn't it?"[6]

In the late 1970s, the Cambridge City Council passed an ordinance that banned parking on the streets around the Longfellow Park chapel, severely restricting members' ability to use the building. Several wards and branches shared the building, which was packed to overflowing every Sunday.[7] A new meetinghouse was desperately needed and a site was selected in nearby Belmont. Local Saints needed to raise over three hundred thousand dollars to come up with their third of the funds required for the new building. Much of the membership was made up of students and a good proportion of the remaining Saints lived on tight budgets. The amount seemed unobtainable.

Fund-raising projects, bazaars, and other money-generating events went into high gear. Employed members were asked to pledge three to five percent of their income to the building fund, on top of amounts already paid to tithing and the ward budget.[8] The sacrifice was significant. As one member noted, "Every dime that we didn't spend to actually keep life and limb together was real money gone."[9]

Sister Helen Rhodes was in her late seventies when fund-raising for the Belmont chapel began. A faithful, unmarried woman who had joined the Church later in life, Sister Rhodes took work at the local library, filing books and doing other odd jobs to earn money to help pay for a chapel she would never attend.[10] Another sister, Evelyn Ames, provided home day care services to bring in income while her husband attended law school. Setting a bit aside each month, she gradually accumulated enough to purchase a sewing machine for her family. When the request for building funds arose, however, she contributed her precious savings without hesitation. "It was truly a widow's mite," said a fellow ward member of these examples. "Someone who didn't have any financial resources beyond what [was] absolutely needed to live on. . . . It . . . inspired everybody else . . . to reexamine what their priorities were and to make sure that they were giving the right amount to be able to build that building as well."[11]

Jan and Paul McKinnon shared memories of their years attending church in Massachusetts, recounting extraordinary challenges they had faced and lessons they had learned as members of the Cambridge First Ward. When the interviewer realized they had talked exclusively about the years they'd spent in Cambridge, he asked the McKinnons to reflect on the time they spent in a more established ward in the Boston area. The McKinnons grew quiet, finally breaking the silence with more Cambridge-based stories of service and spiritual growth. When the interviewer pressed Jan and Paul once again for memories related to their service in the other ward, they could not recall a single story. Paul shrugged and said, "I guess we just never felt like we were needed in the [other] ward."[12]

The McKinnons' years in Cambridge were characterized by demanding callings and massive fund-raising goals. In days prior to the consolidated schedule, church activity required carpooling through traffic, traveling long distances, and weeks where every day seemed to involve some type of Church gathering. These realities required members to make meaningful sacrifices in almost every area of their life as they worked together for a common cause. The McKinnons' inability to equate the time they spent in their two wards was not a slight toward the experiences they had in the latter ward or the friendships the McKinnons formed there. Instead, the fact that many of the McKinnons' defining moments occurred in Cambridge is a reminder that we grow most when we are stretched most. "We spent a lot of time together," said Jan of that period of her life. "I think we're all very well aware of the sacrifices people were making. . . . I don't know what it was about the friendships we formed then, but they've been lifetime friendships."[13]

## A Day of Sacrifice

Things have changed since the years recalled by Naomi Cranney, Ed Berg, the Dunns, and even the McKinnons. In most of the United States, including New England, distances between meetinghouses and members no longer require the travel and time Naomi and the Dunns expended to fulfill their callings. The consolidated meeting schedule limits the number of days we attend Church meetings and the hours of the Sabbath spent in communal worship. While we still tithe, non-tithing contributions are voluntary and congregations are no longer required to meet specific budget and building fund allocations. Buildings are constructed using general Church funds and members no longer devote months of labor to worship in a chapel.

"I was very happy when we went to Sunday," one sister admitted, noting how the consolidated schedule reduced the number of commitments filling her weekday schedule. "But also you lost something. You lost the feeling of being more of a community, because you would see these people constantly."[14]

"It was certainly a lot more expensive to be a Mormon in the old days," said a brother who joined the Church in 1955. But many blessings came from that, he acknowledged thoughtfully. "A lot of devotion was required."[15]

With smaller ward and stake boundaries, more accountability for our schedules, and less ecclesiastical demand for our earnings, the things we are asked to sacrifice on behalf of the Lord's kingdom are not always obvious. But although the type of sacrifices the Lord requires has changed over time, the imperative of sacrifice has not changed. Speaking to Joseph Smith, the Lord stated, "I, the Lord, require the hearts of the children of men. Behold, now it is called today until the coming of the Son of Man, and verily it is a day of sacrifice" (Doctrine and Covenants 64:22–23).

Consider the reflections of one individual who worried that despite a life of faithful service within the Church, his efforts were not what they could have been. He questioned the value of his contributions, suggesting that the service he rendered could have been supplied by others.

When taken in the context of our covenant to consecrate all in becoming a more effective tool in the Lord's hands, I wonder whether we have taken the right path. If we had started life with the objective to consecrate all, would we have been led along a similar trajectory?

. . . We had the option to locate in many Boston-area neighborhoods. If we had asked the Lord where we might make the greatest difference, our trajectory, our opportunities, and our impact might have been much different. This is not to say we have not had impact. Wherever one is, in whatever circumstances one finds oneself, there is service to be given and callings to be completed. That, for the most part, we have done. But by locating based on worldly opportunities and comfort, we may have limited our impact. . .

If I had begun the process of settling in the Boston area by covenanting with the Lord that I would consecrate all (even our family's comfort and worldly opportunities) in becoming the tool he needed in the place he needed it, we may have landed in a very different place. Our impact may have been much less generic.[16]

In some ways, prior calls on members for funds, labor, and time made the principle of sacrifice easier to live, providing clear demarcations as to what was expected. Called to live the same law as our predecessors, but subject to fewer explicit calls to sacrifice, we must each determine for ourselves what we are willing to give to build the Lord's kingdom.

## Here Am I

Bill Fresh was living in New Jersey when he received a strong impression that he and his family would soon be returning to Massachusetts, where he would be called as bishop of the Lynnfield Ward—a ward in which his family had lived a few years prior. With advance notice from the Spirit, Bill was not surprised when, three days later, he was asked to return to the Boston area to head his company's New England division. Bill was house-hunting when he received a call from the president of the Boston Stake, Wilbur Cox. "Bill," said President Cox, "I understand you're moving back to Boston. Would you have lunch with me?"

Over a meal, President Cox asked where the Fresh family was likely to live upon their return. Uncomfortably, Bill admitted he was looking at homes in Lexington, Wellesley, and Weston where there were strong Scouting and Young Men programs for his sons.

"Have you thought about going back to Lynnfield?" President Cox prodded.

"I have, President," replied Bill honestly. "I suppose I'm a little like Jonah."

"Well, they sure need the leadership back there," President Cox continued.

"President," said Bill, with some resignation, "if you want me to go to Lynnfield, I'll go to Lynnfield."

"No, no, no," President Cox stated firmly. "I can't make that decision for you."

Left alone with his conscience, Bill felt too guilty to continue looking at houses elsewhere. Bill purchased a home in Lynnfield and the Fresh family returned to Massachusetts in September. Bill was ordained bishop of the Lynnfield Ward at the beginning of October. Barely six months later, Bill Fresh succeeded President Wilbur Cox as president of the Boston Stake—setting him down a course that profoundly influenced his life and the lives of his family members.[17]

Individuals willing to serve where the Lord asks are still needed. George and Marci McPhee were happy in their ward when they were asked to attend a meeting regarding a reorganization that would affect several congregations. George was a convert who had never attended another ward, and the proposed realignment would put Marci in the same ward as her ex-husband. Full of trepidation, they decided to attend the meeting but agreed not to commit to anything while there.

Things were proceeding well until the stake president stood and said firmly, "You go to the ward whose boundaries you live in, or you need permission from the First Presidency, the stake president, and both bishops." George caught his wife's eye just as the president went on to say, "All members of the Weston 1st Ward, please stand up." Looking at each other and nodding, George and Marci rose to their feet—acknowledging membership in their new ward.

"I feel like there have been so many incredible blessings [that have] come to us because at that moment we said, 'I will go and do,'" said Marci. "I feel, when I look back on my mortality, that will be one of the moments that I'm most proud of. At that moment, when the Lord said through his servants, 'This is where you're supposed to be,' we didn't hesitate. At that moment we said, 'We're here.'"[18]

Today the Church is sinking roots in areas where it wasn't even recognized a few decades ago. In the 1980s and early 1990s, the Boston Stake organized a number of small branches in downtown Boston and outlying communities. Recent converts comprised the majority of these branches, some of which were established to serve members who did not speak English. The stake presidency decided to identify wards as "sister units" to make sure each branch had adequate leadership and administrative support. Branch presidents could call upon their assigned sister ward to provide support the branch lacked internally, and mature wards took care of administrative record-keeping tasks. "My experience," stated Mitt Romney, then president of the Boston Stake, "is not only did these sister combinations strengthen the small units . . . but perhaps just as importantly they strengthened the stronger, larger sister units as well because we had to stretch in a way we never had to stretch before."[19]

John Wright was one of many long-time members asked to serve outside his home ward when he was called to be bishop of the Revere Second Ward in a community populated by large numbers of Cambodian immigrants. In reflecting on his experiences serving within the Church, John referred time and time again to his experiences in Revere, despite the fact that he had filled many ward and stake callings previously. "Revere is, in my mind, where the Church is . . . happening today," he explained. "It brings together . . . people from very diverse socioeconomic backgrounds—newer and very, very untried Church members on the one hand with some young couples who have now moved into that area of Boston because it's much less expensive than some of the old traditional places. . . . In the time I've been in Revere, I have really begun to see where the Church is going to grow. I can see where the vision of the Church in the future is.[20]

"I have seen people in the Revere Second Ward whose lives are really devoted to giving service," remarked Bishop Wright. "They came there knowing that they would have to serve a lot," he continued. "One of the characteristics of that ward is that the people who elected to move into it in many cases came there looking to serve in the Church.

"If I had it to do again," said John of his prior service as bishop of an established suburban ward, "I think I would have tried to find ways to stretch us more and to involve people in service more than we did. . . . [In Revere], you feel like you've got the opportunity . . . to affect lives. . . . It's so rewarding. It's such a blessing to be involved in that kind of service. It's fabulous."[21]

The Church's growth in downtown Boston and other urban communities is similar to that occurring in other large cities in the United States. Observing the experience his son and daughter-in-law were having in the city years after his tenure, Elder Dunn commented on the opportunities for sacrifice and service this expansion brings. "They're seeing the whole diversity of culture that I suppose was always there but that we were never a part of because we never really got down into the inner city. That's all changed now. . . . The gospel is there to minister to these people as well, and the needs are greater. For a lot of these young people, . . . their involvement in these units . . . changes their lives and becomes almost as worthy, in some respects, as the formal education they're getting. . . . You come out of that setting and you're never quite the same."[22]

At one point during his term as stake president, Mitt Romney received a call from a survey group engaged by the Church to evaluate stake leaders' experiences with urban branches. The individual conducting the survey indicated that many stakes were finding such branches problematic and burdensome, due to common factors such as lack of leadership, limited priesthood holders, financial strains, and lackluster growth. After absorbing the proffered data and examples, President Romney responded, "Our experience has been somewhat different. This is the best thing that ever happened to our stake—the explosion in these small branches that we could support. It caused our tired Saints who had thought they had given all they could and done all the work they could for the gospel to somehow lengthen their stride. . . . We couldn't have been more pleased."[23]

## Contributions of Faith

William Knecht attended the original Boston, Cambridge, and Worcester Branches as a child and appreciated the substantial commitments individuals and families made to live the gospel. Even so, the Atlantic District presidency's push to construct meetinghouses during the 1950s caught him off-guard. In a Sabbath-day priesthood meeting, President Wilbur Cox testified that the building program was so essential to the Church's future that it was worthy of unusual efforts. He asked the brethren to commit to raise more money to build chapels within New England, even if it meant mortgaging their homes. Brother Knecht's eyes strayed to the man seated next to him. The man's legs were crossed, exposing a visible hole in the sole of his shoe that was awkwardly patched with a piece of cardboard. William watched in wonderment as the brother raised his arm to the square to support President Cox's call to action. William, in contrast, kept his hands in his lap, convinced that he could not support the district presidency in this request when the congregation was clearly full of individuals with pressing monetary needs.

In time the money was raised and the planned chapels built. Looking back, said Brother Knecht, those meetinghouses proved a great boon to the Church's growth.[24]

"A religion that does not require the sacrifice of all things never has power sufficient to produce the faith necessary unto life and salvation,"[25] Joseph Smith taught our pioneer forebearers, many of whom were asked to lay all they had upon the altar of sacrifice. Discipleship that requires us to forego those things we associate with security and comfort takes faith and helps us understand the measure of our own commitment.

Shortly after Kevin Schmidt was called to serve as a bishop, he learned that only three of his ward's six missionaries serving in the field were being supported financially. Many members were unemployed, underemployed, or in the midst of other economic struggles. Without sufficient funding, the amounts needed to support the missionaries were being deducted from the ward's budget, and the ward was operating in the red. Needing an additional $375 a month to close the gap and left with few alternatives, the new bishop called families into his office one by one to ask if they would be willing to commit five to ten dollars a month for the missionary fund.

Sensing the bishop's concern, many agreed to give up small personal expenditures to help meet the ward's needs. Others asked for time to determine how much they could give. In a meeting with one family already living hand to mouth, the father looked at the bishop and said, quietly, "We're just not sure about our financial situation. We'll get back to you."

The following day, the bishop's wife, Sue, called the mother of the family on an unrelated matter. As their conversation ended, the mother said, "Tell Kevin that we will give him the money, even if we have to take out a loan." Sue asked what she meant. "The missionary money," was the reply. Still puzzled, Sue asked how much money her husband had asked of them.

"$375 a month," said the mother simply. "The bishop explained that it costs $375 a month to keep these missionaries in the field. We're not able to do it within our current budget, so we're willing to take out a loan. We were up all night—I couldn't sleep. But we'll take out a loan. We'll give Kevin his money."

"I think you had an Abrahamic test," Sue said meekly, as she digested the misunderstanding that had occurred and the faith of this humble family. "And you passed."[26]

Other than tithing and fast offerings, demands on our resources are relatively infrequent when compared to any other period of the Church. Combine this with the relative prosperity we enjoy today, and it is clear that even when we give of our funds, we can miss the spiritual significance and power associated with the law of sacrifice.

Jamie Lyon was bishop of a university ward composed mostly of single students when Saints were asked to donate money to the building of the Washington D.C. Temple. In accordance with Church policy, each stake in the new temple district was assigned an amount.

Bishop Lyon realized there was more at stake than the assessment when the call for funds went out. "The essence of the gospel is sacrifice," he stated, adding his belief that the experience of contributing to the temple fund should involve more than simply writing a check.

With sacrament meeting talks, Sunday School lessons, and priesthood and Relief Society classes focused on the meaning of sacrifice, Bishop Lyon challenged every member of the ward to find a meaningful way to give of themselves. Instead of focusing on a specific dollar amount, Bishop Lyon suggested that each individual assess his or her life to determine what would constitute a significant sacrifice and dedicate that to the temple. Meeting personally with members after issuing this challenge, one of the few married couples in the ward reported that sleep was the thing they would miss more than anything else. With this awareness, both husband and wife took temporary night jobs that left them only a few hours of sleep a night. The money earned at those extra jobs became the proceeds they donated to the temple building fund.

A young professional with a successful career approached the bishop to ask what an appropriate contribution might be in his circumstances. Challenging him a bit, Bishop Lyon observed that he had never served a mission. The man acknowledged this, explaining that he had not had the opportunity. Bishop Lyon knew something of the brother's financial means and asked, "How would you like to contribute to the Washington Temple fund the equivalent amount it would have taken for you to support yourself for two years on a mission?" The bishop did not name an amount, but after prayer and contemplation, the brother wrote a check for an amount in excess of what a mission would likely have required.

"Dozens of times our members . . . internalized the principle of sacrifice," said Bishop Lyon. "The result was that the university ward contributed more to the building fund than any other ward in the Boston

Stake." For Bishop Lyon, the dollars donated were simply emblematic of the devotion and commitment he saw in so many of the young members with whom he served.[27]

The dollar value of our contribution does not matter to the Lord. After all, it was He who declared the widow's mite to be of more worth than all the gifts cast into the treasury by worshippers of greater means (Luke 21:1–3). As such, the attitude and willingness with which we give is as important as, if not more important than, the offering itself—a lesson demonstrated by, of all things, a ping-pong table.

Clayton Christensen had arranged to borrow a ping-pong table for a Mutual activity. Borrowing a truck, Clayton retrieved the table and set it up in the cultural hall, where the youth had an energetic tournament. At the evening's conclusion, Clayton asked the boys to take the table down while he pulled the truck around to load it. "In the process of taking the table apart," Clayton groaned, "the boys dropped it and split one leg off. I was devastated because this was a brand new table . . . and I had promised to return it in as-new condition."

Embarrassed, Clayton took the ping-pong table to his home for about a week until he devised a way to reattach the leg. He tried to make the table look as good as possible with the help of some green paint, but could not disguise the broken leg. Finally he took the table back to its owners and admitted what had happened. The husband's response was one Clayton would never forget. "When my wife and I first were married," he said, "we made a decision that we would never get upset about losing something that could be replaced with money. The only thing that would upset us is if this caused you not to come back to us and ask us for anything else."[28]

## If You Won't, Who Will?

When we think about sacrifice, too often we imagine our response to the big request. Like Naaman the leper, who was disappointed when Elisha's servant sent him to bathe in the river Jordan (see 2 Kings 5:1–13), we fix our sights on the call to do some great thing. In reality we are rarely proved by the grand gesture. True tests are often disguised by their ordinariness. Will we accept a calling that is inconvenient? Do we serve those outside our immediate circle? Are we willing to ask the Father's will when the answer may lead us down a different path than the one we are pursuing?

Chase Peterson had just assumed an administrative post at Harvard University when his stake president asked him to serve as president of the

Cambridge University Branch in 1974. Chase didn't know how he could accept such a significant commitment given the high profile responsibilities and demanding travel schedule his new role entailed. After some thought, he told the stake president that he didn't think he could do it. Chase shared the exchange with his family upon his return home. As he finished speaking, his twelve-year-old daughter looked at him through tear-filled eyes and asked, "Well, Daddy, if people like you don't take jobs like that, who will?"

Convinced that his daughter spoke with the wisdom of the Almighty, Chase asked his stake president to ask again so he could accept this time. "That was the answer," Chase stated.[29]

The fact that many members come to Boston in connection with academic pursuits results in a long-standing challenge, observed one former stake president. Thrust into a competitive environment and used to being among the best and brightest, some conclude they must refuse callings to succeed. "There are some folks that say, 'This is my time to study and then when I leave and I get a real job, it will be my time to serve in the Church,'" he explained. "Of course, it never works out that way because life just gets busier; it doesn't get simpler."[30]

Another stake leader recalled large numbers of families who came to the area with lots of promise, much of which went unrealized because they failed to sort their commitment to the Church out from the backdrop of other demands. These members had no shortage of excuses for refusing a call, rejecting a particular doctrine, or simply assigning priorities elsewhere. "It was interesting," he remarked. "There are several of them that just kind of hung on while they were here, and since they've left, they've all taken nosedives in their Church beliefs."[31]

There is no room for complacency when it comes to our willingness to heed the Lord's call, even in small things. With each response, we establish patterns of faith and obedience that ultimately determine the strength of our spiritual foundation. One sister, explaining why her time in New England had been so important, said, "For me, it was the first time I have ever really just thrown my whole heart and soul and all my energy and time into the Church."[32] Another woman recalled a visiting teaching route that took her into neighborhoods she'd always avoided and required the better part of a day to cover. "I remember that I grew from that," she said. "That was the first time I had ever really sacrificed something for a Church calling."[33] A brother described the juggling act he and his wife performed during graduate school while he served in a bishopric and she served in a Relief Society presidency. "This made us extremely busy," he noted, "but it was one of the happiest and most fulfilling periods of our lives."[34]

The demands of life were pressing upon Edna Thibault when she was asked to serve as an early-morning seminary teacher. Struggling to keep up, Edna sat up late one night, studying the epistles of Paul in preparation for the next day's lesson. As she reviewed the class materials and assigned verses, Sister Thibault found herself drawing insights and making connections she had never seen before. "As I thought about how wonderful it was to understand this so much more deeply," she said, "I realized that the person who was benefiting the most from this early-morning seminary assignment was me. Even though it was very hard and very inconvenient, I was actually having the best Church service experience of my life."[35]

Reflecting on her callings within the Church, Jo Maitland recalled how much she cherished her time as compassionate service leader in the Relief Society. "I really loved the service that I was able to render and the testimonies I could share with the sisters," she said. When the call came, however, she almost didn't accept it. "I remember praying about it," said Jo. "The Lord said He could not give me the blessings He desired to give me if I did not accept that calling. And I did accept it. And I received great and wonderful blessings from that calling. It was the most wonderful experience, as far as callings go, that I ever had in the Church."[36]

When Valerie Anderson's bishop called her into his office and asked her to teach the Gospel Doctrine class, she was so horrified that she burst into tears and cried for half an hour. Sure that she could not do what was asked, Valerie began flipping through the ward directory, suggesting others more suited for the call. Unmoved but sympathetic, her bishop finally shook his head and said, "No, Valerie. I'm sorry. It's you."

"After I got over being petrified," said Valerie, "I loved it. It was the most rewarding calling in the sense that I really had to study. I studied every night from 11:00 to 1:00 a.m. after the kids were in bed. I could sit down and think. . . . I learned all kinds of things. It was marvelous. I loved it. I was really unhappy when they wanted to release me.

"I remember one thing that really struck me," Valerie continued. "We were talking about one of the periods when there was a lot of persecution in the early church, and the Saints just prayed and prayed for relief. Well, the Lord gave them three revelations: pay tithing, send the men on missions, and build a temple. I'm going, 'Excuse me. This is not my idea of relief.' I am thinking lightning bolts from Heaven . . . , yet as you saw it unfold and you saw how making these sacrifices drew the Saints together, obviously the Lord was smarter than I was."[37]

Speaking on this topic, President Harold B. Lee said "I [am] persuaded of one great truth: Whenever the Lord has a great blessing for one of his children, He puts that son or daughter in the way to make a great sacrifice."[38] This truth notwithstanding, sometimes when we're asked to give things that are truly significant, the associated blessings are not immediately evident.

Like many of their peers, Kim and Sue Clark were asked to assume a variety of demanding callings while Kim was finishing school and beginning his academic career. As challenging as those years were, a greater trial presented itself when Kim was asked to serve as bishop of a congregation away from their home ward. Sue had experienced the test of raising young children with her husband in a bishopric, but having him lead a ward separate from the one his family attended was even harder. Between the evenings Kim spent on work obligations and the nights he spent meeting with members of the ward over which he presided, Kim and Sue rarely saw each other. The Clarks had seven children under age eleven, the youngest of which were twins. "I was really bitter," Sue admitted. "I couldn't understand why Heavenly Father would ask us to make that kind of sacrifice when there were other men in the ward who didn't have so many children." Despite the hardships, Kim kept repeating, almost as a mantra, "We'll be blessed. Whatever sacrifices we're asked to make, we will be blessed."

Recalling how they survived those years, Kim said, "We had to change. We had to change really significantly. . . . It was the hardest thing either one of us has ever done. I hope it's the hardest thing we ever have to do. The Lord really blessed us during that time. He didn't bless us by removing us from the situation; He blessed us by helping us to change."

"And we have been so blessed," said Sue, reflecting on events since that period. "Blessings and sacrifice don't always equal each other in any one given time," she pointed out, "but blessings far outrank the sacrifices you make at another time in life. You can't stop sacrificing and stop giving just because it's hard. Because another time in your life when you really need the blessings, the blessings will come and they'll be there."[39]

The Clarks' experience is similar to one Elder David A. Bednar's wife, Susan, has shared. Reliving an evening many years ago when the stake president knocked on her door to inform her that David was being called as his counselor, she recalled focusing on how often her husband would be away from home and their three young boys. Describing her feelings, Susan said,

> I did support him, though not always enthusiastically. I just found myself viewing my support of him as an extreme sacrifice on my part. I focused on all the things that I was having to give up . . . I was enduring, but not cheerfully. I finally decided that some changes needed to be made, that I needed a change of both mind and heart. As I pleaded with the Lord, as I studied, as I pondered, as I prayed, gradually I came to know and understand the difference between sacrifice and consecration. Sacrifice . . . is what we give up to build the kingdom of God. Consecration is what we give. . . . And once I understood that better, I was able to support him more effectively.[40]

Sacrifice is what we give up and consecration is what we give. Whether it be a ping-pong table, our desires, or our time, we are asked to sacrifice so we might learn to give that which is ultimately required—the broken heart and contrite spirit that come when we consecrate ourselves by submitting our will to that of the Lord.

## Unlocking the Blessings of Heaven

The principles of sacrifice and consecration are often discussed in terms of time commitments and temporal forbearance, but they are also crucial keys in seeking inspiration and spiritual sustenance. Too often we, like Oliver Cowdery, seek sacred privileges and communication with the divine without taking any thought, save it is to ask (see Doctrine and Covenants 9:7).

This common mistake was highlighted for Brent Lambert when Elder Gordon B. Hinckley, then a member of the Quorum of the Twelve, visited Providence, Rhode Island, where Brent was serving as stake president. Elder Hinckley needed to call a new stake patriarch during the stake conference and, mindful of this responsibility, had asked President Lambert to provide the names of three worthy candidates. During the ride from the airport, Elder Hinckley asked the stake president to provide a detailed description of each man. Last, Elder Hinckley asked that each brother offer a prayer during the Saturday meetings of the conference.

After a long Saturday, Elder Hinckley excused himself at midnight and retired to his room. Greeting the future prophet at 6:00 a.m. the next day, President Lambert casually asked if Elder Hinckley had enjoyed a pleasant night. Elder Hinckley shook his head. Seeing the stake president's concern, Elder Hinckley explained that he had been on his knees until four in the morning, praying to know the Lord's will so he could call the next patriarch of the stake.

Recounting this rare glimpse into the life of one of the Lord's special witnesses, President Lambert admitted his surprise. "Here was an apostle of the Lord," he explained. "You'd think all he would have to do is ask and it would be given, because he is just doing the Lord's work. But he had to pray for four hours to find out who it was. That was very interesting to me."[41]

If the Lord's anointed are required to labor to know His will in what are presumably routine matters for them, why should we expect inspiration to come more easily for us? As with Elder Hinckley, the Lord asks us to do our part: study the matter out; pray with real intent; and approach Him in an attitude of humility, that our heart and mind may receive light and knowledge.

Ken Hutchins described a complicated decision-making process that he and his counselors were required to undertake as a stake presidency. "I came to understand," he said, "how each one of us has a responsibility to work through a process and not have an expectation that the Lord is just there to rubber stamp our calls or the things that we want to have decided right away. There is wisdom in the scripture where it talks about in the Lord's due time. I really think this is one of the principles that is lost on a lot of members of the Church." More than once, the presidency grappled with an issue to no avail. But because they approached the Lord in prayer and fasting, there were times when direct answers came unbidden in following days. Although the process to understand the Lord's will was onerous and time-consuming, said the former stake president, "It was a great learning experience. Some of the decisions that we make in life, it doesn't bother me anymore that the answer doesn't come easy. [I don't] feel abandoned by the Lord. It's like, 'I haven't got this right yet.'"[42]

The phenomenon that caused the McKinnons to wax eloquent about their Cambridge years, John Wright to focus on lessons learned serving outside his own suburban ward, and Jo Maitland and Valerie Anderson to cherish the callings they almost turned down is directly related to the significant ways each was asked to sacrifice to fulfill responsibilities associated with that period of their lives. The lesson for us is that happiness is not found in complacency. The admonition to be "anxiously engaged" in a good cause (Doctrine and Covenants 58:27) is perhaps not so imperative for strengthening the foundation of the Lord's kingdom as it is for building our own.

"I think the whole gospel as we understand it is focused around what we consider sacrifice—obedience and sacrifice," said a former New Hampshire stake president, emphasizing the relative nature of sacrifice. In almost any area, he observed, we can sacrifice much more than we are. "The sacrifices in the gospel . . . are not really sacrifices in my way of thinking," given that they always bring great blessings. "These blessings return to us in terms of friends, fellowship, understanding, communication, spiritual insights, and the ability to live better lives."[43]

Lee LaPierre had been called to serve in the bishopric of a new ward when the windows of heaven seemed to close above him. The dynamics of the new ward were unfamiliar, and Lee was amazed at the number of issues the bishopric was asked to resolve. Sundays had previously been a time of renewal, but now they were draining and emotionally exhausting. Lee felt his spiritual bearings slipping and realized he was at a personal crossroads. Against these challenges, Brother LaPierre said, "I made a decision that really affected the rest of my life to this point, and no doubt will for the rest of my life to come. . . . I decided if I was going to have a testimony and have the kind of spiritual enrichments and experiences that I wanted . . . I was going to have to take responsibility for that. I couldn't depend on going to church . . . to be soothed or encouraged. If there were issues that I couldn't quite understand or matters that needed to be resolved, I was going to have to find a way to come to some sort of spiritual understanding on my own."

Having come to this conclusion, Brother LaPierre decided he needed to spend considerably more time in the scriptures to study and seek specific direction regarding matters on his mind. "I needed the spiritual bearing," he explained, "so I began. Over the course of time, I found that it worked. It was amazing. I had some of the most marvelous experiences that I have ever had as a member of the Church in my own room, studying, thinking about the gospel, pondering, asking the Lord in prayer."

As he pursued this course, an interesting thing happened. The tension and issues Lee had felt with other members subsided and things that had frustrated him lost their importance. "I found myself making friends where before it was contention," he said, recalling how the new ward began to feel like home. "Those are days never to be forgotten. As I look back, I clearly see a purpose that took place in my life that I don't think could have taken place in any other way."[44]

"Without sacrifice," warned President Hinckley, "there is no true worship of God."[45] Recognizing this truth, Brother LaPierre said his most serious concern in a subsequent stake calling was the number of individuals and families that failed to sink their own spiritual roots. "You can live for a while in the Church off of the love and affection and enthusiasm of the others . . . but there comes a day when it's time to pay. If you haven't been doing some of the personal things in your life that make the difference, the day will come that the sun will be hot enough that your roots are going to dry out. That's often what happens. For some it comes sooner, for some it comes later.

"As we work with these units, I guess I'm not so concerned about getting all the records just right and making sure that we have proper meetings and so forth. What I hope is happening is that these families are going home, they are using the scriptures, they are learning to study them on their own, they are learning that prayer is a real resource, and that they are having their own personal experiences that way. That's what will bind people to the Church—when it becomes alive on their own knees in their own home."[46]

Born and raised in Massachusetts, Jonathan Williams saw the growth of the Church in New England firsthand as he accompanied his father on visits to the scattered congregations his father served as a high councilman, stake president, and regional representative. Being a member of the Church seemed different then, Jonathan observed, remembering how it felt to be the only deacon in his ward and the ambitious long-term goals and attendant financial burdens undertaken by such a small group of Saints. "[The Church] seemed to have a bigger impact on everybody because we were so spread out. It seems like a lot of effort was put in to make sure everything went well."

Given the circumstances, you wondered how it could ever come to fruition, Jonathan noted. But with each member contributing their part and then some, every goal was met.

Taking this in, a listener interjected. "What an inspiration that must be—to you and all the others—to see the growth of the Church and to see the fruits of all the work and all the time that the early members put in to make it grow. . . . Now it seems so solid."

Jonathan nodded in agreement, "You get relaxed."

"But it must not have been solid back then," the listener pressed. "It must have been fragile."

Hesitating only a moment, Jonathan's response speaks volumes about what happens when we commit ourselves to the Lord's work: "But it never felt that way."[47]

# 4

# BY WEAK
# AND SIMPLE THINGS

THREE YEARS after the formation of the Boston Stake, S. Dilworth Young of the First Council of the Seventy was sent to preside over a stake conference held at the Cambridge chapel in 1965. Elder Young entered the Relief Society room at the conclusion of the meetings to find a roomful of people waiting for him. Glancing at his watch, Elder Young declared, "I've got to catch an airplane. So I'm just going to set you apart. I won't say any words of blessing because if you do your job, you'll get the blessings."

True to his word, Elder Young made quick work of setting new stake leaders apart. Then a young man newly called to the high council stood. Something about him made Elder Young ask whether they'd met before. No, the new high councilman said, but his brother had served a mission in New England during Elder Young's tenure as mission president. S. Dilworth shook his head and declared, "You need a blessing." With hands on the young man's head, Elder Young ordained him a high priest, set him apart as a high councilor, and pronounced the following words, heard by all in the room:

"Now as you go throughout this area, you will find that the Lord has to do with what he's got. You'll find the leadership is really nothing but a bunch of rascals. But I bless you that if you will pray and be humble and study the scriptures and stand to the office to which you've been called, He will reveal to you that you are nothing but a rascal too."[1]

Few would go on record referring to any of the Lord's anointed as "rascals," but most of us have had the experience of questioning an individual's credentials as they were sustained to a new position. When it comes to callings, Elder Young's unique counsel provides two pointed reminders. First, we should not—and cannot—judge who is best suited to labor in the Church. Second, each of us is called to the work, despite (and sometimes because of!) our weaknesses.

The scriptures are replete with examples of individuals with questionable qualifications called to play key roles in the Lord's kingdom. Enoch was hated of the people, Moses was slow of speech, the Galilean fishermen were asked to embark on a radical and instantaneous career change, and the uneducated farm boy was chosen to bring about a "marvelous work and a wonder." If anything, the Lord has continuously demonstrated that one's ability to serve has nothing to do with being well-regarded, well-spoken, well-heeled, or well-educated. "Look not on his countenance, or on the height of his stature," He instructs, "for the Lord seeth not as man seeth . . . but the Lord looketh on the heart" (1 Samuel 16:7). Given the Lord's infinite capacities, it should be no surprise when ordinary men and women do extraordinary things in partnership with the Lord.

In 1976, a small group of Spanish-speaking Saints began meeting together as a Sunday School group. After a few years, the Sunday School was reorganized as a dependent branch of the Cambridge First Ward. Sister Carmen Francisco Quintera, one of the few Spanish-speaking missionaries in the area, was assigned to the new branch. In that capacity, Sister Francisco and her companion helped bring many people into the Church, most of whom were women. Carmen moved to Massachusetts after her mission because she felt her work in New England was not done.[2] She was asked to serve as Relief Society president of the Cambridge Spanish Branch, the adult population of which was comprised of approximately forty active women and six active men.

Realizing that the congregation could not grow and progress without priesthood strength, Sister Francisco asked the sisters of the Relief Society to spend a weekend in fasting and prayer. Uniting their faith, the women prayed that God would send a man who could act as a leader and serve as a means for bringing other worthy priesthood holders into the branch. Sure enough, a stranger walked into the chapel foyer that very Sunday. But instead of the mature, capable leader for whom the sisters felt they had prayed, the newcomer was a scrawny, boyish-looking illegal immigrant named Jaime Valarezo. Jaime was young and had recently joined the Church. He stuttered so badly that he was almost impossible to understand. Shaking her head in disbelief, Sister Francisco asked one of her counselors, "*This* is the answer to our fast?"

Unaware of the stir he had caused, Jaime made himself part of the branch in his quiet, unassuming way. The gospel was Jaime's first priority, and he was willing to dedicate hours upon hours to the Church. Whenever anything needed to be done, Jaime was there to do it, whether that meant handing out hymnals, arranging the Sacrament table, filling the baptismal font, or sweeping floors. If a child fussed during services, Jaime would attend to him so the mother could listen. Jaime was able to pray clearly despite his ordinarily debilitating stutter and when he offered the invocation or benediction in a meeting, people commonly remarked on the Spirit that filled the room. The missionaries began taking Jaime on splits because he was always available, which enabled them to teach more people. Before long, baptisms in the branch began to increase.

One afternoon the missionaries were trying to teach a family at the meetinghouse. Partway through the discussion, the elders asked Jaime if he would look after the small children so the parents would not be distracted. Jaime had a natural affinity for children and the children enjoyed their time with him so much that they begged their parents to return to "Jaime's church." Eventually the entire family was baptized. Soon Jaime was spending hours at the Cambridge building, tending to the needs of young boys and girls as the missionaries taught mothers and fathers in back-to-back appointments. With Jaime's assistance, the missionaries were able to make more appointments and teach more effectively. Very quickly the dependent Spanish branch began out-baptizing all other units in the stake, averaging two to three baptisms a week. Investigators attending the branch could sense the Spirit and enthusiasm among new members and the branch began to swell and strengthen.

By this point, it was obvious to all that Jaime was an invaluable asset. Sadly, however, the man who talked easily with God and children still struggled to converse with adults. Undaunted, after four years of scrimping and saving, Jaime approached the stake president and asked to serve a mission of his own. The stake president readily agreed and blessed the future missionary that he would be fluent of tongue as he proclaimed the Lord's word. Jaime's personal commitment, humility, and selfless service inspired branch members to rally behind him, many of whom contributed their own humble means to help Jaime purchase necessary items for his mission and support him in the field. The first Hispanic member of the Church to serve a mission from the Boston area, Jaime reset expectations among his fellow Saints by challenging their unspoken assumption that lack of funds, education, and experience within the Church made full-time missionary service an unattainable goal for their sons and daughters.

Jaime returned to Cambridge following a faithful mission and delivered a powerful, Spirit-filled talk in sacrament meeting. The meek boy who could barely speak had returned a man. Following the closing hymn and benediction, the presence of the Holy Ghost was so palpable that no one rose to leave the chapel. After several minutes passed, a fifteen-year-old youth stood up and spontaneously bore his testimony. "I just wanted to thank Jaime for all he has done for me," he said. "And I want Jaime to know that when I turn nineteen, I'm going to fulfill a mission just like he did." Another boy rose and made a similar vow. One after another, each of the young men in the congregation stood and promised to follow Jaime's example by serving a mission for the Church. Twelve of the thirteen young men present at the homecoming ultimately fulfilled their pledges.[3]

Today there are three Spanish-speaking congregations within the Cambridge Stake. Many of the men leading these congregations and sitting in the chapels with their families are Jaime's boys—men who served honorable missions, married in the temple, and returned to further strengthen the Church in the area where they were raised. The prayers and fasting of the sisters of the Cambridge Spanish Branch Relief Society were answered more powerfully than they could have dared hope, although not in the manner they originally anticipated.

In September 2002, the presidency of the Augusta Maine Stake was being reorganized. As the two visiting authorities interviewed local priesthood holders, stake and ward leaders were asked how they came to be members of the Church. A startling number gave the same answer: "My parents were baptized into the Farmingdale Branch in 1963 when I was a boy." Curiosity piqued, an inquiry revealed that over 650 people had joined the Farmingdale Branch between 1962 and 1964! How was such a thing possible? At the outset of the 1960s, Maine was part of the large Atlantic District with only a handful of branches in the state. Membership was sparse, and infrequent visits from missionaries and area authorities were practically all that kept small pockets of Saints in contact with the body of the Church. The answer behind the mass conversion riddle that radically changed this landscape was found in George and Karline McLaughlin.[4]

George and Karline joined the Church in 1951, after Karline's mother opened her door to a set of missionaries on a snowy Maine evening. Karline's parents had spent decades searching unsuccessfully for Christ's church. When the missionaries presented their message, they used a photo of the Salt Lake temple—a building Karline's mother had seen in vision many years prior. Tears running down her face, she said simply, "I know who you are. We have been waiting for you."

The McLaughlins traveled to Logan, Utah, following their baptism to be sealed as a family. Other Maine converts had moved west to provide their children more opportunities within the Church. The McLaughlins had young children and thought about following suit, but were urged by Church leaders to stay in Maine where they could be the means of attracting other families to the gospel. Trusting the inspiration of their leaders, George and Karline stayed put.

George served as a counselor in their small branch before he was called to serve as president for approximately thirty Saints who gathered in a small newly-built chapel in Farmingdale. George was humbled to meet in one of the only Church-owned buildings in the state and felt strongly impressed that his primary responsibility was to help the Church grow in this small corner of the vineyard. A milkman by trade, George wondered what he could do to advance this cause and found himself increasingly preoccupied over how to bring the gospel to the people of Maine.

Approaching the Lord in earnest prayer, George asked for guidance that would accelerate missionary efforts. In the midst of a two-day fast, the new branch president frequently stopped his truck along his milk route to pray for inspiration. On the second day of his fast, George pulled onto a little-traveled road and found a secluded spot where he could kneel. Under the trees, he poured out his desires to build the Lord's Kingdom. When George returned home, he quietly told his wife, "I know what I've got to do now." Sitting with a pen and paper that evening, George carefully outlined the course of action—which he called the U-nite Program—that had been described to him through the unmistakable inspiration of the Holy Ghost.

President McLaughlin opened the Book of Mormon at the next sacrament meeting of the Farmingdale Branch and reviewed the account of Ammon's missionary labors. He then described the plan the Spirit had revealed to him and explained the role each branch member would be asked to fill. Three families were called to serve as "proselyting families." Each proselyting family was asked to bring a non-member family to the church on Wednesday of the following week, the first of a series of what George called "U-Nights." Visitors present at that evening meeting were shown a movie about the Church, after which President McLaughlin made some remarks and bore his testimony. Over the next few days, the missionaries visited each non-member family's home to teach the first discussion, and the second discussion was taught at the next U-Night. The proselyting families were responsible for meeting with their chosen non-member family twice a week, once at U-Night and once in their home, until the investigating family was either baptized or no longer interested in learning about the gospel. If an investigating family chose not to continue, the responsible proselyting family was asked to find another family to attend the next U-Night.

Each of the three initial proselyting families arrived at the chapel that first Wednesday night accompanied by a family they wanted to introduce to the gospel. Each of those first three investigating families joined the Church, following which President McLaughlin promptly called the new members to serve as proselyting families as well. Almost overnight, branch membership increased exponentially as members rallied behind their branch president and looked enthusiastically for ways to share the gospel. The importance of missionary work was emblazoned in the hearts of the Farmingdale Saints. "They could feel the Spirit," Karline answered, when asked how so many ordinary members overcame their natural hesitancy to invite others to hear the gospel. Week after week these men and women faithfully sought out and brought new families to church, often bringing several at a time.

George McLaughlin called President Truman G. Madsen of the New England Mission, not long after implementation of the U-nite Program, to invite him to an upcoming baptismal service. When told that the mission president had a conflict, President McLaughlin persisted. President Madsen sensed the branch president's insistence and asked how many people would be baptized. "You've got to come up and see," George replied vaguely.

When President Madsen walked into the Farmingdale chapel on the appointed day, his eyes quickly settled on three rows of people dressed in white, all waiting to be baptized. Quietly weeping through the service, the mission president watched as twenty-eight individuals entered the waters of baptism, one after another. At the conclusion of the meeting, President Madsen stood and said, "You know, I shall probably never see anything like this again in my life."

The baptisms continued and membership grew. As the number of proselyting families increased, U-Nights were altered so that each classroom could be used to accommodate a different missionary discussion, while another area was used to show an introductory film to families attending for the first time. Every family in the branch was eventually involved in the U-nite Program. Within the first year of the program's launch, 451 people were baptized into the Farmingdale Branch. The following year, 190 people were baptized.

George McLaughlin believed his greatest responsibility as branch president was to help new members develop lasting gospel roots. Entrusting administrative matters to counselors and auxiliary leaders, George focused on helping new converts become strong members of the Church. George held a training session before each baptism to explain the organization of the Church and how callings worked. He initiated a Church history class and a priesthood program to provide additional instruction, along with a temple preparation class for all newly-baptized members.

When President McLaughlin extended callings, he took time to teach members how to succeed in their roles, whether that meant sharing effective teaching methods or providing instruction on how to prepare a room for a meeting. He coached individuals on giving talks in Church and studying the gospel in their homes. Many converts came from humble circumstances and President McLaughlin and his counselors worked to help individuals improve their personal and economic circumstances as well. Most important, President McLaughlin stressed the significance of temple covenants, doing all he could to help couples develop and fulfill a desire to attend the temple, undeterred by the fact that the closest temples were in Alberta, Canada, and Salt Lake City, Utah. "Instead of leaving them," said Sister McLaughlin, "he took them and included them . . . trained them and gave them help." The most important element, she said in summary, was "to genuinely love people, and be prepared to spend time with them."

George McLaughlin never served as a bishop, stake president, or counselor in a stake presidency. He was not a professional educator or man of public distinction. But because of George's great desire to serve the Lord, his diligence in seeking guidance from the Spirit, and his faithfulness in following the counsel he received, by 1968 there were enough members and sufficient leadership for Elder Harold B. Lee of the Quorum of the Twelve to organize the first stake in Maine. When the original high council for the stake was organized, ten of its twelve members were men who had been baptized into the Farmingdale Branch through the U-nite Program.

Years later, a man who had grown up watching George's unwavering example approached Brother McLaughlin at a stake meeting and asked, "Does it bother you at all to see me and these other young men leading the stake?" George looked at him and smiled. "No," he replied, "this is what I've worked for all of my life—to see this. Most people have to die before they get their reward, but we're seeing ours."[5]

Elder M. Russell Ballard referred to George McLaughlin in a general conference address, saying that his was "one of the great missionary stories of this dispensation."[6] George was prayerful. He was teachable. And he was valiant. When such an individual is paired with God, nothing is impossible.

By the world's standards, neither Jaime Valarezo nor George McLaughlin was imbued with characteristics immediately associated with dynamic leaders or compelling missionaries. But they were committed to serving the Lord and labored diligently to fulfill His purposes. President David O. McKay referenced Section 4 of the Doctrine and Covenants in describing the essential qualities of those entrusted to bring about the Lord's marvelous work. "These qualifications [are] not the possession of wealth, not social distinction, not political preferment, not military achievement, not nobility of birth," he observed, "but a desire to serve God with all [our] 'heart, might, mind and strength'—spiritual qualities that contribute to nobility of soul."[7] Filled with righteous desire and richly possessed of faith, hope, charity, and humility, Jaime and George did not worry about their credentials but simply went to work.

With these attributes in place, the Lord qualifies those whom He calls. While attending an area university, Clayton Christensen felt impressed to share the gospel with an academic colleague, Jack,* and invited him to hear the missionary discussions. Jack accepted. Unfortunately, the elders assigned to teach Jack seemed ill-equipped for the task. One was new to

---

* Name has been changed for purposes of this account.

the mission and ill at ease. The other struggled with English and spoke with a thick accent that was distracting and difficult to understand.

Whenever Jack asked the missionaries a question, Clayton was quick to interject so as to spare everyone the embarrassment that would undoubtedly arise when the missionaries were unable to respond articulately. A pattern developed over the course of the discussions. The elders would introduce a gospel principle, Jack would ask a question, and Clayton would answer it. This continued until one evening when Jack asked a question that caught Brother Christensen off guard. As Clayton paused to formulate an appropriate response, the young missionary who could barely speak English provided his own answer—one that was clear, humble, straightforward, and self-evident as to its truth. The next time Jack asked a question, Clayton purposely waited to see what the missionaries would do. Again the elders followed through, delivering a powerful and Spirit-filled response. In that moment, Brother Christensen realized that he had temporarily forgotten that the elders sitting in his home were specifically ordained, set apart, and called of God to preach the gospel. Sent forth with this authority and working to fulfill that charge to the best of their abilities, those two young men could be trusted to magnify their calling in a manner that those without that same divine mandate could not.[8]

It is easy to make the same mistake Brother Christensen did if we do not remember who it is that calls the laborers to the field. The Lord's primary qualifications are a desire to serve, humility, faith, and diligence. God can and will take care of the rest. Surely Joseph Smith must have been reassured when he translated Isaiah's prophecies in 2 Nephi and encountered the Lord's promise that Joseph's weaknesses would not jeopardize His purposes. "I am able to do mine own work," He explained (2 Nephi 27:20). His capacity has not changed.

When Elders L. Tom Perry and Robert Wood were charged with reorganizing the Boston Stake in the early 1990s, they interviewed a large number of local priesthood leaders who fit all the marks for traditional stake president material. They were thoughtful, articulate, experienced in affairs of the Church, successful in professional and personal pursuits, and possessed of leadership and administrative skills that would make them effective guardians of the stake.

Kenneth Hutchins was a Massachusetts native. He was a convert who had made his career in law enforcement and was then serving as a police chief. Ken had served as a bishop, had experience in the stake, and was a counselor in the stake presidency. Ultimately, both Elder Perry and Elder Wood found themselves comparing everyone they met to Brother Hutchins. Kneeling together in prayer, they asked the Lord to confirm that Ken Hutchins should be the next president of the Boston Stake. Elder Wood described the assurance that came as the "most powerful manifestation of the Spirit" he had experienced to that time in connection with a calling.[9]

The visiting authorities called Brother Hutchins and told him the Lord had made it obvious that he was to serve as the next stake president. Although he was no stranger to Church administration, Ken was stunned. He knew he didn't fit the pattern of professionals and academics who had previously served in the position, all of whom had been lifelong members and had come from outside the state. He worried he didn't measure up to his distinguished predecessors, one of whom was L. Tom Perry. Ken appealed to the Lord for guidance and received his own witness that the call was inspired. With this confirmation, he squared his shoulders, saying, "I don't understand why, but I'll do what the Lord wants me to do."[10]

Kenneth Hutchins had a tangible love and affection for the people within his stake, and under his leadership, the Church moved into a new period of growth and establishment in eastern Massachusetts.[11] President Hutchins presided ably over the years during which the Boston Temple was announced, constructed, and dedicated—a time of intense public scrutiny. Given the Lord's foresight, one might have expected a stake president with more public speaking experience, press savvy, or political connections. But the Lord knew what was needed and Ken's humility, enthusiasm, sense of humor, and unwavering commitment to the gospel and those he served were sufficient.

Because this is the Lord's work, extending a calling is not the same as hiring an individual to fill a job requisition. Yet all too often when we need someone to teach a class, lead an auxiliary, or serve as a counselor, we revert to a similar type of résumé review and look to members who have already proved themselves equipped to serve comfortably in a variety of roles. The "STP Problem," as coined by Clayton Christensen, then sets in—the Same Ten People routinely fill key leadership positions within a congregation. After a few years, each is released in due course, but they are soon called to serve in other critical roles. A musical-chair pattern results in which the same people exchange and rotate responsibilities within a ward or stake. Members on the periphery are overlooked and those in the fray grow tired of doing all the work. Leaders and non-leaders alike are denied opportunities to grow, while dynamics and activity within a congregation may stall and stagnate.[12]

When we rely on our own selection criteria instead of the Spirit, we limit our ability to receive inspiration. Unable to see the potential within our fellow Saints, we risk overlooking the next Jaime Valarezo, George McLaughlin, or Kenneth Hutchins.

Herbert and Damie Forrest joined the Church with their children in 1921 in Halifax, Nova Scotia. Only the third family to be baptized in Nova Scotia in the twentieth century, the Forrests moved to Massachusetts and began attending the tiny Boston Branch, meeting downtown in a rented hall. Herbert and Damie were stalwart members who faithfully attended the early Boston and Cambridge Branches. Over those years, neither Herbert nor Damie was asked to assume a Church calling, according to their son. It was not an issue of worthiness, he stressed. It was just that the early Cambridge Branch was led by people, many from Utah, who had a great deal of schooling and long experience in the Church. "My [parents] were not educated people. I guess Mother and Dad finished grammar school. But that's about all." Herbert Forrest had minimal schooling, was a convert to the Church, and worked as a carpenter. He did not fit the leadership role, his son surmised.[13]

The Forrests were casualties of the STP Problem. If extended a calling, surely Brother and Sister Forrest would have magnified it, grown spiritually, and blessed the lives of many. How fortunate that they remained steadfast in their church attendance; how sad they were never given the opportunity to share their solid, quiet faith.

This tendency to overlook able servants in our midst makes the splitting of congregations a blessing because it dramatically increases opportunities for service. When the Wayland Branch was split from Cambridge in 1961, everyone was needed. In many instances, branch president Robert D. Hales found it necessary to ask individuals to fill multiple callings. Long-time member Lois Earnshaw was filling several roles in the Primary when she became acquainted with an earnest young convert named Stella,* who had a great willingness to serve. "I could not help but think she would have been overlooked in Cambridge," Lois stated. The oversight would not have been intentional—the vast pool of people and talent in the ward simply limited needs. In Wayland, in contrast, Stella was

---

* Name has been changed for purposes of this account.

needed. And given the opportunity to participate, Lois observed, "She blossomed like a rose."[14]

Short of splitting established wards into units small enough to involve everyone out of necessity, how can leaders avoid the STP Problem? The Church is filled with thoughtful bishoprics that spend long hours worrying over members who are new to a congregation, uninvolved, or just underutilized. Ensuring that everyone who is willing to serve has a meaningful calling can be a daunting task for the ward blessed with a large and active membership base. Gordon Williams served as bishop of the Cambridge Ward from 1970 to 1974, a period during which the ward was possessed of an incredible amount of talent. The bishop and his counselors felt a keen responsibility to focus on those who might ordinarily be marginalized in such a large congregation, and purposely approached ward needs looking for individuals they thought could gain the most from a calling. In particular, they focused on recent converts and others who were new to leadership roles, rather than starting with the people traditionally at the top of the list.

Bishop Williams credited his counselors, Hal Miller and Kent Bowen, for this approach. Hal's attitude was always, "I'll take anyone." As they went down the roster and identified individuals without callings, whether or not there was consensus that the person could do an effective job, Hal was willing to take them, train them, and find a place for them in the areas of the ward for which he had responsibility. Not to be outdone, Kent used the same philosophy, which made for interesting bishopric meetings when it came time to staff the ward. Extra counselors were called to auxiliaries in an effort to spread responsibility, and additional people were incorporated within the administrative structure. All the while, the bishopric made sure they interspersed enough experienced members to teach and model leadership skills. By deliberately increasing involvement, they developed an approach to train and shepherd those who might not otherwise be asked to serve. "Just off the top of my head," Bishop Williams stated, "there's probably out of that group at least a half dozen bishops, probably a dozen Relief Society presidents and stake leaders, either here or elsewhere who were 'marginal' at the time."[15]

When opportunities to serve, teach, and lead are spread throughout the membership, the gospel takes root in the lives of the people and the Church as a whole is strengthened. President Henry B. Eyring remarked on the importance of this depth when he described his experiences serving in the presidency of the Atlantic District while a graduate student.

There were always people of great talent and aptitude in the Atlantic District, he mused, but the Lord made the members in New England wait quite a while before a stake was organized. Although the top level of leaders was impressive, priesthood and other leadership beyond this group thinned noticeably and the branches outside Cambridge were weak. President Eyring's last Sunday in New England was May 20, 1962, the day on which the Boston Stake was organized. This event could not occur, he suggested, until the general membership within the region was sufficiently strong to assist in the growth of the Church and the proclamation of the gospel. When building His kingdom, President Eyring observed, "the Lord doesn't do it on the first tier." [16]

When we raise our hand to the square and promise to sustain fellow Saints in their Church responsibilities, we are acting on the Lord's errand, just as we do when we call individuals to positions within the Church. Because this is the Lord's work, the only safe bet is to assume that all righteous men and women are capable, through faith, of working mighty miracles (see Mosiah 8:18). With that understanding and a willingness to receive and act upon promptings of the Spirit, the Lord can confirm His divine guidance in preparing those called to tend His vineyard. As former bishop and stake president Lloyd Baird explained, "You never know who the Lord is going to magnify." [17]

Just as we must be willing to trust the Lord's wisdom when He chooses others to do His work, we need to trust Him when He calls us. It is often hard to believe the Lord's mercies and promises apply personally, even when we readily accept their application to others. We read the Lord's promise in Ether 12:27 that He will make "weak things strong" but fear that our own weaknesses are beyond hope. Or perhaps we simply worry, often correctly, that the Lord's transforming process may entail more discomfort and effort than we'd prefer.

Randy Gaz was a young father, a surgical resident, and a counselor in the Cambridge Ward bishopric in the early 1980s, drowning in the demands associated with his chosen profession and struggling just to make it to his many Sunday meetings. Despite Randy's obvious time and resource constraints, Bishop Lloyd Baird told Randy that he wanted to see an explosion of growth within the downtown Boston area, then devoid of any wards or branches. Bishop Baird thought it expedient to start with a basic Church unit, to be initially comprised of the four active families living in the city. Brother Gaz, he continued, would be responsible for organizing and shepherding it. The first order of business was finding a place for the group to meet.

Randy wondered how he could possibly fulfill his bishop's request. "I felt like Jonah when he was asked to go preach to Ninevah. . . . I just wanted to turn and run the other way." Knowing, however, that he would have to see the bishop the following Sunday and report, Randy determined to find a way. "I would've much rather been swallowed up by a whale," he explained, than admit he had not tried.

Carving out a small niche of time on Saturday afternoon, Randy came home in his hospital garb, spread a map across a desk, and announced, "I have one hour to find a location." He drew a triangle connecting the members who lived downtown and decided to look for a meeting place in that area. Driving into the city, time passed quickly. Randy still hadn't found anything definite when he turned onto a street he had driven on past occasions. There in front of him was a Knights of Columbus Hall. Stopping to talk to a man in the parking lot, Randy enquired whether it would be possible rent a room for use on Sundays. The man indicated this could be done, and within two weeks Randy began organizing services there.

Finding a meeting place for the embryonic branch was just the beginning. Knowing embedded leadership was critical to the congregation's future, Bishop Baird identified local resident Joshua Smith to head the group, believing Joshua had the needed spirit and tenacity, if not experience, to establish the group. Brother Gaz was asked to extend the call.

"I remember interviewing him in his home and pleading with him to take this calling," said Randy. "I could see this painful look on his face. It was like asking him to get in a rocket flight to the moon. It was something that he felt was totally impossible for him." Joshua was very reserved by nature, but with the support of his wife (Lillian), Brother Gaz, and the other city members, Joshua went on to serve as a member of the Boston Branch presidency and later bishopric for many years. Joshua's sensitivity to and familiarity with the members laid a foundation for the growth that has since taken place in downtown Boston. In the course of this service, Joshua and Lillian Smith ceased being spectators in the Church and became leaders.

"As I look back, it's very enjoyable to see how that has flourished," Randy Gaz stated. "It was a very rewarding experience—hard and doing something [I'd] never done before." Overwhelmed and unsure how to accomplish his priesthood leader's direction, Randy was totally dependent on the Lord to provide answers and direction, as were others, like Joshua Smith, who were so timid that they didn't want to offer a prayer, let alone lead a meeting. "To see them grow and learn how to do these things was one of the most powerful miracles I have seen," said Randy, "—to see something magnificent come out of nothing."[18]

Because we naturally focus on our limitations, it is easy to discount our ability to contribute to the Lord's cause. Tim Chopelas learned of the Church while serving in the army. Seven years after joining the Lynnfield Ward, Tim's stake president asked him to serve in his ward's bishopric under Bishop Warren Jones. Tim went to the church early the next morning and knocked on the door to the bishop's office. When the bishop answered, Tim quickly said, "Bishop Jones, I want to thank you for having confidence in me to call me to serve as counselor."

Bishop Jones looked at Tim and paused. "Tim," he finally said, "there's one thing you have to understand right now. I didn't call you. The Lord did."[19]

Randy Gaz accepted the assignment to establish a branch in Boston because of his conviction that Bishop Baird's request was inspired of the Lord. Joshua Smith and other members of the tiny original Boston group likewise grew into their stewardships because they knew the author of their calls. When we are asked to accept and magnify callings for which we do not feel suited, we must remember Bishop Jones's counsel and the One who calls us to the vineyard.

"A calling in the Church is both a personal and a sacred matter," observed Elder Loren C. Dunn, "and everyone is entitled to know he or she has been called to act in the name of God in that particular position. Every person in this church has the right to know that he has been called of God."[20] If we understand the source of our callings and seek this confirmation, we will not only be able to square our shoulders and say, "I'll do what the Lord wants me to do"—as Ken Hutchins did when he was asked to lead the Boston Stake—but we will also know where to turn as we seek to fulfill our responsibilities, confident that the Lord can do His own work.

In 1962, while still in his early thirties, Truman Madsen was called to preside over the New England Mission. In connection with the assignment, Elder Boyd K. Packer informed Truman, "We are sure that you have been called all right, but we don't know why." As this pronouncement sunk in, Brother Madsen suspected Elder Packer might be thinking, "And we can't imagine why." Whether he had any actual misgivings or not about the Madsens' youth or suitability, Elder Packer followed his statement with a powerful challenge, stating, "I suggest you go home and get on your knees and find out."[21]

Ann Madsen had her own misgivings. Reflecting on the women that preceded her in the New England Mission, Ann felt that she possessed few, if any, of the talents and abilities those sisters had brought to the task. At their farewell, Ann confided her fears to Truman's former New England mission president, S. Dilworth Young. "Oh, President Young," she exclaimed, "What can I do back there? I'm not Gladys Young, I'm not Margaret Jackson, and I'm not Hattie Maughan. I know these women—they are all great women." Cutting Ann off before she could go any further, President Young said matter-of-factly, "If the Lord wanted Gladys Young back there, he would have called me to go back. He wanted Ann Madsen back there."[22]

There are all kinds of reasons we may believe we aren't suited for a particular call. But God, our Heavenly Father, knows us better. He wants us to be ourselves, and He extends callings to us precisely because of who we are and what we can become. We are called for what we *can* do, not for what we *cannot* do. Just as the Lord wanted Ann Madsen to bring *her* insights, experience, and testimony to the New England Mission, He calls *us* for the unique attributes we bring to our corner of the vineyard and to prepare us for other assignments to come.

"I know this," stated Helen Low, who served as Relief Society President of the Atlantic District and Boston Stake from 1959 to 1969, "if you are set apart for a job and you do it and you pray about it a lot, you don't even have to know what you're going to say. You open your mouth and it comes out. . . . The Lord doesn't let us fail because it's His Church and His gospel."[23]

Mauricio Paredes's first calling was initially terrifying. A native of Guatemala, Mauricio was baptized into the Cambridge Ward on a Saturday in 1978, before the first Spanish-speaking branch had been established in the area. The next day, Brother Paredes arrived at the bishop's office for what he assumed would be a get-to-know-you interview. Instead Bishop Kent Bowen recounted his search for inspiration to know who should teach the Spanish Sunday School group. "According to my prayers," Bishop Bowen informed Mauricio, "it is you. Would you accept the calling as a Sunday School teacher [and] teach the doctrine to the

Spanish members? There is a manual, and you can take the manual to guide you."

Stunned but anxious to serve where asked, Brother Paredes replied, "I accept, but I need time to be prepared. Could you give me a month so that I will know what I am going to teach?"

Shaking his head sympathetically, the bishop said, "Brother Paredes, I think that a month is too much time."

"Could you give me two weeks?" Mauricio asked hopefully.

"Brother Paredes, I think that two weeks is too much time."

Resigning himself to his fate, Mauricio bowed his head and said, "Bishop Bowen, I think that if you give me the manual, I could study the lesson and then I can be prepared for this coming Sunday."

Smiling, Bishop Bowen produced the Sunday School manual and said, "Brother Paredes, the truth is that the Sunday School class is to begin in about twenty minutes."

Although unable to recall what he taught that first Sunday, Mauricio Paredes went on to teach Sunday School for five years. In that time he learned to enjoy his calling as a teacher.[24] Full of love for his brothers and sisters, always enthusiastic, and completely loyal to the gospel, Mauricio Paredes has been a stalwart Saint and a key figure in the growth and establishment of the Spanish-speaking units in the Boston area. "He became the nucleus for creating [the] branch in the Lynn Spanish area," remarked former stake president Mitt Romney. "We couldn't have done that without Mauricio Paredes."[25] And yet, looking back, Mauricio admitted that at the time of his baptism he wasn't sure he would remain with the Church more than a year. While his willingness to serve was a blessing to many, ultimately Brother Paredes's willingness to teach that Cambridge Sunday School class was an essential piece of his own conversion.[26]

By the wisdom of the Lord, the vast majority of callings to serve within the Church are temporary. We are asked to support fallible members as they strive to serve the Lord to the best of their ability and, when it is our turn, hope that our offering might be found acceptable too.

The Lord does not call us to do things that fall neatly in our comfort zone precisely because His plan is to build us as we build His kingdom. Despite a strong testimony, Ned Wheeler, former president of the Nashua New Hampshire Stake, found that his faith in the Lord's purposes did not offset his fear of public speaking. "When I was growing up, . . . I was not [a] very sociable person. . . . To give a talk in church was equivalent to going to the dentist," he said ruefully. Notwithstanding this natural reticence, "As soon as I got old enough to get callings, the Lord would call me to positions that required me to talk in church." The only way to get over the fear was by relying on the Lord, Brother Wheeler observed. "When I was called to be . . . bishop that was a very frightening thing. Of course I pleaded with the Lord to help me, which He did. The Lord always makes us equal to whatever he calls us to do."[27]

Even when we feel suited for an assignment, initial calm often proves fleeting as we come to appreciate the responsibilities entrusted to us, the limited time we have to serve, and the powerful potential for good inherent in any calling from the Lord. Elder Packer attended a meeting during his tenure as president of the New England Mission where a man in the congregation was called to take on a critical leadership position. Asked to bear his testimony, the man essentially testified that he was truly the man for the job and the Lord really knew what He was doing. Elder Packer leaned over to the stake president and observed dryly, "He'll get over that."[28]

When we truly recognize our dependence on the Lord, our ability to support others in their callings and the effectiveness of our own labor are both increased. No matter the circumstances of a specific congregation, we are each needed for our individual gifts. The Apostle Paul taught this principle to the Saints in Corinth: "For the body is not one member, but many. . . . If the whole body were an eye, where were the hearing? If the whole body were hearing, where were the smelling? But now hath God set the members every one of them in the body, as it hath pleased him" (1 Corinthians 12:14, 17–18). As we learn to recognize the diverse talents in our midst and the nobility of soul that distinguishes willing servants of the Lord, we will discover greater depths of love for our fellow saints. That, in turn, will give us strength.

Jan McKinnon remembered feeling overwhelmed and underqualified when called to serve as Relief Society president. "We all fumbled with what we were asked to do," Jan admitted. "I was certainly serving women who were far more capable." Jan relied on the Lord and the sisters with whom she worked to accomplish the tasks asked of her. The Spirit expands your talents, she agreed, but ultimately "you were willing to get out and do something because you felt so loved." Swallowing back tears, Jan continued, "You knew that even if you made a fool of yourself . . .

there was just so much trust. . . . They were just behind me one hundred percent."[29]

We are all weak and we are all simple when measured against the capabilities of our Savior and King. Regardless, He invites us to His side, with the promise that miracles await when we are willing to seek His wisdom and trust His plans. "Verily, verily," the Lord says tenderly, "ye are little children, and ye have not as yet understood how great blessings the Father hath in his own hands and prepared for you. . . . Nevertheless, be of good cheer, for I will lead you along" (Doctrine and Covenants 78:17–18, 20). As we strive to build the Kingdom, let us trust in the Lord, let us support His servants, "let us cheerfully do all things that lie within our power; and then stand still, with the utmost assurance, to see the salvation of God, and for his arm to be revealed" (Doctrine and Covenants 123:17).

THOU ART OUR ROCK, OUR FORTRESS, AND OUR MIGHT;

THOU, LORD, OUR CAPTAIN IN THE WELL-FOUGHT FIGHT;

THOU, IN THE DARKNESS DREAR, OUR ONE TRUE LIGHT.

# 5

# BEARING ONE
# ANOTHER'S BURDENS

THE LARGE influx of students that descended on Cambridge each autumn was always accompanied by an avalanche of calls from individuals seeking help with housing. Local members organized committees in the 1940s and '50s to welcome newcomers and help them get situated.[1] As the number of families moving east for school and jobs continued to increase, what began as an informal service became a necessity.

Robert Hales was serving as elders quorum president in the late 1950s. His concern was the number of LDS students who came by the chapel once or twice only to disappear, lost in the shuffle of those critical weeks after term began. To attack this problem and ease the transition for new arrivals, President Hales helped formalize what became known as "Project 48." The idea behind Project 48 was simple: Individuals and families moving to the area could stay in members' homes for their first forty-eight hours as they looked for their own housing. Local hosts could offer tips and guidance to young couples traumatized by the high price of housing on the East Coast and help them get settled more quickly than they could on their own. By offering this service, Robert Hales recalled, "We got to know virtually everyone who came into the area."[2]

Bonnie and Gerald Horne arrived in Cambridge with their infant daughter in 1960. Bonnie clearly remembered meeting Luanne Van Uitert as they left the ward that first Sunday. "[She] invited us to come and stay at her house," Bonnie recalled. "That was the first time I ever heard of Project 48, . . . To meet this gracious woman who just said, 'Come and spend the night'—we were a little overwhelmed with that!"[3] Word of the program spread to BYU, the University of Utah, and throughout the Church Institute system. An occasional stay exceeded forty-eight hours, but those involved in the program could not recall any real abuse. "We put up people in our home just about every year," said Bishop Van Uitert. "It create[d] some delightful friendships."[4]

Project 48 was so successful that it continued for the better part of two decades, producing lasting benefits that far outweighed temporary housing assistance. "What a powerful influence that was in integrating into the ward," Gael Ulrich said, recalling how Dorothy and Jamie Lyon had hosted his own family—the start of a life-long friendship. "[It] was just a terrific way of fellowshipping. If you came into the ward, whether you had been active or not in the past, it would be hard not to be active after you'd spent forty-eight hours taking advantage of somebody's hospitality."[5]

"There was a sense of community and watching out for each other that extended to the whole group of students who were back there," Jamie Lyon remarked. "It's one of those things where the by-products are greater than the initial goal you set out to achieve."[6]

When the Cornwall family moved to Massachusetts in 1974, Project 48 was still going strong. Grateful to be sheltered by a family in the ward, they went on to offer the same hospitality to others new to the area. "This was just something you did in the ward," said Carter Cornwall. "I thought that was really neat. This was the essence of the Church as far as I was concerned."[7]

Sue Clark reluctantly accompanied her husband Kim east to finish his undergraduate degree in 1971. Born and raised in rural New Mexico, Sue found it difficult to adjust. "I'd heard a little bit about Boston in studying American history," Sue acknowledged, "but in my mind all I could think about was the Boston Strangler, city life, and fast-paced living. I was quite scared to come. The first year was hard because I also felt like I just wasn't as smart as everybody else. . . . They were so bright, and I just wasn't bright like that. So I was really self-conscious."

Their second year in the area, Sue was called as Relief Society president. "That really cured me . . . of my self-consciousness," Sue stated. "I had to look outward and think about everyone else. I learned that there were a lot of people who felt the way I did."

Sue was serving in another Relief Society presidency some years later when a family with three little boys, one of whom was legally blind, moved into the ward. It was clear that the family was struggling to get settled, so Sue made an effort to help the mother find local stores and invite her to activities. One evening not long after the family's arrival, Sue went to bed thinking about this sister. She woke in the middle of the night with the young mother's name still on her mind. Unable to get back to sleep, Sue called the sister when morning finally came to see if she would be coming to a class a few hours later. No, the woman said. Things were much too hectic at home. Sue offered to pick her up, but the young mother demurred. Sue asked if she could come over and help unpack boxes, but the sister again said no. Fighting the impulse to give up, Sue asked if she could simply come by and visit. The sister finally agreed.

Uncertain what to expect when she arrived, Sue was surprised when the mother tearfully greeted her at the door. "I had the hardest night last night," she gulped. "The only thing that saw me through was that Heavenly Father told me that you would come today." Grateful that she had heeded the Spirit's prompting, Sue learned that the family's blind son was terminally ill. Doctors at their prior home had given him less than six months to live. Reluctant to share this burden with their new ward, the mother had harbored her terrible grief alone.

Miracles occurred once her secret sorrow was out. Individuals in a position to help within the ward stepped up as they learned of the boy's prognosis. Leveraging medical expertise within the congregation, the husband and wife met doctors who envisioned different possibilities for their son. Years after the family left the area, the young boy called Sue to tell her he had passed the sacrament on his own for the first time. He went on to graduate from high school, become an elder in the Melchizedek priesthood, serve as a home teacher, and work as a tutor for blind children before he passed away at the age of twenty-one, a lifetime more than doctors had originally projected.

"The faith of the mother, combined with the faith of this little boy, were just wonderful lessons for the whole ward," said Sue. "Their pure faith and their willingness to rely on other people who wanted to help . . . was really a great experience. We love [this] family. We love them for coming here and letting us have that experience."[8]

Ward Low, who served in the Boston Stake presidency and as a stake patriarch, told of a time when his commitment to the Church was anything but a given. It was 1957 and Ward's wife, Helen, had just given birth to their last son. The birth was difficult and the doctor was attentive, but it was unclear if the baby would live. The obstetrician beckoned to Ward and said quietly, "We've done everything we can. If you have anything you can do, now's the time to do it."

Overwhelmed, Ward couldn't think who to call. He wanted to give his son a priesthood blessing, but he had never given one before. In desperation, Ward contacted Bill Cox of the Cambridge Branch and relayed their plight. Hurrying to the hospital, Brother Cox arrived and anointed the baby. Ward sealed the anointing. "After the process was over," Ward recalled, "the room was quiet. . . . Everybody had felt the Spirit, perhaps I most of all.

"That was the beginning of my rapprochement with the gospel of Jesus Christ," he continued. "Up until that moment, . . . I was leaning out and away from the Church." What occurred in that hospital room, Ward explained, was like a clap of thunder to him. Immediately, he recognized something real was present. "I did not realize what was involved. It was contact with the Spirit in the extremest."

Ward credited Bill Cox for playing a vital role in his personal conversion, noting that everything in his life had followed from that experience. "He was key to everything that happened to us," Ward stated matter-of-factly. Just before he died, I wrote him a letter . . . [and] told him of the criticality of the role that he played in our lives. . . . He wrote back to me and said, 'You give me way too much credit, but thank you.' . . . He was the sled on which I rode to the gospel."[9]

The programs of the Church encourage us to serve one another in simple ways, almost without thought. We welcome new members, bring in dinners, support service projects, and serve as home and visiting teachers. An infamous form of service is found in the moving assistance elders quorums commonly provide, particularly valued in college towns like Boston. "It seemed like every Saturday there was somebody to move," said a man of his early years in the area, recounting stories of rogue pianos escaping down stairwells and a move where a large hide-a-bed couch suspended above the road spontaneously sprang open in midair while the quorum was trying to raise it into a third-floor apartment using a rope hung through an upper-story window.[10]

"I . . . cannot tell you the numbers of refrigerators I have hauled up narrow staircases," one brother groaned.[11] "We moved so many people, we started laughing about it," another chuckled. "When I was in the military, if you were a noncommissioned officer, you would get stripes on your sleeve for years you served . . . we thought we should have a sweatshirt with stripes for every move that we made!"[12]

When Alma described the baptismal covenant to his little flock at the Waters of Mormon, he explained that the children of God must be "willing to bear one another's burdens, that they may be light" (Mosiah 18:8). The fact that we are willing to literally bear one another's burdens by giving up our Saturdays to move unwieldy appliances is a tangible indicator of a greater truth. One of the most remarkable things about the Church, stated member Darrell Rigby, is that when you move, "instantaneously there are 200 to 300 people who feel like family members that will help you do anything!"[13] Refrigerators and couches are some of the easier loads we are asked to help carry when compared to the other burdens we heft along this mortal course. The knowledge that we need not lift such weight alone can make all the difference.

## A Religion of Saving Souls

The morning after Brigham Young learned that the Willie and Martin handcart companies were stranded on the plains of Wyoming, he strode to the podium of the Tabernacle and told the Sabbath assembly that the subject of his address would be the rescue of their brethren and sisters. "That is my religion," President Young stated. "It is to save the people." Calling upon the bishops and elders in the Tabernacle, Brigham Young said there was no time to waste. Mule teams, wagons, teamsters, food, and supplies would be prepared immediately. Closing his remarks, President Young sent the congregation off to follow his direction with the following admonition: "I will tell you that all your faith, religion, and profession of religion, will never save one soul of you in the Celestial Kingdom of our God, unless you carry out just such principles as I am now teaching you. Go and bring in those people now on the plains."[14]

Our admonition has not changed. As members of the Church, each of us is invited to watch over individuals in our midst, to nurture and lift, attend to needs, and, on occasion, bring them in from the plains. "There was a wonderful woman who was Relief Society president," said Linda Hoffman Kimball, of the period following her baptism. "She introduced me to the concept of visiting teaching. I had never heard of that before. She made it sound so wonderful . . . the chance to reach out to women and have a unique opportunity to just be with them and share soul comments. . . . I've always thought visiting teaching is really the heart of the gospel. [It] is where a lot of the richest, most valuable, soul-saving stuff happens."[15]

Walter Dolan served as a home teacher to the Einreinhofer family for over twenty years. Walter had been reassigned occasionally over that period, but when each reassignment resulted in the Einreinhofers not seeing anyone, Brother Dolan always returned to his priesthood leader to say, "These folks need to be home taught. I'm going."

"Even during the days when we were inactive, Walter was there," said Jo-Ann Einreinhofer. "Always there. Never pushing us, just there as a friend, all the time." Echoing his wife, Roy Einreinhofer added, "He has certainly been someone who has inspired us [and] really shown what the home teaching program is all about. It's not about hammering a lesson down your throat once a month. It's just to be there and let you know he's there if you need him."[16]

When Tom Nally joined the Church in Gardner, Massachusetts, Ted Baker was assigned as his home teacher. Recognizing the sacred charge contained in his assignment, Ted was concerned about Tom's well-being, visited him often, and helped Tom through a critical period as he gained his gospel footing. Acknowledging what Ted's friendship had meant to him, Tom simply said, "Because of that, I'll love him forever."[17]

Gordon Williams had the opportunity to observe many home teachers from his vantage as bishop, stake president, and regional representative, but it was a new convert from western New York who epitomized for him what home teaching is all about. As one of several LDS medical professionals in the area, it was not uncommon for Brother Williams and other similarly situated local Saints to provide support when members came to the city for serious medical treatment. On one such occasion, Brother Williams was asked to look after an eight-year-old girl who had come to Boston with her mother. The girl underwent several tests before she was diagnosed with cancer. The surgeons told the mother that her daughter's leg would need to be amputated. The girl didn't know much about cancer, but she knew if she had a leg removed she wouldn't be able to climb trees, ride bicycles, or do many of the things she loved. A renowned endocrinologist, Gordon understood the girl's medical needs. "I spent a lot of time talking with her," he reported, "but it didn't do any good." She didn't want anything to do with the surgery.

With no family to call upon, the little girl's mother grew increasingly concerned, unsure how to help her daughter understand the need for the life-preserving surgery. Their home teacher telephoned to see how things were progressing, and the mother sadly reported that they had reached a stalemate. Without waiting another moment, the home teacher hung up the phone, got in his car, and drove from Albany to Boston. Upon reaching the hospital, he went in to talk to the daughter, after which the little girl came out and announced, "Okay, I'll have the operation."

"It was interesting," said Brother Williams. "I couldn't do it. . . . The surgeon couldn't get her to do it. Her mother couldn't get her to do it. This home teacher was able to get her to do it. The thing that was remarkable, besides the fact that he had driven 120 miles to be with her during this time, is the fact that he had only been a member of the Church for about eight or nine months." Prior to his baptism, the home teacher explained, the missionaries taught him that he would be responsible to care for and nurture individuals and families assigned to him. When this mother and daughter needed him, he was there the next day. He went on to drive 250 miles round-trip on a weekly basis for three months to support a sick child in a family for which he was accountable. He called every day to find out how things were going. "He assumed that was what he was supposed to do," Brother Williams stated. "He didn't have time to learn that there's another way to do home teaching."[18]

Sharing tender accounts of service rendered by visiting teachers and priesthood blessings administered by home teachers, Judy Dushku stated, "My interpretation of Mormonism is 'You are your brother's keeper, and you do everything you can to help everyone around you to the fullest extent possible.' . . . It's certainly the guiding personality-shaping aspect of Mormonism that came from my Church experience. And I attribute it to being . . . a visiting teacher."[19] Becoming reflective, Judy concluded, "When I've had any impulse not to be as dedicated or fervent in my activity in the Church, the single thing that calls me to the whole Church experience has been the home and visiting teaching program. . . . I think it's one of the uniquely incredibly successful and beautiful programs that we have in the Church now. I have benefited from it both from being one and from being served by others, all my life."[20]

## Just Do It

The home teacher from Albany lived the religion President Young professed. He did not wait for the morrow, and his immediate action made him a rescuer to the family for whom he was steward. Most of us want to serve, but too often we wait to be asked or shown what to do, worried that we might otherwise offend or impose. "What I've learned from the service of others," Ruth Ray Kelleher stated ardently, "is seeing a need and meeting it without being asked is the most effective way to serve." Citing an example from her life, Ruth told of a time, more than forty years past, when she suffered a severe allergic reaction that rendered her completely immobile and confined her to bed. Ruth's Relief Society president, Helen Low, showed up at her door. "She didn't come and say, 'What can I do?'" Ruth emphasized. "She came in, diapered the kids, took the laundry, cleaned the house, and brought back the folded, clean laundry with a meal."[21]

Tona Hangen internalized a similar example while participating in an effort to provide care for a member who was dying of AIDS. Hoping to provide as much hands-on care as possible in the family's home, the ward sponsored training meetings so packed that extra chairs had to be added. "That apartment became a hub of activity," Tona recalled. "There were always people coming and going and meals coming and going." Amidst all the activity, however, one simple act stood out. The family at the center of the project had a broken answering machine, which made things difficult as the wife had numerous calls and issues to juggle each day. Although nothing had been said, a sister in the ward showed up with her own answering machine. "She didn't ask, 'Do you want to borrow my answering machine?'" Tona noted. "She just brought hers over, elbowed everybody aside, and plugged it in herself to make sure it was going to be there."[22]

Fred Bowman and his wife were baptized in 1969. The Bowmans had only been in their ward a few weeks when their home teacher, Victor Ludlow, learned they were trying to implement a program called "patterning" for their four-year-old son, who suffered from tuberous sclerosis with frequent seizures. Patterning was a labor-intensive form of physical therapy that required the involvement of multiple people, several times a day. Unable to fathom how they could ask for so much assistance, the Bowmans were stunned when Brother Ludlow stood at their first fast and testimony meeting and announced: "Brothers and Sisters, we have a young couple in the ward who are recent converts. They have a young child who has some difficulties. They are going to be going into a physical therapy program that's going to require four people twice a day, seven days a week. Any of you who feel you can participate in that, see me after service in the Relief Society room."

Over 130 people signed up to help, Fred recalled. "I knew that we needed people," he said, "and I knew that I could never have asked for that." Over the course of several months, groups of volunteers staffed regular physical therapy shifts at the Bowman home, while others babysat children so young parents could participate. As ward members worked together with volunteers from the community, friendships developed, gospel discussions took place, and many people were exposed to the Church for the first time. There was such a warm feeling associated with that effort, Fred recalled. Sunday services were particularly touching for the Bowmans when they entered the chapel and saw all the people who had been assisting them.[23] It was an enormous ward project, said one sister of her own participation. "Everybody in that ward helped . . . many for a long time. . . . It was quite amazing. It touched a lot of people."[24]

Perhaps a reason King Benjamin describes service as one of the "mysteries of God" in his masterful discourse (see Mosiah 2:9), is that no matter your part in the transaction, you come out ahead. Sometimes it can be difficult to distinguish the giver from the recipient. As a former bishop observed, "What, in my younger days, I would have considered the recipient of the service was often as much the giver as the recipient. It depends on your perspective. You think of yourself as doing service, and you look back twenty years later and you say, 'I learned a lot from that person. I thought I was helping him at the time, but he was really helping me.'"[25]

"The lesson that I learned is that growth comes through service," said Ruth Ray Kelleher, shaking her head. "I don't think there's been any element of my life that I haven't felt both the receiving and the giving. I think that flow becomes a natural part of being a Church member."[26]

This exchange means some of the most profound lessons come from unexpected sources. Bruce Porter was attending a ward in Cambridge when a young couple with a baby moved in. The parents were recent converts who had been introduced to the Church while serving in the army. They looked a bit out of place, and Bruce suspected the city would be challenge enough for the family. He wondered if the couple would stick with the Church, given all the obvious changes in their life, or simply become another set of faceless names on the rolls.

Bruce was excited when he was asked to home teach the new family, believing he could really make a difference teaching the couple how to live the principles of the gospel. On the evening of the first appointment, Bruce and his companion drove forty-five minutes into the city to the family's small apartment. When they entered they found the couple holding family home evening with their baby propped up in an infant seat. Bruce expressed surprise they would have family home evening when the child couldn't possibly appreciate it. "Well, we want to start early," the father replied. "We want to do what's right." As the parents closed their lesson, Bruce made a mental note that he and his wife needed to be as faithful in holding family home evening.

The home teachers were preparing to share their message when the husband brought out the genealogy he and his wife were doing. The only members in their respective families, they were anxious to share the gospel with their ancestors and spoke reverently about what temple work meant to them. Bruce squirmed. This was another area where he could be more diligent.

The visit concluded and the home teachers stood, only to be beckoned to the back of the apartment by the husband. There, in a screened-in porch, Bruce was dumbfounded to see towers of ten-gallon ice cream containers filled with wheat, honey, flour, salt, sugar, and other staples. This couple had managed to amass a complete year's supply of food, despite being students with little in the way of material goods. "I always thought students were exempt from having a year's supply," Bruce admitted. "But this couple was too new in the Church to have all the sophisticated excuses the rest of us make. . . . The prophet said do it, so they just went out and did it."

Bruce was thoroughly humbled. As he turned to leave, his eyes caught a picture of the Washington D.C. Temple hanging by the door. Jolted, Bruce recalled the counsel of the prophet, then Spencer W. Kimball, that every Latter-day Saint home prominently display a picture of the nearest temple. With sinking heart, Bruce realized there was no such picture in his home. He had excuses for not having family home evening, doing family history, or having food storage, but Bruce couldn't think of one reason to explain why he didn't have a picture of the temple.

Bruce could not sleep when he arrived home. Deep in thought and filled with the spirit of repentance, he began rummaging through closets, bookshelves, and drawers before finally locating an out-dated German missionary tract, from which he cut a tiny photo of the Swiss temple. Bruce affixed the cutting to the wall with tape, eyed his handiwork, and whispered, "We're going to have a picture of the temple in this home no matter what."

"When we look at the picture of the temple in our home today, we think not only about the covenants we make in the temple, but we think about a young couple, brand-new in the Church, who taught us what it meant to follow the prophet," said Elder Porter. "That experience really told me something about how we, as members of the Church, get so comfortable in our testimony and the traditions we've grown up with that we start to neglect simple counsel from the prophet. We think, 'I'll get around to that.' Here is a couple that just did it."[27]

## When Being There Is Enough

The Coppins family came to the Malden Branch from a student ward where, in David's words, "you pretty much had a homogenous group of people." Their new Church family, in contrast, contained an eclectic mix of people with diverse and often overwhelming needs. "Service," said Carol, was "the biggest lesson I learned." Up to that time, the family's primary experience with service was preparing meals for someone who could use a helping hand. In Malden, "we were very much serving people who absolutely needed it every day, every week," said David. The Coppins had been asked to fill multiple callings in other congregations, just as they were in Malden, but the emphasis on meeting life needs was something new.

Many branch members navigated lives scarred with dysfunctional relationships, filthy homes, bizarre challenges, and tragedy. "To get them out of that situation for just a few hours a week really made a big difference," Brother Coppins observed. "All of our efforts were trying to get people to go to church. That is when we started to make the distinction between what is the true gospel and what is cultural." It didn't matter so much what people wore to church, if they stopped at the grocery store afterward, or if they drank a little coffee, he elaborated. While meaningful, those details could be worked out later. "You just wanted them to get there," David explained. "What is really important starts to become really obvious."[28]

"The things that these people overcame to attend church—you couldn't even fathom," sighed Denise Barnett, a founding member of the branch and wife of the branch president. "We may have done a lot and spent a lot of time, but I had a husband who was strong in the Church, I had children who went to [good schools]. They had friends who were LDS." Most of the Saints in the branch had no such support, and their challenges were of a whole different level.[29]

The needs were constant and there were no easy answers. People new to the branch had a general tendency to overestimate their ability to change things for the better, observed Carol. When change didn't come as quickly as expected or individuals continued to make bad decisions, discouragement set in. Those with the best of intentions often burned out, seeing little response to their efforts. "You think, 'Oh, it's not worth it,'" she explained. "'I'm giving everything I have.'"[30]

When faced with intractable challenges or problems that exceed our ability to remedy, how can we succor our brothers and sisters? There is comfort and guidance in the gentle, poignant admonition of our Savior found in these familiar verses:

> For I was an hungered, and ye gave me meat; I was thirsty, and ye gave me drink; I was a stranger, and ye took me in;
> Naked, and ye clothed me; I was sick, and ye visited me; I was in prison, and ye came unto me. (Matthew 25:35–36)

Sometimes we can load the wagons with flour and sorghum and rescue those stranded on the plains, but more often we cannot remove the suffering or burdens of those for whom we care. In those latter cases, where we cannot heal and we cannot remove the imprisoning chains, we must remember that we are not asked to make everything all right. That is not our job. We labor to relieve the needs we can, but sometimes all we can do is to visit, to come unto—to be there. And sometimes that is the best service.

Jan McKinnon was Relief Society president when a child in her ward was diagnosed with leukemia. In hopes of preserving life, the family entered into an intensive battery of medical treatments. "I thought that we were doing everything possible," said Jan reflectively. "We were taking meals in every night for their family." The family was often at the hospital and people wanted to avoid imposing, so meals were frequently left with another family who lived below them in their two-family home instead of being delivered directly. "I'll never forget," Jan said, recalling the period after the little boy passed away. "[The mother] said, 'We could've done without the food. We needed someone to talk to.' . . . I was afraid to go talk to them about what they were going through. I didn't know how to comfort them. I didn't know what to do. I thought, 'I wish I could do that part over.'"[31]

Rarely can we eliminate the challenges of mortality or the consequences of a lifetime of decisions. A bishopric counselor recalled a service project spearheaded by an enthusiastic elders quorum president who was determined to clear a sister's filthy apartment of accumulated garbage and years of collected junk. After a weekend of sorting, discarding, and scrubbing by volunteer laborers, the young quorum leader was devastated to find the sister's home regressed to its former state when he visited a short time later. "We found," the bishopric member explained, "that once you gave [people] the support, they really had to raise themselves up. We could provide the Church, but we couldn't go in and change [their life] or clean up their house."[32]

"If you went to an inner-city unit like [Boston] and thought that you were there to serve and rescue them from their environment," cautioned former Boston bishop Justin Lindsey, "you would not have the right type of experience." As an example, Justin recalled a young man who was living on the streets to escape an abusive situation at home. Well-meaning members approached Bishop Lindsey and offered to send the youth to Utah to live with a strong family happy to take him. With some trepidation, the bishop approached the youth but was not surprised when the boy forcefully declined. "What he wanted," Justin explained, "was none of that. He just wanted to be living back at home with his family and for things to be better. If you take the swoop-down-and-move-them approach, it is not the right program."[33]

Real change must come through application of the gospel, observed Bishop Lindsey, quoting President Ezra Taft Benson: "The Lord works from the inside out. The world works from the outside in. . . . Christ changes men, who then change their environment. The world would shape human behavior, but Christ can change human nature."[34]

The gospel can help people remove themselves from bad situations, Bishop Lindsey added. "Sometimes that means they move, but sometimes the slums are transitioned to a place they want to be." Members needed their own spiritual oasis, he continued, and for many world-weary Saints, the meetinghouse became home, providing a solace they could not find within the walls of their apartments.[35]

When needs are profound, our simple willingness to give of self can make a great difference. Greg and Kristiina Sorenson were newlyweds when they began attending the newly established Boston Branch in 1987. Missionary work was booming and growth was rapid. "The problem with growing a branch at that time wasn't that there weren't members," Greg said, laughing. "It was that there were almost too many members!" With twenty missionaries assigned to the branch, Sunday meetings were crowded with investigators and new converts, yet it was almost impossible to find someone who could lead music. On a typical Sunday, it was not uncommon to arrive at the chapel and be asked to give the opening prayer, after which you might speak, lead the music, and teach one of the classes. Afterward, said Greg, you would likely clean the facility and make refreshments for a baptism or fireside. Most important, you were always picking people up to make sure they got there and taking them home afterward.

The branch presidency was working hard to integrate new members and help them learn to serve, but with such constant change in branch composition, observed Greg, "you needed some people who were dependable and reliable—some sense of glue." In prior wards, Greg had seen members divided by political leanings, views on Church history, or opinions on Church administration—things that were completely irrelevant in the branch. "What mattered was could you get to church, and were you willing to just be there?" he explained. "If you were just willing to show up and hold the hand of a couple of three-year-olds, that made you a valuable member of the branch. . . . A lot of those people, merely by their sheer presence, made a huge impact because . . . you could count on [them] to be there. . . . They are really minor things, but yet they are really the core of what makes or breaks a branch or ward.

"It was a little exhausting. It was exhilarating, in a way," Greg admitted. "You really felt like what you were doing mattered." There was nothing magical about it, Greg concluded. "It wasn't anything anybody else couldn't have done. . . . It was just a matter of being willing to love those people and show up. Isn't 90 percent of success just showing up? That was kind of it."[36]

Understanding that we are not asked to eliminate trials can actually enhance our capacity to offer relief, as we forego the responsibility to solve each problem and learn to appeal to the true Deliverer. "[John Hartley] was our home teacher when we discovered [our son] was deaf," said Ann Romish, acknowledging the devastation they felt for their baby, who they already knew was blind. "He came to us as our home teacher and said, 'Could I fast and pray with you, as you fast and pray about your son?' I don't think anyone has ever more sweetly or more eloquently offered us love and kindness. . . . We were blessed to have him as a home teacher."[37]

When the Lord called Peter Whitmer on a mission with Oliver Cowdery, He counseled Peter not to fear. He then instructed: "And be you afflicted in all his afflictions, ever lifting up your heart unto me in prayer and faith, for his and your deliverance" (Doctrine and Covenants 30:6). The Lord does not expect or ask us to be able to provide all the answers, but He does ask us to be willing to take up some small part of others' suffering, just as He took upon Himself the suffering of all mankind. The Savior, who has power to heal all wounds of body and spirit, first wept with Mary and Martha upon learning of their brother Lazarus's death (John 11:35). He who is perfect knows perfect empathy. The Lord asks us to follow His example. He asks us to be there with heart and hands.

## Things of Lasting Import

A mother and father were asked if they had done anything notable when their children were young that had helped them stay strong in the gospel. The father shook his head with bemusement. "Sometimes you don't realize it until after the fact," he responded. Nodding, the mother admitted she was frequently surprised by things her grown children credited as having made a difference. They were often minor events that she didn't remember. In most cases, both father and mother agreed, pivotal experiences for their children had appeared quite commonplace as they were occurring.[38]

Rarely can we know the import of our actions in the moment, since things of significance only become evident with the passage of time. As such, we cannot be weary in well-doing since something as simple as a sympathetic ear or the right word at the right time can make all the difference. Edna Thibault was a mother of five and a relatively new convert who had been baptized with her family. When her older children were facing trials, Edna worried that her decision to join the Church had aggravated their struggles. At a Relief Society activity, Edna confided her fears to Ruth Tingey, asking, "What did I do? What did I give them?" In a voice warm with empathy, Sister Tingey responded, "You gave them eternity."

It was what she needed. "I went on that for many, many years," Edna said gratefully.[39]

Dorothy Nielsen was visiting a grown daughter who lived out of state. While attending her daughter's ward, Dorothy met a woman with whom she had apparently interacted many years prior in Cambridge. The woman had had great difficulties while in Boston, Dorothy's daughter reported. "She's told me about your friendship with her. Now . . . she has seen the difficulties that I have gone through. . . . She has befriended me like a mother. You'll never know what kind of influence she has been on me, and I think it's because of your relationship years ago."

"She told me some things I don't even remember doing for this woman," said Dorothy, admitting she didn't even remember the sister's name. "But that doesn't really make a difference. When someone comes into . . . our lives, we can reach out and make all the difference."[40]

David Coppins was serving as elders quorum president when he encountered a man who had joined the Church in his youth, the only member in his family. He had served a mission but felt directionless and unneeded after returning home. The young man wandered onto other paths, which led to heartbreak and eventual bitterness toward the Church and God in particular. David began visiting the man regularly as a home teacher. The man had lots to say, and the two started meeting over breakfast every Saturday morning at 7:00 a.m. David asked questions, listened, and took notes. The man had a long story, and it was clear he needed to share the entire account before he could listen to any feedback. At the end of his tale, concluded many meals later, the former elder announced that he hated God for what He had done to him.

"This was a particularly difficult statement for me to take, and I don't think I took it particularly well," David admitted. "I kept home teaching him and kept coming back, but it took a long time. I had some very specific things that he needed to do. . . . Eventually he decided he would try. He said that every time he read the scriptures he found inconsistencies. Every time he went to church he felt like everyone was a hypocrite. It was just a very bitter, difficult time for him. I just spent a lot of time with him, and eventually he came around. . . . He is now back completely, [with] all of his blessings. He is married to a wonderful woman. He has got his job back on track. His wife . . . joined the Church. All her children . . . are all members now and are very active. It is very exciting . . . a big, big change in their lives over a period of a few years. He said it was when he was ready to learn."[41]

Returning to his memories of the Boston Branch, Greg Sorenson recalled the branch president, Keith Knighton, taking individuals into his home, one after another, as they faced financial or other difficulties. "Many of those people have now established themselves, a decade later, as strong members of the Church. It surprised me, actually," Greg confessed. "A lot of those people I thought were destined for failure. . . . They were in a place in time when just a few little things made all the difference. I think there's no way of projecting to the future to see how the little things we do are going to impact people. . . . You can't tell now. You can't tell in the next five years. Sometimes you can't tell for ten or fifteen years."[42]

## He Knows How to Succor His People

Paul and Kristen Anderson were new to the area when their toddler became seriously ill. Despite great support from families in their ward, the succeeding months were frightening and lonely as the Andersons watched over their small son in the hospital. During that time, Kristen reflected on a priesthood blessing she had received just before her son got sick. In it, she'd been promised that she would grow closer to her Father in Heaven and gain a greater appreciation for divine parental love as she cared for her son's needs, even when it was painful for her.

"As situations like this happen," the blessing had stated, "you will be able to remember that Heavenly Father goes through the same thing with all of His children. Sometimes He is forced to allow His children to suffer in order that they might grow, because He understands their needs and He understands what will be best for them in the long run." After weeks at her son's bedside, coaxing him through myriads of prods and pricks and trying to stay calm and reassuring in the face of his immense discomfort, Kristen said, "It really gave me a deeper understanding of how our Heavenly Father must feel when He watches us suffer."[43]

Justin Lindsey witnessed countless struggles and tragedies as he served as a counselor and bishop in downtown Boston, characterizing these events as the most painful and most spiritual experiences of his life. It was particularly wearing to work day-in and day-out with people he loved and watch them continue to make bad, often destructive, decisions. Nevertheless, Justin continued, "The number one thing I learned about the Atonement is what the Lord means when He says I will succor my people according to their infirmities. It is a fact that the Lord understands our problems and can deal with them. . . . I know the Lord loves those people. He has great things in store for them. As we look on their hearts and their spiritual capacity we will see a different vision of the people. . . . They have a spiritual strength that is amazing."[44]

There is no challenge or sorrow we are asked to bear alone. The Lord asks us to serve one another in love, but it is He who will heal the wound and make all whole. "It is because of the sacrificial redemption wrought by the Savior of the world that the great plan of the eternal gospel is made available to us," President Hinckley stated. "In our own helplessness, He becomes our rescuer, saving us from damnation and bringing us to eternal life. In times of despair, in seasons of loneliness and fear, He is there on the horizon to bring succor and comfort and assurance and faith."[45]

Just two days after sending a son to the Missionary Training Center, Kim and Sue Clark received a call from the stake president, informing them that their son would be returning home to clear up some things in his life. Sue paced the house all night, depressed and angry. As they prepared to pick up their son the next morning, Sue suggested she stay home because she was so upset and hurt. In response, Kim put an arm around his wife's shoulders and said, "You know what? This is about Michael. It is not about you."

"That put it in a whole new perspective," said Sue. "When he did that, I remembered that I had recently borne my testimony in church and had felt inspired to thank Heavenly Father for His unconditional love. I had also hoped that I might be able to love unconditionally. . . . I thought, 'That's what I have to do. I have to love unconditionally. This is his experience, not mine.'"

Over the next few months, the Clarks watched and prayed as their son prepared to return to the mission field. "It was one of the most amazing spiritual experiences of our lives," Elder Clark observed. "It was very difficult; he got very discouraged [and] frustrated. But he was really committed to getting himself worthy to go back and to be prepared. We would have long talks about the gospel and about the Atonement. We would read scriptures together; he would ask for blessings. The Lord told us very clearly . . . that this young man was going to be a mighty elder in Israel. Our job was to support him, love him, and be a good example for him. It was a profound experience because we lived in a house with a young man who was being molded by God right in front of our eyes. The Atonement was having its impact on him. . . . We could just watch it work."

After a period of time, the young Clark returned from meeting with a General Authority, totally alight. "He knew that he was worthy to go on a mission," his father explained. "There was no doubt in his mind. Shortly after that, his call came." It was a great experience in retrospect, Elder Clark stated. "But it didn't start out with us thinking, 'Oh, this is going to be a great experience."[46]

The gospel of Jesus Christ is, at its core, a message of rescue, with the Savior providing the one sure means of deliverance. When we reach out to our brothers and sisters, we can be confident that the Lord will be by our side, since it is His yoke we are taking upon ourselves. "Wherefore, be faithful," the Lord instructs, "[and] succor the weak, lift up the hands which hang down, and strengthen the feeble knees. And if thou art faithful unto the end thou shalt have a crown of immortality, and eternal life in the mansions which I have prepared in the house of my Father" (Doctrine and Covenants 81:5–6).

# 6

# TAKING THE LEAP
# OF FAITH

JIM AND JO ANNE Neal were living in Sudbury, Massachusetts, when missionaries knocked on their door. The Neals felt something as the missionaries taught them, but after the third discussion they asked the elders not to come back for a while. They wanted time to think.

The missionaries returned six weeks later. The elders went through the remaining discussions while the Neals engaged in independent study, earnestly seeking to understand the principles being taught to them. As Jo Anne read *A Marvelous Work and a Wonder*, Jim studied the New Testament, comparing its teachings to those of the missionaries. As Jim gained confidence that the doctrines of the Church were consistent with the Bible, he prayed for a witness to know that Joseph Smith was a prophet and the Book of Mormon was true. The Neals had declined repeated invitations to attend the local ward, but agreed to meet with mission president Paul H. Dunn and his wife. Their discussion gave Jim much to think about. Praying for guidance as they drove home that evening, the prompting Jim received was powerful and direct: "You feel good about this and this is all you're going to get for now."

Recognizing this answer as a call to faith, Jim was baptized with his wife two days later in November 1968. "I just accepted that as the answer for the time being," said Jim, "but not the final answer. . . . Then after I was baptized I had a spiritual experience that was like the one spoken of in Moroni, which was a real confirmation of what we had done." It didn't come immediately, he emphasized. It came after continued study of the Book of Mormon, sincere prayer, and an intense desire to move beyond intellectual conversion. The answer required continued faith and diligence after baptism, and it came in accordance with the Lord's timetable, rather than Jim's.[1]

❧

Fred Bowman was working in his yard when missionaries first approached him. Confused by their talk of ancient American civilizations and distracted by the needs of his severely disabled young son, Fred politely excused himself. A year later, another set of elders came to the house. Fred and his wife, Carole, were consumed by tasks associated with their son's care and told the pair they could return on two conditions: (1) they had to come after 10:30 p.m. so their son would be asleep and (2) they had to teach everything in one night. Worried about these requirements, the missionaries contacted President Dunn, who said simply, "If I were you, I'd take a nap."

The first discussion did not end until 6:00 a.m. Although it did not cover everything, the principles taught intrigued the Bowmans and they agreed to meet with the elders again. Fred decided to put Moroni 10:4–5 to the test since the elders kept quoting it. Offering a prayer, Fred admitted he was not sure God existed, but if He did, would He let Fred know of His reality and if the message was true. "If you'll let me know that these things are true," Fred promised, "I'll act on it." Almost immediately, Fred received his answer—one he knew he could not deny. "That scared me to death," he recalled, "because I didn't know what I was getting into . . . but I knew that I made a commitment which, if I didn't follow through on, I would be accountable for." Fred and his wife were baptized soon after in 1969.

A few months later, Fred approached his bishop with a weighty concern. Every year he had to borrow substantial amounts of money to pay his son's medical expenses. Giving a tenth of his income to the Church would force him to borrow even more. Economically, he couldn't make tithing work. Soberly, the bishop replied, "Well, Fred, it's not my law. Let me read you what the Lord says." The bishop opened the Book of Malachi and read the Lord's words about opening the windows of heaven. Concluding the verses, he said, "Fred, it's the Lord's promise. Go prove him."

Fred relayed the conversation to his wife. Carole listened and replied, "Well, Fred, if we're going to be Mormon, let's be total Mormons. If tithing is part of it, let's tithe." Nodding his assent, Fred said it just meant borrowing more money, which he did.

The Bowmans began paying tithes in April. As a young faculty member, Fred was looking for ways to supplement his family's income over the summer. Within a month, Fred had four job options, only one of which he'd sought. Fred chose one that commenced a long-term career and allowed him to begin pulling out of debt. "Today I'd be afraid not to tithe," he admitted, "because my income was clearly a consequence of tithing. If I were not tithing, I don't think I would've had that same experience."[2]

Dick and Marsha Lavin had two children when they began adopting, aware that any children born to them had a high probability of inheriting a serious neurological disorder. Over time, the Lavins adopted seven African American children. They were anxious to raise their children in a church that would include their whole family, but each one they visited disappointed for one reason or another. Occasionally Dick and Marsha found a congregation they enjoyed, but when it became evident that their children were uncomfortable there, they continued looking.

Marsha encountered missionaries during a cross-country flight in 1977 and felt an instant connection. The Lavin family began taking the discussions and liked what they heard. They enjoyed interacting with members and attending church meetings, but once they learned black men were not eligible to hold the priesthood, baptism seemed out of the question. "I just couldn't see myself joining something that just wasn't going to be open to all of us," Dick explained.

For six months the Lavins wrestled with the issue, as well-intended members and missionaries tried in vain to explain the policy. Dick knew he wanted to join the Church, but became more frustrated with every dead-end conversation. He had almost given up when he was invited to meet with Gordon Williams, then president of the Boston Stake.

It was a hot spring day when the two met. Dick listened as President Williams talked, watching sweat bead on the man's brow. Finally, Dick could take it no longer. "How long are we going to suffer with this?" he asked impatiently. "Nothing is making any sense at all to me!"

President Williams sat back in his chair. "All this might not make any sense at all, but there are two courses of action," he replied. "You can sit and wait and when . . . [the priesthood] becomes available to all people, then you can join and feel good about it. Or you could exercise faith."

The Lavins responded with faith. Baptized in April 1978, the family prayed that the policy on blacks and the priesthood would change. The family awoke early one morning in June, as was their habit, to prepare for school. On that morning, Dick offered a particularly heartfelt plea during family prayer that the prohibition would be lifted. A few hours later Dick received a call from Fred Bowman, a fellow ward member, asking, "Have you heard the news? There is no more ban."[3]

The Neals, the Bowmans, and the Lavins are three of nineteen families who joined the Church in Weston, Massachusetts, from 1968 through 1978. Since that time, baptisms in the Weston wards have continued, but at a much slower pace.[4] Life-long members and converts alike describe that decade as a time when there was a tangible feeling of growth and enthusiasm for the gospel. "That was a wonderful time for all of us," said Hannah Goldberg, baptized during that period. "I think there were more converts in the ward than there were people that were born in the Church. There was just a very special spirit among us."[5]

Surges in missionary work occur from time to time. Worcester and Lynnfield, Massachusetts, both experienced great increases in membership and activity levels when their meetinghouses were being constructed. The exponential growth of the Church in Maine that came out of George McLaughlin's U-nite Program in the 1960s was more than remarkable, and in the 1990s, the Boston Branch was out-baptizing most stakes, let alone wards!

To what can we attribute these bursts of missionary activity? Occasionally you can point to events that have raised awareness of the Church within the community. More often than not, however, it's hard to identify specific factors that cause missionary work to take off at a particular time or place. Although we cannot discern the Lord's timing to know with certainty where and when the next phase of growth will occur, we can prepare by developing and emulating attributes and attitudes that foster inclusion, activity, and retention when the Lord harvests His field.

The characteristic most fundamental to our ability to share the gospel is the same attribute vividly illustrated in the conversion stories above:

faith. Just as Jim Neal was willing to act on the Lord's quiet assurance, Fred Bowman was asked to trust the Lord's promises regarding tithing, and the Lavins were baptized as a witness of faith despite a seemingly inviolable barrier to full participation in the gospel, we too must exercise faith to successfully share His good news. Of all the qualities that qualify us for this work, the Lord lists faith first (see Doctrine and Covenants 4:5).

"It's a faith-based effort," stated Mark Johnson, who joined the Church in Belmont, Massachusetts, just prior to the temple dedication in 2000. "You . . . must believe that you can talk to people and the Lord will guide you in what to say and that things will be okay."[6] To be effective messengers, we must have faith that the Lord has prepared people to hear and accept the truth, faith in our message and the Spirit's ability to convert, faith to persist when the outcome is unclear, and faith to follow through with the harvest.

## Faith that the Lord Has Prepared Individuals

George McPhee was born and raised in Waltham, Massachusetts. Life had been challenging, and in the mid-1980s George was fighting alcohol dependency and the disintegration of his marriage. A young couple, Mike and Mary Jane Smith, lived in the same apartment complex. While a dark rain cloud lingered perpetually over the McPhee home, the Smiths seemed to bask in bright sunshine. They smiled, they laughed, they had many friends, and their children were bright and cheerful. Through casual conversations, George knew God was a central figure in their lives. Curious, he began asking Mike about the teachings of the Church. George's marriage ended as the Smiths were preparing to leave Massachusetts. Loading his truck, Mike turned to George and said, "Well, maybe now's the time to investigate the Church."

"At that moment, my body just reverberated from top to bottom as if I had been rung like a big gong," George stated. "I checked myself for goose bumps, to see if it was an actual physical reaction, but there was none. But those words just rang me like a bell."

Two weeks after his wife left, George began meeting with the missionaries weekly. He was baptized fourteen months later by Mike Smith, who came back for the event. George was surprised to learn that although the Smiths had been involved in the Church during their time in Boston, they'd worried that their contributions were not what they should be because they had been so immersed in Mike's doctoral program. "But their example was marvelous," George stated. "That's what attracted me to the Church. They had something that I didn't have, and I wanted it badly."[7]

The Smiths may have questioned the quality of their influence, but the Lord knew who and where they were. George McPhee may not have seemed a likely candidate for baptism, but the Lord knew George's needs and heart. Mike and Mary Jane were instruments in the Lord's work simply by being open about the role that the Church and its teachings played in their family.

What struck Hannah Goldberg about her fellow converts in the Weston Ward was that they had all been looking for spiritual answers.[8] Bishop Keith Knighton found the same thing in the Boston Branch. People who were attracted to the Church, he said, were "people of integrity who wanted desperately to change their life for the better—who wanted to find peace for themselves and peace with God and who wanted direction and couldn't find it in what they had seen up to that point. They were simply looking for something better."[9]

Edna Thibault was searching for a way to teach her children spiritual things. A pair of missionaries tracting in the area was preparing to return home when a prompting caused them to turn around to try one more house. The Thibaults' home was blocks away, but it was the house the elders chose. A few months later, Edna and Tom Thibault joined the Weston Ward with all their children who were old enough to be baptized. The Thibaults were ready and the Lord arranged a way for them to find the answers they were seeking.[10]

Helen and Ken Cutler raised eight children, all of whom were filled with missionary zeal, introducing friends, neighbors, and acquaintances to hear the gospel and attend Church activities. Sharing some of their missionary experiences, Helen mentioned a summer afternoon when their daughter Christine, fresh off a mission, visited her father's office. While there, Christine met a woman and gave her a Book of Mormon and a pamphlet on its origin and teachings. Another daughter and son got involved and soon the woman was taking the discussions in the Cutler home. "She joined the Church," Helen stated. "It's made all the difference in the world to her."

"So why was Christine there that one day?" Helen asked, noting that it was the only visit Christine made to her father's office that summer. "Things like that happen."[11]

How many people around us are kept from the truth only because they know not where to find it? (Doctrine and Covenants 123:12) The

Lord knows His children and wants all of them to have the opportunity to hear His words. In the first decades of the Church's existence, many New England converts were prompted by an inexplicable spirit to put themselves in a position where they could find the gospel. Thomas Marsh, first President of the Quorum of the Twelve, was one of those. Living just outside of Boston with his family in Charlestown, Thomas was dissatisfied with his Methodist faith because he could not reconcile it with the Bible.

In 1829, Thomas was filled with a strong desire to travel west. Leaving his family at home, Thomas resolved to follow the Spirit and eventually arrived in Lima, New York, where he spent three months seeking information that could explain why he had come. Discouraged, Thomas finally started back to Boston on foot. After lodging with a family the first night of his homeward journey, Thomas was preparing to leave when the woman of the house asked if he had heard of the golden book found by Joseph Smith. Thomas knew nothing of it but was anxious to know more. His hostess directed him to Martin Harris in Palmyra. Thomas immediately turned west again and found Martin Harris in the printing office, where the first sixteen pages of the Book of Mormon had just been printed. When Martin Harris discerned Thomas's intentions, he gave him a proof sheet to keep and took him to the home of Joseph Smith Sr., where Thomas met Oliver Cowdery and stayed two days. Returning home, both Thomas and his wife gained a testimony of the Book of Mormon by reading the proof sheet. After a year of correspondence with the Prophet, Marsh moved his family to Palmyra following the Church's organization on April 6, 1830.[12]

Thomas Marsh was led to find the Church when it didn't have the resources to find him. We see a similar phenomenon in our day as people from countries with little missionary activity are led to cities where they can find the truth. As president of the Boston Branch, Keith Knighton kept a world map in his office, on which the branch presidency affixed a star for each country represented in the congregation. "There were stars all over the world," he noted.[13]

"Something that we have no doubt about," said April Munns, whose husband presided over the Massachusetts Boston Mission in the mid-1990s, "is that the Lord brought people from all corners of the earth . . . to be introduced to the gospel."[14]

John and Rani Roberts had come from India to visit their daughters in Watertown, Massachusetts. With their girls gone for the day, John and Rani were watching television when they saw an advertisement for the

Book of Mormon. John had been a minister for thirty-five years and felt impressed that he needed this book. Unsure how to operate the phone, the Roberts waited impatiently for their daughters to return so they could call the 800 number.

The book consumed John's days upon its arrival. When John went to bed, Rani read it through the night. Returning the volume to her husband one morning, Rani said, "This is a true book. The things I have read in here I have always believed, but I have never talked to you about them because there was nothing in the doctrine of our religion that supported these beliefs."

Conferring together, the Roberts decided they needed to talk to someone from the Church. A few minutes later, the phone rang. A representative from the Missionary Training Center was calling to see if they'd received the book and find out if they wanted to speak with a missionary. Their assent was so emphatic that a pair of elders was knocking on the Roberts' door ninety minutes later. John and Rani were baptized within the month.

Before their return to India, Brother Roberts bore a powerful testimony in which he noted he had converted thousands of people to his former religion. Noting that he now had the authority to baptize, he felt the responsibility to return and share the truth he had received. "I don't have thirty-five years this time," he noted regretfully, shaking his head.[15]

The Lord places His children in situations where they can be exposed to His plan for happiness, but He needs us to reach out, speak up, and actively look for those ready to hear the word. While the Roberts family may have been required to travel halfway around the world to be introduced to the gospel, the same should not be required of our neighbors. People everywhere seek assurance that God is real, truth exists, and they can have a personal relationship with Deity. The Lord proclaims that the field, or world, is white and ready to harvest—not just a portion of the field (see Doctrine and Covenants 6:3 and Doctrine and Covenants 33:3). We need to accept Him at His word.

The New England Mission had a goal of achieving one thousand baptisms in 1965. On December 31, the mission was one short of its target. Exercising faith in the mission president's inspiration, Ed Berg of Lynnfield knocked on the door of a sister in his ward. When her non-member husband answered, Ed asked if he would be baptized. The man had helped build the Lynnfield chapel and, confronted with such a bold proposition, agreed. He was baptized that night.[16]

The Lord prepares His children to hear and accept the gospel, and He places these individuals along our path. Because we cannot recognize them by sight alone, we must listen for and follow promptings of the Spirit, ready to be the type of example the Smiths were for George McPhee and ready to go out on a limb, if necessary, as did Ed Berg. If we are willing to do our part, the Lord will lead us where we need to be.

## Faith in Our Message

Camille Foster was new to Massachusetts when an acquaintance innocently inquired, "What do you believe in your church?" Stumbling through a couple of Articles of Faith before drawing a blank, Camille realized she needed to be better prepared for questions about her religion. The Fosters had a set of neighbors with whom they were close, and Camille tried to be proactive in sharing *Ensign* articles that might be of interest to her friend, inviting her to Relief Society meetings, and creating opportunities to talk about the Church. Her neighbor was receptive and seemed hungry for truth.

Camille realized she needed a plan. In prayer, she committed to be bolder and invite her friend to take the discussions. As a result of Camille's resolve, her neighbor began investigating the Church and was eventually baptized.

"[We] had had a lot of opposition in trying to purchase our home," Camille said. "I feel that one reason why may have been that the adversary knew that [she] was ready and waiting for somebody to bring her the gospel message. I feel like I was an instrument in the Lord's hands in that particular case. That was a brand-new experience for me doing missionary work. It was exciting."[17]

Pam Eagar joined the Church while attending college in Virginia. Partly because her boyfriend, Tom, was attending MIT, Pam decided to transfer to Boston University. Pam was anxious to tell Tom about the Church, but he was active in his religion, and Pam wasn't sure how to share her new faith. Richard Bushman was serving as bishop of Pam's ward. When Pam explained her dilemma to him, Bishop Bushman simply said, "Just invite him to come to church."

"Oh!" gulped Pam. "What if he doesn't like it?"

"Don't worry about that," soothed Bishop Bushman. "Let the Lord take care of those things. You just have to invite him."

Tom Eagar joined the Church before the winter was over.[18]

Most of us are like Pam. The gospel is precious to us and our testimonies are personal. We feel uncomfortable sharing the gospel with people we interact with regularly out of fear of offending or simply creating an awkward situation. We worry so much about rejection that we often stay quiet and, by so doing, reject the message for them!

"It's all about perspective," said Mark Johnson, who was introduced to the gospel by a colleague. "We need to always make sure that we're not constraints in the way of the Lord. . . . Don't be so fixated on whether or not they say yes to the discussions, but realize that just your testimony and the way you touch them could change their path."[19]

When George McLaughlin described the member missionary program that led to the conversion of over six hundred people in the Farmington Maine Branch during the 1960s, his interviewer expressed amazement that families were so willing to accept assignments to share the gospel. How did he get members to invite and bring a nonmember family to church each week?

The answer was simple, according to George's wife, Karline. When George introduced the program, he prepared branch members by reading from the Book of Mormon and explaining what members would be asked to do. "They could feel the Spirit," she stated. "They can feel it and they . . . respond to that. They will respond to it."

"You're not going to get anything done without the Spirit, least of all preaching the gospel," George said, agreeing.[20]

It is the Spirit that converts. There is enough power in the word that we need not fear being the messenger. We just have to invite.

The missionaries knocked on Jim Sloan's door in 1967. A student of mathematics and philosophy, Jim was interested in talking about the "great questions." What began as intellectual curiosity eventually led to baptism, due to a statement the elders made up front: "If you pray, you will be answered."

Jim observed a similar attitude among students at an Institute class: "There's something personal here. We have it, [and] you can too." That kind of individual witness and contact with Deity struck Jim powerfully.

"That goes beyond philosophy," he explained. "That's not talking about, that's talking with."[21]

We do not have to be eloquent to share truth. As long as we carry the fire of testimony, it is enough. Tom Thibault's first spiritual experience was the testimony of a young missionary who had just landed at Logan Airport, straight from the MTC. His first evening in the field, this elder visited the Thibault home and bore his testimony about Heavenly Father. "It so touched me," said Tom, "[that] the next day I stopped smoking and drinking. I knew that [it] was true." That first witness was so strong, he continued, that it was almost fifteen years before he could discuss it.[22]

Carmen Rivera's brother had joined the Church. He invited her to accompany him to meetings every Sunday, but Carmen usually found excuses not to go. Surprising even herself, however, she agreed to hear the discussions. The missionaries asked her to pray to know if the Book of Mormon was true, and Carmen tried to do so but found she could not. Carmen began crying when the elders asked if she had prayed for confirmation. "I can't," she sobbed. "This is the book of God. I don't want to challenge God. I don't want to make Him upset at me because I am doubting that this is [His] book." The Spirit accompanying the Book of Mormon was so strong that Carmen had acquired a deep, confirming testimony before she even asked the question.[23]

Bill Cortelyou joined the Church in 1974. The day after his baptism, Bill began working for a cab company, a career he continued for over thirty years. As a cab driver, Bill met people from all over the world and all walks of life. His car housed a box filled with copies of the Book of Mormon and pamphlets about the Prophet Joseph sorted alphabetically by language. Bill made it a habit to talk about the Church as he drove and would give books or pamphlets to four or five of his passengers in a typical day. Occasionally he invited people to attend church or asked if he could send the missionaries to visit. "I create opportunities for missionary work," Bill stated. "I don't really push. I'm just offering."[24]

Every Sunday at church, Bill shared a missionary experience from the past week. Approaching another member of his branch, Bill handed him a pamphlet on the Book of Mormon and encouraged him to find ways to share his testimony. "You are so much more talented and experienced than I am," Bill stated. "You can do this too."[25]

"People don't often turn down my offer," Bill explained, "because the Spirit helps me." Over the years, Bill has given away more than 6,000 copies of the Book of Mormon and 10,000 pamphlets. He rarely learned the outcome of his efforts but was not discouraged. "My missionary work," he stated simply, "is to create opportunities for someone to make the choice about learning the truth of the gospel."[26]

Bill Cortelyou is not tentative about missionary work because he knows his role is simply to offer. We should not be tentative either. As members of the Church, too often we fail to realize what we have. "There is so much to share that people are looking for," said Helen Cutler. "If you have it and don't give it to others, then one day they will ask us why—why didn't you share?"[27]

Camille Foster's husband, Dave, was asked to home-teach an inactive brother who had a wife and a nine-year-old stepdaughter. The husband had been away from church many years and his wife and daughter knew nothing about the gospel, so Dave decided to take a "20 Questions" approach to his assignment. "Why don't we just start out with questions you might have about religion, about life, and see if I can answer them from the point of view of the gospel?" Dave suggested. The family agreed. "They had lots of questions," said Dave.

After a little while, Dave told the family, "You are getting pieces of the gospel . . . , but you really need the big picture. How about we bring the missionaries over and you can take the missionary discussions with me here?"

"We had a wonderful experience with the missionaries," Dave reported. The daughter answered the missionaries' questions with child-like brilliance, often startling her parents with her answers. The father was soon reactivated, his wife and step-daughter were baptized, and the family became major contributors to the ward.

"I don't take credit for that so much as just being available to show up," Dave said, smiling. "The Spirit did it."[28]

## Faith to Persist

Betty and Gus Manderino met during World War II, while Gus was stationed in Utah with the military. Betty had been raised in the Church, while Gus grew up in Arlington, Massachusetts, surrounded by his large Italian Catholic family. Before they married, Gus agreed that Betty could raise their children in the Church, certain he had nothing to fear since he was sure there were no Mormons in Boston. Betty had done her homework, however, and after arriving in Massachusetts, made Gus drive her along Cambridge's historic Brattle Street. As soon as she spied the yellow home that housed the early branch, she cried, "Stop the car! There's my church!"

Betty attended meetings faithfully over the years, traveling across town using public transportation with her children in tow. Gus never showed interest in joining the Church, but he was supportive in reinforcing principles Betty taught at home. He read his children stories from the

*Children's Friend* magazine, helped them practice talks for junior Sunday School, and attended daddy-daughter activities and basketball games.

After the Manderinos' second son expressed a desire to serve a mission, Gus paid a visit to his family's bishop. Apprised of the responsibilities and obligations associated with a mission, Gus agreed to let his son go and agreed to provide financial support.

Gus was well known in the ward and witnessed the power of the gospel in his family's commitment to the Church and priesthood blessings that brought healing to his home. By the time his youngest son was serving a mission, Gus was getting tired of staying home while his family went to church. Out of the blue, Gus told Betty, "I think maybe I should get baptized." After thirty years of marriage, Betty thought he was pulling her leg. Gus insisted he was sincere, so they went to see the bishop, whose reaction was similar to Betty's. When Gus's baptism was announced, a number of people were shocked to learn he wasn't a member already!

It took three decades for Gus to join the Church. During that time, he never felt pressured by his wife and always felt she respected him for who he was. "Some people crawl, some people run, and some people trot. I was a crawler," he stated. "I promised her that if we got married that she could raise the children. She's done a great job. She converted me too along the way."[29]

Most conversions do not take thirty years, but the calendar for conversion does not always follow the missionary's wishes. A stake missionary who helped teach George McPhee recalled leaving one of their meetings deeply discouraged. George had been investigating for almost fourteen months, and he feared it was all wasted effort. That night, the stake missionary had a dream in which he saw George standing at a podium, conducting sacrament meeting. The dream strengthened the member's desire to continue helping George learn the gospel and gave him renewed confidence, knowing that the Lord knew George and knew George's potential.[30]

Having confidence in the investigator and his ability to recognize truth is critical. When Jim Neal was introduced to the Church, his careful study of the New Testament confirmed to him the truth of the missionaries' message. "The thing that was important to my conversion," Jim said, "was that the missionaries let me investigate the Church according to my own pattern, rather than trying to fit me into their pattern. They would come to teach the lesson . . . and I would start to ask questions and then they would answer my questions. They eventually got through all the discussions, but not in order. This was important because they were addressing my concerns."[31]

We can have confidence in people simply knowing they are children of our Heavenly Father and inheritors of divine attributes. This kind of confidence is invaluable when an investigator or individual doesn't appear to exhibit characteristics indicating receptivity to the gospel. A former bishop recalled a young woman who had been excommunicated. She was very angry and wanted nothing to do with the Church or its members. Her Relief Society president, a sister from the singles ward, assumed responsibility for staying in touch despite the fact that the young woman had made it clear she wanted to be left alone. Month after month, the Relief Society president persisted, engineering opportunities to meet her by "chance" on a regular basis. After a year, the hate and anger subsided and the woman became willing to talk about the gospel. She was eventually re-baptized and went on to serve a mission in the Midwestern United States where she was involved in the conversion of fifty to sixty people. "When you think back on it," the bishop stated, "if this Relief Society president had not adhered to 'Love thy neighbor'—even those who have fallen—and nurtured this woman back to full fellowship in the Church, there are fifty or sixty people who would not have been exposed to the gospel."[32]

Like Bill Cortelyou, we rarely know the results of our efforts to act as the Lord's emissaries. "I think of it as a glass with water filling up," said a sister. "Eventually when it gets to the top it will flow over, but it may take several contacts with different people. . . . Eventually enough water gets in that cup, that when that cup is full, that's when Heavenly Father can open up areas, because these people . . . [are] ready."[33]

## Faith to Follow Through

Weston's era of missionary work is illustrative not just for the number of families baptized, but also for its high convert retention. "It is so important," President Gordon B. Hinckley stressed, "to see that [newly baptized members] are converted, that they have in their hearts a conviction concerning this great work. . . . It is a matter of the heart and its being touched by the Holy Spirit until they know this work is true."[34] To assure that conversion, President Hinckley taught, each convert needs a friend, a responsibility, and continued nurturing with the good word of God.[35] The families who joined the Weston Ward between 1968 and 1978 were received and embraced as President Hinckley counseled, providing a vivid example of what can happen when we follow through.

*A Friend*. Bishop Elbert Johnson presided over the Weston Ward during the early 1970s. A large man, he was known for his hugs.[36] "Everybody felt special," said a sister who moved into the ward shortly after being baptized. "He just made you feel so welcome."[37]

"No matter who or what . . . you just knew you were accepted and loved," added another convert. "He just oozed it out of every pore."[38]

The ward mirrored Bishop Johnson's love and warmth. "When visitors walked into one of our meetings," recalled Victor Ludlow, "it was like bees coming to honey. Members just went up to them, made them feel welcomed and important. Fellowshipping really happened."[39]

That said, fellowshipping was never left to chance. Home and visiting teachers came to baptisms, as did Primary leaders when children were involved. Families invited new members to dinner, family home evenings, and other events. Each person coming into the Church was assigned someone to look after them—their attendance, progress, and callings. You didn't feel monitored, stressed Fred Bowman; you felt special and valued.[40]

Almost all the families who joined the Weston Ward had young children and teenagers. When a family visited for the first time, a perceptive ward mission leader, Keith Knighton, made sure he knew the ages of their children so he could introduce each child to his or her teacher before services began. By taking this simple step, parents knew their children were taken care of, each child knew his teacher, and the teacher was aware of her visitor. When children reunited with their parents, they were enthusiastic about their experience. "The children wanted to come back," Keith smiled. "What are the parents going to do? They're going to come."[41]

The overall effect of these actions infused the ward with warmth. "You really felt like they wanted you there," said Leon Elliott. The Elliotts were blessed with a couple who took a personal interest in their progress prior to and following their baptism. The husband served as their home teacher and visited every week to see how the Elliotts were doing. His wife took Marti to Primary meetings. "They'd stay as long as we wanted them to stay and answer questions," Leon recalled. "[They] just had a sense of what our needs were. . . . We got well-entrenched in the Church, which made it easier to stay."[42]

Phil Potvin joined the Church in Lynnfield, eight years after marrying his member wife. During those years, he was continually impressed by the way people in the Church treated one another and those they didn't know.

"I remember the kindness, most of all," he said. "I remember the non-pressuring people who were there to be friends with me for who I was and not for who they wanted me to be." They didn't try to change him, said Phil, who was Bishop Potvin at the time of his interview, but "they did make me different through their actions and their examples. Even today I'm thankful to my Father in Heaven for being associated with them."[43]

"All missionary work largely is done one on one," said Fred Bowman, from his perspective as a convert, ward mission leader, and gospel essentials teacher. "I don't think you do missionary work in big groups. I think . . . fundamental missionary work is done one on one."[44]

*A Responsibility.* Carmen Rivera was called to be a counselor in both her branch's Primary and Relief Society shortly after baptism. "I really loved it," she said. "I was running from one room to another. I was spending the first class in the Primary and the second class in the Relief Society. I had to be reading a lot. I felt like I wanted to learn more about God. I needed to be closer to Him because I had been away so far for so long. . . . I wanted to be where He was."[45]

"[Converts] come into the Church with enthusiasm for what they have found," said President Hinckley. "We must immediately build on that enthusiasm."[46] A responsibility helps a new member feel needed and valued, and provides an opportunity to develop gospel roots. Their zeal for the gospel is magnified when they are given an opportunity to share it with others. Jo Anne Neal remembered lifelong members saying, "You all have something that other people wish [they] had. What is it?" Answering the question, she said, "It was an excitement for new knowledge, an excitement for learning and living the things we had found."[47]

"You're a part of us now," Bishop Johnson would declare at each baptism. "I used to stress the fact that [new members] had the responsibility to welcome other people into the Church," Bishop Johnson remembered. "They weren't just to sit back. . . . We wanted them . . . [to] help in the welfare, provide for the people . . . and so forth."[48]

New members welcomed this way didn't think twice about being asked to jump in with both feet. "We were all so new at it," reflected Hannah Goldberg, "so whenever we were given a calling or asked to do something, we just did it. I don't think we ever stopped to think about whether we were capable of doing it or not—we just did it."[49] One new member was called to serve as Bishop Johnson's counselor before everyone in the ward even knew his name.[50]

Not all converts are ready to serve in two auxiliary presidencies or a bishopric, but they all have something to share in terms of testimony, perspective, and a thirst for truth. Sensitive leaders prayerfully consider meaningful responsibilities that will bless the lives of new members and prepare them for future service in the Lord's Kingdom. "It may be ever so small," said President Hinckley, "but it will spell the difference in his life."[51]

Keith Knighton was branch president in Boston when he asked a newly baptized member to teach Primary. The sister asked to be released shortly thereafter, expressing feelings of discomfort and inadequacy. President Knighton realized the branch leadership needed to help people learn they could serve. "It wasn't that they didn't want a responsibility," he clarified. "They needed to have a responsibility that they could handle."[52]

A significant legacy of the U-nite Program in Maine was its leadership training. When a family joined the Church, they were asked to participate in the branch's missionary efforts by inviting other families to weekly meetings. When he extended a calling, the branch president took time to make sure the individual understood what was expected and had the knowledge and materials necessary to succeed. This improved the quality of service rendered and taught individuals that they could learn and better themselves. Many joining the Church found that the skills they acquired serving in the branch improved their temporal circumstances as well. "It immediately changed their lives," said President McLaughlin.[53]

***Nurturing with the Word***. Because baptism is merely a gate to discipleship, President Hinckley emphasized the need to nourish new members with the meat of the gospel, the sustenance that builds converts, long-time members, and wards alike. The lasting commitment exhibited by converts in the Weston Ward came, said Jo Anne Neal of herself and her peers, from understanding gospel principles.

An important contributor in this regard was Victor Ludlow, who taught a series of post-baptismal lessons, in which many of the Weston converts participated. Classes rotated among the participants' homes, and people often stayed late into the evening, enthralled by the subjects they were exploring together. The meetings gave new members an opportunity to discuss questions and concerns in an atmosphere where you didn't have to have all the answers. "Everybody was willing to talk about it," said Jim Neal, "so there was a lot of discussion going on. We were all new to the gospel; we were all learning something new; we were all curious about it. We built on each other's enthusiasm as we were doing that. There was no question that wouldn't be addressed . . . no sense there that anything was off-limits."[54]

Describing the powerful influence of those lessons in his life, Fred Bowman said they gave him a sense of what Mormonism was all about, what was expected of him, and the kinds of changes he needed to make in his own behavior to better live the gospel.[55]

All the couples who participated in the class remained active in the Church. "Unbelievable service," was how Marti Elliott characterized the lasting influence of Brother Ludlow's classes.[56]

There are many ways to nourish with the word. One couple spoke appreciatively of a family who frequently invited them into their home and taught them how to hold family home evening.[57] Some mentioned home and visiting teachers, while others recalled testimonies that other members had shared during ordinary exchanges.

"I remember how I felt when I learned a new principle and how I would place that into my superstructure of understanding," said Fred Bowman. "I remember who it was that gave me the particular insights. . . . They've become, to me, mentors. And I appreciate that."[58]

Kristen and Paul Anderson were called as stake missionaries. To involve more people in the work, they made sure new converts were invited into ward members' homes on a weekly basis. Paul remembered new member discussions in which a recent convert frequently raised topics she'd been pondering and ask, "What do *we* believe about this?"—indicating that she had accepted the answer even before it was given. "It was one of the highlights of our time in Boston . . . to get to know them and answer all their questions," Paul stated. "We had the easy job; when we met them, they were already converted."[59]

Spreading responsibility beyond the stake missionaries and home and visiting teachers made a difference not only to converts but to the ward as well, said the Andersons' bishop. "As the seed of the gospel began to take root . . . there were just a large number of people who truly, personally became involved and viewed nourishing the word as their own responsibility.

"When a focus in the ward is on truly reaching out to those who join the Church, there's a desire to not just welcome them into the ward, but welcome them into the flock, into the brotherhood and sisterhood of friendship," the bishop continued. This helps individuals become converted, taste of the gospel, and prepare to go out and make their own contributions.[60]

Mauricio Paredes first encountered the Church as a Boy Scout in Guatemala, where he was impressed by the caliber and conduct of young men from an LDS Scout troop. This positive impression was corroborated a few years later when Mauricio saw similar attributes in a young woman who sang in a choir with him. The young lady invited him to church and gave him a copy of the Book of Mormon, which Mauricio read for the history it contained.

Mauricio began attending sacrament meeting, even after his friend from choir stopped coming. For three months, he attended meetings alone, hoping in vain that someone would reach out to him. On the last Sunday he visited, Mauricio decided he was ready to partake of the sacrament. As the bread made its way down his row, Mauricio reached for a piece, only to be rebuked by the woman next to him who whispered, "This is only for members." Apologizing profusely, but receiving no further explanation or encouragement, Mauricio stopped coming.

Seven years later, in 1971, Mauricio moved to the United States. Attending school and the Catholic Church, Mauricio made many friends, but he was restless. Looking in the telephone directory, Mauricio found a listing for The Church of Jesus Christ of Latter-day Saints and decided to visit. The sacrament talks left him confused. When the meeting concluded, a brother offered to introduce him to a Spanish-speaking member from Central America. The introduction was made, but the two did not hit it off when the topic of the Catholic Church came up. Mauricio felt alienated and criticized. He left, vowing to remain satisfied with the church of his youth.

Despite his resolution, Mauricio remained curious about Mormons. In December 1977, Mauricio was shopping with his wife and daughter when a voice in his head encouraged him to walk to the end of the mall. At the end of the building, Mauricio saw two young men, trying unsuccessfully to talk with holiday shoppers. The elders were putting their materials away by the time he got to them and did not look up until Mauricio said, "Please forgive me, but could you tell me are you elders, missionaries of The Church of Jesus Christ of Latter-day Saints?" Answering affirmatively, Mauricio asked if they could do him a favor. The missionaries were momentarily wary, but happy to agree when Mauricio provided his name, address, and telephone number and asked if they could visit him.

Mauricio was elated when he returned home, but weeks went by without word from the elders. At the end of March, Mauricio called the mission office. They had no record of his request, so Mauricio again provided his information and asked to have missionaries sent to his home. Another month passed, and Mauricio called again. This time the mission office had his records but explained they didn't have any Spanish-speaking missionaries.

"Send them!" Mauricio insisted. "Send them even if you have only English-speaking missionaries. Send them."

The missionaries began teaching the Paredes family that May. Finally given a chance to learn the gospel, Mauricio and his wife were baptized one month later. Since that date, Mauricio has been a pillar in establishing and solidifying Spanish-speaking units of the Church in Boston.

It's hard to fathom so many missed opportunities to share the gospel. Yet the Lord's work could not be frustrated, for "the Lord knoweth all things from the beginning; wherefore, he prepareth a way to accomplish all his works among the children of men" (1 Nephi 9:6). This is the Lord's work, and He invites us to take part.

"For many years, I was a Catholic because of my parents and grandparents," said Brother Paredes of his conversion. "I am not a member of The Church of Jesus Christ of Latter-day Saints by tradition, but by pure conviction."[61]

"Who said, 'Behold, I cannot speak the smallest part which I feel'?" asked Jo Anne Neal. "That's exactly the way I felt for years. When I follow the gospel . . . I cannot even speak the smallest part which I feel. I love it so much. It just totally changed our lives."[62]

"I think we all have to get a conversion experience—even if we've already had one," remarked Mark Johnson. "Because there are other people out there who can be brought to the gospel. It may seem so unlikely, but yet the Lord knows his flock and . . . those that are passionate because they have a fire burning within will be the most likely to do this work. . . . It won't come from missionaries alone."[63]

When the McLaughlins were asked about the hundreds of people who joined the Church through the U-nite Program, Karline spoke of the blessing George was given when he was set apart to work with the New England Mission presidency. "Lest we get too puffed up," she said, "he was told in the prayer that he was taking the place of someone else that should have done it and failed. . . . The reason we did it was because we happened to be obedient. There were other couples that were already prepared to step in and do this. So it's not us . . . it's the Lord."[64]

O BLEST COMMUNION, FELLOWSHIP DIVINE!
WE FEEBLY STRUGGLE, THEY IN GLORY SHINE;
YET ALL ARE ONE IN THEE, FOR ALL ARE THINE.

## 7

# A LEADER,
# A DISCIPLE

WILBUR COX and his wife, Nora, moved to Belmont, Massachusetts, in 1951. Both were from southern Utah and had been married in the Manti temple, but Wilbur came from a long line of Jack Mormons and was completely inactive in Church matters. A forceful and outspoken man, Wilbur Cox was known to enjoy cigars and the colorful language he had picked up in the Navy during World War II. He was not antagonistic toward the Church but felt he had little use for it. His wife, in contrast, attended every meeting with her three daughters in tow, accepted all callings extended to her, and was surrounded with friends from the Cambridge Branch. Each Thursday for at least fifteen years, Nora Cox fasted that her husband would return to activity.[1]

Wilbur, or Bill as he was known, supported his wife's callings and contributed to the Church's frequent fund-raisers, but he chose to observe the Church from a comfortable distance. When Nora's home teachers visited, Bill would sit in his garage until the men left.[2] Eventually Nora was called as Relief Society president, and this separation became harder to maintain as Ira Terry, the branch president, began holding planning meetings in the Cox home. President Terry had a habit of calling everyone "brother" or "sister," and he deliberately solicited and accepted suggestions from Brother Cox, who acknowledged himself Nora's "third counselor."[3]

Despite his increased involvement in branch matters, Bill resisted any formal role in the Church. When a brother asked Bill if he would accept a calling, Bill Cox simply grinned and asked, "Could I smoke my cigar on the stand?"[4]

Smart answers or not, the Lord had plans for Bill Cox. It was a Saturday afternoon in 1954 when President Ira Terry knocked on the door of the Cox home. One of the Cox daughters greeted him by saying, "President Terry, Mother is not here." Ira Terry was unconcerned. "I don't want to see your mother," he stated. "I need to speak with your father."

When Bill came to the door, the authority in President Terry's voice was unmistakable. "Brother Cox," he stated, "the Lord wants you to give up your bad habits and serve as Sunday School Superintendent of the Cambridge Branch." Having fulfilled his errand and delivered the Lord's message, President Terry promptly turned and left.[5] It was a pivotal moment, not only for Bill Cox and his family but the Saints of New England as well.

Something in the exchange caught Bill's attention. He recognized the truth behind Ira Terry's words and began observing the Word of Wisdom from that time forth. He accepted the Sunday School leadership and took responsibility for the building committee overseeing construction of the Longfellow Park meetinghouse. Bill served as a counselor to Ira Terry, after which he served as president of the Cambridge Branch and then the Atlantic District. Bill Cox served as the first president of the Boston Stake when it was organized in 1962. He was subsequently called to lead the California Central Mission, following which he was ordained a patriarch, served as president of the Sanpete Utah Stake, and ultimately served as president of the Manti Temple. According to his daughter, Martha Ballantyne, President Cox's activity in the Church "began when an inspired and humble branch president issued a call"—a call that carried with it the authority of divine will.[6]

President Cox was a man of action, fully dedicated to moving the Lord's work forward. With his forceful, no-nonsense leadership style, he was instrumental in installing meetinghouses throughout Massachusetts. More important, however, was the influence Bill Cox had on the men and women who served with him as he tended to the needs of the New England Saints within the Atlantic District. The district's boundaries extended from Hartford, Connecticut, to southern Maine, and President Cox spent Sundays crisscrossing the area to visit branches and scattered Sunday School groups. These travels afforded President Cox ample time to discuss matters with his counselors, one of whom was Henry Eyring. One observer of Wilbur Cox's legacy wrote, "the sweeping trips through the New England area transformed the Church and transformed the men President Cox took with him. They drew from his incredible brilliance and energy and commitment to the Church and became a whole generation of visionary Church leaders themselves—from bishops and stake presidents to Seventies and Apostles."[7]

Speaking to the New England Saints on the occasion of the Boston Stake's formation, President Cox bore fervent testimony of the Lord's work. "Brethren and sisters," he said, "the gospel of Jesus Christ is our most priceless possession. It is the way to eternal progression and exaltation, and our responsibility as servants of the Lord is to defend this faith in those who are members and bring the gospel to those who are not. . . . I love the gospel of Jesus Christ. I firmly believe, without question, in the divinity of the Prophet Joseph Smith, and the fact that he restored this gospel in this land in this last dispensation of time. Let us make it the beacon light of our lives, and in our efforts, make it the beacon light in the lives of all those who will listen to it."[8]

In the last pages of the Book of Mormon, Mormon addresses his listeners by stating, "It is by the grace of God the Father, and our Lord Jesus Christ, and his holy will, *because of the gift of his calling* unto me, that I am permitted to speak unto you at this time" (Moroni 7:2, emphasis added). One of the gifts we receive as members of the Lord's Church is the opportunity to be called by one in authority to take part in His work. Little room exists for passive membership in a vast organization entrusted to volunteers. Charged with a work infinite in scope, we are asked to tend our own corner of the vineyard, which, if we do faithfully, will prepare us for the kingdom.

What is marvelous about this process is the Lord's use of ordinary men and women to accomplish His purposes. Bill Cox was an ordinary man who became an integral part of the Church's growth in New England because he heeded a call to serve. President Cox was a dynamic man by nature, but the characteristics he exhibited in his stewardships are attributes that can be modeled by all. President Cox recognized the Lord's call, extended through the voice of a mortal servant. Once called, he was obedient to the Lord's instructions. President Cox loved the individuals he served and recognized his duty to prepare them to carry on the Lord's work. Most important, Wilbur Cox never forgot that the labor in which he was engaged was the Lord's.

## "Have You Prayed about This?"

For most of us, the extension of a calling is not the central turning point it was for President Cox, and we regularly accept responsibilities within our branches, wards, and stakes. If we take time to seek confirmation of the source of these calls, however, our understanding of the Lord's purposes is enlarged and our capacity to serve is increased as we come to appreciate our role in His plan.

When President Cox was called to preside over the California Central Mission, necessitating his release as stake president, Elder Boyd K. Packer asked Bill Fresh to lead the Boston Stake. Brother Fresh listened numbly as he was handed a list of names and told he had two hours to choose counselors. Slightly traumatized, Brother Fresh found a quiet space away from the meetinghouse and prayed for guidance. He immediately felt impressed to ask Don Parker, one of President Cox's counselors, to continue serving in the presidency. As Brother Fresh continued his prayer, his eyes were drawn to a name that appeared to stand above the plane of the page he'd been given, as if the letters were on stilts. The name meant nothing to Brother Fresh, but he recalled counsel that this is the Church of Jesus Christ and we ought to let Him run it. Convinced this was the Lord's will, the new president returned to report. When Elder Packer asked if he had his counselors, President Fresh said yes, but admitted there was a problem: "I haven't the foggiest idea who L. Tom Perry is!"

"That's no problem," Elder Packer assured him. "We'll just ask him to offer the closing prayer in the Saturday night session." When Brother Perry stood to offer that prayer, it was President Fresh's first glimpse of him.[9]

There is great assurance in understanding we have a Father in Heaven who knows us by name. Every time a call is extended through inspiration, it is a reminder that He is mindful of us and He knows our capabilities, even when we do not.

Brent Lambert was living in eastern Massachusetts in 1975 when he was called into then stake president Richard Bushman's office. President Bushman welcomed him with the query, "I suppose you know why you're here?" Brother Lambert said he did not. "Well," President Bushman began, "as you know, the bishop of the Hingham Ward has been released."

Detached, Brent merely nodded, murmuring, "That's interesting."

Raising his eyebrows and looking directly at Brent, President

Bushman cleared his throat. "I'm here to call you as the bishop of the Hingham Ward," he stated.

Shocked into attention, Brother Lambert caught his breath and forgot to address the president by his proper title. "Dick, have you prayed about this?"

President Bushman laughed. "As a matter of fact, I have Brent. And you're it."

Some years later, after serving as bishop and a stake president himself, Brent Lambert recalled his own experiences extending callings on behalf of the Lord. In one instance he needed to call a bishop for the Newport Rhode Island Ward. He interviewed the seven high priests in the ward, all of whom were qualified. The ward's soft-spoken elders quorum president, on the other hand, had been a member for just eighteen months and appeared inexperienced and naïve as to matters of Church administration when compared to the others. Yet the Holy Ghost told President Lambert that this elders quorum president was the new bishop. "I wanted to reject that information," President Lambert admitted, "because it didn't make any sense, but I couldn't. . . . I turned to my counselors and told them the impression that I had gotten was undeniable. They said, 'We received the same.'"

Over the course of his service, said President Lambert, "I had . . . a series of marvelous experiences where the Lord in an unequivocal way was directing the affairs of His Church through me. There were multiple examples. . . . He made it abundantly clear at every sort of turn in the road what His desires were."[10]

Stewardships within the Church are not a series of promotions contingent on past positions. Instead, they reflect the Lord's understanding of the things we need to learn and the unique ways we can contribute at a particular time. Commenting on the diverse attributes of Church members, Mitt Romney remarked, "Among the leaders of the wards, there are some Joseph Smiths and there are some Brigham Youngs. Brigham Young probably didn't hug many Saints. But he helped build the Church in important ways. . . . Some [are] more loving and individual, and some [are] more organizational or dynamic. The Church rolls forth, in part, I believe, because of these different styles and different personalities."[11]

Rosemary Fletcher knew few people in the area when she was called to serve as stake Relief Society president, prompting her to ask the stake president for advice in choosing her counselors. The stake president suggested some names and counseled Rosemary to pray about it, promising she could have anyone she wanted. Rosemary took a list home and read it over and over as she fasted and prayed. When the answer came, Sister Fletcher said it felt as if the Lord had literally spoken to her. She had three unmistakable names.

Only one of individuals was on the list the stake president had provided. The second name was that of a woman Rosemary had met briefly. The third had no source beyond inspiration. When Rosemary took the names back to the stake president, he eyed her choices with curiosity and asked why she had chosen the third sister. Rosemary responded honestly: "I don't know." The stake president cleared his throat and said, "Well, she's completely inactive. She won't do anything."

Rosemary was taken aback but sure of the answer she'd been given. She asked if she could pray about her decision again and then speak with the woman on the phone. Permission was given, and Rosemary called the sister in question. The woman on the line began to cry as Sister Fletcher introduced herself. "I've been praying and praying and praying," she explained, "for something I could do in the Church." The prompting of the Spirit confirmed, the third sister accepted a call to the stake Relief Society presidency, where she served faithfully for three years.[12]

When we recognize the Lord as the source of the calls we accept and extend, it changes the spirit of our service. It reminds us that we have an Eternal Father who personally entrusts portions of His divine work to us, helps us better understand our relationship with God, and allows us, like Mormon, to see such calls as holy gifts.

## Do It with Exactness

Recognizing the Lord's will in his branch president's admonition to change, Bill Cox re-aligned those areas of his behavior that were inconsistent with the Lord's commands when he agreed to lead the Cambridge Sunday School. In so doing, Bill Cox exhibited humility and showed the Lord he could be trusted. To serve the Lord effectively, we too must be willing to heed His directions, whatever the task. To lead in the Lord's kingdom, we must follow.

Spencer W. Kimball visited a training conference in Maine while serving in the Quorum of the Twelve. Near the close of the meetings, Elder Kimball instructed George McLaughlin to ask the mission president if he could drive Elder Kimball to the airport in Boston without inconvenience. Brother McLaughlin knew the mission president was already hoping to take Elder Kimball to Boston, so instead of relaying the question, he simply told the president the arrangements were set. When lunch ended, Elder Kimball asked Brother McLaughlin, "Did you do what I asked you to?" George said yes, but Elder Kimball shook his head. "Oh no, you didn't," he replied. Looking closely at Brother McLaughlin, Elder Kimball counseled, "When one of the Brethren asks you to do something, you listen very carefully, and you do it exactly—exactly as they tell you to do it."

When the next conference took place, George McLaughlin was one of many priesthood leaders who arrived early to assist with set up. As they prepared the room, the visiting General Authority saw that the public address system needed to be plugged into an outlet behind a piano bench. Addressing Brother McLaughlin, the visiting authority asked, "Would you get down under the piano bench and plug that in for us?" A brother standing nearby noted it would be easier to simply reach over the bench. Despite the logic of this suggestion, George remembered Elder Kimball's instruction. He picked up the electrical cord, crawled under the piano bench, and plugged it into the wall. When it came time for the visiting authority to talk with area priesthood leaders, George's name was not on the interview list. George was confused and asked if there had been a mistake. The visiting authority smiled and replied, "No, I've already interviewed you."[13]

Humility and obedience are necessary prerequisites to personal revelation. If we are not willing to accept and follow guidance from the Lord, there is little reason for the Holy Ghost to provide instruction. When we are faithful in the small things, we demonstrate that we can be trusted with larger tasks as well.

Bert Van Uitert was a man worthy of such trust. Paul McKinnon served on the high council with Bert for several years. "Bert was always the Scout guy," Paul recalled, noting that for the better part of two decades, Bert attended all the councils, camps, and meetings. "I always thought of Bert as being Mr. Dyed-in-the-Wool-Scout-Guy. . . . Not only did he attend every meeting, but it was always by the book."

Paul recalled an occasion when he had become frustrated trying to explain an opinion he'd voiced. "I don't like Scouting!" Paul had exclaimed. "I don't like doing it. I don't like Scouting like you do!" Bert's response was calm and straightforward but unexpected. "You think I like this?" he asked with bemusement. "I don't like it at all. I don't enjoy doing all this stuff. I don't enjoy going to these camps. I do it because I'm supposed to do it, and I think that's what my call is. But I don't like it."

"I was stunned," Brother McKinnon admitted. "Never was there any indication with Bert that it was anything other than a pure pleasure to be doing it."[14]

"Bert did not like living in the outdoors," said Gordon Williams, admitting that he'd been the bishop who had called Bert to serve as ward Scoutmaster—the beginning of Bert's twenty-year relationship with the Boy Scout organization. "Why did we call him? Because we were concerned about the kids," Bishop Williams explained. They needed someone to be an example, to wear the uniform, and get things going, "[Bert] did not want to do it, because that was not . . . the sort of thing that he thought he could do well. But he took on the responsibility and when he took it on, like all other things Bert did, he took it on with gusto. . . . He did it, and he did it to a tee."[15]

At some time or another, we all receive callings for which we feel ill-suited. When that happens, suggested a former bishop, "You get on your knees and say, 'Lord, I know you want me to do this. Help me and tell me what to do.'" Get out the manual, he continued. "It tells you what you're supposed to do." If you are obedient, "Bam! You catch the spirit or the vision of what you're doing and miracles happen. People around you start feeling the influence of what you do. It is humility first, realizing that you need the Lord to tell you what to do. Second is being obedient . . . [and doing] your best, even though it's hard and awkward. . . . The Lord fills in the rest."[16]

## "Love. Just Love"

"Wilbur Cox was by far one of the nicest men that I have ever known in the Church," said former Cambridge Branch member Penny Holton. "He understood people. . . . He believed in all kinds of people. We loved him dearly."[17]

When we serve our fellow Saints, we are proxies on behalf of our Savior, whose every deed was motivated by His pure love for the Father and His children. President Cox followed the example of the Great Shepherd as he spent his time among the Saints in New England. "He was an individual who cared enormously about the individual person within the stake," said Gordon Williams, who served with President Cox as a young man. "Many of the people within the stake knew him very well, not only because he was a leader, but also because of the type of individual he was."[18]

When Christ visited the Nephites, he invited them to come to Him one by one (see 3 Nephi 11:13–17). Ordinances in the Church are likewise performed individually. The gospel is eternal in scope, but it is not about efficiency. Its power is found in the change that is wrought when the Spirit touches one heart at a time.

In the late 1970s, the Cambridge First Ward had a number of Spanish-speaking members and had organized a Spanish-speaking Sunday School. A priesthood leadership meeting was convened to discuss what ward leaders could do to assist and strengthen these members. After an extended period of general discussion failed to lead to any concrete action items, Steve Wheelwright, a counselor in the bishopric, broke in saying, "You know what strikes me is that I never remember our having had a discussion about the English-speaking members of this ward. We always refer to them as individuals and families, yet here we are referring to the Spanish-speaking members of the ward as a group."

The tenor of the meeting changed abruptly with this simple observation. Over the next forty minutes, the group identified six families they believed had the potential to become leaders of an independent Spanish branch. They then selected and released six couples in the ward from their home and visiting teaching assignments and assigned them to prepare these Spanish-speaking families to become the nucleus of a future Spanish-speaking congregation. Within a period of months, the stake presidency organized a Spanish-speaking branch. Today both the Cambridge and Boston stakes have strong Spanish-speaking congregations.

"I have often thought of that experience when we hold discussions in our leadership meetings about non-members, about inactive members, about single adults, and so on," said Clayton Christensen, a participant in the Cambridge leadership meeting. "We will be much more productive in all our work if we recognize everyone as an individual."[19]

Asked about things she did as a Young Women president, Mary Finlayson identified only one thing. "I felt like the most important thing I could do was to let those girls know I really cared about them. . . . What goes on in a class means much less than how you feel when you're in there. Lots of times kids won't remember what happened, but they know . . . if the leader loved them and cared about them. . . . I remember the individual girls and trying to support them individually."[20]

What is true in the Young Women organization is true for all of us. After a major reorganization, the Arlington Ward was created with members drawn from four different wards.* Bob Chandler was called to serve as bishop of the new congregation. One of his counselors at the time remarked, "We didn't know ninety percent of the people . . . [and with time] the magnitude of the change became apparent." There were strong differences of opinion and people who felt left out. "Being in the bishopric, I saw a lot of the issues that came up. . . . The arguments were strong and powerful and the feelings were deep. It was clear early on that taking fist-pounding stands saying 'This is the way it is,' wasn't going to work, at least in terms of keeping the ward together."

Bishop Chandler was not a strong administrator, but he had a personality that discouraged anger and soothed hurt feelings. "No matter what he does," the counselor explained, "people accept it for fact that he's done the best he can with the sincerest of hearts. Over the course of time, he enabled the ward to hang together. . . . Whether he knew how to hold a meeting, whether he knew how to administer, whether he knew how to handle the finances of the Church, frankly it didn't matter. Not that he didn't know how to do any of those things, but they clearly weren't first in his priority list."

In particular, the counselor grew to appreciate the bishop's gentle way of asking people to help out and participate. "I found myself being very careful about how I approached things, tried to do it gently, and tried to be very honest about it," the former bishopric member concluded, "trying to follow the example of Bishop Chandler."[21]

Uniting the membership of the new ward was a daunting assignment, but Bishop Chandler was successful because he loved the individuals he was called to serve and they returned that love. This personal concern was enough to bridge divides when logic and persuasion could not. "Bob hadn't had a lot of management experience," former stake president Mitt Romney observed, "[but] I can't imagine a bishop more loved and cared for than Bob Chandler."[22] When President Romney asked another priesthood holder to take on a similar challenge and preside over a diverse, struggling urban branch in downtown Boston, he had only one piece of advice: "Love. Just love."[23]

No matter where we serve, this trait should be the hallmark of our charge. Richard Bushman heard intimidating accounts of General Authority visits when he was called as a stake president—tales where

---

* The Arlington Ward was organized in 1984, drawing members from the Lynnfield, Weston, and Cambridge First and Cambridge Second Wards.

leaders were drilled on statistics, administration, programs, and goals. Thus forewarned, President Bushman armed himself with facts and figures and, where needed, excuses as he prepared for his first visit. To his surprise, the anticipated interrogation never occurred. "I got two very strong impressions," said Brother Bushman of his experiences with visiting authorities. "One, they wanted to know how I was. . . . There was an awful lot of really good listening. . . . The second thing I got was testimony from those brethren—not just in the meetings, but to me. They wanted me to be reassured that this is the work and they loved it, . . . Not a word about the structure of the organization."[24]

"The best training was clearly the one-on-ones," Mitt Romney said of the time he spent as a stake president working with other stake leaders. "Kneeling down and having [a] prayer with a bishop once a month and going through all the families in the ward that were having difficulties and issues. . . . I wouldn't really call it training. We need to get buoyed up by one another. There's no job that's tougher than being bishop. Everybody thinks you're doing it wrong."[25]

Ken Hutchins was president of the Boston Stake in 1995 when he arrived home at the close of a particularly long Sunday that had started at 5:00 a.m. His relief at being home was short-lived, since the phone began ringing as soon as he stepped through the door. Call after call came in for the tired leader, and President Hutchins despaired of any reprieve as the hour grew late. To make matters worse, his teenage daughter was desperate to make a call. She became increasingly distressed as the phone continued to ring for her father. In an attempt to appease his daughter and get a moment's rest, President Hutchins finally told her to use the phone and take a message if another call came for him.

Ten minutes had not passed when President Hutchins heard his daughter's disgruntled voice from the other room. "Dad, the phone is for you!" she groaned. Weary to the point of exhaustion, Ken reminded her to take a message. "Dad," she called again, with more urgency. "It's the Prophet."

Ken was sure that his daughter was pulling his leg, but she was insistent. A skeptical President Hutchins picked up the phone only to hear the Prophet's executive secretary ask, "President, do you have time to talk to President Hinckley?"

The assent was barely given when a familiar voice rang over the line: "President Hutchins, how are you doing? Have you had a long day? Are you tired out yet?" Stunned that the Prophet was speaking to him in his living room, Ken stammered that he had been tired but, truthfully, this was no longer a problem. President Hinckley empathized, saying he too had a hard day, and it wasn't done yet. After asking about President Hutchins' well-being, the Prophet went on to inquire about members of the stake he had met at a regional conference a few months previous.

"I put the phone down," recalled President Hutchins, "and thought, 'Here is a man who has jurisdiction for the earth, and he is calling this remote stake president out here in the state of Massachusetts and taking up his time and expressing his love and concern for individual members of the Church.' It taught me such a great lesson about how you should never consider yourself in a calling so far away from an individual member that you can't have personal touch with them and make sure they feel the love from you that they need to feel."[26]

## Learn through the Experience of Serving

The majority of Saints scattered throughout New England during Wilbur Cox's tenure as president of the Atlantic District were new to the Church and far from a critical mass of members. "One thing I learned," said Patriarch Gordon Williams of his days traversing the Eastern Seaboard with President Cox, "is the importance of follow-through. When you delegate a responsibility to someone, you shouldn't assume that they will necessarily do it. . . . [President Cox] would always [say], 'Now, what we need to remember is that they probably haven't done what we asked them to do, but don't let that bother you, because with time and effort on our part, following up on them, they will gradually learn how to lead.'

"The other thing I always remember," Gordon continued, "he said, 'Even though you don't think the job is done right from your perspective, what you ought to do when you talk to them is find something positive about what they've done. The critical element is to let them know . . . what they've accomplished, because they are struggling against so many odds anyway. . . . Our role is to energize them.'"[27]

Delegation and stewardship are fundamental to the Church's organization. The gospel is a "learn by doing" program, as is our entire mortal journey. "Jo Anne Neal was the first Relief Society president I knew [in Massachusetts]," said Camille Foster. "She was just so energetic and excited about everything. I remember the first time [my neighbor] came to Relief Society. . . . She asked me if Jo Anne and other women like her had to go to special training to learn how to be a Relief Society president, like a special school or something."

"No," Camille told her friend. "They just learn through the experience of serving."[28]

In the 1980s, suburban members of the Cambridge wards began attending newly created units in Belmont and Arlington. Those left in the Cambridge First Ward were primarily young married students, and the ward's bishops were called to serve from other congregations. Don Hangen was the first bishop to be called from the ward's membership in 1994, and he was shocked by the call. "It was a big surprise for everyone in the ward," his wife admitted. "I think we had all just assumed that Belmont would always provide the leadership for that ward," due to the youthfulness and transient nature of the Cambridge congregation.

"In many ways I didn't feel quite ready, as far as my Church experience," Don stated. "I felt like I was too young, too inexperienced. . . . I was really shaken.

"I spent a lot of that morning in tears," Don continued. "But I knew immediately who my counselors would be. . . . That answer came so clear to me that I thought, 'Maybe if that works, maybe I am supposed to be bishop.' . . . I think it was good for our ward, in the fact that there was no longer a 'they.' It was more of a 'we.' We were certainly in this together. . . . we felt like we were growing up a bit. There was no longer this sort of generation gap that our fathers or other people's fathers were providing the leadership. It came from within our ranks."[29]

In 1984, Bishop Lloyd Baird asked Randy Gaz to organize Saints living in Boston into a group that could become a branch. Randy felt overwhelmed. After all, a similar attempt at a downtown branch had ended after two years in 1974. Bishop Baird remained involved "in a non-interventional way," asking questions and making suggestions as Randy reported to him each Sunday. It was clear to Randy that the fledgling group was constantly on the bishop's mind, but he allowed Randy to lead the charge. "That's one of the things I admired about him," said Brother Gaz. "He would put people in places of responsibility. He could've done a much better job than I did, but he didn't have time to do that and he knew I would grow. . . . That's a lesson I needed to learn. . . . I'm sure one of the reasons he was called to be bishop was because he knew how to motivate people [and] pick opportunities or situations . . . where he thought they might be successful. Then he would stand back. . . . He is good at letting people try and fail, or try and succeed, and, in the process, grow. That's part of being a good leader."[30]

Bishop Baird's leadership style became the model for the new Boston Branch. The first attempt at a city branch, suggested one brother, had been hampered at times when those who needed to learn to lead did not because others did the work in an effort to avoid failure. "I learned," he said, "that a lot of times you're not looking to do things efficiently. You're trying to teach people to learn from their experience and learn to take responsibility."[31]

Mitt Romney recounted a leadership meeting where a visiting authority pulled him aside and said, "You know, sometimes, President, we come into stakes that are perfectly organized and it's just remarkable how well they run." He concluded bluntly: "Those usually aren't the best ones."[32]

Unfortunately, our impatience to see results and our fear of failure often outweigh our motivation to help others grow into a role. Stake president Ken Hutchins once visited a unit where a high priest had been called to serve as elders quorum president because of a shortage in leadership. "That's fine," the stake president said, "but that's not the goal. [The goal is] not to have somebody who already knows how to do it. The goal is to train them to do it themselves."[33]

Even congregations focused on building self-sufficiency often rely too heavily on experienced members, Carol Coppins observed. There's a hope that established leaders will provide a strong example for others to follow, but "if you do exceedingly well, [others] think, 'I can't do that.' If you take too much on yourself, [others] don't have the experience to take over themselves." In a training situation, she suggested, it can be effective to call proven leaders as counselors to provide support, rather than run the program. A call to lead bestows a trust that is a powerful motivator. You feel needed if you are asked to lead, Carol pointed out. "Most people rise to the occasion."[34]

Delegation does not entail an abdication of responsibility, but rather a heightened accountability. The leader is no longer directly responsible for the assigned task but is now responsible for a more important outcome— the development and growth of an individual.

"We never had enough Relief Society teachers," said Shelley Hoffmire of her years in the Boston Branch. "We never had people who had experience to teach, so we did team teaching all the time. We would pair a convert up with somebody who had some experience. . . . We combined two or three [classes] together with a strong teacher and two teachers-in-training. . . . We had somebody who was responsible for the lesson, but

[who] was also responsible to [make sure] the teachers-in-training [taught] an aspect of the lesson. After people were in that position for six months, they were ready to take it on their own a bit."[35]

"That was clearly one of the keys to the success of the Boston Branch," said Brother Gaz. "The people who were the foundation were involved and were leaders and doers. . . . They put their souls in it. Because Church didn't happen unless they were there and ran it, they knew they had to be there. If the Church depended on them, it gave them a reason to be there.

"Your capacity to do things in the Church is magnified by your calling," he continued. "I had one of my [medical] residents . . . ask me why the Mormon Church was growing so fast. I said . . . you have to be a participant and everyone has a responsibility. . . . Either you get with the program, you're active and grow and learn in the Church, or you don't."[36]

The Lord is the Master Delegator. He entrusts His kingdom to us, asking us to seek His guidance and learn our part. Dottie LaPierre vividly recalled teaching a class where things went badly awry. Devastated that the lesson had not gone as intended and fearful that she had disappointed her leaders, Dottie prayed for guidance. Not long after her plea, Dottie received an impression that informed her what she'd done wrong. "There was nothing meanly said, but just a feeling of: 'You didn't do this, and you didn't do that.' It was very gentle but firm, and it was right on," she stated. "There wasn't any skirting around the issue. . . . I don't think the Lord works that way. . . . He does want you to know what it is that you need to do if you want to succeed."[37]

## "We Saw the Hand of God Moving"

A final attribute Gordon Williams described in President Cox was the way he took time to reflect on the quality of programs members had managed to establish within their small congregations, despite their lack of experience, resources, and even skills. "Quite clearly," President Cox would say on their return trips home, "this is evidence that the Lord's hand is involved because . . . they couldn't accomplish what has been accomplished [on their own]."[38]

There were three stakes in New England when Bill Fresh was called to fill President Cox's shoes as president of the Boston Stake. Working with leaders in Salt Lake City, President Fresh was instrumental in creating a fourth stake in New Hampshire. Approval for the new stake was granted, but its organization was delayed until President Fresh moved his family to New Hampshire in connection with a new job. When President Fresh was released as president of the Boston Stake, Elder L. Tom Perry was installed in his stead. Six weeks later, the Manchester New Hampshire Stake was created with Bill Fresh as its first president.

Describing the lessons he learned through this and other experiences, President Fresh said, "First, the Lord knows His children quite well. And second, this is His church and He's going to run it if we let Him. . . . I believe sincerely that He cares about us as individuals. I think He knows us by name. He knows us far better than we know ourselves. He has a plan for each of us, if we'll let Him . . . direct our lives. Therefore, He cares where we go to school, He cares about our education, He cares about our spouse and our children, He cares about where we live.

"[Something that] has been borne out over the years of Church service," President Fresh continued, "[is] the Lord has His own transfer system of those who are willing to serve. Where people are needed, it is not that unusual to see someone prayed into a ward or a branch to accomplish what was necessary."[39]

"The thing that stands out most in my mind . . . is how important [the Church] is to the Lord," Brent Lambert remarked. "The Lord isn't passive on this at all. He is vitally interested—this is what comes across so strongly. I never called a bishop that the Lord didn't specifically tell me who he wanted. I never called a counselor that the Lord didn't actually speak to me in a very direct way. I'm not one of these people that is guided every step by the Lord—about 99.9 percent of my life, I just go on my own way and hope that the Lord will bless me if I live the commandments. But in the affairs of the Church, it has been so direct and poignant as to be undeniable."[40]

The power that accompanies a call from the Lord—when hands are laid upon our heads, and we are set apart for a particular purpose, place, and time—is real and tangible. As expressed by Sister Julie B. Beck in a general conference address, "The blessings of the priesthood make it possible for every person who is set apart to serve in any office in the Lord's church to receive authority, responsibility, and blessings connected with their office."[41] Because the Lord is so concerned about this work, none of us need fear that we will be left to our own devices when we heed the call to labor in the Lord's vineyard, so long as we invite Him to serve with us.

Reflecting on his own experiences serving in the Atlantic District with President Cox, President Henry B. Eyring said, "The thing that affected me most deeply during that period of time, and is probably having the most effect now as an Apostle . . . [is] simply the notion of the closeness of God. . . . We saw the hand of God moving to help us when we were in difficulty. . . I saw President Cox get revelation. . . . I saw the power of God moving in his priesthood and among the sisters with great power. That [resulted in an] optimism, that even a pretty thin operation with God's help can make it through most difficulties. It's a very interesting kind of optimism. It's not that everything will go well. On the contrary, it's that there will be a lot of troubles, [but] by and large troubles you can face with some equanimity. He is building His kingdom. [Boston] was a stake when I left. If you had asked me the day I walked into the Atlantic District, 'Could it possibly have made it in four years?' I would have said no.

"I guess what I'm saying," President Eyring finished, "is that if faithful people will try hard and get help, the Lord can raise them up tall. I saw that in New England. To me it's an optimism that is probably going to bless me for the rest of my life. . . . It looks as if the Lord can take very humble, ordinary people and very rapidly bring them along."[42]

Germaine Simon was a Haitian convert. Only a few years after her baptism, Sister Simon was called to serve as a Relief Society president. After her sustaining in sacrament meeting, Germaine promptly went to shake the hand of her first counselor. "I am so glad to be serving with you," Sister Simon greeted the woman. "I think you will be a great president."

The counselor quickly corrected Sister Simon: "You were called to be the president, not me."

No, Sister Simon protested, that wasn't possible. Certain there had been a mistake, the bishop ultimately had to advise Sister Simon that she had indeed been called to lead.[43]

Sister Simon found the bishop's assurances inadequate and returned home to pray. Receiving confirmation that the call was inspired, she accepted. "I accepted that calling," Sister Simon explained, "not because I knew what I was going to do, but because I wanted to learn and I wanted to grow. . . . I come to love the Church. It is the people that make the Church that I love. . . . They accepted me. I think that showed me that the Lord loves me—by choosing me to work in His good Church."[44]

"[She] taught me a lot about leadership and what is required to serve in the Church," said Justin Lindsey, who served as bishop of the ward.

"Sister Simon took this calling like few I have seen. All the activities weren't well-organized, and that bothered some people, but in my opinion she was all anyone could ever want in a Relief Society president."

A few months after Sister Simon was sustained, Bishop Lindsey's wife gave birth to their daughter Sariah, a little girl who died shortly after birth. "While [we were] in the hospital," he shared, "Germaine Simon would ride the bus for one hour to come and visit. . . . We were in the hospital for about one month. In these situations you don't know what you can really say or do to comfort the person. I remember when she would come she would just hold LeAnn's hand. . . .

"When people ask me about all [the] administrative qualities [of] a Relief Society president, I don't think of those. I know they are important, but Sister Simon is what I would want in any Relief Society president. . . . There was a feeling when she was there of love and commitment."[45]

# 8

# WE GATHER TOGETHER

IN 1937, Oscar E. Johnson accepted a job transfer to Providence, Rhode Island. A Providence Branch had dissolved ten years previous due to poor attendance, so the Johnson family spent the summer traveling 120 miles each Sunday to meet with other Saints in New Bedford, Massachusetts. That autumn, two missionaries asked Brother Johnson if he would be willing to serve as president of a new branch in Providence. He accepted immediately.

The Providence Branch was organized to serve approximately fifty members. Meetings were held in members' homes and attracted an average of twenty-five people. The group gradually outgrew parlors and began renting temporary space. Over the next few years, members gathered in facilities of varying quality until branch and mission leaders decided it was time to secure a more permanent meeting place. Efforts to find a facility began in 1941, but were unsuccessful until a writer for *The Providence Journal* grew curious about the group's repeated advertisements. The journalist talked to the missionaries and wrote an article about the branch. A reader contacted local leaders and suggested that the Church purchase a private library attached to his home at 295 Benefit Street.

The Rhode Island Saints had hoped to find a meeting place but had assumed they would lease space since there was only one Church-owned chapel in all of New England. Worried that the proffered realty would slip away, branch and mission leaders sent a letter to the First Presidency and requested permission to purchase the property.

Permission was granted, and the library was purchased. The members of the Providence Branch began work to renovate and repaint the building for its new purpose.[1] In late spring of 1944, the Saints learned that Elder John A. Widtsoe of the Council of the Twelve would be conducting a series of branch conferences throughout the mission that summer. If the remaining work on the chapel was finished, it could be dedicated during his visit. Branch members enlarged their efforts, devoting evenings and Saturdays to the renovation, aided by LDS servicemen who joined in to install wallboard, plumbing, and other fixtures on their days off.[2] All told, the small band of members put in more than eighteen thousand hours of work to beautify and restructure the building.[3]

On a Wednesday evening, June 14, 1944, seventy people met together in Providence to attend a Massachusetts-Rhode Island District Conference and participate in the dedication of the newly-converted chapel. In addition to dedicating the Providence chapel that summer, Elder Widtsoe dedicated meetinghouses in Lynn, Massachusetts; Bridgeport, Connecticut; and Springfield, Massachusetts. In each case, the dedicatory prayer included the following petition:

"Inasmuch as thou has said to thy children that they should meet together . . . Father, we pray that this little branch of thy church may increase in numbers. May those who live here be directed to the members of the branch and to this place. . . . When strangers enter the door, may we meet them with open, loving hearts, and an understanding of the urgent need of all men for eternal truth."[4]

Over a dinner at Bishop Bert Van Uitert's home in the mid-1960s, the bishop raised an issue that concerned him. It seemed a shame, in a ward like Cambridge, that there was no efficient way for the new students who arrived each year to benefit from the collective wisdom more experienced ward members had amassed about the area. Ward member Laurel Ulrich suggested compiling a pamphlet with practical information about Boston and its environs. If done right, she continued, this collection might also be useful to others in the community and present an opportunity to raise funds.[5] Bishop Van Uitert was enthusiastic and presented the idea in ward council, only to be rebuffed by the business school students in the elders quorum. Such an endeavor would require publishing and marketing experience, as well as money, they pointed out. It would be labor-intensive, it wasn't practical as a ward project, and it was unlikely to be successful even if they were able to pull it off.

Unmoved by the men's protests, Bonnie Horne, the Relief Society president, turned to the bishop and said, "That's okay. The Relief Society will do it."[6] Laurel Ulrich was asked to organize the project. Sisters in the ward were given research and writing assignments covering museums and historical attractions, local traditions, activities for children, shopping, restaurants, and geography. Using time when her children slept, Laurel wrote large portions of the text and edited information other women supplied. Another sister oversaw artwork, and Luanne Van Uitert spent weeks typing the manuscript. Paste-up was done by hand, and Bishop Van Uitert personally provided the money for the printing.[7] The resulting publication, *A Beginner's Boston*, was no modest pamphlet but a full-fledged guidebook. "I think everybody at that time in the Relief Society was involved with something," Bonnie Horne observed. "We were not very sophisticated, but it turned out to be a charming book."[8]

The first printing of a thousand copies took place in the fall of 1966. The women hoped to sell enough copies to friends and neighbors to recoup the costs of publication and, with a bit of luck, cover the Relief Society's annual $300 budget assessment.[9] With no funds for marketing, Laurel and Bonnie visited the women's page editor at the *Boston Globe* to see if she had any interest in their undertaking. A glowing article appearing in the next day's *Globe* declared the sisters' project the first real guidebook to Boston. Unaware, the Cambridge Relief Society had assembled for its weekday meeting when the meetinghouse phone began ringing. Every caller wanted to know where they could get a copy of the book! The first printing was done with "fear and trepidation" according to Bishop Van Uitert, but sold out before it was delivered.[10] *A Beginner's Boston* went through three editions, the last printed in 1973, before it was finally retired as a ward project.[11]

The funds generated by *A Beginner's Boston* satisfied the Relief Society assessment and produced enough cash to support a variety of ward projects over the course of its publication, but its benefits were more than monetary.[12] "It was collaborative and fun and really exciting," Laurel stated, crediting Bonnie Horne's "amazing confidence" as key to the project's success.[13] A subsequent bishop observed that several women involved in the project had reluctantly accompanied their husbands to the area for school. *A Beginner's Boston* was an effort that all members of the Relief Society could put their energies into, and many came to embrace their new home as they discovered the city for themselves. "I think [*A Beginner's Boston*] uplifted and really changed the lives of a lot of people here," he concluded. "In fact . . . instead of wanting to go back West, some of them said, 'Why do we have to leave?'"[14]

Projections for the Belmont Massachusetts meetinghouse entailed a million-dollar construction budget. The 30 percent allocation for which congregants were responsible might as well have been the entire million dollars, given the number of members in school or on fixed incomes.[15]

Seeking ways to raise funds, the ward organized groups to perform inventories for downtown department stores. The inventories were time-consuming and inconvenient, running late at night into the wee hours of the morning. "I remember we would go," said Paul McKinnon, "we'd work down there for the whole evening . . . [and] you'd make [about] $7 for the ward."

The meager earnings raised questions for some. At one point during an evening inventory, a ward member with a lucrative career pulled his bishop aside. "Doesn't this strike you as crazy?" he asked. "Let me go consult three or four days and let me pay you. I'd be happy to devote a certain number of days every year that I'll consult. . . . But having me work for $2.25 an hour is sub-optimization at its worst." Without batting an eye, the bishop responded, "You're missing the point. It's not just about making money. It's about contributing to a cause."[16]

It was always interesting to look around at who was there, a brother observed. People who earned hundreds of dollars an hour in their professions were on their knees sorting boxes and working side by side with individuals who had no other way to participate in the building fund. "You are not looking for efficiency all the time," he concluded. "You are actually looking for the opportunity for people to serve. . . . It was a camaraderie for everyone."[17]

The bishop's insistence on providing ways for everyone to contribute influenced the fund-raising projects that were organized for the new chapel and allowed members with very different means and opportunities to contribute, regardless of personal circumstances. "It brought people together," said one brother. "We always had a good time doing it."[18]

"I don't know how much money we ever made," Brother McKinnon admitted. "It couldn't have been very much. . . . [Yet] the feeling we always had was that everybody was equal."[19]

Elder Widtsoe's dedicatory admonition to greet all "with open, loving hearts" is as important today as it was to the fledgling New England branches desperate for growth. In his heavenly petition, Elder Widtsoe said we are to bring others into fellowship so they might "receive the joy and comforting assurance that come to those who receive the Gospel of Jesus Christ."[20]

How do we attain the sense of collaboration, camaraderie, and equality described in the accounts above? Historically, a significant contributor to the Saints' sense of belonging was the sheer quantity of time spent together. Sundays required multiple trips to church prior to the introduction of the consolidated schedule. Members often prepared their midday meal at the meetinghouse or shared dinner in the homes of families living nearby to minimize travel between Sunday School and sacrament meeting. With Scouts one evening and Mutual on another, Primary on Wednesday, and Relief Society on Thursday, seminary each weekday and stake meetings on weekends, "[church] was an everyday activity," one member declared. "It was all day, every day!"[21] Strong bonds formed as a result of these shared experiences, a sister noted. "It seemed like we were traveling back and forth to church several times a week. It was the core of everything that went on."[22]

Fund-raisers for budget assessments and building projects took time too. "There was a lot of donated labor," one brother explained, "because there wasn't much in the way of funds."[23]

The Worcester Massachusetts branch received permission to construct a meetinghouse in 1961. The facility would be built in four phases so that financial goals could be staged and construction could begin as early as possible. The first phase required approximately $30,000. Although the branch encompassed over two hundred members, sacrament meeting attendance averaged sixty and money was scarce. The branch presidency sent a letter asking all families to consider giving one to three dollars a month per family member, depending on family size and income. There was no way the branch could raise the required sum relying solely on internal resources.

To make up the shortfall, Worcester members held bi-weekly bake sales, sponsored community suppers, and sold bread and other food items. Priesthood quorums painted homes and did carpentry and demolition work. Several men hired themselves out to build a chalet in Vermont, a project that took a year of weekends and evenings, but brought in $10,000. Once they had enough funds to start the first phase, branch members provided the labor under the direction of a church service missionary.[24] Some plumbing and brickwork was subcontracted, but the rest was done by volunteers. Ironically, by the time the first phase was complete, the Worcester Saints had already outgrown it. Energized by a common cause, sacrament meeting attendance was burgeoning and convert baptisms were increasing.

In Lynnfield, Massachusetts, the branch made paper certificates representing bricks in their future building, which they offered door-to-door for a dollar. The Relief Society made fudge, and the elders quorum fried cashews, which were sold from the back of a station wagon to factory workers at the local General Electric plant. The women sold cakes, pies, and handmade teddy bears. "We had all kinds of projects you could think of," said member Louise Harper.[25]

The completed meetinghouse was a blessing, but the harvest was the unity that developed within the branch as members labored together raising funds and rafters, said branch president Ed Berg. In the course of constructing the meetinghouse, the branch tripled its sacrament meeting attendance and enjoyed 100 percent home teaching for two years following the building's dedication.[26]

A teenager who participated in a stake construction project over the same period recalled weekends spent working alongside older members. All the youth came, he remembered. "As we labored together physically and watched the things happen and grow and become real, we really felt like we were part of something important."[27]

"In the Church, you go willingly when compelled," one member quipped.[28] Said another, "If there's a reason, people generally with a little push will do it. These fund-raisers and things seem to be that push that got us together."[29]

## Becoming Knit Together

When Alma the Elder organized Christ's church by the waters of Mormon, he instructed his followers to assemble together "as often as it was in their power," that they might have "their hearts knit together in unity and in love one towards another" (Mosiah 18:21, 25). We meet on Sundays to worship and partake of the Lord's sacrament, but we also lend our faith, testimony, and support to one another as we do so. This interaction helps us grow individually and collectively, becoming more fully rooted within the Lord's vineyard.

Church budget policies and meeting schedules have changed over time, bringing important blessings and opportunities. Meetinghouses are now built with tithing funds, allowing the Church to expand rapidly. Saints in diverse nations and regions enjoy greater equality of opportunity with the centralization of budgetary planning and allocations. The consolidated schedule reduced travel and time away from home. Yet we may have lost something too. "I think people pull together more when they are working on [fund-raisers and] things like that," remarked Addis Murdock, a founding members of the Wayland Branch that grew into the Weston wards. "It bonded people much closer together. Now we have to work to get that bonding."[30]

Closeness comes with common experiences. A sister who attended church in Cambridge during the 1970s, when traffic restrictions made meeting at the chapel extremely difficult, observed that lasting friendships sprung from united causes—"even fighting for the parking spots on Brattle Street!" she laughed.[31] We have many common causes as we worry about our families, seek to hear the Spirit's promptings, and strive to live our covenants. We may not be asked to mortar bricks or install wallboard, but we are all called to labor in the same building project our predecessors did.

Clayton Christensen was a relatively new bishop of the Cambridge University Ward. On a routine business trip, Bishop Christensen attended sacrament meeting at an English-speaking ward in Tokyo. After introducing himself, he was asked if the University Ward was still a place where the mysteries of the gospel were plumbed each week. The inquiry caught the bishop off guard. Just the day before, he'd read the Savior's words in John 13:35: "By this shall all men know ye are my disciples, if ye have love one to another." The words of the scripture played over in his mind, as Bishop Christensen considered the University Ward's reputation on the other side of the globe.

Bishop Christensen was certain the Lord wanted something different for the University Ward. Christ's words set a clear criterion for his disciples. The singles ward should not be a place where unknowable principles were debated but rather an assemblage where true Christianity was practiced—a congregation of people who truly loved one another.

Infused with a sense of urgency, Bishop Christensen reserved an entire sacrament meeting to share his vision of what the University Ward could become. The ward then set out to transform itself, working together in ward councils and classes. "To do it," Clayton said, "we really needed to give opportunities for every member of the ward to express their love one to another. . . . We decided that we would have to expand the scope of the ward in order to give every member a chance for meaningful service."[32]

One area that was enlarged to expand opportunities for participation was the ward's Activity Committee. Under the leadership of Rick Rawlins, a number of small committees were formed, each focused on unique ways to create valuable group experiences ranging from traditional socials to community service. Assessing the ward's makeup, Rick saw that many of the students who came to the area to study art and music seemed to gravitate to the fringes of the congregation. An arts committee and a concerts committee were organized to highlight the contributions of these members and foster greater interaction among the ward as a whole.

The Concerts Committee sponsored monthly events featuring performances by ward members and their friends of other faiths, and the Arts Committee began planning a ward art show. As the date approached, stake leaders asked whether other wards could participate. Within days, the scope of the exposition had grown too large for the Longfellow Park Chapel. Spearheaded by artists in the University Ward, the event was moved to a larger meetinghouse and showcased paintings, photographs, and sculpture contributed by all congregations within the stake. The show commenced with an invocation and an anthem, composed specifically for the occasion. "It was an unbelievably inspiring event," Bishop Christensen said, recalling his emotions as he sat in the audience. "I was just overwhelmed with the talent of the members of the University Ward. It was such a blessing to associate with them."[33]

As opportunities for participation increased, a stronger sense of belonging took root in the ward, and missionary work increased as members invited friends to activities. Speaking of that period, a sister said of the then Activities Committee Chair, "I think Rick Rawlins will look back on that and think, 'Oh, that was sort of a joke that I was spending so much time on parties,' but a lot of people went to those and felt it was a place where they could be included. . . . I think we minimize recreation and socialization, when that's such a huge part of people feeling included."[34]

The familiarity and friendships created through Church socials and other activities should not be discounted. In the early years of the Atlantic District, the Cambridge Branch was the hub of activity, hosting dances, dinners, and an annual production that required everyone's efforts, whether writing a script, constructing sets, playing in the orchestra, or acting. The annual luau was famous even outside the church for its sit-down dinner, costumes, and decorations (complete with an active volcano erupting on the stage one year).[35] Every area has its own traditions. In New England, the annual clambake still observed by many wards dates back to the 1930s. William Knecht was a boy when the Church was still in its infancy in Massachusetts. "Through those picnics," he said, "we developed a spirit of family and fellowship that simply couldn't be replicated in any other way."[36]

A sister baptized in her twenties said the thing that kept her strong early on "was the overwhelming sense of being accepted, of friends, of fun activities. . . . For me, it was really that feeling of being drawn into an extended family . . . Anybody was welcome with open arms."[37] That acceptance is vital, another convert agreed, noting that Church membership can create distance with family and friends. "If you are going to stay active in the Church, you need to belong there," she stated emphatically. "Everybody needs to feel like they belong somewhere."[38]

A founding member of the Spanish Sunday School in Cambridge expressed a similar sentiment. "When we came to this country," he stated, "we had no relatives to speak of, no real friends." As his family began attending Church, "we saw the need that we had for that companionship, for that friendship, and for that brother and sisterhood. I think there's a lot of us like that here. We miss our relatives, we miss our country, and we only find solace with each other."[39]

Needs, interests, and priorities change over time. Some of the traditional events held by early Boston-area Saints have stood the test of time, fostering a spirit of inclusion and collective identity, while others have been replaced or adjusted to incorporate the needs and traditions of more diverse congregations. In downtown Boston, soccer games replaced some of the traditional ward basketball games, and dances took on a decidedly international flavor. "We'd play Haitian, we'd play American, we'd play African," said one sister. "Everybody danced. It was so much fun!" Every holiday was a celebration, often marked with a potluck dinner featuring an eclectic array of dishes that provided members another way to share and explore together.[40]

Every ward has the opportunity and obligation to assess the needs of its members and create opportunities for people to share their talents. When we work, play, and interact outside our Sunday meetings, we become more than a congregation—we forge ties that unite us, in LDS parlance, as "ward families." We see people in a different light and recognize strengths that we might otherwise overlook. As one member said of such activities, "It's important to let people shine."[41]

## Success by Any Other Measure

Events do not need to be elaborate or perfectly executed to achieve their purpose. "An extremely important part of the history of the Cambridge Ward in the 1960s was food," noted one member. "Food was really taken seriously."[42] Indeed, many waxed nostalgic remembering dinners featuring lobster soufflés for two hundred, fish stuffed with cucumber-bread pudding for five hundred, and flaming puddings at ward Christmas parties.[43]

Against this backdrop was the infamous beanie-weenie casserole dinner put on by the elders quorum. Far from elegant, it generated as many collective memories as any gourmet feast. Describing the event in detail, one attendee said, "Somebody brought the beans and somebody brought the weenies. They stirred them all together and served that up. . . . It was awful!"[44] Remarked another, "That was truly the worst dinner I've ever had in my life."[45] Smiling, a sister summed up the evening, stating simply, "It was memorable."[46]

The stake farm of the 1970s was an inexpertly executed project. "One is always somewhat reluctant to refer to certain projects that the Church takes on as ill-conceived," admitted participant Carter Cornwall, but "if there were ever a project on the margin of being ill-conceived, it would be the stake squash farm." Seeking to encourage self-sufficiency, the stake identified public land for use and then worked to identify the easiest crop to grow, since no one knew anything about farming. Research suggested the answer was butternut squash. "We got it all plowed, we planted the squash, and then it was sort of a chore to get folks over there to weed the squash, and then weed the squash some more," Carter said, chuckling. "This seemed to me to be the absolute dumbest project that one could have—the whole concept of having all of these people out on Saturday morning weeding squash. But that was what we were asked to do, so we did it. . . . The return was clearly not going to be requisite with the effort put forth."[47]

Once the squash was grown, organizers planned to sell the crop to local grocers to raise funds for stake coffers. "We grew this squash, not very well. Then we needed to harvest it, so we were down there harvesting it, and we didn't harvest it very well," former stake president Kent Bowen groaned. "It was a real comedy, here all of us Easterners that couldn't do anything with this squash, but lots of labor."[48] As luck would have it, it was a bumper year for squash. With no demand for butternut squash, the hard-earned harvest sat in a shed until it froze and became unusable. "We didn't get much squash selling done," Brother Cornwall stated matter-of-factly.[49]

Although dramatically unprofitable, the squash farm yielded dividends of another type.

Philip Barlow recalled his time working on the farm fondly, stating, "I would feel that sort of loving democracy of the welfare project, being surrounded by custodians, homemakers and budding students working side by side with well-known scientists, scholars, and business leaders."[50] Both Carter Cornwall and Kent Bowen agreed that the camaraderie gained in working together was worthy of the effort. "I don't mean this was ill-conceived in the sense that it was not worthwhile," Carter explained. "It was ill-conceived only in the sense that it didn't produce money. . . . There are some things, odd though they may be, that make for the kind of spiritual growth and togetherness that just otherwise would not be there, but everybody knows that this is the stupidest thing you could possibly do. . . . Something so amazingly bizarre, so dumb, that it was actually good."[51]

The early Saints' experience with Zion's Camp is a reminder that success cannot be measured by the realization of specific expectations. Members of the camp marched over 900 miles in the heat of the summer, suffering great deprivations, only to arrive in Missouri and be told in revelation that Zion could not be redeemed at that time (see Doctrine and Covenants 105). Although the group did not achieve its political objectives, when the Prophet organized the Quorums of the Twelve and the Seventy the following year, nine of the apostles and all of the Seventies came from the ranks of Zion's Camp.[52] Whether our objectives are serious or light-hearted, we need opportunities where we can "stand fast in one spirit, with one mind striving together for the faith of the gospel" (Philippians 1:27). We build unity and fellowship as we work together, not as we sit together.

In 1986, the Boston Branch met in borrowed space at a mental health facility, with an average of twenty to twenty-five people in attendance each Sunday. Eight years later, the branch had grown into a vibrant ward with its own meetinghouse. Reviewing pivotal events during that critical transition period, John Hoffmire focused on a questionable investment of time and money that helped set the stage for the branch's future.

Few members in the city had the economic resources to be homeowners. One family had stretched to purchase a building in a rough neighborhood, intending to use it as a rental property. A week after the purchase, the basement filled with sewage and the tenants left. The property had never been desirable, and the extended abuse from tenants had left the building in bad shape.

A small team of members decided to help the family and renovate the property. Together the group raised funds and contributed labor, devoting evenings and weekends to repairing the property. As the elders quorum president, John Hoffmire was convinced the branch leadership needed to get to know one another on a deeper level. "There were a number of us who felt that the best way to get to know one another was to work together elbow to elbow. So we collectively chose this project and decided we were going to do it even though [others] were . . . opposed. . . . It was a very big project, and they felt it would be worse to fail at this than to just let it go. There were enough of us who felt, even if it did fail, that the process was an important one. So we fixed that house."

The renovated building proved an asset to the family and the branch for a time and was often used to house members who had no other place to go. This positive notwithstanding, John said bluntly, "It's important to acknowledge over the long-term that project didn't work out from an economic perspective." A slump in the real estate market decimated the building's value and it was ultimately repossessed when the owners were unable to refinance or sell the property.

"One could say that it was a mistake," John admitted. There was a level of dedication among the participants that might not have developed absent that experience, but "the people who participated in that project, they were probably going to play significant roles in the Church anyway," he acknowledged. Nevertheless, "those kind of projects cement people," said Brother Hoffmire. "It was wonderful. Our best friends in the world grew out of that project." The camaraderie within the branch encouraged young families to move into its boundaries, providing leadership for a youth program that in subsequent years led to a significant surge in missionary work. "I think it was important to lay down that foundation," John concluded. "It was through that process that we saw enough strength to start building other programs."[53]

## The Ninety-Nine and the One

Although we talk of "strength in numbers," scarcity can be a powerful, unifying force. Paul Rondina joined the Church in Providence, Rhode Island, in 1967. "Mormons were few and far between," he said of that time. "Boy, we stuck together like glue! They'd have a meeting—a missionary correlation meeting—everybody in the ward would show up. There'd be refreshments. It was like the Saints just wanted to be with each other. . . . We were all struggling. I can remember the branch president getting up in priesthood and he said, 'I need ten brethren right now who can donate $100. Right now, who can write me a check for $100? The finances are such that we need this money right away.' I always had the feeling that I was joining some poor church that didn't have two nickels to rub together," he said, chuckling.[54]

A sister in Marlboro, Massachusetts, remembered the welcome her family received when they moved to the area. "I think when there are fewer of you in a town, you get very excited when someone else is moving in," she explained. "You don't just disappear into the woodwork, but you are brought in and usually put right to work. You are made to feel you are needed."[55]

In 1988, Kim Clark was serving as bishop of the Cambridge First Ward. Concerned about the number of inactive families in adjacent towns east of Cambridge, he felt impressed that the Church needed to come to them. Bishop Clark released one of his counselors, Brent Barnett, and reassigned him to work specifically with these members.

Looking for ways to meet the Saints' needs, Brent held a brainstorming meeting, attended by fifteen people, at the home of one of the sisters living in this area. A series of monthly firesides attracted the same general crowd. Those attending were enthusiastic, but their attendance in the Cambridge ward building did not increase. Bishop Clark challenged Brent to have the group hold its own sacrament services by the start of the new year. With no budget, the group began meeting at a Knights of Columbus hall on a week-to-week basis, subject to cancellation by the owner on important days such as Super Bowl Sunday. A small portion of another facility used for training handicapped adults was secured for

Sunday service–use only. This location proved more predictable for the not-quite-a-branch, but they still lacked a dedicated space. Each Sunday the little group dragged chairs up to their allotted space on the second floor of the building, together with songbooks, a keyboard, a podium, and all materials needed for sacrament services. After meetings, they loaded everything back into cars so that they could return and do the same thing the following week, a cycle familiar to many acquainted with the challenges of starting a new branch.[56]

While people got used to this routine, it was never easy. When the group officially became a branch, they learned they could obtain funding for their own space if sacrament meeting attendance grew to sixty. The number captured everyone's attention, but attendance had never been close to sixty. Determined to change things, branch members set up twenty chairs for sacrament meeting the next Sunday. After the meeting, branch leaders and missionaries huddled together to discuss the chairs that sat empty and ask, "Who should have been here who wasn't?" Each took an assignment to call missing members and investigators. Every call included similar questions, "Are you okay? Is there anything we can do for you? Do you think you could come next week? Because we really need you."

As soon as there were twenty people in sacrament meeting, the branch set up forty chairs, going through the same exercise each Sunday. Who could have been here who was missing? How can we get them here? Members with vehicles organized to drive people who didn't have access to transportation. Others invited friends to increase the numbers, even if they couldn't imagine their friends being interested in the Church. When attendance reached forty, chairs for sixty were set out. "What I loved about that branch," said Cari Schreck, who served in the Primary presidency, "was that there was a face to every one of the names on the branch's list. The attitude was, 'We need these people.'" Every person was as critical to reaching the branch's goal as the next.[57]

By the beginning of 1993, the branch had secured a permanent lease and received a set of Church standard-issue equipment, including chairs, a pulpit, sacrament trays, Primary furniture, and library materials. "We were just in heaven!" Brother Barnett recalled.[58] Yet there was more to aspire to. If attendance reached one hundred, the branch could apply for its own building. Again, those present each Sunday set chairs out for the number of people they needed, working together throughout the week to fill them.

With such conscious attention to every member, "there was nobody that you didn't know," recalled branch members Dave and Carol Coppins. Branch activities were fully attended, often attracting people who were not present on Sundays. Every temple recommend holder participated in branch temple trips, even though such events required travel to Washington, D.C. "I remember sitting in that sealing room," said Sister Coppins. "It was so exciting just to . . . have that whole branch family there."[59]

In accordance with standard practice in the Church, ward clerks count the number of people sitting in pews during each sacrament meeting and enter that number in the ward or branch statistical report, after which members divide for Sunday School and auxiliary meetings and return home. The members of the Malden Branch took the opposite approach. While they never took the Saints in attendance for granted, they followed the Savior's example by focusing on the names of the individual sheep missing from the fold. After identifying the lost, they went out and found them. The branch's growth reached 100 and then 120. In less than ten years, the congregation went from having fewer than twenty people regularly attend Sabbath meetings to the dedication of a brand-new meetinghouse in Revere, Massachusetts. Michael Schreck, who had served as branch mission leader and in the branch presidency during this period of growth, compared the much-anticipated chapel dedication to that of a temple. "There were more tears than we have ever seen," Cari Schreck added, noting that the veil felt very thin that day.[60]

Ironically, once members were sitting in traditional pews in the new Revere chapel, there was no longer a need to set up chairs on Sundays. The clerks counted the number of sheep present in the fold, per statistical requirements, and there were no more meetings after church to identify those who should have been there but weren't. The motivation that had pushed branch members to actively look outside themselves for those who might have unmet needs was gone. Without that push, membership in the congregation stalled at 120–130 for the next several years.[61]

The Lord has promised that "where two or three are gathered together in my name, there am I" (Matthew 18:20), but usually there is room and need for many more. The gospel is a team event, one brother aptly observed. "It is not an individual sport, so to speak, being a Christian. You cannot succeed by yourself. The more people that you take along with you . . . the better your team is. . . . [Your happiness] depends on serving other people and seeing them succeed."[62]

The occasions and requirements that cause us to gather together may change over time, but the innate need each person has to be known, valued, and included does not. Everyone needs encouragement, and everyone wants to belong.

A husband and wife spoke about their experience attending a new ward after being active in several other area congregations. The members were kind, they said, but they felt out of place because they lacked common experiences that had tied them to other congregations in the past. "I guess we got here too late in life," the husband said, sighing. "We never really got involved with the ward. We'd go on Sunday, but . . . it was never like [our former ward]."

"You were in the bishopric," the interviewer noted with surprise, "and yet you feel like you weren't really involved in the ward?"

"The ward has always had more talent than it ever needed," the brother explained. "Every calling I ever had in the ward, I never had to do. Everyone always did it. It was like they gave you a calling because they had to fill the position, but you really didn't have to do anything."

"I don't think you feel real needed there," his wife summed up.[63]

"Over the course of time I've been surprised, astounded sometimes, at who falls away from the Church," said Lee LaPierre, former counselor in the Boston Stake, noting that some dwindle away, while others leave abruptly, despite the fact that many have experienced the confirming witness of the Spirit accompanying a testimony. On the other hand, President LaPierre continued, "There are people who come into the Church and you wouldn't think they'd last a week. Somehow they keep hanging on. . . . There's a growth [that] takes place, there's a warmth and acceptance that they feel and they really bind to the Church. . . . Woven into the Church is probably the best description of it. They feel a part of it."[64]

Dorothy and Talmage Nielsen arrived in Cambridge just after World War II, in 1946. They were excited to embark on a new phase of life and looked forward to participating in the small but intimate Cambridge Branch. Visiting the mission home where the branch met, they were greeted by local leaders, as they were the following Sunday and the Sunday after that. Every week, however, the greeting was discouragingly similar: "And now you are Brother and Sister . . . ?"

Weeks turned into months. Still no one seemed to remember their names, and no one had befriended them. This impersonal experience, the stress of Talmage's responsibilities, and the amount of time it took to travel to church without a car began to wear on the Nielsens. "We began to think, 'Well, nobody really knows us over there,'" said Dorothy, "'It's a long way. Maybe we won't go this time.'" With growing ambivalence, the Nielsens continued to attend Sabbath services until a Sunday when a sister in the branch unexpectedly invited Dorothy and Talmage to come to her home for sandwiches after the meeting. "I think that was the beginning of our activity in the church," Dorothy stated. One person willing to reach out opened a door that helped Dorothy and Talmage meet other people and come to feel they belonged.

"It might just very well be without the influence of that one person, I may not be where I am in the Church today," Dorothy stated ardently. "I don't think we can stress enough the importance of reaching out. . . . I realize at this point in my life that part of my missionary work, part of the things that the Lord wants me to do, is to befriend everybody who walks into the church so that no one feels like I did those first three months—no matter who they are."[65]

Judy Dushku always wanted to go to the temple but felt that door had closed when she married a non-member. After a divorce some years later, Judy found that a sense of mistrust and unease had eroded her prior yearning. For the next twelve years, as regular as clockwork, bishops and other priesthood leaders approached Judy and asked her to think about preparing to attend the temple. Each time the question was raised, Judy said she was not interested. A primary deterrent came from the fact that the inquiry rubbed her wrong. "I had a lot of people say things to me along the lines of 'How can we fix you so you can go to the temple?' or 'How can we get you worthy to go?'" she explained. "I was shocked and surprised," she continued with emotion, when Gary Crittenden approached her shortly after being called as bishop of the Belmont Ward and asked, "Judy, what would the temple have to be like in order for you to want to be there?"

Judy had never been asked that question. She considered the inquiry both beautiful and serious, and it made her think about the temple in a new way. Presented with such a query, Judy wanted to answer properly. She told her bishop she needed to go home and think about her response. He invited her to come back and talk after she had done so.

Judy knew she wanted to enter a deeper covenant relationship that would reinforce promises previously made to the Savior. For so many years, however, she'd seen the temple as unappealing—a place where she would be required to jump through hoops to please other people. Confronting her concerns, Judy returned to talk with her bishop. Recalling that meeting, Judy stated, "I said I wanted it to be a place that felt welcoming and inclusive and not a place where I felt that there were walls to keep people out. I wanted a place that felt like it had its arms open to all who love the Savior." Looking closely at Judy, Bishop Crittenden said, "Guess what. That's what it is. And it's there waiting to bring you all those things that you're looking for—you just didn't know that it was there."

Tears running down her cheeks as she remembered that turning point in her life, Judy described the associated events as a beautiful experience, a gentle and sweet preparatory time for which she would always love her bishop. "Once it sounded inviting, I was excited to go. It was a wonderful experience."[66]

"I stand at the door and knock," said the Savior (Revelation 3:20), but sometimes when we open the door, we don't recognize Him. Instead we see a stranger, an elderly woman, a middle-aged couple, an unsure convert, an unkempt teenager, a struggling parent, or someone else to whom we don't relate, or we feel too busy and careworn to try. There are no strangers in the Lord's Kingdom—He embraces all, just as we can if we have eyes to see, recognize, and act on the divine heritage that unites us all in the family of Christ.

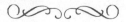

# 9

# THAT OUR CHILDREN
# MAY KNOW

ON SEPTEMBER 23, 1956, the Longfellow Park chapel in Cambridge, Massachusetts, was filled to capacity, as were the adjoining cultural hall, the balcony, and the foyer. The redbrick meetinghouse, with its tall, ascending spire, was complete and ready to house the Cambridge Branch, which encompassed Saints from Rhode Island, Massachusetts, and New Hampshire. President David O. McKay had come to dedicate the building, and over 1,200 members had gathered from all regions of the Atlantic District to see the prophet and to participate in the momentous event.

When President McKay stood to address the congregation and offer the dedicatory prayer, he noticed something odd about the assembled Saints. Scanning the faces filling the pews and overflow seats, he asked, "Where are the children?"

The children, President McKay was informed, were in the basement, kept busy in the Scout room so that they would not disturb the solemn proceedings in the chapel. The Prophet shook his head vigorously and said, "We don't want that." At President McKay's kind but firm direction, the children were invited upstairs and seated up front beneath the pulpit. Smiling down at the girls and boys before him, President McKay explained that he would be speaking directly to the children, and the adults could listen if they liked. Following the offering of the dedicatory prayer and the singing of the Hosanna Anthem, David O. McKay stood at the chapel door to look into the eyes and shake the hand of every person who passed, particularly the children.[1]

President McKay's actions hearken back to a lesson taught almost two millennia before, when well-intentioned disciples asked parents to keep their children back, so as not to divert the Master's attention from the weightier matters of His ministry. When Jesus discovered this, "he was much displeased." The Gospels record that He then "said unto them, Suffer the little children to come unto me, and forbid them not: for of such is the kingdom of God" (Mark 10:13–14).

There is nothing peripheral about teaching our children and preparing our youth so that they may become acquainted with God. Explaining the importance of the sacred records he'd been commanded to keep, Nephi wrote: "And we talk of Christ, we rejoice in Christ, we preach of Christ, we prophesy of Christ, and we write according to our prophecies, *that our children may know* to what source they may look for a remission of their sins" (2 Nephi 25:26, emphasis added). Truly, there is no other task in which we can invest our time and energy that is more likely to hasten the establishment of the Kingdom of God in our midst.

## Worth Any Inconvenience

Bert Van Uitert served as the second bishop of the Cambridge Ward. The vice president of a major insurance company and a respected businessman, Bert was a pragmatic, straight-arrow man who was effective and efficient in addressing the demands of the diverse and burgeoning ward for which he was responsible. Despite his tight schedule, each Sunday Bishop Van Uitert spent much of his time between meetings kneeling in the foyer, folding small squares of paper into elaborate origami birds and animals. Children crowded around him, anxious to see what would emerge from their bishop's hands, hoping to receive one of the intricate creatures. When asked why he spent so much time crouched on the floor folding paper, Bert expressed sympathy for the little children who were forever wandering amidst a forest of legs, and said simply, "You've got to get down to their level."

The boys and girls who received Bishop Van Uitert's paper birds have long since grown, but former ward member Gordon Williams observed that they all remember Bishop Van Uitert as a great bishop, even though most of them can't say exactly why. "I strongly suspect [it] was because he understood what their needs were," Gordon posited. "He was moved by the Spirit," Gordon explained, "that this is what was needed for those young people, and that's what he did."[2]

Formal Church programs for young members of the Church within the New England area were not established overnight. Even after Primary and youth programs were present in most wards and branches, small numbers, distances, school boundaries, and other circumstances forced youth to stand alone more often than not. To address this reality in the early 1970s, Bill Fresh—former stake president of the Boston Massachusetts and Manchester New Hampshire stakes—found it incumbent to provide youth conferences, dances, camps, road shows, and other activities that would bring young members together. "We put tremendous amount of emphasis on the youth, to build the testimonies of young people," he explained. By holding such events, a youth could go home knowing that while he might be alone at school, there were hundreds of teenagers who "all carry the banner of Christ and believe."

President Fresh valued the short-term benefits this camaraderie produced but was inspired by a loftier goal: "That they will prepare to go to the temple and have temple marriages," he stated matter-of-factly. Given that the nearest temple was in Salt Lake City, this was ambitious. Through the inspiration of his calling, President Fresh understood that only by being provided vivid examples of the gospel in action could the youth "make those choices and [develop] the self-mastery and discipline [to] be worthy to enter God's house and partake of those sacred ordinances contained therein."[3]

Elder L. Tom Perry's daughter Linda was the only LDS student in her school in Weston, Massachusetts. The companionship of other Church members was a solace and a strength to her, and whenever something was going on at the meetinghouse, that was where she wanted to be. "If it was Primary day in the afternoon—and even though I wasn't in Primary anymore—I still came over, and my friends still came over. It seemed that every time the church was open, we tried to get a ride to be here. . . . To leave the contrast of [school] and . . . be truly accepted for what you are. . . . They were truly the best friends."[4]

In order to get the youth to places where they could be nourished with gospel instruction and friendships, many wards organized programs to collect the children and youth within their boundaries and bring them to Church activities. For one sister, the recollection of the hours she spent with her mother picking up children for Primary in their VW van every Wednesday are as vivid as any memories of Primary itself.[5]

Kathy Bowen served in the Cambridge Primary program during the era of weekday Primary. Each week, she and other Primary leaders left their homes shortly after lunch to begin collecting children from outlying communities whose parents were inactive or did not have access to transportation. Primary would end just in time to fight rush hour traffic during the return loop. Between the time spent sitting in traffic and the inevitable parking tickets collected in the line of duty, said Kathy, "it would make you feel like, 'Is this really worth it?' But yet the next week we would do the very same thing."[6]

Taking his turn on the rotating team of adults who were asked to drive teens to early-morning seminary, Clayton Christensen spent a year picking up two sisters in East Cambridge. The girls' parents were not members, the family had no telephone, and every morning there was a strong likelihood that while Clayton sat outside the apartment complex in his car, the girls would remain sleeping upstairs—a scenario that played out regularly. Following graduation, the girls attended Ricks College, but neither graduated. Over time Clayton lost track of them.

Several years later, during a visit to the Cambridge Spanish Ward, Elder Christensen was surprised to see one of the sisters walk in with a baby and a man who was a returned missionary and faithful member of the Church. Both she and her sister, he learned, had married in the temple. "I just sat there and cried," Clayton recalled, "thinking of all the time we had spent driving this young woman and her sister back and forth, seeing that indeed she had kept the faith."[7]

Kathy Bowen and Clayton Christensen are two of the innumerable individuals who spent hours chauffeuring young members to and from Church meetings, hoping their efforts would make a difference. "The kids were the only thing you had," explained Gordon Williams. "The kids are the ones that you grab hold of, [hoping] that it will be the next generation . . . that will be able to overcome the problems of the environment in which they were raised." The idea that driving youth to and from Primary and Mutual once a week would help them attend the temple seemed remote compared to the immediate inconvenience and costs associated with such efforts. Yet, while not all remained faithful, Bishop Williams estimated that half of the teenagers in the Cambridge Ward from the late 1960s to early 1980s went on missions and married in the temple. It would not have happened, he stated, without individuals willing to drive a hundred miles every week to pick up everyone willing to come.[8]

Confirming that several of the children she and others picked up for Primary went on to college and married in the temple, Kathy Bowen concluded, "You feel that you've participated in something. . . . I wouldn't change it for anything."[9]

## Out of That, Everything Else Will Come

Following a trouncing at a stake scripture chase, the humiliated seminary students of Worcester, Massachusetts, returned home determined not to suffer such a defeat again. Intensely motivated to learn the designated scriptures better than anyone else, they divided assignments among themselves, practiced on their own time, and devised clever scripture marking systems, going so far as to sleep on their scriptures at night so the books would fall open to the correct pages on their own. The Worcester Ward soon dominated seminary scripture chase challenges and a strong camaraderie grew among the Worcester youth. When other wards struggled to hold early-morning seminary classes, the Worcester youth would talk with their peers, sharing their infectious enthusiasm for the program.[10]

"It was the youth themselves that took the initiative," one father pointed out. They generated an excitement and enthusiasm that mushroomed into the whole ward.[11]

"If you look around the stake where there's a vibrant ward, it's because they have a vibrant youth program," observed stake president Kent Bowen. "If you were a bishop and you took charge of a ward that didn't have much energy in it, focus on the youth and get them to bring their friends. And out of that, everything else will come."[12]

In the early 1990s, over twenty missionaries were assigned to the Boston Branch, equipped to teach in English, Spanish, and Haitian. Membership was growing, but the lack of a youth program posed a challenge, as investigators and new converts lost interest when their children didn't want to attend. The branch president was concerned about the problem, but lacked manpower to staff additional auxiliaries. Consulting with the mission president, the branch president received permission to call some of the missionaries to help establish a youth program. A new convert was called as the Young Men president, another was called to lead a Young Women program, and a handful of elders were asked to organize a Scouting program, help staff the new auxiliaries, and get youth out to church.

Initially, only three boys were members of the branch, none of whom remained active. One of the women in the congregation, however, had a son with a strong group of friends, two of whom were brothers, Jason and Henry Astwood. When the missionaries invited the boys to participate in activities at the church, they accepted. The parents were not interested in talking with the missionaries but were grateful that their sons were spending time at church as opposed to other pursuits that could lead to trouble.

Because children and teens living within the city were reliant on public transportation and could not travel safely at night, the elders would arrive at the meetinghouse early in the afternoon on Mutual days to enable the youth to come to church straight from school. The missionaries provided help with homework and held an early Scout meeting, followed by a Mutual activity for the teenagers. Within a year, the Young Men program had grown from three to twenty. The boys began bringing their friends and before another year passed, there were almost sixty young men participating in the Boston youth and Scouting programs.[13]

"We had some great experiences there," said Justin Lindsey, who got involved with the youth program soon after he and his wife moved into the branch. "Every Mutual, we had whoever got off the bus. We had members and nonmembers alike. . . . The youth just naturally shared the gospel with everyone they interacted [with]."[14]

"We had fifty people in our Young Women's and Young Men's program before we could even bat an eyelash," said Dick Lavin, who served as bishop of the congregation after it became the Boston Ward. "Before we had people to do it. And it was just great how all that happened. That happened over a period of two to three years."

"All these youth without their parents," added his wife, Marsha. "We had all the youth that just came off the street."[15]

Before long, this large and enthusiastic group of youth formed a core that began to draw in others, creating a positive cycle that increased retention and opened additional opportunities for missionary work. "They told their friends, and their friends would show up," explained Elder Jimmy Fish, one of the missionaries assigned to work with the youth. "It started off with three boys, and it just grew. They told friends. People joined the Church. More people got baptized." With Mutual programs in place, parents joining the Boston congregation were more likely to stay active than adults who joined alone. "We were getting contacts to meet parents through youth," Elder Fish continued. "Parents of kids who weren't members of the Church just were flabbergasted by the idea that the kids wanted to go to church in the middle of the week. So they would send their kids with them, and we'd make all kinds of contacts that way. We had a chance to do a lot of teaching."[16]

Two of the earliest invitees, Jason and Henry Astwood, invited their eight-year-old sister Milly to accompany them. Baptized at age fourteen, Milly met Jonathan Ubri a month later and invited him to a youth dance. Jonathan enjoyed it so much that he came to church with her the next day, and after that, he just kept coming.

Eventually, Jonathan approached the bishop after sacrament meeting and said, "This all seems familiar. I wonder if I have been to this church before?"

A quick check of Church records showed that not only had Jonathan attended the LDS Church, but that he had been baptized at nine years of age with his brother and his Dominican mother, all of whom went inactive a month after their baptism.[17]

Re-committed at an age where he could better appreciate the fruits of the gospel, Jonathan began working with other active youth to reach out to inactive young men in the branch as part of an effort they dubbed "Operation Mormonation." Jonathan developed a calling tree used to contact anyone missing from class and assigned each young man responsibilities that would help him feel welcome and useful, such as assisting with lessons, setting up for Mutual activities, and teaching with the full-time missionaries. Quorum presidencies used the same system to remind people of activities, and each young man was expected to report on the status of his assignments.[18]

One of Jonathan's priesthood advisors attributed much of the growth within the youth of the congregation to Jonathan's efforts and the way he continually followed up with and encouraged his peers. "This is a young man who met with the bishop, missionaries, Young Men's leaders, and the other youth and said, 'How can we grow this branch?'" his leader stated, noting that at least three of the young men in the group were converts who Jonathan had invited to Church.

Within the stake, Jonathan reached out to other congregations and built friendships across the inner-city and suburban wards, where cultural differences sometimes loomed large. "There is not a youth in this stake who he hasn't reached out to," Jonathan's leader continued, noting the way Jonathan had reached out to support youth from two inner-city units on the far side of the stake in Worcester, Massachusetts. Waiting for Jonathan to join him in watching a football game one evening, the advisor instead received an email that read: "Sorry I didn't come over tonight, but Milly and I were on splits with the sister missionaries in our ward. It was really important that we were there to share a member's perspective to the lessons."[19]

An invitation to Henry and Jason Astwood was extended to their sister Milly, who extended it to Jonathan, who continues to extend it to others as he serves a mission for the Church. "It's a pattern, and it's pretty incredible if you think about it," said Milly.

"There's a chain of people we affect with our actions," Jonathan agreed. "Not just one person."[20]

## The Spirit They Bring Is Overwhelming

"Serving as a bishop," said Phil Potvin, "I think my choicest moments are interviewing the Primary children," referencing his practice of interviewing each child and youth on their birthday. In conjunction with these interviews, the Primary girls would receive a flower, a candy bar, and a blessing. Boys got a wooden truck, a candy bar, and a blessing. "The candy bar, the truck, and the flower gives them something to look forward to," explained Bishop Potvin, "but then it gives me the opportunity to talk with them about gospel principles."

This yearly event created great excitement in the Primary. For children who have reached another milestone, said Jackie Potvin, "it's like, 'It was my birthday. When is the bishop coming for me?' They watch for him to poke his head in to take them."

One Sunday, Bishop Potvin decided to test a girl who had just turned six, to see what their yearly appointment meant to her. Visiting with her briefly, he gave her the expected flower and candy bar and then stood, saying "Come on, I'll bring you back to class."

Refusing to budge, the little girl looked up imploringly and cried, "Bishop, my blessing!"

"I just wanted to see if she would know," Bishop Potvin explained. "And they know. They look forward to it, and the Spirit that they bring into my office—it's overwhelming."

Going on to describe the thoughtful discussions he had with the youth during their annual interviews, Bishop Potvin concluded, "The kids from the Primary to the young men, young women, have done more for me than I think they'll ever imagine. Those are the ones I look at now, those are the people I look up to, their sweet spirits. It's a joy."[21]

The Spirit present in our children and youth has import for all of us, not just bishops and youth leaders. In an address to members of the Church, President David O. McKay informed his listeners, "The spirituality of a ward will be commensurate with the activity of the youth."[22]

James Alexander, who grew up in the Weston Ward, was asked about a period of unprecedented missionary work during the 1970s. "I think the core of the ward was the youth," said James of that time. "The youth program at that time was huge."

"It seems like there was a symbiosis between the teens and the adults," he continued. "[The youth programs] drew the parents there as well. The social circle became larger. As we grew spiritually and bore our testimonies, we strengthened each other. It created this cohesiveness that was incredible. . . . We learned how to live the gospel with robust gusto."[23]

The Garbutt family moved to the Weston area with a son who was six-foot-nine. Devastated when he was told he was too late to try out for the school's basketball team, he accepted the invitation extended by the Weston youth to join their ward team. Up to that time, the young men had been losing games regularly. They did not lose another.

The teen began attending Mutual and invited his sister. Their younger brother joined the Scout troop. Before long, the three approached their father and asked for permission to be baptized. The father was active in his own faith and said no. While he would not prevent them from attending events at the LDS Church, he warned them he did not want to hear anything more about it.

One of the Garbutt's daughters had serious spinal problems. Unable to join her siblings in their Church activities, she was eager to hear and accept the gospel principles that her brothers and sister brought home. One night, her father came upstairs and found his little girl crying. When he asked what had upset her, she answered, "What if I die, and we're not an eternal family?" The father could not take his daughter's tears. Coming downstairs, he asked his other children what she had meant. One thing led to another and the entire family was baptized and later sealed in the temple.[24]

The strength within the Mormon Church, suggested a former seminary teacher, is what we do with our youth. "We give them a vision of who they are. They are each a child of a Father in Heaven who loves them. They have a mission upon this earth that they are to complete. They have an eternal perspective."[25]

In a culture consumed with immediate gratification and the urgency of the now, this perspective is life-changing. Speaking of the youth he worked with in downtown Boston, Jimmy Fish noted, "It's so hard for these boys to have any type of eternal perspective when they are worried about whether or not they are going to live from day to day."

Watching his boys stand up to the challenges around them strengthened Jimmy in ways he did not anticipate. After completing his mission, Elder Fish spent only a short period at home in Georgia before he returned to Boston to pursue an education, find work as an interpreter, and continue working with the youth in whom he had become personally invested. Being a missionary had not prepared him for how expensive the city would be, and with no funds, things were very difficult. Unable to secure a place to live, Jimmy spent a significant period living out of his car.

"It was tough to get started and make it," he explained. "Those boys really kept me going." [26] These were young men who would skip lunch on Friday so they'd have money to ride the bus to church on Sunday. They would do the same thing in the middle of the week so they could attend Mutual. "I just remember that being a tremendous example to me," Brother Fish stated.

The boys wanted to fulfill their priesthood responsibilities, but the obstacles were daunting. The ward had worked to procure white shirts for the young men to wear to Church to pass the sacrament, but no matter how much the adults cajoled and scolded, they wouldn't wear them. Unable to understand why this was such an issue, Jimmy finally sat down with one of the boys and asked why he wouldn't wear his shirt.

"If I look like I have any more than my peers do," the boy explained, "I'll get beat up. Anything could happen to me."

Comprehension dawning, the ward began keeping white shirts in a closet by the baptismal font so the boys could change clothes after they arrived at the meetinghouse to perform their duties as Aaronic priesthood holders. [27]

"I was amazed with the [youths'] desire to come to church," remarked Justin Lindsey. "It was something they wanted to do. There was no question about that. They would wear casual clothes on the bus and wear a backpack with their church clothes inside, which they would then change into."

Recalling a trying period during which his wife spent weeks in the hospital, Bishop Lindsey continued. "Those same boys who wouldn't wear their church shirts out in public brought the sacrament to my wife. . . . My favorite picture of that will always be a collection of very big, rough-looking inner-city boys walking down the [hall] with sacrament trays in their hands, coming to do their job as Aaronic priesthood holders. I will never forget that."[28]

"It makes it all worth it," Jimmy Fish summed up. "As hard as it was to make it on my own in Boston, I had those boys. When I felt like giving up . . . , if I felt like doing something I knew I shouldn't do as a priesthood holder, my thoughts would immediately be with those boys. I knew that I would have to face them every Sunday and every Wednesday, so I would keep going."[29]

In the 1980s, the towns east of Boston, including Lynn and Revere, became home to thousands of refugee families from Cambodia, Laos, and Vietnam. The Boston Stake organized an Asian branch in the early 1990s when individuals in these communities began accepting the gospel. What made this branch unique was the average age of its members: most of the converts were eight to twelve years old.[30]

"The youth were the ones that were coming into the Church," explained April Munns, wife of then-mission-president Ranier Munns.[31] The idea of so many children joining the Church on their own gave the stake leadership serious pause. In addition to concerns as to whether the youth could stay active in communities that were plagued by crime and gang violence, there were practical issues around getting these children and teens to meetings and activities.

"With the Cambodian Branch there was a lot of soul-searching," said then-stake-president Mitt Romney. "We would have a hundred people attending church there, with maybe four or five adults. So it was a massive Primary. We wondered if there was any way this would accomplish any good. How could we keep all of these youth? We knew that . . . we would lose many of them. At some point during this time, the Spirit whispered, 'If we could save but one of these youth . . . it would all be worthwhile."[32]

At times sacrament meeting looked more like a combined Primary and Mutual event than it did a ward. Evaluating the situation, a visiting authority observed, "We don't see the big picture from our vantage point, but obviously the Lord knows how to spread the work. . . . In decades to come, this foundation of youth who are joining the Church will [be] the core of our leadership. They will disperse throughout this country and go back to their native lands with leadership expertise and bless their own nations." With this perspective, the stake committed to do all that it could to help these youth gain a foothold.[33]

In 1999, John Wright was called as bishop of the Revere Second Ward, which had been combined with the Cambodian branch. "The strongest component in the ward in Revere is the youth," he stated, noting that the ward had a baptism almost every weekend. Typically the only members in their family, "these [youth] . . . will be leaders in their day because they are motivated to come to church on their own," Bishop Wright continued. "They . . . have to do it themselves."[34]

Chea Touch (pronounced Cheea Tooch), lived in Lowell, Massachusetts, another community home to many southeast Asian families. Chea found the Church and was baptized on his own at the age of eleven. Within a year, Chea's love for the gospel had led directly to the baptisms of fifteen friends and contributed to the conversion of others. Explaining his actions, Chea said, "I've always known I have a Heavenly Father who loves me. It's been wonderful to learn more about him and know what I must do to return to him. I want my friends to know the truth so they can have the happiness I do."

Chea's family had immigrated from Cambodia, where they suffered great privations. Chea's introduction to the missionaries in Lowell was accidental, as the elders were looking for another family when they knocked on the Touch family's door. Chea was the only one in the home who spoke English, and in the course of his conversation with the missionaries, he told them that he loved Jesus, wanted to find a church, and made them promise to take him to church the following Sunday. Chea had already visited several denominations but hadn't felt right in any of them.

Chea recognized truth as he heard the discussions and attended sacrament meeting. Following his baptism, he became inseparable from the elders, who lived nearby. Often he would arrive at the elders' apartment with a list of friends and relatives he wanted them to visit. "Sometimes we had a hard time keeping up!" one of the missionaries declared.

Said Chea's Primary president, "Each Sunday he would bring a different friend to church. He'd introduce them to me, spell their names, tell me their ages, and sit with them until they felt comfortable. Then he would go to his own class. He did this every week for a whole year!"

Saveth Vong and her three children were one of several families Chea introduced to the missionaries. As the elders taught the Vongs, Chea helped translate the discussions and explain gospel principles from his perspective. "Day after day," one of the elders wrote in his journal, "Chea sat quietly by Saveth, helping her understand the things we taught. He never seemed to tire of the message of the gospel."

Chea's approach to sharing the gospel was simple and non-intimidating—he simply told his friends and acquaintances that he wanted to share teachings that would make them happy. Speaking of the happiness he'd found himself, Chea said, "As I learn the scriptures and read the Book of Mormon, I can feel Heavenly Father's love for me." [35]

## Nothing Too Small

Shortly after missionaries began a fledgling Scouting program for the Boston Branch, the boys comprising its small troop began clamoring for a camping trip. Having practiced myriad outdoor skills, they were anxious to put their newfound knowledge to work, but a camping trip was out of the question. The elders serving as troop leaders did not have cars and were not permitted to travel outside their assigned area. The Scouts themselves had few funds for activities and were entirely reliant on public transportation.

The missionaries tried to talk the boys out of their impossible request, but their efforts went unheeded. The boys could not be dissuaded. Unable to placate the young Scouts and realizing that a solution was beyond their own abilities, the missionaries explained their dilemma in prayer and turned the matter over to the Lord.

A few days later, the elders were riding the subway, when they got on the wrong train. Getting off at an unfamiliar stop to retrace their route, they came face to face with a poster advertising camping on the islands of the Boston Harbor for a low promotional rate. Startled, the missionaries realized that this was an option that would allow them to go camping with the boys, using public transportation and without leaving the city. After obtaining permission from the mission president, the elders soon found themselves back on the train, accompanied by Scouts and piles of backpacks and sleeping bags. Taking the subway to the harbor, they boarded a public ferry and spent an unforgettable weekend camping together with Boston's financial district in clear sight across the water. [36]

There is something wonderful about knowing we have a Father in Heaven who cares about a camping trip for ten-year-old boys. He understands and values the concerns of all his children, and is particularly attuned to those things that matter to His youngest supplicants.

At the conclusion of a conversation with Elder L. Tom Perry, the interviewer suggested that Elder Perry's instinct in matters of programs and teaching was to focus on the youth. "Absolutely," Elder Perry agreed, referencing the responsibilities he had for the Church at that time in Europe. "If I do anything that is successful . . . it will be with the young adults and youth. . . . That is where our emphasis should be.

"They are an age group that is searching, looking, and is inquiring," Elder Perry continued. "These young people are the ones that will really make a difference."[37]

The Lord has often called young men and women to fulfill critical stewardships. The Lord called Samuel as a prophet while he was still a child, and Samuel went on to anoint a young shepherd boy as king of Israel (see 1 Samuel 3 and 1 Samuel 16:13). A fourteen-year-old boy in upstate New York was chosen to commence the Restoration, and the angel Gabriel visited a young Galilean woman of approximately the same age to tell her that she would be mother to the Son of God. "I know of no age limit described in the scriptures or guidelines announced by Church leaders restricting . . . important service to mature adults," Elder David A. Bednar has observed.[38] There is no such thing as "too young," in the Lord's kingdom, and we all have a personal interest in the success of our youngest brothers and sisters.

"When I had returned from my mission," Clayton Christensen admitted, "I remember making a statement to the Lord in one of my personal prayers that I would be happy to serve in whatever assignments He gave to me, but that I really hoped that those assignments weren't in the youth programs of the Church. I didn't feel that my temperament or talents were well-suited to working with the youth. It turned out that over the next fifteen years the *only* assignments I ever had were to work with the youth, either as an adviser or as a counselor to our bishop. I found it to be enormously rewarding—whereas adults are so set in their ways . . . I found that an amount of effort spent to mold the lives of our young people really does create change."[39]

Nearly three decades following his Mutual years, James Alexander still expressed a special fondness for that time in his life. "At the . . . time, we were having a lot of fun with road shows and camping. We were having early-morning seminary where the teacher was great and loved us. We knew he loved us. Our testimonies were growing. It was a renaissance time in my life. It was an awakening to the beauty of the gospel and its importance. It was a time when we all developed our testimonies."[40]

Said a mother of the important role youth temple trips, girls camp, youth conferences, and other activities had played in the lives of her daughters, "[They] allowed them to really formulate good friendships within the Church. . . . It allowed them this special time to be what they wanted to be and to be themselves."[41]

Following a ward split, fourteen-year-old Megan Hopkin learned to serve in ways she hadn't anticipated and, in so doing, became firmly woven into her new congregation. One evening shortly after the reorganization, one of the counselors in the bishopric called and asked Megan if she would be willing to serve as ward organist. Megan had never played the organ, but she agreed without hesitation. The next Saturday, Megan accompanied her mother to the chapel for an introduction to the organ. Megan's mother characterized the following Sunday as a miracle. Despite Megan's inexperience, "we just had this beautiful, full-sounding organ music from the very beginning," she explained.

Although the new ward had a dearth of teens, there was a large group of children under the age of five that Megan befriended. Soon she had a number of close friends older and younger than she was, and she considered herself an important part of the ward. Megan's willingness to extend herself and a leader's invitation to serve benefited the ward and solidified Megan's perception of her own role in the Lord's work. As a student at BYU a few years later, Megan frequently referenced her experiences, describing how it felt to internalize the teachings of the gospel by contributing to her ward's worship as a youth.[42]

In the tender years of senior Primary and Mutual, our youth decide whether to obey the Word of Wisdom, who and how to date, whether to remain morally clean, whether they will serve a mission, where to attend school, what vocation to pursue, and sometimes even who they will marry. They are sinking spiritual roots. When they are wavering or uncertain during this critical stage of life, adults outside the family circle can offer crucial support and encouragement. There is no more important time to become grounded in the eternal truths of the gospel, and each of us has the power to help or hinder that process.

Ben* was still of Primary age when he joined the Church with his parents and older brother. His older brother enjoyed Church and loved to study the scriptures, but the youth in the ward were critical of one another, and the relationship between the seminary teacher and students was acrimonious. Having watched his brother be marginalized and misjudged, Ben was already apprehensive about his own involvement in the Church when he turned twelve. One Sunday Ben accompanied his father, who

---

* Name has been changed for purposes of this account.

served on the high council, to another ward. The deacons there greeted Ben enthusiastically and expressed excitement that Ben could help them pass the sacrament. Their welcome cooled, however, when the bishop of the ward unwisely rebuked the twelve-year-olds in front of Ben, stating that Ben could not pass the sacrament with them because they didn't know whether he smoked or drank. Humiliated and offended, Ben never returned to church again.

Ben's experience contrasts sharply with that of Jonathan Clark, son of Kim and Sue Clark, who also wrestled with his feelings toward the Church. Jonathan was a member of a band, and as part of an effort to involve him, he was invited to play at a Church dance. Jonathan and his friends, who were not members of the Church, spent their Saturday setting up, adjusting the sound system, and making sure everything was perfect. They had barely performed their first number when a stake leader unplugged their speakers, saying simply, "Sorry—this isn't appropriate music for a Church event." Jonathan was embarrassed and angry. Arriving home that night, Jonathan told his parents he was never going to church again. Sure enough, the next morning, as the rest of the family left for Sunday services, Jonathan announced he was not going. Sue and Kim decided to leave him at home. Bruce Porter, Jonathan's priest quorum advisor, noted his absence and left sacrament meeting to drive to the Clarks' home. When Jonathan answered the door, Bruce said, "Jonathan, what happened to you last night was not right. I am going to work on this and make it up to you. It is going to be all right. Now get dressed, I'm taking you back to church."

"We're just so grateful that he had a youth leader who was sensitive enough to take the time and the effort to go and pick him up to bring him to church," Sue Clark stated. "That made a big impact on his life."

Today Jonathan is a devoted husband, father, and worthy priesthood holder.[43] A faithful youth advisor understood that there was no time to waste when Jonathan failed to show up to church that Sunday. His willingness to immediately act upon a spiritual prompting, together with kindnesses shown by other adults and leaders over the years, has blessed not only Jonathan's life, but that of his wife and young children as well. We never lose or save a soul in isolation.

If we want to build the Lord's kingdom on earth, we must look to its natural heirs. We have been admonished to "teach [our children] to walk in the ways of truth and soberness . . . to love one another, and to serve one another" (Mosiah 4:15). The purpose of declaring the doctrines of Christ, said Alma, is to bring salvation to the people, "that they may prepare the minds of their children to hear the word at the time of his coming" (Alma 39:16). If we do this, surely nothing can stop the kingdom of God from filling the whole earth.

Bruce Porter was working on his doctoral dissertation at Harvard University during the summer of 1979. Because many members of the Cambridge Second Ward left for the summer, the Primary president approached Bruce and asked if he would be willing to teach Primary for six weeks until some of the teachers returned. Primary met in the middle of the week, so Bruce was reluctant to accept because he was busy with research. Hemming and hawing until things got uncomfortable, the Primary president finally asked if Bruce would be willing to teach a class for two weeks. Still reluctant, Bruce agreed because two weeks was better than six.

When the first class rolled around the following Wednesday, Bruce was studying world politics in Widener Library, absorbed in what seemed to be terribly significant issues. The Primary class he'd agreed to teach seemed unimportant in comparison and an inconvenient distraction. Delaying for as long as he could, Bruce finally pulled out the manual and skimmed the lesson twenty minutes before Primary was to begin. Leaving the library, Bruce walked slowly toward the Cambridge chapel on the opposite side of Harvard Square, fixated on the time he was being asked to sacrifice. Walking in the shadows of ivy-covered buildings, Bruce could think only about the great seminars, conferences, and classes taking place around him, while he was left to attend to the ordinary, simple task of teaching a small group of children.

Arriving late at the meetinghouse, Bruce made his way up to the Primary room on the second floor, where opening exercises had already begun. As he stepped through the door of the room, the children began singing a hymn he had never heard before:

> *As I have loved you, love one another.*
> *This new commandment, love one another.*
> *By this shall men know, ye are my disciples,*
> *If ye have love, one to another.*[44]

As the music faded, Bruce continued to stand frozen at the door, transfixed by the hymn's beauty and message. His eyes filled with tears as the lesson he had not been seeking became clear.

"It struck me with great force that I was looking at the most important class taking place in Cambridge, Massachusetts, that day," said Elder Porter. "Back on the campus, all kinds of great issues were being discussed. People were searching for answers to the world's problems, but I was looking at the answer to the world's problems. This was the stone carved from the mount without hands that would roll forth to fill the earth. This was the Lord's way of fixing the world's problems. Not political or economic schemes, but teaching little children one by one so that they would grow up in righteousness."[45]

AND WHEN THE STRIFE IS FIERCE, THE WARFARE LONG,

STEALS ON THE EAR THE DISTANT TRIUMPH SONG,

AND HEARTS ARE BRAVE AGAIN, AND ARMS ARE STRONG.

# 10

# TENDING THE VINEYARD

WHILE SERVING as president of the New England States Mission from 1965 to 1968, Boyd K. Packer asked a small group of priesthood leaders to join him on the observation deck of the Prudential Tower, a fifty-two-story skyscraper in downtown Boston. As the men looked over the city below them, President Packer shook his head. "We're in New England, but we're not really in Boston," he said. "We're a church in the suburbs."

Taking advantage of the solitude found at the top of the building, the men bowed their heads and President Packer offered a prayer of dedication, asking the Father that the blessings of the gospel might spread and the Church might grow to serve all residents of Boston.

Loren C. Dunn was present that day. "We didn't really see the fulfillment then," he said of the rededication, "but the blessing was never lost." Considered too dangerous for missionaries at the time, attempts to root the Church within Boston were fraught with challenges for many years. Three decades later, however, Elder Dunn's son was called to the bishopric of an urban Boston ward. "The Church is established there, and the wards are established there," said Elder Dunn, smiling. "I look on that as a fulfillment [of] the blessing that was pronounced at that time. It was prophetic."[1]

## Boston Branch—Take 1

Fred and Jolene Rockwood made the cross-country drive from California to Boston in August 1972 to attend graduate school. Almost immediately, they heard rumors of a new branch being formed. If the Rockwoods were unable to find housing in the Belmont-Watertown area, some warned, they might not be able to attend the vibrant Cambridge Ward that served as a social hub for married students. Despite this caution, daunting rental costs convinced the couple to choose an apartment farther out than the majority of their LDS peers.

Sure enough, on their second Sunday in the area, Bishop Gordon Williams asked Fred to serve in the presidency of the Boston Branch, which was being formed as a dependent unit of the Cambridge Ward. For good measure, Fred was also asked to lead the elders quorum. The branch was officially organized on October 1, 1972, with E. Earle Silva set apart as branch president. Not since the Boston Branch of the early 1900s had a unit of the Church existed within the city of Boston.

The new presidency rejected a number of locations deemed unacceptable before renting an old Unitarian church where the first services were held on Sunday, October 15, 1972. "We still remember this meeting," Jolene said, "because we felt many people from beyond the veil were present to witness the beginnings of the branch. It was an incredibly spiritual meeting, more like a testimony meeting than a sacrament meeting, and a great beginning."[2]

The inactivity rate in the city was high, and the branch was considered experimental, as few urban congregations existed within the Church at that time. Membership rolls showed approximately one hundred members within the branch's boundaries, but initial attendance averaged ten. "Fred and I had a real sense of excitement about the new calling," Jolene wrote in her journal. "We were anxious for the challenge. In many ways it seemed like a mission call."[3]

Priesthood holders were sparse, and most of the individuals attending meetings had little to no experience serving in the Church. The lack of male membership and unstable family units posed challenges, raising early questions around the blessing of illegitimate children and the propriety of women serving in callings traditionally held by men. To prevent members of the branch presidency and their wives from having to talk every week, speakers were recruited from Cambridge for the first few months.

President Silva was a loving man who was adept at inviting individuals into the fold, but active members were stretched thin as they struggled to meet the administrative and temporal needs of the branch. Home teaching was done by married couples, and the Rockwoods' responsibility for seven families (only one of which came to church) was representative of others' assignments. On a typical Sunday, Fred taught elders quorum while Jolene taught Junior Sunday School and played the piano. Jolene then taught Relief Society and played the organ for sacrament meeting, where either she or Fred (or both) would speak. Afterward, Fred spent hours with the branch presidency trying to address needs that never abated. "Thank heavens we haven't formed our own MIA yet!" Jolene wrote in exhaustion at the close of one Sabbath.[4]

To bolster the ranks, a handful of young couples from Cambridge were called to attend the Boston Branch nine months after its organization. Among them were Jeanne and Randy Gaz. "We were called as what would now be stake service missionaries," Randy explained. "It was fun to go down there because it gave us an opportunity to feel like we were in the mission field." The additional help was appreciated, but needs were still plentiful. "Between Randy and I," Jeanne stated of their year in the branch, "we had eleven church jobs."[5]

Many people attending the branch had not been to church in years due to language barriers, lack of transportation, poor health, feeling out of place, or simply falling through the cracks. With a branch attuned to their needs, they began coming again. As lives were brought into harmony with gospel teachings, goals and aspirations changed. Such changes were a double-edged sword for the branch, as families able to improve their financial circumstances often moved into better neighborhoods outside the city. While a blessing for those members, these losses were hard for a congregation struggling to establish a stable base of adult leaders.[6]

One stalwart family was that of Richard and Priscilla Lowe. An African American, Richard was not able to hold the priesthood, but he participated in all elders quorum activities with other black males as a prospective elder. Richard served faithfully as Sunday School superintendent and filled a number of other non-priesthood callings while Priscilla served as Primary president and wherever else she was needed. Their large home sheltered many people, including foster children, who had nowhere else to go. Although she often cared for up to thirty people at a time, Priscilla's home was spotless and her children clean, well-dressed, and well-behaved.

"Richard and Priscilla Lowe were some of the most Christlike people we have ever known," Jolene noted. In a testimony meeting, Richard assured his fellow congregants that although he did not understand why he could not hold the priesthood, he accepted it on faith and was willing to wait for further revelation from the Lord. In the meantime, he was grateful for brothers within the Church who came to his home and shared the priesthood with his family so that they did not want for anything. Certain that this blessing would come to him in time, Brother Lowe testified that he was striving to live a celestial life so that he would already be living as a worthy Melchizedek priesthood holder when the blessing finally came.[7]

By June 1974, the branch had outgrown the old Unitarian church and procured space at a private school in a nicer area of Boston. Recent baptisms had added families and priesthood holders to the congregation. Anticipating boundary changes, branch members hoped to welcome additional families who would add permanent strength. Looking forward, Jolene wrote, "Fred feels he may have finally reached the point where his counselor job won't be so demanding. . . . I am still teaching the Gospel Doctrine class, and . . . playing the piano in Junior Sunday School, but I am not overburdened for the first time." A letter from President Earle Silva a month later spoke of a baptism attended by sixty-three branch members. "We also had ninety-six at sacrament service today. Remember when that was the whole membership?" he marveled.[8]

The branch was developing marvelously, said Cambridge bishop, Gordon Williams. The potential was obvious, as the majority of baptisms in the stake were coming from the Boston congregation and a dependent Spanish branch also supported by the Cambridge Ward.[9]

Notwithstanding these positive signs, the Boston Stake's foray into the city came to an abrupt halt just two years after the branch's organization. In October 1974, the Cambridge Ward was split into two. There were not enough members to staff the new Cambridge Second Ward and the Boston Branch, so the branch was folded back into the Cambridge wards. The decision was met with mixed emotions, and some who had just begun to participate in church activity drifted away anew. "That's the sad part of wards dividing and being created," Bishop Williams stated, "particularly when there is something unique that is holding [a congregation] together."[10]

"So many things have happened in the branch," Jolene Rockwood wrote in 1972. "Fred and I have had more miracles and spiritual experiences . . . in the past few months than we have had in two years."[11] Asked whether the attempt to establish a congregation in the city was a failure,

Jolene responded emphatically. "The Boston Branch ended not because it failed, but because it was successful. It grew into a significant part of a ward," she stated. "The branch blossomed and grew with many baptisms, but also saw success when many of the members who were reactivated found their lives changed. . . . The end of the Boston Branch was very sad for us because we loved the people in the branch as though they were our own family members."[12]

## Boston Branch—Take 2

Randy Gaz was serving as a counselor to Bishop Lloyd Baird in the Cambridge Second Ward when the next attempt to establish a congregation within the Boston city limits occurred approximately ten years later. Bishop Baird worried that the ward wasn't adequately meeting the needs of an important segment of its members and asked Randy to organize a group composed of the four active families then in the city. Living in Mattapan and Dorchester, all had joined the Church since the dissolution of the earlier Boston Branch.

Joshua Smith, one of the local members, was asked to lead the group with support from Brother Gaz. Initially, the group held a sacrament meeting at a Knights of Columbus hall once a month and came to Cambridge for the remainder of their meetings. Weekly sacrament meetings commenced after a year, and within two years they were holding Sunday School, priesthood, and Relief Society, a gradual process in which the members were asked to take increasingly greater responsibility for the unofficial unit.[13] Growth was slow. "The first year we only baptized four people," said Joshua Smith. "We only had two missionaries and they worked so hard. They just couldn't get them to say yes."[14]

"The way the Boston Branch started," Bishop Baird admitted, "it didn't start as a branch, it just started as a twig."[15]

Interestingly, another reorganization provided an opportunity for the reestablishment of a branch in downtown Boston. In May 1984, two new wards were created by taking membership from seven area congregations, including the Cambridge First and Second Wards. As part of this realignment, the two Cambridge wards were collapsed into one congregation. The change had a dramatic impact on members remaining in Cambridge, as the vast majority of experienced leaders, including both bishops of the former Cambridge First and Second Wards, lived within the newly created Belmont and Arlington ward boundaries.

Brent and Denise Barnett were members of the recombined Cambridge Ward, composed almost exclusively of married student couples with a few singles and a handful of families. Membership rolls showed large numbers of inactive members in the city and outlying communities. Of those names, said Brent, "We knew maybe a fourth of the people on [the] list."

Brent was serving in the elders quorum presidency. With few alternatives for meeting the ward's members, Brent took the membership roll and drove into unfamiliar neighborhoods to knock on doors, often accompanied by one of his children. Denise took her Primary presidency into burned-out buildings in inner city communities to find children they did not know, while the Relief Society did the same, hoping to locate faceless sisters on a list. Working in tandem, ward leaders traversed many neighborhoods within the geography of the unofficial city unit.

Brent took it upon himself to document the results of their travels, charting the ward's membership on a large road map sprinkled with color-coded dots to show the locations of singles, couples, and families with children. In time, the map garnered attention outside the ward, and former bishop Lloyd Baird, now in the high council, asked if the stake leaders could get a copy. "We knew then," said Brent, "that they were going to separate off the Boston Branch."[16]

Mitt Romney was a counselor in the stake presidency at the time and recalled some concern that disbanding the prior branch had been a mistake. "The Spirit came back knocking on the door a little more forcefully saying . . . 'We need to organize a branch in Boston.'"[17] The Boston Branch was officially reorganized in February 1986. Many of the people the Barnetts and others within the Cambridge Ward had devoted long hours to finding would now be invited to join with the little group of Saints already meeting together in the city.

Gordon Williams, bishop in Cambridge when the earlier Boston Branch was formed, was serving as stake president. In this capacity, he called Keith Knighton, who lived in an outlying suburb, to attend the branch with his family and serve as a counselor in the branch presidency. "Brother Knighton," he explained, "the Lord wants this branch to be established in Boston. See to it that it happens." The words echoed in Keith's ears as he thought, "Me? See to it? I'm not the branch president." Two years later, Brother Knighton was asked to lead the branch.

Initial attendance, including missionaries, was twenty-five to thirty. "The first year we struggled, we really struggled," Brother Knighton said, sighing. "The second year, things began to change. We began to get young couples moving into the branch. . . . They came and served where they were needed."

When a Haitian family began coming to the branch, Jeff Dawson, a doctoral student who had served a mission in Haiti, agreed to teach Sunday School in their language. Word spread among the Haitian community and people began coming out of curiosity, including previously unknown members who had immigrated to Boston. Violence in Haiti had recently led the Church to evacuate missionaries from that country, which resulted in a number of Haitian-speaking missionaries called to serve in the Boston area for the first time. Between word-of-mouth referrals and the missionaries' tracting, Brother Dawson was soon serving as a quasi-branch president for his growing class.

Francisco Anleu, a long-time member attending the branch, asked to organize a Spanish Sunday School. President Knighton agreed, so long as Brother Anleu taught it. Twenty-five people attended the Spanish-language class its first Sunday. A week later, the class had doubled and never fell below fifty again. Within a year, the branch was holding sacrament meeting in Spanish in the Relief Society room and Haitian-Creole services in the Primary room. At 10:00 a.m. each Sunday, the branch conducted sacrament meeting in three different languages.

"It was obvious," President Knighton said, "if we were going to grow, we needed to have missionaries." The mission president was on board and multiple sets of missionaries speaking Haitian, Spanish, and English were soon brought into the city.[18] If Boston were ever to have a temple, the mission president opined, it needed organized congregations within its core.[19]

By 1991, several Haitian-speaking missionaries were pressing for the creation of a Haitian branch. They had prepared their proposal carefully by cleaning up membership records, verifying addresses, and documenting all priesthood holders in the group. President Knighton listened thoughtfully and responded, "Let's pray about it." At the conclusion of the prayer, the branch president looked up and shook his head. "I just don't think it's time right now," he said.

"We felt like that was a setback," said Jimmy Fish, one of the elders who had advocated for the new branch. "It turned out to be a lot of wisdom." With additional time, a number of members were reactivated and took on responsibilities that allowed them to become key leaders when the time was right.[20] Strong missionary work produced upward of one hundred converts a year, and the Boston Branch became the Boston Ward in 1995. Three short years later, a Spanish and Haitian Branch were organized, and the Boston Ward was split into two wards, the harvest of what fifteen years prior was four lone families—six individuals—supported by a handful of committed Saints and leaders.

## Distinguishing Patterns for Growth

Although we know the ultimate outcome of the Lord's work, the fate of any one area can feel as uncertain as it did for the initial pioneers of both Boston Branch attempts. Bill and Addis Murdock moved to Needham, Massachusetts, in 1955. Even in Cambridge, the long-established hub of Church activity for the Atlantic District, things felt precarious as members moved in and out. "We were lucky if we had forty-five people," said Addis. "The Lord seemed to help us. He would move strong people in. We'd get the wards going. This was the pattern all over New England. You would see it time and time again. . . . It seemed that it was gradual, but it was very definite."[21]

Jay and DeLene Holbrook were in Worcester, Massachusetts, during a pronounced surge in missionary work and baptisms. "Most of these people who joined around that time remained true to the faith and became leaders," DeLene noted. The ward had only a small, first-phase building so "there wasn't even room enough for us all to fit in the same room for sacrament meeting," she said, laughing. "One of our Relief Society classes met in the ladies' restroom—that's how crowded we were! Yet that's when all these people came in and stayed with us."

"Activity was splendid and the sacrifices were many," Jay recalled. Asked what produced such growth, he shrugged. "I'm convinced that the Lord prepared the time and the place," he said. "There were just people [who were] ready. That seemed to be the right moment for these special people to become members of the Church. . . . I think it was almost nothing that we did."[22]

Growth is not always linear, nor is it always measurable. In any congregation, there are times when activity is high, missionary work is productive, and the Spirit is abundant, but there are also times when the harvest seems lean for the effort invested. Deciphering traits that distinguish one period from another can be puzzling and frustrating.

Mitt Romney referenced Parley P. Pratt's mission to New York when asked to discuss attributes leading to growth. After six months, Elder Pratt had little to show for his labors. Gathering with the few area Saints for a prayer meeting before he left, the Spirit was manifest. In Elder Pratt's words, "The Lord said that He had heard our prayers, beheld our labors, diligence and long suffering towards that city; and that He had seen our tears. . . . Our labors and sacrifices were accepted. We should tarry in the city, and go not thence as yet; for the Lord had many people in that city. . . . And there should be more doors open for preaching than we could fill." Elder Pratt stayed on and saw this promise fulfilled, preaching to packed audiences and baptizing almost daily for the next several months.[23]

"I recognized in that example," said Brother Romney reflectively, "that there are times when the Lord is expecting us to serve, to put our head down, to sacrifice, to labor, and perhaps there's very little that comes of it. Then there comes a time when the Holy Ghost opens His Spirit to the people and people join the Church in great droves.

"In the . . . growth of the Church worldwide, you can watch the Holy Ghost doing that in different parts of the world. . . . The Holy Ghost and the timing of the Lord seems to move upon an area and dwell for some period of time, and then . . . it slows down. I don't know if there is anything more or less holy about the people during that time . . . , other than it is always incumbent on us to do our best and . . . hope that those sacrifices are accepted. . . .

"I also believe that while missionary work is one of the great manifestations of the Holy Ghost, there are other great manifestations," Brother Romney offered, noting that some congregations see periods characterized by member reactivation or the strengthening of their youth. "How the Lord works and in which ways He's working . . . is sort of hard to know."[24]

A convert who joined the Church during a decade of remarkable missionary work in the Weston area shared another insight. "There had been an awful lot of preparation laid for a long time by a lot of people," he suggested, "some of whom were probably completely unknown to us. During the period when maybe the missionary work had not been so successful, there were people here who were faithful, living the gospel, and committing their lives in a very serious way to making the gospel grow in this area. I'm bound to think that in some way what happened later had to be a result of the foundation that had been laid by those people."[25]

## Growth through Division

We often view the division of wards and stakes as a product of growth, with new units created when a congregation grows too large for administrative practicality. But just as often perhaps, the act of division is an essential, if somewhat painful, catalyst of growth.

Through the decades leading up to the formation of the Boston Stake in 1962, the Cambridge Branch boasted the largest congregation in New England. Hugh Forrest's family joined the Church in the 1920s and was one of the few families in the branch not from Utah. For thirty years, the Forrests met with other Saints in a variety of rented halls and modified homes until the Cambridge chapel was dedicated in 1956. Less than three years later, Hugh and his wife, Alice, were asked to leave the new chapel, for which they'd sacrificed and labored, to attend services in Billerica where meetings were held in an old barn.

The newly formed North Middlesex Branch served a number of members living on the New Hampshire border who rarely made it to Cambridge. All but a small handful of congregants were recent converts. Despite the bats flying overhead during sacrament meeting and classes held in a hayloft, "somehow or another, I got more enthused about working in the Church," said Alice. "For one thing, I felt freer. . . . The people that were in the little red barn were very warm and close. . . . Out here we all had to have two to three jobs. We just all worked together like a family."[26]

Not long after the formation of the North Middlesex Branch, Robert Hales was asked to lead a new Wayland Branch. Meeting in an American Legion Hall that needed to be cleared of beer bottles and ashtrays each Sunday, Elder Hales said, "It was remarkable how many people there were. We went out to all the people who had been members of the Church, the real Massachusetts natives. As our church began to grow, many of those came back to activity because we . . . had a church that was near them. Cambridge was viewed by a lot of the locals as more of a student and a Western church, and they felt that they weren't really needed."

A sense of two separate cultures had occasionally been present, Mary Hales acknowledged. As the Church extended into other communities, said Elder Hales, "I saw us losing that division, that separatist kind of feeling. We needed everyone. . . . I would go into the homes and say, 'We need you,' and they responded."[27] Only a few of years after North Middlesex and Wayland had been split from Cambridge, sacrament meeting attendance among the combined three congregations nearly doubled what it had been in Cambridge alone.[28]

The same thing happens today. As units are divided, opportunities expand among individuals and congregations. Asked why individuals would sacrifice and endure inconveniences to attend the Malden Branch when they'd been inactive in prior wards, Carol Coppins cited the branch's size as a significant motivator. "It was this close-knit family that did everything together and relied on each other," she explained. "You know that if you don't show up, there is not somebody else that can do your job. . . . There are not enough people."[29]

Kerry Hopkin was a bishop in Weston when his ward was split and combined with a portion of another unit to create a new congregation in 1998. Having chosen two young counselors from the other ward, the fledgling bishopric sat down with a new ward council to staff the ward top to bottom—something akin to an NFL draft exercise, Bishop Hopkin suggested. The number of callings that needed to be filled meant nearly every active adult would need to contribute. And they did, the bishop stated. "People come prepared to serve. . . . That's one of the miracles that we just take for granted every Sunday."

"There was an energy that was infused in this ward that I've never seen before," said Bishop Hopkin, noting that many of those called as instructors and leaders were younger members who had been underutilized in prior wards. "People were experiencing personal growth like they had never experienced before. . . . They felt good about themselves. They felt the Spirit in their lives. They were able to reach out."[30]

Paul Anderson was a graduate student who served as Bishop Hopkin's first counselor. "It was hard work to try to pull the whole ward together," he said. "For the first little while you'd sit there and you could look out at the ward and tell that people felt uncomfortable and that they didn't know what to do. It was hard having different groups of people . . . all shoved together in one chapel. But it didn't take long before the ward members felt comfortable with each other."[31]

"I'm in favor of splitting wards," Bishop Hopkin concluded. "I think blessings come from sacrifice. I think if you need to have two or even three callings to fully staff a ward, it's better to do that. . . . I'm in favor of smaller units that give everybody a chance to serve and to stretch, even if they don't feel like they are capable of serving in that particular calling. Nobody is. On their own, nobody is. . . . Let them grow in their calling and pretty soon they're every bit as capable."[32]

A sister recalled the uproar a recent division in her stake had created. "People were moaning and groaning about it, but that is what strengthens us as more people are given the opportunity to serve."[33]

## Identity within the Fold of the Gospel

A case study for individual and congregational growth is found among non-English-speaking members in the greater Boston area. The Boston Stake made its first foray into organizing groups by language under the auspices of the Cambridge Ward in the early 1970s when a Spanish Sunday School class was organized to better serve and facilitate the participation of a growing Spanish-speaking population. Although hardly unique today, the endeavor ran contrary to the total integration approach common at the time, which was leading to the loss and inactivity of a number of Spanish-speaking members.[34]

The class had an impact, and pressure built to hold sacrament meeting in Spanish as well. A dependent branch of approximately six active families was formed under the ward's umbrella in 1979. The group was enthusiastic, but its size led to frequent personality issues that were difficult for leaders to address. The branch had baptisms, but a high inactivity rate as well. Attendance would increase, only to fall back following a disagreement or change in leadership.

Almost a decade after formation of the branch, stake president Mitt Romney worried that the group was not progressing. Missionary work had slowed and there was contention among the members. Leaders wondered aloud if language was a reasonable basis for keeping the group separate and talked of reintegrating the branch. A former bishop of a Spanish ward in Chicago encouraged President Romney to press forward. Two things were necessary for the Church to grow among the Hispanic members, he counseled. First, leaders had to recognize that Spanish-speaking members were not a homogeneous group—they identified themselves by nationality and culture. To address differences, a new identity within the gospel fold must be established. Instead of regarding themselves as Guatemalan, Nicaraguan, or Peruvian, congregants needed to see each other as members of The Church of Jesus Christ of Latter-day Saints.

Second, he insisted, stake leaders must have the same expectations of a Spanish-speaking congregation as they did of English-speaking wards and branches. "Don't treat us as a group that needs to be coddled and given special attention," he counseled. "Expect us to do our fair share in stake callings. Expect us to have the same home teaching percent[ages]. . . Expect us to contribute as much in terms of tithing percentage as the other units in the stake. And you will see that the Spanish-speaking people will rise to the challenge."[35]

Acting on this advice, the stake adopted a radically different strategy than the one it had been considering. Instead of dissolving the Spanish branch, additional units were formed to meet specific needs. Spanish, Cambodian, and Portuguese branches were organized, along with English-speaking branches created to serve members in outlying areas. Each was initiated with the expectation that it could ultimately become a center of strength. At one point, said Brother Romney, "We had nine units . . . that required leadership or help from other units in the stake, four [of which] were not English-speaking."

Taking a cue from the old "dependent branch" structure, the stake paired branches with established wards that could help provide manpower and administrative experience, so branch leaders could focus on people. In addition, the stake presidency made adjustments in its priorities, delegating many tasks to the high council. "We spent all our time working with the units," Brother Romney explained, emphasizing the focus his presidency placed on strengthening the branches. "We didn't have any time to work with the auxiliaries."[36]

Kent Bowen was assigned to provide direction to a few of the branches from the stake level. The change in approach was spectacular in retrospect, he stated. Attending meetings in Spanish and Portuguese, often assisted by a member who could translate, "it was just absolutely marvelous, the strength of those people and how much they cared for each other and [took] on those responsibilities."[37]

Having watched over the beginnings of the Spanish congregation in Boston, Keith Knighton admired the capabilities of its members when they were provided with a place where they could act comfortably with self-confidence. "Language was the only barrier," he explained. "Integrity? No, that was not a barrier. Testimony was not an issue. It was [an issue] of functioning in an English language . . . [T]hey could function perfectly well in their own language in their own setting."[38]

Nancy and Jim Arias joined the Church in Venezuela. Arriving in Cambridge in December 1980, they found five Hispanic families holding the one and only Spanish branch together. Less than twenty years later, five Spanish-speaking congregations existed within the same geographic area. Sister Arias compared the first branch's setbacks to those encountered by the pioneers. "They had ups and downs and they had . . . disagreements with each other, but the movement was forward." In a typical English-speaking ward, she noted, many of these dedicated but economically challenged Saints would be on the receiving end of ward service efforts. Having their own branches gave them opportunities to serve. Even today, "some of them have to pray literally for food," Sister Arias pointed out, while others forego necessities to attend church via public transportation. Yet these same individuals are eager to share what they have and were the first to fill temple buses en route to Washington, D.C. "It shows a tremendous amount of faith."

Opportunities to serve create temporal as well as spiritual changes. In the workforce, Sister Arias observed, individuals who are not proficient in English are often forced to take low-paying jobs and expected to keep quiet. "Suddenly in the Church they're given responsibility," she said. "They're told not only you have responsibility, but we value you and we value your input. There's a transformation that carries over into their secular lives and with their jobs and [you] see the people move up economically. . . . It's a funny phenomenon, but the more faithful the people are, the more the people who are coming in . . . want to be a part of it. Because they want to be a part of it, the Church grows. As it grows, more callings are needed, more people have work to do. The more work, the more people themselves are transformed."[39]

The Lynn Asian and Lynn Spanish branches were initially formed as dependent branches of the Lynnfield Ward, which had approximately 350 members. With the dependent branches' rapid growth, the ward's combined membership soon exceeded 800! "There are all sorts of people that weren't in the Church twenty years ago," said Lynnfield bishop, Steven Evans. "People who have recently immigrated to the United States and are joining the Church by the hundreds. . . . I think we see that starting now. I think that's going to be the way it is here for a long time."[40]

Prior to the formation of a lasting branch downtown, the Boston Stake's strength had been concentrated in the outer suburban wards. As attention shifted toward building strength in the city, leaders envisioned the stake as a tree, where the center needed a sturdy root and trunk to support the growth of new branches.[41] This shift facilitated the creation of urban and outlying congregations to serve individuals and groups who had not found a place in the old model.

"If you look at the stake, most of our units are not standard units," remarked former Boston Stake President Lloyd Baird, referencing the singles wards and language-based wards and branches. By 1999, the Spanish-speaking units alone had grown large enough that the stake was holding a Spanish stake conference for five hundred to six hundred attendees."[42]

Many wards today began as small branches and Sunday Schools

organized to serve active members who had joined the Church in other countries and on whom the Spirit was working with great power, said Brother Romney. Due to transportation problems and language barriers, existing wards were not providing adequate support for their testimonies. "There was something special about the places that these branches were organized," he asserted. "There was something that was quite compelling there. The branches would start . . . and then wane away, almost disappear, and you'd ask yourself, 'Should we disband this branch?' . . . And yet the decision kept coming back, 'No.' . . . Now I look back and I just marvel. I would have never imagined we'd have two wards in Boston, we'd have a Spanish-speaking ward, we'd have two wards in Revere. . . . I always thought that they would be just places for maybe ten or twenty families to come together. . . . Now [they've] grown into full-fledged active strength in the Church."[43]

## Branching Outward

Boundary changes, divisions, and reorganizations facilitate growth, but they are rarely easy. Elder Robert Wood recalled a case where a branch was made a ward by taking bits and pieces of two other congregations, resulting in something many considered a Frankenstein monster—they didn't want to be there. Over time, reluctance faded and that ward has since been divided into two congregations, each with their own identity. "Now they don't even remember from whence they came," he said wryly. "It's a whole different character. I say that's been true of the growth in New England generally. . . . It takes a little bit of time for people to settle in and then there's a whole new surge of growth and different sorts of people and conversion."[44]

"There was a lot of gnashing of teeth when they split the ward in Cambridge into Cambridge First and Cambridge Second," a brother observed. "Friendships were torn apart. . . . You couldn't imagine how anything was ever going to be the same. Two weeks later, there you go."[45]

Although there are different ways to calculate it, since its organization, the original Cambridge congregation has been split at least eight times, resulting in more than twenty-five wards and branches that can trace their origins to it.* This "growth by division" strategy was not accidental and was particularly effective, Gordon Williams suggested, because the area always had a pool of enthusiastic, bright, young people

---

* See Congregational Growth Chart on page xviii.

who were willing to serve. "They were delighted, for the most part," he said, "to go and man the outpost," providing important support as new units established roots. In addition, Brother Williams offered, there was a philosophy among stake leaders that "the stake should be a seed for integrating outward" and their primary responsibility was helping others take hold of the gospel.[46]

Today there is a tendency to let congregations get larger before they are divided. This reduces administrative loads and provides a broader base of leadership within congregations, but it may also impede the growth that comes from stretching. When asked if growth could have been increased had the stake divided other wards as aggressively as it had in Cambridge, Brother Romney was thoughtful. "It's hard to know what would have happened," he replied. In many areas where branches were formed, local members were reliant on public transportation and their opportunity for activity increased greatly with the creation of a unit close to their homes. In other areas of the stake, proximity was not nearly as determinative. Still, he said, "I'm convinced that we probably could have done better missionary work had we organized smaller branches out in some of those areas."[47]

## One Becomes Two

When Mitt Romney was released as stake president in 1994, Ken Hutchins was called to preside over the Boston Stake. Almost immediately, his presidency set a goal to double the size of the stake in five years, facilitated by the tremendous missionary work being done in downtown Boston and the other young branches. Building on work done under Presidents Williams and Romney, the new stake presidency believed there was potential to create another stake in very short order, a goal for and upon which they began praying and focusing. Within four years, the stake grew from eleven units to nineteen wards and branches.

This growth did not come without challenges. Every change, whether a boundary alteration or the creation or division of a congregation, disrupted lives. "It was more hard than it was easy," President Hutchins stated. "But you can see the wisdom in the way the Lord orchestrated [it], especially in the growth of our language units and how they just prospered."

By 1996, the Boston Stake was having serious conversations with the area presidency and surrounding stakes about the possibility of a split. For months they answered requests for information focused on membership and the effect of a split on youth and language units. "It did not happen rapidly," President Hutchins said, laughing. "I think I naïvely had the view that it's obvious . . . something needs to be done, so let's just . . . get it done."

The first formal proposal for division involved the disruption of an adjacent stake and was rejected. After meeting with presidents of three area stakes, another proposal was made and rejected. Working on a third iteration, President Hutchins received a call from an area authority who acknowledged the work, time, and prayers that had gone into the prior proposals but informed the tired president that yet another detailed piece of information was needed from each branch and ward before a split could be considered.

The requested data was collected, and the presidency submitted a proposal that involved splitting one ward into three congregations and altering boundaries of three others. Although complicated, it was accepted. "There were probably five hundred phone calls at a minimum that went back and forth over the length of this two-year process and discussion," President Hutchins estimated. "I learned an incredible principle through all of this. I learned that . . . [approvals] on these kinds of decisions don't come easy. . . . The finite details of concern that [the general authorities] have for individual lives of members and the impact it has on families . . . are a manifestation of their love for the Saints and their wanting to do the Lord's will in this. . . . It seemed pretty crisp and clear to us at the outset, . . . [but] we really needed to make a presentation that was honed to a finite degree so that these brethren who love us could in all honesty petition the Lord and ask for His blessings to allow that to happen.

"I'm so impressed lately with the emphasis on the world-wide church. . . . These brethren in their priesthood responsibility are so careful not to make a decision that would throw the Church out of kilter in any area. . . . That's one of the reasons why it sometimes takes an incredibly long period of time to get what appear to be relatively simple things accomplished."

The split, which resulted in a Cambridge Stake and a Boston Stake, each responsible for eleven units, "was done in an attitude of prayer and fasting from start to finish. It was a great learning experience," said President Hutchins. "There were times when I was frustrated because instead of getting a clear answer, I was sent back to the drawing board. Then I would say to myself, 'Well, there's a reason for that, so cut it out!'"[48]

## A Double-Edged Sword

"The changes are dramatic," said Robert Wood of the Massachusetts congregations he first encountered in 1961 as compared to those today. "There are fourteen stakes in New England where there was only one. . . . It's a much more diverse stake . . . ethnically, linguistically, and otherwise." People still come east for school and work, but the major transformation is the growth of the Church among the local population and immigrant groups that have settled in the area.[49]

"When we first came in 1971," observed Jeanne Gaz, "the people that were here were mostly Utah transplants. There were a few that grew up in the area, but they were far and few between. . . . If you looked at the characteristics of the wards, they were very white Anglo-Saxon, frankly. Now you . . . are translating stake conference into five or six languages. . . . This growth has all occurred since we have been here. It is so exciting to see."[50]

The Church's growth in New England mirrors its worldwide expansion and demonstrates an ironic side effect. While the process of establishing wards and branches in underserved areas and providing meetings in various languages has helped broaden our diversity as a whole, individual congregations often become increasingly homogenous. As a ward or branch's geographic boundaries grow smaller, there results a sameness in background, education, and socioeconomic status among those with whom we most frequently worship, particularly in suburban congregations. Until the late 1970s, the Cambridge Ward stretched across Boston and myriad outlying communities, serving members of every stripe.

"When I arrived in 1949 everybody was mixed up together," said Richard Bushman of the branch that included young students, families of every stage, lifelong transplanted members, and local converts new to the faith. "It had the sense of a big, happy family and also a band of brethren in the wilderness. We knew we were pioneers out on the edge of the world."[51]

Said another member of his experience, "The opportunity to interact with truly a wide range of people, tremendous diversity on every parameter, gave . . . me a deeper appreciation for the applicability of the gospel to absolutely everyone and helped us see the fundamental power of the principles of the gospel in everyone's lives."[52]

"When I look back," a former bishop stated, "I remember us just having this huge, diverse set of people. People with lots of problems just

living life. And yet a cadre of servants that were just unbelievable. . . .
I think the great lesson out of that experience was how wonderful the
Church works when it represents the breadth and diversity of humanity. I
think that's why it was so wonderful. . . . We were capturing some of the
ideas about a Zion people."[53]

Growth led to congregational divisions, beginning with separate
wards for students and families. "Those of us who had been there in the
old days," remarked Brother Bushman, "always mourned the loss of that
mixture—instead we were all isolated into our specialized groups. . . . We
were now no longer sort of a pioneer bastion in the wilderness, but a
pretty well-established ward that did the job."[54]

"When people have reflected on the time of their lives here where
they enjoyed the Church the most, it goes back to the diversity," observed
Clayton Christensen. "As the Church has grown stronger and stronger,
each of the wards [has] become progressively less diverse." Not only has
this taken something away from the communal worship experience, he
noted, but "it's harder for people that don't fit that mold to feel welcome."[55]

A branch striving to nourish new members and a ward stretched thin
to meet never-ending needs face obvious challenges. But the greater risk
may lie in the "well-established ward that does the job" and grows complacent in its traditions, losing sight of the fact that this work is all about
change, discomfort, and continually reaching beyond our current capacity to become what the Lord intends.

"As you view what is essential to build the kingdom of God," a former
stake president observed, "the first ingredient is truly converted, committed Latter-day Saints."[56] In downtown Boston in 1984, there were six.
New to the Church, each stepped forward when asked. Sundays were
long. After holding their own Sunday School service, they traveled to
Cambridge for sacrament meeting. When they began holding their own
services after a year, Joshua Smith blessed and passed the bread and water
as the only priesthood holder every week.

Small in number, each Monday the group gathered for family home
evening. Lessons came straight from the scriptures with each reading in
turn until the chosen chapter was finished. Home and visiting teaching
were a similar communal experience in which everyone gathered on an
appointed evening to visit and offer encouragement and support.

"We had started so small," said Joshua, "[but] we never [got] any feeling that we shouldn't go on." With little growth to show in the first years, a stake leader approached Brother Smith and asked if the group would prefer to fold back into one of the wards. "No, I don't think I should stop," Joshua replied carefully. "We'll grow. We'll carry on."[57]

Missionary efforts gradually bore fruit and the foundation established by these chosen few proved fertile. "These four families were loving friends," said Randy Gaz, who was initially charged with shepherding the little group. "Their friendship and their joy in doing gospel activities served as an example for the investigators . . . an example of love, friendship, and reaching out to others as they came." They were doers, Brother Gaz concluded. "They put their souls in it."[58]

Today Boston is home to two diverse and energetic wards, as well as a Haitian-Creole branch. "The Lord's work will prosper," Lillian Smith said simply. "When I joined the Church in 1978, I didn't even realize that there were churches in Russia and in Africa. . . . I thought it was only in America. Then you see how the Lord blesses the Church and it just takes time."

Asked if they got discouraged early on, Sister Smith said that they fasted often. "During the time when we were struggling, we were just praying and fasting for Heavenly Father to bless us that the work would get [off] the ground," she shared. "We had to really depend on divine intervention. . . . Pray for the wisdom to carry on. . . . I think He answered the prayer."

"My greatest experience over the years since I was baptized," Lillian's husband, Joshua, observed, "[is] the work of the Lord—no one can stop it from going forward. . . . It's the Lord's church, He's at the head, and if you believe in Him, there's no turning back."[59]

"I think stories here in Boston are wonderful," a former member of the branch admitted. "[But] I don't know if they are any more miraculous than anywhere else in the world. It's just the hand of the Lord doing what it usually does."[60]

# 11

# ENLARGING
# THE BOUNDARIES

TONY KIMBALL grew up with his relatives' stories of Harvard University and Cambridge, Massachusetts. When Tony applied to graduate school, Harvard was the only school on his list. Fortunately, he was accepted. "The day I arrived, it was almost like falling in love," Tony reminisced. "I think I'd been here maybe . . . ten years before I realized I would never go back to Utah."[1]

In 1963, there was one ward in Cambridge consisting of members of every age and position, a trait that suited Tony just fine. Welcomed by a core group of Latter-day Saints who had lived in the area for decades, Tony was energized by the vibrant exchange of ideas that filled his new environment and the constant stream of people flowing in and out of the Cambridge Ward.[2]

Tony's status as a relative newcomer and his passion for his new home imbued him with sensitivity for young students in the congregation. Larry Wilson had just finished high school in Pocatello, Idaho, when he arrived in 1968. Tempted to spend Sunday exploring the wonders and oddities of Harvard Square, Larry ultimately decided to walk the extra few blocks to the Longfellow Park Chapel, where he met Tony Kimball in the foyer. Soon thereafter, Tony began dropping by Larry's dormitory and intercepting Larry on his way to and from class to see how he was doing.

"During my freshman year," Larry recalled, "I spent a great deal of time trying to decide . . . whether or not to serve a mission for the

Church. Tony had served in Germany and commented regularly about his experience there. . . . In large measure, because of the collective impact of my many interactions I had with Tony, I decided to go on a mission. That experience proved to set the course of my life in many important ways."[3]

Jim Jardine was another beneficiary of Tony's friendship. A new student at Harvard Law School, Jim found himself overwhelmed by the city, his studies, and his lodgings—consisting of what was surely the smallest room in the Harvard housing inventory. "What struck me then, and now," said Jim, "was how completely open [Tony] was to making friends with someone new on the scene, even though he had an amazing number of other friends with whom he kept in regular touch. He immediately took an interest in me, offering ideas for acclimatizing to the area. . . . At the end of my first year, as I was preparing day and night to take the one and only test in each of my five first-year classes, Tony brought a container of hot lentil soup to my dorm room to sustain me. It was an act of kindness quite extraordinary in retrospect, but quite typical of Tony."[4]

Kim Clark, current president of BYU-Idaho, arrived in Cambridge in 1967. The counterculture movement of the 1960s was flourishing in Harvard Square and its effects were felt within the university. "It was a really difficult year," said Kim of his freshman experience, when LDS undergraduates were few and far between. "I was far away from home. I'd never lived in a city like this and had never been in a place that was anything like this place." University policy required freshman to live on campus, but after walking into his room to find people cutting bricks of marijuana on his desk, Kim had reached his limit. Without saying a word, he packed his belongings and left. School records continued to show Kim as a resident of Harvard Yard, but he spent the remaining four months of the term at Tony's apartment. "He became a very good friend and tremendous mentor," President Clark stated. "The Institute program and church on Sunday were . . . my anchor. And Tony Kimball was the guy who kept everything together."[5]

Tony's intellectual curiosity and understanding of gospel principles left a similar impact. "He presented the gospel with such freshness as I had never seen before (nor often since)," Brother Wilson explained. Tony demonstrated time and again that the case for belief in the gospel of Jesus Christ was at least as reasonable as the alternative, but "one of his maxims," Brother Wilson continued, "was 'anything you can be reasoned into, you can also be reasoned out of.' Ultimately, spiritual knowledge came from a source that involved reason but subsumed in it an experience with the Spirit of God."[6]

Bill Cortelyou was baptized in 1974. "The one thing that [stands] out," said Bill of Tony's example, "was that you don't have to leave your brain at the door when you live the gospel. . . . You live charity, you live kindness, you live good, but you also think deeply, use your mind. . . . The gospel is the heart and the mind."[7] Said Jim Jardine, "His thoughtful faith inspired me and others to be better scholars, including gospel scholars."[8]

"He never ducked from tough questions," said another who attended Tony's priesthood class. "He would ask questions that he didn't know the answers to, and we could talk about these things." Because it was absolutely clear that Tony had a testimony and was committed to the gospel, Tony's students learned that they did not need to fear difficult questions. "That's a great lesson," finished the student.[9]

"Through the years," said Larry Wilson, "I have discovered that Tony Kimball touched the lives of many Harvard undergraduates, just as he had mine. In many respects, he was a guardian angel for those of us who were at a very formative stage of life."[10] A prolific correspondent, Tony did not lose touch when missions, schooling, or professions took individuals out of the area, and his home served as an informal reunion venue, allowing former residents of Cambridge to connect with others just embarking on their Massachusetts experience.

BYU law professor Cole Durham grew reflective as he attempted to summarize Tony's influence. One unique aspect, Brother Durham posited, was how Tony reflected and magnified the influence of others, constantly initiating introductions between individuals, communities, and even works of literature. "It is as though through Tony I had the influence not only of Tony himself, and his incredibly generous mentoring," said Brother Durham, "but also insight into countless others . . . who could help [my] efforts to understand the gospel in greater depth, without 'looking beyond the mark.'

"I wonder how much the kingdom depends on 'kingdom expanders' such as Tony," Brother Durham mused. "People who mediate to others and magnify in the memories of others the countless stories of the impact of Christ in the world: stories concerning which John wrote, 'if they should be written every one . . . even the world itself could not contain the books that should be written' (John 21:25)."[11]

Tony's arms-outstretched approach to individuals and ideas is worthy of emulation, but because we're forced to reconcile competing demands for our time and energy, the easier path encourages us to stay within familiar bounds. Commenting on "tokens of inclusion" within the Church, Doug Orton noted that "the natural human tendency is to turn inward." We seek friendships with people we admire and want to be like—someone who has characteristics, viewpoints, or a background we recognize. "But that doesn't help in a church context," Brother Orton pointed out. "What helps in a church context is to turn the other way. . . . Love for fellow man is different than love for self. Love for self tells us to go insular, to protect ourselves, to go with people whom we trust. Love for fellow man, I think, is to stretch, to test our limits, and see how comfortable we can be" with people who do not look or act like us.

We are too quick to categorize, Brother Orton suggested, specifically referencing our labels of "active" and "inactive." "Most of my life I've been intrigued by people who are active on some dimensions and inactive on other dimensions. I always thought there should be a larger range. . . . We are a relatively black-and-white boundary kind of church. People are either in and they have temple recommends, lots of kids, they pay tithing, they believe everything, or they're out. . . . In real experience being a member, I think most of us are fringe and we're passing for central. We pretend that we're 100 percent active, but all of us [feel] guilty that we're not doing more." We acknowledge our admonition to bring the gospel to all the world, but our behavior, Brother Orton proposed, often suggests "that we really don't want that many new members, because that taxes our capacity to love, it taxes our capacity to have a routine that we're settled into."[12]

When we put artificial boundaries on the reach of the Lord's kingdom, we deny ourselves opportunities to discover truth and may inadvertently alienate those earnestly seeking the good part who do not fit within our self-defined strictures.

## A Receptive Mind

Notwithstanding the familiar phrase "the glory of God is intelligence" (Doctrine and Covenants 93:26), a wariness occasionally surfaces in discussions regarding faith and reason. If there is anything designed to challenge, it is the process of question and examination followed in most universities. With over fifty institutions of higher learning in the Boston area, it is an appropriate place to test the compatibility of intellectual inquiry with the experiment upon the Word that Alma taught (see Alma 32:26–43). The very reemergence of the Church in Boston began in 1891 with a small group of Saints who came east for schooling. As a result, observed Tony Kimball, "You had [an] unusual group of people coming back who were characterized by an appreciation for intellectual inquiry and who were willing to experiment, to try and do things the best way, who are always questioning. . . . That may be the primary influence on the Church culture in Boston."[13]

Within area congregations, said Richard Bushman, skepticism "simply didn't ever dominate or ever become very pervasive. . . . The tone of . . . meeting[s] was always very faithful, very inquisitive. There were no holds barred on anything that was to be discussed. No sense of off-balance subject, but always the presumption of faith and conviction."[14]

"If you keep your covenants," said Loren Dunn of the pursuit of faith and knowledge, "you can have it all. . . . If you start making choices, if your intellect gets ahead of your testimony, then you begin to limit yourself to the opportunities. . . . As long as you can keep your priorities straight, from a Church point of view, it's great."[15]

We do not need to fear for truth or its pursuit, but we need to remember its source, and seek after it with humility. Brigham Young once said, "We believe in all good. If you can find a truth in heaven, earth or hell, it belongs to our doctrine. We believe it; it is ours; we claim it."[16]

## The Power of a Good Question

Toward the end of his life, Dr. Talmage Nielsen of Salt Lake City was asked what he had taken away from his years of study in Cambridge, many decades previous. "I came personally to reverence the question," he responded. At the college he had attended in the West, the emphasis had been on the answer and knowing how to supply it. Out east, in contrast, "the orientation . . . was to ask a good question because the answers to a good question keep changing. The good question leads to those answers.

"I began to realize," Dr. Nielsen explained, "that even the dispensation of the fullness of times was ushered in on a very good question that was long in being asked: . . . 'Which church should I join?'"

The key, Dr. Nielsen stressed, is the intent of our inquiry. "If your basic orientation is to be a skeptic . . . [or] purpose for inquiry is to destroy an idea," he warned, "it will lead you nowhere. If you [follow] Moroni 10:5, you're asking with real intent and wanting to know sincerely, a question will never lead you into falsehood. It will always lead you on the right path."[17]

Asking good questions is an essential skill in our quest to understand truth. Modern revelation reminds us that we "are commanded in all things to ask of God" (Doctrine and Covenants 46:7). The importance of questions is so great that it is the first thing missionaries teach investigators after introducing the Book of Mormon.

"Living the gospel needs a lot of explaining," said Ruth Ray Kelleher bluntly. "It needs a lot of personalizing. It needs a lot of communication with the Lord to know exactly what [it] means. . . . Blind acceptance is sometimes in ignorance, not in knowledge. I think if we just accept things blindly without backing it up or supporting it with knowledge of our own study, our own prayers, our own striving to understand what we're accepting, then something's going to pop us off that block and you can run into some problems."[18]

Learning to ask questions that will lead to truth is, itself, an exercise in humility and spiritual discernment. Relating an experience that gave him an appreciation for this process, Kent Bowen told of a fireside given by Boyd K. Packer, who served as president of the New England Mission during the Vietnam Era. President Packer took questions from those at the meeting, some of whom were growing impatient with the Church's unwillingness to take a public stand on the unpopular conflict. As the questions progressed it was clear the congregation was of two camps—those who sympathized with the anti-war movement and those who professed a duty to support the country's leaders. The discussion was getting divisive, recalled Kent, when a brother in attendance "asked one of the most spectacular questions. It stuck with me all of these years. He stood up and said, 'Well, President Packer, we're all here and we're asking all kinds of questions, but what questions should we be asking?'

"It was just a profound notion," President Bowen reflected, "that if you come to learn from someone who is very wise, you come with all this energy and your agenda, but the real . . . insight is to ask, 'What questions should I ask?' I thought many times as a teacher or [in] a leadership role, if we all learned to ask those questions, then we'd all be way ahead."[19]

The Savior did much of His teaching by responding to and asking questions of His followers and critics. Precisely because His audience did not always ask the right questions, His answers, often in parables, addressed the subject of the inquiry while providing greater substance for those willing and humble enough to search deeper.

Mimmu Hartiala-Sloan joined the Church in Finland. As a teenager she attended a Sunday School class composed primarily of converts. The class had many questions. The teacher was not always sure of the answers and approached the mission president for advice. The next Sunday the entire class was invited to the president's home, where he responded to questions and addressed the role of inquiry in the gospel. "He said to us it is very important to ask questions," said Mimmu, but advised that "you need to be able to evaluate whether these things are that important . . . by asking another question. That question is, 'Does this affect your salvation or not?' If it does, then you put all your energies and focus into that until you find the answer. But if it doesn't, and most of the questions in life that we ask really do not affect our salvation, then you can put those . . . [on] the back burner.

"[That advice] has been very, very good for me," Mimmu observed. "When I find myself getting very excited about something that seems so wrong or so right . . . I ask myself, does this affect my salvation? If it doesn't, then it is really not worth that much."[20]

When we ask questions in the spirit of humility, we acknowledge that we do not have all the answers but are willing to learn. One of the greatest experiences, said Elder Robert Wood of his service as a general authority, is to sit with the members of the Twelve when a question comes up where the answer is not clear. "I've had this in meetings with Elder Packer," Elder Wood went on, "and the answer he gives is 'I don't know. I just don't know. . . . I can wait. There are some things we don't know, we don't understand.'

"That takes a high degree of confidence," said Elder Wood, and an understanding that "you don't have to have every answer to every question. You just need the key answers to the key questions, and that we have. . . . Therefore we can accommodate intellectual, rational discussion, observation, [and] study."[21]

## A Receptive Heart

The same confidence that assures us the gospel can withstand inquiry increases our ability to accept and embrace those whose ideas and behaviors are different than our own. Congregations where this confidence is present have a broad tolerance for different views, Richard Bushman observed. "No one was upset or troubled if someone had a crazy idea," he said. "They didn't feel challenged by it. On the other hand, there was a steady confidence that if you just wait and think about it, you'll realize that the truth of the world is right here in this gospel." Referencing his college experience, Dr. Bushman said, "We felt like once we had created this little nest of people who believed in the doctrine, we trusted each other's belief in the doctrine."[22]

Karl Haglund expressed appreciation for others' commitment to fundamental gospel principles, which manifests itself in "the love that members . . . have for an enormous range of people inside and outside of the Church." That love, he continued, results in a congregation "that takes in many sorts of people and has room for many different beliefs or for people who are still . . . sorting out what they believe." On a personal level, Bishop Haglund noted, this communal experience had enlarged his own perspective. In worshipping with people who saw things differently, he was less prone to assume his opinions were correct and, at times, felt prompted to reconsider and reexamine his own views. "I think it has made my own beliefs stronger."[23]

"During my life," said Robert Fletcher, "I have had a few major experiences with the Holy Ghost, which I tend to treat as milestones in my spiritual development." The first such experience occurred during World War II, while he pursued studies and research in Massachusetts. Robert had served in several capacities within the Cambridge Branch when he was called to serve as a branch missionary in 1944, a role in which he was expected to supplement work that would normally be done by full-time missionaries who were unavailable due to the war. Asked to proclaim the gospel, Robert struggled with doubts he harbored about the truth of the message he'd been asked to share. With regret and embarrassment, Robert asked for a release.

What happened after the release had lasting effects. "When I found I couldn't continue with my branch mission because of a weak testimony," Brother Fletcher said, "I was not treated as a heretic, but . . . continued to receive calls to serve [including as a] Gospel Doctrine teacher and second counselor in the Atlantic District Presidency. I met my fiancée at the branch, married, went on to graduate school at MIT, and had two children before leaving Cambridge. I finished this period of my life with a firm commitment to live the gospel as taught by the Church as well as I knew how."[24]

When James Lyon entered Harvard College in 1952, his parents worried he would lose his testimony. Not only were their fears not realized, but James was also called to serve as the first bishop of the University Ward fifteen years later. Associating with people who were "learned and smart and faithful" had influenced him for good, and this combination proved just as potent for others in the University Ward. In the four years spent shepherding his flock, said Bishop Lyon, "We never had a Latterday Saint undergraduate . . . who was active when he [or she arrived] who went inactive." In contrast, he recalled many young adults who came to the area having already fallen into inactivity as teenagers. "They'd come out and check the waters," the bishop explained, "and we had literally dozens that came back to activity." They didn't reach everyone, Bishop Lyon acknowledged. "But if they were active when they came, they stayed active. [And ] many [were] brought back into activity because . . . they felt comfortable in the Church—many of them for the first time in their lives."[25]

Judy Dushku happily acknowledged her liberal viewpoint and tendency to challenge the status quo. That said, Judy admitted to struggles with Church leaders she felt would have preferred her to act and think differently. "That was hard for me," Judy confessed, "but that's been the exception." Most of her leaders made her feel not only tolerated, but also loved and embraced. "I think that that happens all over the Church," Judy stated. "I don't necessarily think it's unique to Boston, but possibly there's a bit more of an atmosphere of wanting to accommodate different people."[26]

A profound example occurred when Sonia Johnson, a vocal feminist and critic of the Church, made national news for her excommunication in 1979. Although Judy was not acquainted with Sonia Johnson, she was distressed, wondering what repercussions this event might portend for her own opinions. In the midst of this internal turmoil, Bishop Gordon Williams phoned and asked Judy if she would meet with him Sunday. Full of trepidation, Judy wondered how to respond if her bishop broached the topic of excommunication. She need not have worried. As soon as she sat down, Bishop Williams smiled and said, "I just wanted to talk to you to let you know how much you're appreciated in the stake and in the ward, and how much we need you. . . . And just to let you know that we love you and we care for you."

Pondering that interchange years later, Judy was still touched. "What a sensitive man that would know that I was sitting home in my living room being stressed over the whole issue of feminism and the Mormon Church. And he just called me as my bishop to tell me I was fine. That was one of the sweetest things. I've always remembered that."[27]

When Christ passed through Samaria and paused at Jacob's well, he encountered a woman who had had five husbands and was living with a man to whom she was not married. Such a history would raise eyebrows today, as it did then. Her presence at the well at midday evidenced her status as an outsider in society, yet it was to her that the Savior bore His first recorded witness that He was the Messiah. She, in turn, bore witness of the Savior to her townsmen, many who came to believe upon Him (see John 4:5–42).

In a conversation with his stake president, a branch president complained about a man within his congregation who sported a number of piercings and an unconventional haircut, but often participated in blessing the sacrament. Offended by the brother's appearance, he burst out, "Should those people really be in sacrament meeting and blessing the sacrament?" The stake president responded simply, "I can't think of any place they should be other than sacrament meeting."[28]

Whether influenced by real or perceived differences, how many of our brothers and sisters leave the Church because they do not believe they have a place within our congregations? Whatever it is that causes exclusion, we must find ways to focus on "tokens of inclusion" that really count. The work of the Lord requires more "kingdom expanders" and fewer gatekeepers. While there are many ways to reach out and enlarge our boundaries, the following accounts provide a few examples where groups of Saints have addressed potentially divisive differences that have helped to strengthen the whole.

### Sisters in Zion

The anti-war protests and women's movement of the late 1960s and early 1970s ushered in an era during which there was enormous pressure for women to redefine themselves. As the dialogue grew more strident, Mormon women, in particular, felt caught in the crossfire. "There was so much change taking place about the role of women that it was a very complex time and women needed support," remarked Grethe Peterson. "We were all somewhat conflicted about going to a party at Harvard and having a professor say, 'Well, you mean to say, all you are doing is taking care of children?' As though that was not enough."[29]

As social discourse bounded from one argument to the next, a dozen or so LDS women began meeting together to share thoughts and ideas in an attempt to understand how the public debate affected their personal aspirations. With children and babies in tow, "we talked and talked and talked and didn't get through talking. We decided to meet the next week and the next and the next," said Laurel Ulrich.[30]

An Institute class focusing on women in Church history was initiated, involving many of the same women. Because there was no existing curriculum, the first semester was spent researching selected topics and individuals, in order to share the results during the second semester. Taking advantage of resources available to them, a number of women began meeting at Harvard's Widener Library. Waiting to convene one day amidst the library stacks, a sister grew curious about the volumes in the bookcase she was leaning against and opened one. The group was stunned to find copies of *The Woman's Exponent*, a monthly newspaper published by Mormon women in Utah from 1872–1914, which became an influential platform for women's rights and suffrage. None of the Cambridge sisters had heard of the publication or were aware of its existence.[31] Describing the moment when they realized what they had found, Judy Dushku said, "For all of us it was like a spiritual experience." To have such a treasure delivered at such a time, "it seemed like the heavens were opening."[32]

Inspired by the work of their predecessors and anxious to share things they were learning and discussing, several women felt impressed to write about their experiences to make sense of the changes and continuities in their lives and reach women outside their immediate circle. Linda Hoffman Kimball, who joined the Church in college, found the outspoken, lively, and bright women behind the women's Institute class and new publication a remarkable fringe benefit of being a Latter-day Saint. "This is a wonderful, wonderful place to be and so exciting to be a woman in this group, in this Church," Linda thought. "It is so much how God wants us to be." Others worried about the publication and the agenda it might promote. Shaking her head ruefully, Linda acknowledged this conflict. "Boy, surprise, surprise, when I . . . found out that there are other ways to view what women can and should do."[33]

While some individuals involved in the paper fell away from the Church, others credited the group for providing a forum for discussion and strengthening women who might otherwise have felt marginalized.[34] No matter where women sat on the public debate, suggested Laurel Ulrich, LDS women shared more commonalities than differences. "By definition," she observed, "if you are a Latter-day Saint woman, you are committed to preserving some very important values like family, motherhood, the value of domestic life, [and] the importance of ordinary people."[35]

By the late 1980s, the fervor around women's rights had receded, but there were still concerns and issues, some of which were playing out in Church meetings. Attuned to currents within the Boston Stake, stake Relief Society President Helen Claire Sievers approached Mitt Romney in his capacity as stake president and stated bluntly, "We're offending many sisters . . . by doing things that are culturally acceptable, that we've done for a long time, but that are not part of the gospel."

Respectful of Helen Claire's insights and recognizing the need for a different approach, President Romney called a meeting for all adult members of the stake. The appointed night arrived, and the chapel was packed. Conducted as a group council, the assembly convened to discuss issues impacting women's participation in the Church and what members of the stake, both male and female, could do to be more inclusive.

President Romney and President Sievers shared responsibility for the meeting and placed a number of blackboards at the front of the room. "We're going to put three columns on these boards," President Romney explained. "One column is for things that we do in our stake that we can change and that we should change to make people feel more comfortable here. The second . . . column [is] for things that are doctrinal that . . . we can't change. The last [is for] things which may not be doctrinal, but they are things that are decided by people outside our stake who we follow and respect as leaders that we also can't change, and won't change." While Helen Claire Sievers led the discussion, President Romney manned the chalkboards and determined which column a comment fell into so the group could avoid spending time on items that could not be changed.

More than 100 suggestions were offered. "Many of them were suggestions about things that we couldn't do anything about," Mitt Romney admitted. "But the majority were things that we could do something about—things that we just never thought of." Where there was no good reason for the status quo, practices changed.

"I think that diffused, to a great extent, the tension that a lot of people felt about women's issues in our stake," said President Romney of the evening's lasting effects. By providing an outlet for valid concerns to be raised and discussed, the meeting strengthened dedication to gospel teachings. "We never had any interest in changing anything that the Church had taught us," he emphasized, but rather "those things that we were doing culturally that had nothing to do with the gospel."[36]

Today's discussions take different forms, yet choices regarding education, career, marriage, and family still divide, particularly when we assume our shared foundation of faith should lead everyone to the same conclusions. With many options come many questions. Jenny Atkinson reflected on the struggles she'd faced in determining the ways her faith should shape the details of her life. In doing so, she found comfort in women who could listen without reproach and help her work through questions in a gospel context. Relief Society can provide that support, Jenny observed. "I don't see a lot of places in the world where people who are different [can] come together and really talk. . . . In some ways [sisters'] lives are really different, but they come together to worship God and figure out how to love each other."[37]

As a ward and stake Relief Society president, Laraine Wright found it essential to make sure all lessons were centered in Christ. The only way for women to understand their individual purpose as daughters of God, she explained, was to study the scriptures and seek personal revelation from the Lord. "There really is no other way," she said simply. "No amount of debate—it doesn't work. . . . You have to have that testimony that the Lord loves you as a daughter." Concerned that too many were unable to attend Gospel Doctrine class on Sunday, the stake sponsored a women's scripture class, offered mornings and evenings. There was a noticeable change in spirit at the testimony meeting held among those who had participated at the end of the first year.[38]

In the class Nancy Dredge attended, Nancy accepted the instructor's challenge to keep a scripture journal and record thoughts as she studied. "It's been almost amazing what has happened to my understanding of the scriptures," she remarked, expressing similar appreciation for the ideas shared by the group in the class setting. "It just seems like my understanding of gospel concepts and principles has grown by leaps and bounds.

"The main thing I've come to understand," Nancy concluded, is Christ's teachings show us a way to be, rather than a way to do. "Really what you are inside is what counts."[39]

### Families of One

Chris Kimball was called as bishop of the Cambridge University Ward in 1994, a ward with over six hundred members of record and a high activity rate. Composed of students and professionals, the common congregational denominator was the unmarried status of its congregants.

The number of individual families within the ward made administration almost impossible and sacrament meeting regularly spilled out of the overflow and into the foyer. Faced with this reality, Bishop Kimball spent his first months on a recommendation for splitting the ward. After considering many options, he eventually settled on a split by age, resulting in the creation of an undergraduate student ward and a ward of graduate students and young professionals.

Bishop Kimball was excited to continue serving as bishop of the smaller ward, where all members were at least twenty-five years old. "Almost every topic that came up in the younger half of the University Ward I had been trained for," Chris explained, "[and] I could deal with based on things I had been taught [and my] experience in the Church." In contrast, many individuals within the older ward already understood those answers but were struggling with serious questions and challenges in their lives. "What I found most exciting and . . . most difficult," said Bishop Kimball of the young adults in their late twenties and thirties, "was that . . . almost to a person, their lives had not worked out the way they had expected. . . . They were having to reconsider and redraw."

Re-evaluation fostered self-criticism, often along the lines of "What have I done wrong?" People who followed patterns learned in Primary and youth programs were caught off guard when their lives did not map to the plan laid out. Bishop Kimball repeatedly met with members who had earnestly prepared for temple marriage. "It hasn't happened," they'd say. "And nobody ever talked about what I do with my life now."

There was a lot of loneliness, and individuals were making serious decisions in their lives, the bishop observed. One of those decisions involved church attendance. If a single adult found church unsupportive or perceived no benefit from attendance, he or she would often choose to pursue something they found more meaningful. "It was a phenomenon that didn't fit in the history of my training . . . about inactivity," Bishop Kimball explained, as such inactivity was not spurred by concern over doctrine or offense by a leader.

The lack of social structure for older LDS singles was another challenge. Family home evening groups and other activities that featured prominently in the operation of the younger ward were not as suited to the older congregation, where most members were involved in demanding programs and careers that provided fewer opportunities or reasons to gather the way students attending the same campus were able to do.

Seeking to establish a cohesive identity, the first order of business was a name for the congregation. When "Longfellow Park" was suggested during a ward council, it immediately resonated for all the things it did not say. "It was not a university ward," Bishop Kimball pointed out. "It was not a student ward, nor was it Cambridge. It wasn't geographical. It was single, but nobody wanted to be identified by that kind of label, [which] had a negative feeling."

With a name in place, the bishopric focused on making sacrament meeting the focal point of the ward. "That was the place we came together, that was the place the ward met," Bishop Kimball stated. "We wanted the sacrament meeting to be a place where everybody came and felt welcome. We wanted them to feel that it was an important and valuable meeting."

To support this goal, Bishop Kimball deliberately took advantage of the substantial talents within the congregation. A professional designer in the ward was asked to design a unique sacrament meeting program to emphasize the sacramental ordinance as the center of the meeting. A committee was formed to help the bishopric plan topics and speakers for meetings. By doing so, "we drew from a larger pool of speakers than if the bishopric had been doing it," said Bishop Kimball, and since people were usually given at least a month to prepare, "we had very thoughtful talks."

There were complaints. Some worried the ward was pulling away and "showing off" by forging its own identity. In a way, it was true, Bishop Kimball admitted. "The Longfellow Park Ward could field a remarkably good choir. We had . . . people done with school and with real capabilities. . . . By drawing out some of those abilities and allowing them to be exercised and . . . used, we could do some exciting things." But a unique positive identity was appropriate, the bishop asserted. With no families, youth programs, or Primary, "[t]here was a sense that the sacrament meeting is what we have, and we can do this well." So often the message congregants had received, intentionally or unintentionally, from other members was "You're single, so you're a problem."

"The sense that we tried to convey," he stated, "was that marriage was a good thing and if you had an opportunity to be married, that was good. But being a single adult was an okay thing by itself. . . . Part of the business of the ward and that community was to be figuring out and thinking about how you live as a moral, ethical, religious person in a community that mostly caters to families . . . [respecting] that some people might never be married. Even if they would someday be married, people at that stage in life needed to figure out a lifestyle, a life pattern, that wasn't desperately looking for marriage, [that] had some stability."[40]

While singles wards, by their nature, are attuned to "families of one," most single adults in the Church are dispersed among "family wards," an unofficial but common term that on its face suggests single adults are outliers. Whatever the cause in an individual case, the majority of single adults are not active in such congregations, and the number of active single women over thirty has outnumbered the number of active single men of the same age by five to one for many years. When you consider that approximately one third of adult members in the Church are single,[41] the magnitude of this loss begins to take shape. Although there are many reasons unmarried sisters and brothers fall to the side, one is certainly their substantial under-representation in callings and leadership positions, especially in areas where stakes enjoy an excess of talent.

Clayton Christensen was attending a bishops' counsel where the stake president expressed frustration that a number of stake callings were vacant because bishoprics had been unwilling to release individuals from ward assignments. As he listened, it was apparent to Bishop Christensen that stake leaders had never considered the University Ward as a source for such leadership.

"For some reason," Clayton stated, a view had developed "that the single adult members of the stake couldn't be relied upon to fulfill callings as consistently as the married members of the ward could." Well-acquainted with the abilities and commitment of those with whom he served, Bishop Christensen arranged to have one slot in each stake auxiliary reserved for a University Ward member. In addition, the University Ward agreed to supply stake missionaries to support smaller branches within the stake. Soon there were thirty single adults serving in stake capacities. Their dedication and ability were readily apparent, and a few years later a sister from the University Ward was called as Stake Primary President.[42]

As bishop of the Longfellow Park Ward some years later, Chris Kimball also saw that his ward needed expanded opportunities to serve. As he promoted the use of single adult members throughout the stake, Bishop Kimball felt he was "pushing out some of the best people I had. I think that was a good thing to do." Ultimately three of his counselors were called to the high council. "All three of them had extensive experience," Chris reiterated. "The only reason you might have hesitated . . . was that they were single. We got over that."[43]

"We gave them outstanding people to serve in those assignments and they did a wonderful job and I think taught the leaders of the stake an important lesson," said Bishop Christensen of their efforts to increase the utilization of singles within the Boston Stake. Unfortunately, he admitted, it is a lesson too often forgotten.[44]

### Same Gender Attraction

When a faithful returned missionary in the University Ward approached Bishop Christensen to confide that he was gay, Clayton was astonished. "I had actually not thought much about homosexuality," Clayton admitted. "When this wonderful, worthy young man told me that he was homosexual, I didn't quite know what to think. It was simply impossible for me to say that he was living in sin, because he wasn't. As he described how these feelings had begun emerging in him as early as age ten, it was also clear to me that this was not something that he had chosen for himself."

Over the next several months, a number of young men met with Bishop Christensen, sharing similar accounts. Filled with concerns and doubts, many simply wanted to know if their bishop still considered them worthy members of the Church. "As I talked with and got to know these young men, my whole attitude towards homosexuality changed dramatically," Bishop Christensen stated. "I studied the issue carefully, read as many things as I could about it, and prayed a lot to our Heavenly Father to know how I could help with these young men."

Seeking guidance to counsel those within his stewardship, Clayton realized that so long as these members kept their covenants, they were as worthy to go to the temple and to serve in Church callings as anyone else. Inviting each young man to fast and pray with him individually, Bishop Christensen knelt with all one-on-one. Together they petitioned the Lord that the young man would have the strength to obey the Lord's commandments, would always feel loved and accepted within the Church, and, if possible, would in time be able to marry and raise a family. "Subsequently, some of them have [married] and others have not," said Clayton. "But I'm very happy to say that each one of them with whom I was able to work has kept the faith and is a strong, active, contributing member of the Church today."[45]

After several months spent counseling individual members as to how same-sex attraction impacted their involvement and participation in Church matters, Bishop Chris Kimball determined this was a matter that required consensus from stake leadership. Carefully and thoughtfully, he prepared capsule summaries on a handful of situations that could be characterized as involving a sexual orientation issue. Once complete, he prepared a memo for the stake president, which posed a number of questions and recommendations as to how the stake should deal with such issues within the framework of the gospel.

After reviewing the memo, the stake president asked Bishop Kimball to meet with him so that they could discuss the issues and take them to the high council. "We talked about whether someone could be called on a mission . . . ; whether someone could have a church calling; whether someone could have a stake calling," Bishop Kimball recalled. As long as they were chaste and living in accordance with the moral code, the stake president affirmed, there was no problem. With some satisfaction, Bishop Kimball noted that not long afterward, a self-described gay man was called to a stake position.[46]

Following his release as a bishop, Clayton Christensen continued to seek statements by Church leaders on same sex attraction. His continued study supported the conclusions he initially drew as a result of personal study and prayer. Elder Dallin H. Oaks has said, so long as the homosexual feelings are kept under control, "a person with these inclinations . . . is eligible to do anything in the Church that can be done by any member of the Church who is single. . . . We welcome to that kind of service people who are struggling with any kind of temptation when . . . they are living so as to be appropriate teachers, or missionaries, or whatever the calling may be."[47]

"There is nothing sinful about having homosexual feelings or tendencies," Elder Christensen reiterated. "Learning this was, in fact, one of the greatest blessings of my service as bishop. . . . It subsequently has given me great pain when I've heard . . . disparaging comments about [such] people . . . by members of the Church."[48]

Describing his life before he was baptized, George McPhee remarked on the difference he immediately saw in Latter-day Saints. "They're clear, they're alive, they're bright, they're open, they're sparkling. And it's more than just physiologically—there's a receptivity to the world. It's a positive attitude and outlook that comes from faith."[49]

"That which is of God is light," the Lord revealed, "and he that receiveth light and continueth in God, receiveth more light" (Doctrine and Covenants 50:24). As followers of a God who speaks of worlds without number and descendants outnumbering the sands of the seas, it is clear the Lord does not recognize the limits and boundaries we are prone to impose on the breadth of his Kingdom. "Hearken," he instructs us, "for verily I say unto you, *all* those who receive my gospel are sons and daughters in my kingdom" (Doctrine and Covenants 25:1, emphasis added).

Dick Lavin was often asked how he dealt with all the differences within the multi-ethnic membership of the Boston Branch where he served as branch president and then bishop. In response, he always replied, "You asked the wrong question. We don't deal with differences. What we do is deal with what we have in common. That's the gospel of Jesus Christ. . . . We have our differences, we enjoy our differences. We're different people. Thank God for it. But the thing we have is the gospel, we just grow from that. It worked."[50]

While our differences are real and many, the Apostle Paul counseled us to be "likeminded one toward another according to Christ Jesus: That ye may with one mind and one mouth glorify God. . . . Wherefore receive ye one another, as Christ also received us to the glory of God" (Romans 15:5–7). Reviewing his remarks regarding "tokens of inclusion," Doug Orton recalled an individual who suggested the only inclusion tokens we need are a broken heart and a contrite spirit. "I think that's probably a better way to say what I was trying to say," he said, smiling.[51]

"Acceptance is . . . a major component of meekness," added George McPhee, as if finishing Brother Orton's thought. "I think that's a major component of what the Savior's message is to all of us. He accepted all of us."[52]

# 12

# IN THE WORLD

THE PHONE rang at 3:00 a.m. on August 1, 1984. Kent Bowen answered to hear his friend and neighbor, Gordon Williams, then president of the Boston Stake, say he'd received a call from the Belmont Fire Department. Hastily, Kent dressed and together they drove to the hill where the new Belmont meetinghouse was being constructed. The sky before them was illuminated by an intensely bright flame emanating from a familiar location. They arrived to see the inferno consuming the roof of the nearly completed structure.

Brokenhearted, the two watched the new copper steeple buckle from the heat. "I don't know when I've ever felt lower," Brother Bowen recalled. "So much had gone into that building."[1]

Mitt Romney, bishop of the newly formed Belmont Ward, called the Church Building Department to ask for direction. "We will communicate to our members and to the community that we will not be prevented in this work," came the answer. That afternoon, bulldozers arrived to knock down twisted steel and clear away remnants of the chapel, which had been destroyed by the fire. Trucks followed to haul away charred beams and building materials. Although the chapel's concrete foundation was badly stained, it was declared sound and suitable for rebuilding, and the classroom and cultural hall areas were deemed repairable.[2]

Investigations failed to pinpoint the cause of the blaze, but officials viewed it as "suspicious" from the outset, another casualty in a rash of church fires affecting the greater Boston area. For members in Marlboro, Massachusetts, a town twenty miles to the west, it was all too familiar. Their own meeting place, a stately old Episcopalian chapel purchased in 1979, had just been remodeled when arsonists destroyed the building in January of 1984.[3]

The loss stunned members of the Church and community alike. Although the Church had acquired several properties to support growth in membership, the Belmont chapel was the first LDS meetinghouse constructed in the area since the Cambridge chapel had been dedicated in 1956. Individuals in the affected congregations had worked, sacrificed, and saved for many years to raise the $300,000 required to launch the construction effort.[4]

Pressure to secure a new meeting place had come to a head in 1977. Three wards filled the Longfellow Park chapel to overflowing every Sunday, but the tipping point came with the passage of a by-law by the city of Cambridge that restricted on-street parking to residents only—a rule enacted to prevent commuters from parking their cars on local streets while they took the subway into downtown Boston. Although the restriction did not apply on Sundays, the effect was devastating to evening MIA activities, weekday Relief Society meetings, and afternoon Primary. The Church was allotted only five parking passes for use during the week, which meant members must park miles from the chapel or collect and pay fifteen-dollar parking tickets on a regular basis.

When meetings with residents living near the meetinghouse and a legal challenge failed to alleviate matters, Church leaders decided it was time to find a site for a new chapel. A demographic study conducted a few years prior showed the most rapid membership growth in the suburbs west of Cambridge, so attention quickly focused on towns within that area.[5]

Jan McKinnon was serving as Relief Society president of one of the Cambridge wards. In January 1978, she was asked to serve on a site selection committee and look for property that might accommodate a chapel in the Belmont area. No one she contacted was willing to talk with her about a potential purchase by the Church. Following a ward fast on behalf of those searching for land, Jan got lost driving home and took a route through Belmont that was new to her. In doing so, a sign posted on a tree caught her attention. Although she was alone, Jan distinctly heard a voice tell her to call that number. She stopped and wrote down the telephone number, even though there was no contact name and no mention of the land being for sale.

The phone was ringing as Jan walked in her door. Fellow ward member Nancy Walsh was calling to let Jan know that her family had noticed a sign on a tree during their Sunday afternoon drive. Knowing that the Walsh family had heeded the bishop's call to fast for guidance in finding suitable land for a chapel, Jan was not surprised that the number was the same one she had written down minutes before.

Any hesitation to call the number was gone. Jan's call resulted in a meeting with the owner, who said the land posted for sale would not be suitable for the Church's needs. The owner showed Jan some other parcels, but both agreed they were not large enough. "Then the miracle happened," said Jan. The owner produced a drawing of a seventeen-acre parcel that she also owned. The Church could acquire it, she offered, so long as they purchased the whole parcel. Although the Church needed only five acres, it must purchase all seventeen acres offered or none of them.[6]

Jan took the maps to the next committee meeting and they decided they needed a firsthand look. Walking onto the site for the first time, Jan recalled, "I knew that we were standing on sacred ground."

Convinced that the acquisition was appropriate, a proposal sent to Salt Lake suggested that the extra land could be used to accommodate anything from a mission office to a temple. The Church Building Department was not interested in these options, but after extensive discussion back and forth, Salt Lake agreed that the excess acreage could be held as investment property. The parcel was procured in February 1979.[7]

Initially, local leaders leaned toward placing the meetinghouse in the center of the parcel or atop the hill overlooking the Boston skyline, but as planning got underway a conscious decision was made to place the chapel on a low flat corner that presented the best options for site access. "I wanted to put that chapel on the highest outcropping of rock," said Mitt Romney of the stake presidency meeting where the site was discussed. President Williams shook his head and indicated it should be in the lower corner, despite the fact that no one would be able to see the chapel there. "Something told him, whispered to his spirit that . . . we should save that top corner," Brother Romney said in retrospect. This action left the majority of the parcel empty, including the highest spot atop the rocky ledge.[8]

Discussions with the town engineer and other community leaders went smoothly, as much thought and care had been put into the plans to meet existing building requirements. Ironically, the fly in the ointment was parking. While laws prohibited communities from zoning against construction of a church, the town of Belmont had an ordinance requiring a special permit for any project that required parking for more than three vehicles. As Church leaders began meeting with homeowners along the portion of the site designated for the chapel, it became clear that building a coalition among the neighbors would be onerous, if not impossible.

Patiently, members met with concerned individuals and small groups to explain what the Church needed. Architects and planners revised drawings many times to seek a solution that the neighbors would find acceptable. Just when it seemed that an understanding had been reached with enough parties to go forward, a zoning board meeting was held during which person after person stood to complain, falsely, that they'd been left out of the process and their concerns had been ignored. Within an hour, the support that had been laboriously collected evaporated.

When the Church's request for the needed permit was denied, the Church filed a lawsuit in desperation. Plans were revised once more and local leaders tried to meet with neighbors again, to no avail. Out of options, Bishop Bowen reached out to Bill Monahan, a member of Belmont's Board of Selectmen and a man Kent knew through his children's swim team. Bill was not naturally sympathetic to the Church, since one of his close friends lived adjacent to the planned chapel and was adamantly opposed to the project, but he recognized the Church's plight and agreed to attend a meeting to see if consensus could be reached. At Bill's suggestion, the impacted residents met on the site where construction for the chapel had already begun. Standing atop the flattened ground intended for parking, Church representatives offered to move the lot so that it was at least sixty feet from the borders of the surrounding home sites, ten times the six-foot buffer required by town regulations. "That seems reasonable," Mr. Monahan replied. When plans to shelter residents through landscaping were described, the selectman again declared the proposal reasonable. The neighbors were unusually quiet, as if embarrassed to disagree. After nearly three years of effort, the Church dropped its lawsuit and obtained the necessary permit.[9]

Given the time and effort that had gone into obtaining project approval, Kent Bowen took it upon himself to watch over everything happening on the building site and to see that any effect on the neighbors was anticipated and minimized. Kent walked the site almost daily, tracking the chapel's progress up until it was burned, just months before its scheduled October completion.[10]

The Belmont Ward briefly considered staying in the Cambridge chapel while the necessary reconstruction work took place, but the building's capacity was already taxed from housing four wards, a Spanish-language branch, and a Chinese-language branch. Knowing autumn would bring a large influx of students to further fill the Longfellow Park chapel, ward leaders decided to begin holding services elsewhere. The first Sunday the ward met in the Belmont Town Hall. Members of the new bishopric felt strongly that the tragedy was an opportunity from which blessings would flow.

Indeed, many in the community were horrified that such a crime could take place in their midst, and within days, Bishop Romney had received a number of calls and letters from other Belmont churches offering use of their facilities. Appreciative of this hospitality, Bishop Romney responded to each of the ministers and pastors who had offered their buildings, and the ward ultimately decided to accept the invitation of three local churches, realizing it would increase the Church's recognition in town and help members view their friends and neighbors in a different light as well. "While it would have been far more convenient to use just one building," Bishop Romney explained, "we decided to use every building where the facilities were sufficient for our needs." As a result, the ward spent three months meeting in a basement-level hall beneath a Catholic school, three months using the Plymouth Congregational church, and three months at the Protestant Armenian Church meetinghouse during the nine months of reconstruction. By rotating in this manner, more people would get to know and accept ward members as friends and vice versa. The public dispute over the Church's parking lot had created some bad feelings within the community, and this was an opportunity to make amends.[11]

"That was a great experience," said Bishop Romney. In return for the welcome extended to the Church, "we want[ed] to make sure anybody who attends one of these buildings [would say], 'Those people are the cleanest, neatest people we've ever seen in our life.'" Members regularly stayed behind after classes to pick up chairs, vacuum carpets, and wash blackboards. "Sometimes I worried that we might be compromising the Sabbath a little by the work we would do after Church," the bishop admitted, noting members often cleaned items they hadn't even used. "We made those churches . . . spotless."

"We didn't want anyone to think that we might have left a dirty blackboard behind," Bishop Romney explained. "It was a great thing . . . and it taught us respect for a building. . . . We have a beautiful building [in Belmont], but I think this building receives more respect as a result of the cleanliness with which we kept those other buildings."

These exchanges also brought opportunities for the Saints to see themselves through others' eyes. One Sunday when the ward was meeting at the Armenian Church, the pastor walked into the chapel to find ward members visiting in their normal fashion. She was horrified. The chapel contained an altar for which Protestant congregants showed respect by being quiet. "In the other faiths, they treat their chapel like a sanctuary. They call it a sanctuary," Bishop Romney pointed out. "When I recognized that she was offended . . . I made a much greater effort as bishop to ask our folks to be reverent. . . . It did teach us a sense of reverence."[12]

"It gave us a different feeling to hold church elsewhere," said Connie Eddington. "When we were in the Catholic school, my feelings immediately changed toward every Catholic I knew. Every time I would see one of my Catholic neighbors, I would tell him or her that we enjoyed meeting in their church. I really wanted to thank them for their kindness to us."[13]

"Many of us generated very close relationships with the people in these churches," remarked another ward member. "It was really quite remarkable how warmly received we were in the community as a result of that. Even now we still attend the Armenian Christmas service. . . . [The fire] served to bring the Saints together, but it served more importantly to bring the Church into the community. . . . It wouldn't have come about in any other way."[14]

"Sometimes members of our faith tend to think of ourselves as being quite separate," Bishop Romney remarked. "We have so many meetings and efforts that we do amongst ourselves, we don't have as much time to be involved with the religious community around us."[15]

In addition to literally opening their doors to the Saints, a number of Belmont churches held fund-raisers to assist with the chapel's reconstruction. So many people expressed a desire to help that the ward held a "fire" sale on the town commons where people could donate items to be sold, participate in games, and purchase baked goods. "We were very gratified by the response," said Don Eddington, who oversaw the event with his wife, Connie. "We did little advertising, yet we raised several thousand dollars."[16]

Reconstruction on the Belmont chapel was completed in March

1985, but the ward waited for landscaping and other finishing touches to be done before holding an open house in June to celebrate the chapel's completion and thank the community for its support. The theme chosen for the open house was "Strengthening Families and Leading Them Closer to Christ," and exhibits highlighting the Church's auxiliaries and programs were organized around this central idea. Over the course of the open house, nearly three thousand people came to see the new building, which led directly to one baptism and the eventual conversion of another family who became acquainted with the Church through their visit.[17]

While no one would wish for zoning troubles or the fires that destroyed the Marlboro building and delayed the Belmont meetinghouse's construction, these events served as a wake-up call. Sitting in a planning meeting during the struggle to obtain approval for the Belmont chapel's parking lots, Clayton Christensen recalled a moment when the assembled Church leaders realized they knew none of the town officials. With few exceptions, ward members were not involved in community affairs, and Clayton was struck by how few friendships ward members seemed to have outside the Church. "At the time we really were a very happy and a very insular group," he reported. "As ward mission leader it was clear to me that we could never be effective member missionaries if we were only friends with each other." [18]

The problem Clayton recognized among the Belmont Saints is not unique to that group. "As members of the Church, we are so busy in the Church, and it fulfills our social needs so effectively, that many of us don't even know our immediate neighbors," observed Grant Bennett.[19]

"A number of us . . . made a resolve that we would become very active in the community so that if another occasion arose when we needed to leverage our reputation and our contacts with town officials, we would have a reservoir of goodwill and understanding that we could draw upon," Clayton reported. "At the time we built the Belmont chapel, even though many of us lived in Belmont, we were very much regarded as an alien church and not as a community church." [20]

## The Savor of Salt

Insularity can be deliberate or inadvertent. As a long-time member of the Boston Stake used to say, however, "How do you expect to be an influence in the world if you are only at church?"[21]

"When we first moved here, we moved here with the idea . . . that once [our children] started school, we were going to move back to the west where it was safe to be," said Peggy Brown. "It wasn't until we got out here that I even met anybody that wasn't a member of the Church. You kind of grow up with the attitude that you are the only righteous people around. I think that was a big shock to me to come out here and actually meet people that weren't member[s] of the Church that were really, really good people. . . . That was a real eye-opener."[22]

"We moved to Belmont, to this strong Catholic town, where families were important," said Margaret Wheelwright of her time in Massachusetts. "We loved our Catholic neighbors with strong families, and grandparents and aunts and uncles. . . . with deep, deep roots."[23]

"Living in the mission field has been . . . the best thing our family has done," Kathy Bowen opined. "Having been brought up and raised in Utah, we were brought up with mostly members. [In Massachusetts] most of my children's friends in school were nonmembers. . . . It was fun to see the closeness in school friends that they had and that they will always have."[24]

We needn't worry that by strengthening relationships outside our faith, we'll be "somehow assimilated and destroyed by the contact," asserted Chase Peterson. Many groups maintain their identity by excluding things and people they see as threatening, he acknowledged, but those that maintain their identity and ideals while interacting in the mainstream of society are much more powerful. "It allows our bushel to be seen," he explained. "Our candles are not hidden."[25]

With this in mind, when the Christensen's oldest son was getting ready to join Cub Scouts, Clayton and Christine were one of several LDS families who deliberately enrolled their boys in the pack sponsored by the local elementary school rather than a Church-sponsored pack. Eventually an arrangement was made with the school's Parent Teacher Association to merge the school pack with the ward pack. The elementary school was undergoing extensive renovations, so the ward volunteered its new meetinghouse for pack meetings—an offer that was quickly accepted. "In the process," remarked Clayton, "hundreds and hundreds of members of the community regularly [went] to the Belmont chapel to attend Cub Scout events. This was a small thing, but I don't think it was insignificant. I think it helped many people become comfortable that the Mormon Church was a good institution that taught good values."[26]

As a result of what was ultimately a ten-year partnership, the elementary school's Scouting program was revitalized and members got to know neighbors in a different context. "During the two years that I served," said Kathy Bowen of her work with the Cub Scouts, "there was a lot of bonding as far as parents go. I think that bond will always be there. I think they appreciate what we stood for, and I appreciate what they stood for. That was very rewarding."[27]

"It's been the greatest place to raise kids," said Marianne Hopkin of her family's twenty-plus years in Massachusetts. "We've just been so impressed with the quality of the people . . . not just in the Church, but with our nonmember friends as well. . . . We really have never come across anyone at all who didn't respect us for our religion and how we were raising our kids. . . . People respected us for our beliefs, and I think they really supported our kids in their beliefs."

On one occasion, one of the Hopkins' daughters was given a reading assignment in freshman English class that included language and topics that made her uncomfortable. She approached the instructor to ask if she could read something else, knowing any other option would require her to do a lot of independent work. The teacher agreed to let her choose an alternative book. "It really impressed the teacher," said Marianne, "and . . . that teacher ended up giving her a recommendation when she was applying to BYU. It was an example of her not knowing what was going to happen but wanting to stand up for what she felt was right."

"I know there were challenges," Marianne continued, "but . . . being a minority [and] having to stand up for what you believe, and really knowing—not being like everyone else, but being uniquely different—makes you stronger. . . . The kids . . . have strong testimonies, and they know who they are. They don't have to be rebellious and different, because they're already different."[28]

A common challenge encountered by many was the number of sporting events held on the Sabbath—a problem familiar to LDS families everywhere. When the Hiers family moved to Massachusetts, their daughters wanted to play sports that often required Sunday play. One daughter was adamant about being on the swim team, but attending at least five out of eight meets was a requirement to compete. Only four of the meets were on Saturdays. "She was old enough to make her own decision," said Charlene Hiers. On the Sunday of the appointed fifth meet, Sister Hiers told her daughter she'd have to find her own way to the event, since the family was going to church. "She went [to the meet] and was miserable," Sister Hiers reported. "She learned very quickly that she didn't like the way it felt . . . being there.

"It was interesting that they had to stand out immediately," Sister Hiers said of her girls. "In a way, it was a good thing because it was okay to be different in that way. They earned respect from their friends because they were different. Their friends expected them to live by that code. They would have been disappointed if they chose to do something differently. . . . That made them stronger in a lot of ways. They could stand out."[29]

"It was difficult to not be able to play . . . games on Sundays, no matter what it was," said Dee Dee Williams of her children's experiences. Whenever team events were moved to Sundays, Dee Dee and Gordon pulled their children out and moved them to another sport still held on weekdays. After some time, an individual in the town recreation department approached Gordon to ask if he'd be willing to help start a basketball program for children in elementary and middle school. For over twenty-five years Gordon served as president of the Belmont Youth Basketball Association, during which time a number of members provided support by serving as coaches and board members, ensuring there was at least one sport for children on Saturdays.[30]

Dottie LaPierre was amazed by the attention her children's decision not to play sports on Sundays garnered. One son's choice not to run on Sunday was written up in the newspaper three times. As her boys left on missions, their relationships with people in town continued. Whenever she worried why they didn't write home more often, someone in the community would approach her saying, "Your son just wrote [me] this unbelievable letter. Can you believe a nineteen-year-old could write this letter?" Ultimately she determined her sons were serving their missions at home and abroad. "I think our children are going to be our biggest missionary tools," she stated simply.[31]

"I just think being in such a small, cohesive town as Belmont, and being involved so much in the schools . . . is such a blessing," said Margaret Wheelwright. Sports, drama, and other activities all provided the family an opportunity to share their values and live their religion, whether participating in parent associations or supporting an activity from the sidelines. "For our kids, that made a big difference," said Steve, "because they . . . saw us as not separate from the town because we were Mormons, but very much [part of] the town."

"That is the best thing I can imagine," Margaret continued. "I can't think of any place I would rather have raised my kids than here, being a minority standing out in a crowd because of what we believe. . . . It made our kids better."[32]

## Living the Gospel Visibly

In 1998, the Belmont Ward was split in a way that fundamentally changed its demographics and left a membership that was 95 percent active. Home and visiting teachers had only one assigned family, two at the most. Filling callings was not a challenge, and welfare needs were minimal. Confronted with this new reality, Bishop Grant Bennett worried the ward membership would grow complacent—something he was sure the Lord did not want. Seeking ways to stretch, the bishopric asked each family in the congregation to prayerfully consider what the Lord would like the Belmont Ward to do. Taking this counsel to heart, approximately three-quarters of the ward penned one or more thoughts to the bishopric.

Suggestions were presented and discussed in ward counsel. The emerging theme came to be known as, "Living the gospel in the community," representing the idea that the members should not keep the gospel to themselves but live their religion visibly and share their beliefs with those around them. Each ward auxiliary and quorum was challenged to identify two activities that could be expanded or adapted to involve and benefit nonmembers. Individuals were asked to find personal outlets for participation in the community, whether that meant caring for a family outside the Church or becoming involved in a town organization.

"One of the things the Church does for all of us," observed Bishop Bennett, "is it gives us an opportunity to serve others in an organized, structured way." Realizing that, members of the ward began looking for ways to use that infrastructure to serve more people. In particular, members were asked to identify the things they found most meaningful in their Church activity and consider how those same things could be valued by others in the community.

Bishop Bennett was in a meeting with the manager of the local Council on Aging when he learned that the volunteer coordinators who ran the area Meals on Wheels program struggled to maintain routes when regular drivers got sick or went on vacation. Carefully, the bishop described the Relief Society organization and its emphasis on compassionate service. Such service was not limited to members of the Church, he explained, but encompassed anyone in need. Using the structure already in place, the

Belmont Relief Society produced a list of volunteers for the community group, many of whom became vital to the Meals on Wheels program.

Priesthood quorums discussed the purpose of home teaching through the ward's expanded lens. As a practical matter, many concluded having a home teacher meant you had someone to call for a ride to the airport, for assistance in times of illness, or for other temporal support. Since ward assignments were light, members were asked to consider picking a non-member family to serve in ways they would typically assist their home teaching families.

Brett and Ann Wunderli had come to know a family through their children's school. Inviting them over for dinner, Brett and Ann proceeded to explain the home teaching program and the challenge they had been given. "We would like to home teach you," they said at the end.

"It's okay with us," the couple answered with some bewilderment, "as long as you let us home teach you in return."

Soon Brett learned the family they'd chosen was moving apartments. "Don't do anything other than declare the day!" he exulted. "This is what we do best. This is what home teachers do."

That Sunday, Brett circulated a sign-up sheet in priesthood, announcing that his nonmember home teaching family was moving from the first floor to the second floor in their apartment building. The response was overwhelming and everyone showed up promptly at 8:00 a.m. on the appointed Saturday. Unbeknownst to the group, the wife held a staff position at Harvard Business School. When several prominent faculty members including Kim Clark, the school's dean, walked in to move her boxes and laundry baskets upstairs, she almost fell over in astonishment. The size of the volunteer contingent resulted in a move finished in record time.

The next Sunday, two large floral arrangements sat prominently in the chapel. "We are new to this home teaching stuff and don't quite know how to say thank you," the accompanying note read, "but we thought we would start by sending flowers." Although the family did not join the Church, they became regulars at many ward functions and became familiar with many members of the congregation. "Clearly," said Bishop Bennett, "their life is better as a result of the Wunderlis stepping up and doing home teaching."[33]

Grant Bennett was well positioned to lead his ward's efforts to reach out to the community. Shortly after the fire that destroyed the Belmont chapel, Grant received a call from a sister in the ward who wanted to know if Grant could fill in for her husband at a meeting at the Armenian

Church. The woman was unsure of the meeting's purpose, but Grant agreed anyway. When he arrived, Grant introduced himself to the first man he saw, the minister of a local Lutheran congregation. The man confirmed the spelling of Grant's name and the meeting began.

The event proved to be the annual meeting of the Belmont Religious Council, a nondenominational ecumenical group formed to represent religious perspectives in town affairs and foster greater appreciation for and among different faiths in the area. The agenda included the election of officers for the next year, and Grant was more than a little surprised when his own name was presented for the position of recording secretary. Grant wasn't sure what the group did, but he had a strong feeling this was a wonderful opportunity. Thus began Grant's association with the Council, which lasted twenty years and set a pattern for active participation by local wards that continues today. "As we have gotten involved in [Council] events," he remarked, "it is very clear to me that several people have formed some very close friendships. More importantly, I think, it provides an opportunity for people to see us as we are."

One such opportunity occurred when the Belmont Religious Council sponsored a youth trip where teens rehabilitated homes in a poverty-stricken area of West Virginia. A number of churches had wanted to sponsor a significant youth event, but lacked the critical mass to do so alone. Working together, a Jewish rabbi and a minister from the local Congregational Church agreed to lead a joint project and six youth from the Belmont Ward chose to participate.

Before the group left, the rabbi called Grant. One purpose of the trip, he said, was to help those youth attending gain a greater appreciation for other faiths. With that in mind, could Grant help the LDS participants prepare a short devotional for one of the evenings they were away? Grant readily agreed. He called a young woman in the ward, relayed the assignment, and asked her to think about a devotional, noting it should be simple and informal.

The six young women and young men who went on the trip chose to share portions of King Benjamin's address on service and sing the hymn "Because I Have Been Given Much." Their efforts and insights made such an impression that upon the group's return to Belmont, the Congregationalist minister immediately called Bishop Bennett. "That was perhaps the highlight of the entire trip," he said. "You must have worked for hours with them."

Assuring his friend that he could not take the credit, Grant responded,

"I made a quick phone call and what you see is what you get."

A few months later the minister called to say he'd had the most marvelous experience delivering computers to a Head Start program. An LDS youth had seen a need during their trip and his parents responded by donating the computers. "I have never quite met people who were so willing to help," the minister explained.

"[It's] an example of the kind of interaction that I think really breaks down barriers," Grant stated. "As the Church rises out of obscurity . . . it does not do it with power or fanfare, but in the most important ways, through one-on-one contact."[34]

## Coming Full Circle

In 1995, a temple was announced for Boston, Massachusetts, which would be built on the extra land purchased in Belmont over fifteen years prior. Many ward members had taken on visible roles in community organizations since that time and felt the Church had gained much ground in terms of community support. Speaking of his own involvement in town policies, Brother Christensen said, "I got to know scores of the prominent citizens and they got to know me."[35]

As soon as preliminary plans for the temple were available, a series of meetings were held in members' homes for neighbors of the affected property. "All of those meetings were wonderful," said Bishop Bennett. "We felt nothing but support. Then the zoning hearings began." Thinking they'd given every neighbor an opportunity to comment and weigh in, local Saints were unprepared for the strident opposition raised.

It quickly became obvious that a small group of people had gone door-to-door spreading factually incorrect information regarding the Church and its temples. The underlying theme of their message was that the LDS Church and its leaders were not truthful, and any assurances they provided could not be trusted.

The Church's temple department had asked Grant Bennett to form a local committee to act as a liaison with neighbors and represent the Church at zoning board hearings as it sought necessary building permits. A key question at the outset of the proceedings was whether the Church would insist on answering only those questions related to the issues before the zoning board or whether it was willing to respond to broader inquiries. "We felt very strongly," said Bishop Bennett, "that what we needed to do was answer any question that was asked."

The zoning board was pleased with the Church's willingness to engage in a wider dialog, as its members wanted to provide citizens an opportunity to ask any questions they had during the process. The resulting public hearings were lengthy with many speakers. After the Church made its presentation, those opposing the project would present their perspective, following which attendees were free to ask questions or make statements of their own. Traffic and lighting attracted attention, as did the height of the proposed steeple. Some concerns were sincere and well-founded, while others bordered on ludicrous, such as the presentation that suggested the steeple would create a hazard for birds and cast a shadow causing icing on roads, resulting in traffic accidents.[36]

There were always many questions. "It gave us repeated opportunities to describe what a temple is," Bishop Bennett noted. "It gave us lots of opportunities, when outlandish claims were made, to answer respectfully [and] show a willingness to . . . collect additional information."

As the hearings continued, Bruce Olsen, director of public affairs for the Church, paid a visit to Boston and met with editorial staff at the local newspapers. In preparation for those meetings, Brother Olsen encouraged local Saints to identify a third party who could tell their story and serve as an authenticator for the Church. Bishop Bennett's years of service on the Belmont Religious Council allowed him to pick up the phone and call his good friend Victor Carpenter, minister of the Unitarian church in Belmont and former minister at the Unitarian Universalist Association's headquarters in downtown Boston. Victor's response was immediate when he was asked if he would be willing to accompany the group as they talked to the media: "Absolutely, absolutely." Victor Carpenter sat in on each meeting, and his insistence that the Church should be allowed to construct a temple greatly influenced the long-term tone of the press.[37]

Throughout the process, leaders worked to assuage concerns. When traffic issues arose, the Church hired a traffic consulting firm to collect hard data on traffic patterns around the Atlanta, Orlando, and Dallas temples. When lighting questions were raised, a lighting firm was engaged to take light intensity readings of all the churches in town. In every case, temple landscape architect Jerry Brown said, "We met all the requirements. We went above and beyond."[38]

Initially, the proposed temple was designed as a 94,000-square-foot building with six spires, the tallest of which would rise 159 feet, an exception to the town's 72-foot height limitation. The Belmont zoning board granted the application for a special permit, but the Church continued to evaluate community concerns and determined to scale the temple back to a 70,000 square-foot structure with a single 139-foot spire. Although some still felt they did not go far enough, many neighbors were pleased by the changes. The proposed modifications were unanimously approved by the Belmont zoning board in a twenty-seven-page opinion that followed twelve public hearings held over a nine-month period.[39] "At the end of this whole process," said Bishop Bennett, "all of the key decision makers in town had 100 percent confidence in the credibility of the Church. They had concluded that the Church . . . was simply an organization with deep and fundamental integrity and that there really wasn't any gamesmanship going on. It was an environment that allowed . . . the town leaders [to bear] the brunt of some of the extreme opposition during the construction phase."[40]

"I don't think anyone ever doubted that we would get permission," Jerry Brown stated after approval had been granted. "It was just a matter of *when* as opposed to *if*. We followed all the laws and met all the requirements. Once you cut through all the rhetoric and misinformation that was put out, everything we've done . . . [has been] in keeping with what we should have done or what we were required to do."[41]

Controversy over the temple did not end with the zoning board's decision, despite the extensive public hearings. Two lawsuits were filed, the first of which challenged the zoning board's decision to grant the special permit allowing the steeple. The second challenged the temple in its entirety by asserting that a 1950 Massachusetts law known as the Dover Amendment violated the US Constitution's separation of church and state by exempting religious groups, schools, day care centers, and other groups from certain zoning regulations.[42]

Throughout it all, the support offered by other religious groups in the community was widespread and even enthusiastic. When discussions grew heated, it was often clergy from other sects who wrote letters to the newspapers and corrected misunderstandings among their own congregations.[43] Victor Carpenter, the Unitarian minister and friend of the Church, called Bishop Bennett in frustration one day. "Grant, I have had it," he stated. "There are still people in our congregation who believe that the temple shouldn't be built. I need to preach on this topic from the pulpit. The topic of my sermon is going to be entitled 'Mormons among Us.' I am working on it right now. . . . Would you come by? I want to make sure that some of the facts I have are correct."

"He had done an enormous amount of research," Bishop Bennett recalled. "We talked at great length about Joseph Smith and about certain doctrines of the Church. He is a true friend."

On the appointed Sunday, Grant attended the service with Kent Bowen. The assistant minister introduced the topic, describing a remarkable religious experience of a young man from New England named Joseph Smith and summarized the coming forth of the Book of Mormon. The choir sang "Come, Come, Ye Saints," following which Victor Carpenter presented a powerful sermon, describing Church teachings and beliefs in greater detail. Concluding his message, he stated unequivocally, "We welcome the Mormons. Anyone who subscribes to the creed of the Unitarian Universalists absolutely welcomes the Mormons."

Foregoing the regular adult Sunday School class, the minister asked his LDS guests if they would stay and answer questions. It was astonishing to Bishop Bennett, given the educated nature of the parishioners, how many strange misconceptions still existed. The positive, he noted, was that "it again provided a forum to answer some basic questions. Every time we have an opportunity to communicate what the real story is, they say, 'That's great.'"[44]

Construction on the temple commenced despite the legal challenges pending in court. On one day alone, an individual leading the opposition called the Belmont Board of Selectmen eight times to complain about alleged construction and noise violations. Fortunately, the Church's conduct throughout the lengthy approval process had assured those charged with enforcing the laws that if they made any request, the Church would do its best to comply. This confidence allowed construction to move forward in the face of extreme actions, including a suit brought against the Belmont police for not enforcing noise ordinances (ultimately thrown out as frivolous). "The town officials bore the brunt of a lot of the opposition," said Bishop Bennett gratefully, which they were willing to do because they knew the Church was credible and trustworthy.[45]

The Church's commitment to being a good neighbor motivated local members to do more than was requested. "We'd listen to the extreme claims that were made during public hearings and then ask what more we could do," said Bishop Bennett. A sound-proofing box was installed to dampen noise from the jackhammer used to drill the granite rock supporting the temple's footings. Extra plates were embedded to shore up the ledge on which the temple was built, an elaborate underground system of drains was constructed to catch runoff, trees were planted around the perimeter to shield homes from light, and a water truck kept the ground wet throughout construction to minimize dust. Trucks were washed as they left the site to prevent rocks and debris from being scattered on public roads.[46] When a problem with initial blasting efforts sent rocks and dust all over, members went door to door in the most affected neighborhood, offering to wash windows and clean carpets.[47]

Bill Monahan was a particularly influential town selectman who had been instrumental in brokering the agreement that led to the Belmont chapel's parking permit some years prior. Grateful for his support, Bishop Bennett frequently met with Bill to discuss issues and progress. One evening the town leader noted that one of his lifelong friends lived in a home abutting the meetinghouse and had been a primary opponent of the chapel's construction. In talking together, the friend had asked, "Remember all the controversy about the meetinghouse? Bill, I just want to let you know that I was wrong. The Mormons are absolutely wonderful neighbors."

"He didn't have to tell me that," said Mr. Monahan to Bishop Bennett. "I knew him very, very well. That comment was very helpful to me."

"I don't know who in the ward had been in contact with [the friend]," the bishop admitted. "It might simply have been that the meetinghouse was relatively well maintained and people were generally respectful around there. Lots of those things, I think, really did lay the groundwork."[48]

"My sense of watching the hearings and . . . that whole temple process was that the Church members really pulled together," said one local member. "From my perspective, I've never been so proud to be associated with a group. . . . To see the way the Church leaders, from Bishop Bennett on, stood up before those public hearings that were so contentious and so hard . . . and [spoke] with the conviction and faith that so clearly sustained them. It was palpable."[49]

## Shared Values

Not long after public hearings for the temple began, a group known as Belmont Against Racism (BAR) approached the Belmont Religious Council seeking help to organize a community event around the Martin Luther King Day holiday. The local Episcopal Church had held a Martin Luther King Day service on the Sunday prior to the holiday for a few years, but it was sparsely attended and never gained momentum. "Do you have any ideas as to what we could do?" they asked, expressing frustration that they couldn't generate interest in the town.

The Council suggested a community breakfast. The group was enthusiastic but worried about a location for the event. Without thinking, Bishop Bennett said, "We'd love to host it at the Mormon Church." Members of the Council and BAR seemed surprised but were quick to accept.

Less than two weeks later, Bishop Bennett received a call from the president of BAR. "I need to talk to you about something that is a little bit uncomfortable for me," he said apologetically, "but I feel like I just need to be very direct." After the meeting with the Belmont Religious Council, he'd gone back to the executive committee of BAR. He'd reported that the Council was enthusiastic about co-sponsoring a breakfast and the Mormons had volunteered to host it. The words were barely out of his mouth when a female officer of the group exclaimed, "That was absolutely inappropriate!" Declaring the Mormon Church notorious for racism, she asserted no black would set foot in a Mormon building.

Apologizing again, the man continued, "I didn't get that feeling from you, but I have great respect for this woman. Can you comment at all?"

Bishop Bennett responded thoughtfully. "First of all, if anyone would not feel comfortable coming, then I withdraw the invitation. You certainly shouldn't feel obligated to come here," he said. Addressing the specific issues the female officer had raised, the two had a frank and open discussion about the revelation on the priesthood and verses contained in the Book of Mormon. As the conversation wound down, Bishop Bennett bore his testimony that the Church was not racist but was in fact a very positive influence against such attitudes and behaviors. Pensive, the caller asked to take this information back to his executive committee.

A few weeks later the man called again. "We decided," he said. "It is not a unanimous decision, but we decided to go ahead and hold the service at the church. Given all the controversy with the temple and overtones of religious bigotry, we want to show that we welcome people of different races and different religions in Belmont."

Members of the ward rallied to support the event, many taking time off work. Although the day was snowy, attendance was high and the cultural hall was packed. Members sat, ate, and talked with people they might never have encountered otherwise. Asked to share some thoughts, Bishop Bennett spoke about programs of the Church. He shared a conversation he'd had with some Cambodian youth from Lynn that he'd driven to Belmont for a basketball game. Thinking he was only engaging in pleasantries, he asked a young man about his family and learned that many members of the boy's family had been killed by the Khmer Rouge. Commenting on the radical differences this young man recognized in the United States, Bishop Bennett went on to describe the stake's youth basketball program and other youth activities. He talked about the Spanish-speaking units in the stake and the rich diversity of membership in downtown Boston.

"They realized," Bishop Bennett reflected, "that not only were we not a racist organization, but that we felt just the same way they did about this important topic." At the conclusion of the meeting, Bishop Bennett received a note from a woman that read, "Thank you for a wonderful event. Thank you for hosting it. The highlight for me was that I felt the support of your congregation for this cause which is so important to me." The writer was the woman who had vociferously objected to the event being held in an LDS building.[50]

In another venue, Ann Wunderli acted on the challenge to get more involved in the community by sending her résumé into the town with a note saying she would like to contribute in some way. To her surprise, she was invited to serve on the town's Shade Tree Committee, which seemed to be comprised of retired landscape architects and elderly women. "I really didn't know much about trees," she admitted, "and this [seemed] a little far off field."

Ann had been attending for a while when she overheard some committee members discussing the temple after a meeting had concluded. "Those Mormons are all liars," one individual stated. "They said that about 80 percent of the trees on the site would remain, and what have they done? They have gone in and blasted the entire site. There is not a tree left standing."

Ann knew nothing of the accusation, but identified herself as a member of the Church and expressed her confidence in its leaders. If any promises had been made, she was certain they would be kept. After returning home and conferring with her bishop, Ann invited the committee to hold its next meeting at the Belmont meetinghouse where Jerry Brown, the temple's landscape architect, would walk them through the plans for the temple grounds.

On the appointed evening, Brother Brown showed a number of photos taken of the trees that had been cut down. Each tree was virtually hollow inside. "We all knew that was a rocky ledge," he noted, "but what we didn't know until we got into it was that there was no top soil."

The committee was surprised, and firmly agreed such trees were too dangerous to leave standing. They were impressed with how much of the property would be left in place as Jerry showed them the plot plan. Respect turned to amazement when he pulled out a bill of materials listing 22,000 items to be incorporated into the landscaping.

Jerry walked the group onto the site to show them the storm drain system that would do a far better job of protecting neighboring homes from flooding than the ledge in its natural state. As he explained the process followed to make sure each tree had space for its root structure, a group leader said, "This is going to be the most significant landscaping in the town of Belmont. This is just unprecedented." Committee members asked if people could come to the site to simply enjoy its beauty and were assured all were welcome. A few days later both Jerry and the bishop received glowing thank-you notes declaring the Church's plans absolutely wonderful. "You clearly have spared no expense, and you clearly have given this a great deal of thought," they stated.

Talking with Sister Wunderli after the dust settled, Bishop Bennett said, "Ann, you didn't know why you were assigned to be on the Shade Tree Committee, but what you have done is you have spread the gospel by this group of opinion leaders in their own area. They now know that when the Church says that [it is] doing something, [it] really [is] doing it."

"One thing that the temple has done is give us unexpected opportunities to simply state how we really feel about certain teachings of the Church and what they mean to us," said Bishop Bennett. "The result is almost without exception that those we have . . . met with have had at least respect, and in many cases, admiration for the Church.

"With the benefit of hindsight, it does seem . . . that the Lord has used the opposition for His purpose. What the opposition did was give us an opportunity to act like members of the Church in a public format. That opportunity certainly helped the Church be perceived for what it really is and what it believes in."[51]

"It always makes me feel very good and warm when my nonmember friends ask me how is the temple coming and voice their support," remarked a sister. "They've just gotten to know Mormon families that they really respect, Mormon families that don't set themselves apart as being different [or] better than someone else. You're different, but you're still friendly human beings, fellow human beings. Equal concerns may be carried out in different ways, but they are still concerns about family [and] children."[52]

Speaking of her community involvement, another sister added, "It made a difference for our kids, but I think it also made a difference for the coming of our temple. Every family doing the same things we were doing, paving the way for the temple to be built and welcomed by the community."[53]

John was in his final year at Harvard Business School, looking forward to a trip with his wife following graduation in the spring of 1959. Just before the school year ended, however, John's wife was unexpectedly hospitalized for emergency surgery. Far from their families, John stayed with his wife until the hospital staff forced him to leave around 9:00 p.m., at which point he headed back to their small apartment alone. As he walked toward the student-housing complex in the dark, he saw a man sitting on the steps of the porch they shared with their neighbors. As John approached, the man rose and introduced himself as George Albert Smith Jr.

John was familiar with Smith, since he was an instructor at the business school, but John had never taken a course from him and was surprised the professor knew him. Before John could speak, his visitor said he had heard about the surgery and expressed concern for John's wife. The professor went on to observe that John would need money for the medical procedure. Expecting that John would be reluctant to accept help, he had put some money in an envelope and dropped it through the mail slot in John's door—it could be repaid at John's convenience. As George Albert Smith Jr. prepared to leave, he noted that he'd also dropped the keys to his Volkswagen through the door and the car was parked on the street. He and his wife had two cars, he explained, and could get along with one so long as use of the Volkswagen would assist John while his wife was ill. With that, the professor took his leave and began his walk home.

Those who knew George Albert Smith Jr. were not surprised by this gesture, finding it entirely consistent with his character. For John McArthur, however, the incident was singular in its simplicity, sincerity, and immediately personal nature. Years later, John still wondered how long the professor had sat on his stoop, waiting for him in the dark. John was not one of George Albert Smith's students, nor was he a member of the Church, yet as soon as Brother Smith heard of this student's predicament, he reached out in a way that demonstrated profound caring and trust.

When John McArthur became a professor himself, he vowed to perpetuate the kindness and caring shown to him at a vulnerable time. Serving as dean of the Harvard Business School for fifteen years, he made sure the institution reflected those values as well. As a result, a school that is renowned for its role in perpetuating capitalism is also known to be extremely empathetic and flexible when those in its fold are confronted with severe medical or other family hardships.[54]

We cannot know the potential impact of our interaction with others, but every exchange provides us with opportunities to put the principles we espouse into action. Elder L. Tom Perry said of his years in New England, "You have to find a standard that you must live by that is different from the world, but you must do it in such a way that doesn't offend people and that makes them feel warm and comfortable to be around you. Then you have the opportunity of explaining a higher value to them than they understand and know about. I think that taught me to relate to people of all faiths, colors, [and] nationalities. . . . That was most beneficial to me. I became a citizen of the world out there with a strong gospel foundation."[55]

"We're staying here because we like the Church in Boston," said one brother. "I think people in the Boston area don't disrespect the Mormon Church. It is just one of many, so you learn that your faith needs to be something that you nurture and don't take for granted. And yet at the same time, it is a thing of beauty you can share with others."[56]

"It has been a blessing being able to raise our family here," stated another member. "We have made friends here that will always be our friends. . . . To mourn and celebrate with them, to be a part of their lives has touched and changed our lives."[57]

"We love this community. We have become a part of it," said Jay Holbrook of his family's home in Oxford, Massachusetts, describing municipal groups they'd served on and public offices for which they'd run. "A church that is apart from the world," Jay continued, his voice trailing off as if the idea seemed wrong. "We've tried to integrate ourselves in the communities so that we like members of our community as much as we like our Church friends. We don't differentiate between the two. We treat them as if they are Church members, because they are part of the larger community that we love and enjoy."[58]

From earth's wide bounds, from ocean's farthest coast,

Through gates of pearl streams in the countless host,

Singing to Father, Son, and Holy Ghost.

# 13

# PROMISES
# TO THE FATHERS

DAVID OPAROWSKI was five years old when his parents joined the Church. In 1979, at age fourteen, David returned from a Boy Scout campout complaining that his leg hurt, after which he developed stomach pains that would not go away. David was ultimately diagnosed with non-Hodgkin's lymphoma, requiring intense chemotherapy. Although he was in and out of the hospital and constantly ill, David was acutely aware that members of his Cambridge Ward were laboring diligently to raise money for a chapel in Belmont. David desperately wanted to be involved. When his parents found sheets of precut leather that could be laced into coin purses and wallets, David went to work, selling his handiwork to his visitors and the doctors and nurses who cared for him.

Shortly before his death, David carefully placed his earnings into an envelope, which he handed to his mother with clear instructions: "I want you to give this to the bishop. Here is the money for the temple."

Certain her son had misspoken, David's mother reminded him they were building a meetinghouse, not a temple.

David was undeterred. "Oh, Mom," he responded, "one day there is going to be a temple on that property and Angel Moroni will be on top of that temple for all of Boston to see."[1]

Prior to attending an April 1995 regional conference in Worcester,

250

Massachusetts, Gordon B. Hinckley spent a day looking at property in New York and Connecticut. A temple had been announced for Hartford, Connecticut, two and a half years earlier, but the prophet felt unsettled about the selected site and had been praying for guidance.

President Hinckley was candid about the challenge of building a temple in New England during a meeting with stake presidents prior to the conference, indicating it was a matter of frequent discussion among the brethren. With a large population of Saints around New York City and another around Boston, do you put a temple in each area or one in the middle? Without missing a beat, several stake presidents responded in unison: "You put one in Boston."

Chuckling with good humor, President Hinckley admitted the matter vexed him. Where, he asked the assembled gathering, would they suggest building a temple?

President Kenneth G. Hutchins of the Boston Stake was one of the men in attendance. A long-forgotten conversation from twelve years prior came suddenly and forcefully to mind. Raising his hand tentatively, he said, "I think there's this piece of land in Belmont that would be most suitable for a temple, and it's owned by the Church—I think."

Peering at the stake president, President Hinckley asked, "Can you find out?"

"Give me five minutes," President Hutchins replied.

The prophet nodded, putting his forefinger on his wrist. "You've got five minutes."

Springing from his chair, President Hutchins left the high council room calling for his executive secretary, Tony Kimball. Although he'd been to the Belmont chapel, he'd never been on the upper portion of the lot he'd just suggested to the prophet. "What do you know about the property in Belmont?" President Hutchins asked urgently, as soon as Tony appeared.

"Not much," Brother Kimball answered honestly, "but as far as I know we still own it." Accompanying the stake president into the meeting room, Tony provided basic information about the purchase and suggested they contact Grant Bennett, bishop of the Belmont Ward. As the stake president and his executive secretary walked out to make the call, the prophet shook his head, muttering, "I can't believe I didn't know we had property in Belmont."

Tony dialed the phone while President Hutchins hung over his shoulder, afraid of losing the opportunity unfolding before them. Bishop

Bennett was preparing to leave for the regional leadership meeting when the call came but was able to confirm that the Church still owned approximately nine acres of undeveloped land above the chapel. "President Hinckley is on his way," the stake president stated cryptically. "I don't really know anything about the site other than where it is. Would you please meet him there and see if you can answer any questions?"

Walking back into the meeting, President Hutchins could barely contain himself. Conversation came to an abrupt stop as he entered and the prophet asked, "What did you find out, President?"

The Church owned the site, President Hutchins told the group, describing its location next to a major highway. "How long would it take to get there?" President Hinckley inquired.

The prophet handed responsibility for the approaching priesthood meeting to Elder Neal A. Maxwell and followed President Hutchins and Brother Kimball to Belmont. Arriving at their destination, President Hinckley stepped out of the car and looked about the property. Turning to Bishop Bennett, he asked a number of pointed questions and requested that additional information about the parcel be gathered by the next afternoon. The prophet was particularly puzzled that the parcel didn't show up on the Church's real estate holdings, a list with which he was very familiar. The bishop could not explain this but assured the group that the Church retained title to the land, apart from a few small portions that had been sold for residential use.

Standing on the wooded hill with the prophet, President Hutchins felt his heart swell within him. "I just had an immediate witness . . . there was going to be a temple on that site," he said. The stake president fought the feeling, afraid to "jinx" things, but it persisted. "There's just no doubt in my mind," he said in retrospect, "there was a witness . . . expressed there for me."

The leadership meeting was well underway when the men returned to the conference. President Hinckley made no mention of where he'd gone, but noted in his remarks that he had been fasting and praying about an issue that had troubled him for some time. Unable to sleep the previous night, he'd paced his hotel room at 3:30 a.m. Looking over the assembled brethren, he said, "I think the Lord has just given me an answer to my prayers."

Turning to the man seated next to him, President Hutchins could contain his excitement no longer. "We're going to have a temple in Boston!" he exulted as quietly as possible.[2]

Bishop Bennett took responsibility for assembling additional information, taking photos of the site and obtaining the original files and plot plan from the time of its purchase. A call to Salt Lake explained why the site didn't show up on the Church property listing, as the title had been moved to an investment account for retired Church employees. A few weeks later, Bishop Bennett received a call from a Church real estate employee. The gentleman reported that while the matter was very preliminary and entirely confidential, he had been asked to study the zoning laws in Belmont and had been given the bishop's name as a contact.[3]

Neither President Hutchins nor Bishop Bennett heard anything more on the matter, but President Hinckley recorded his experience viewing the rocky ledge in his journal: "As I stood there I had an electric feeling that this is the place, that the Lord inspired its acquisition and its retention. Very few seemed to know anything about it. . . . I think I know why I have had such a very difficult time determining the situation concerning Hartford. I have prayed about it. I have come here three or four times. I have studied maps and tables of membership. With all of this I have not had a strong confirmation. I felt a confirmation as I stood in Belmont on this property this afternoon. This is the place for a House of the Lord in the New England area."[4]

Plans for a temple in Boston were announced during the priesthood session of general conference on September 30, 1995. President Hutchins was in Provo, Utah, watching the broadcast with his son. Overwhelmed with emotion, the stake president could not control the tears coursing down his cheeks. "I wanted to just share that [moment] with everybody," he said. "I wanted to be back in the middle of the stake somewhere, but I wasn't."[5]

A brother watching from the stake center in Weston, Massachusetts, compared the moment to a touchdown in a critical game. "People were shouting; they were jumping out of their seats!" he chuckled. "They were just so excited they didn't know how to contain it. There was crying, there was laughing, there was screaming. . . . We couldn't hear anything else that was announced. As soon as they said the word 'Boston,' the place just erupted."[6]

Saints in Massachusetts had prayed for a temple from the time Cambridge's Longfellow Park chapel was dedicated in 1956.[7] Shortly after the creation of the first New England stake in 1962, Charles Clayton, a Massachusetts native and convert to the Church was talking with the stake president, Wilbur Cox, and the conversation turned to the subject of temples. "There will not be a temple here in New England during my lifetime," Charles said, sighing. The stake president's response was swift and sure: "You're wrong. There will be a temple here and I can tell you where it will be." With fire in his eyes he described the location of the future temple in great detail, painting a verbal picture of the hill and nearby roads on Route 2 that was so vivid it was emblazoned on Charles' mind ever after.

"I will never forget his utterance of that statement," Brother Clayton said. "[I] left the conversation thinking I've either heard a revelation or been talking to a crazy man. I kind of thought it was a crazy man, but who knew?" Over thirty years later, when location of the Boston Temple was announced, Brother Clayton recalled his private conversation with President Cox. "My immediate reaction was, 'Well, of course," [and] then I thought, 'Well, Bill, you were right. Shame on me for having doubts.[8]

Jae Baliff presided over the Massachusetts Boston Mission during the late 1970s. "Not long before we left," he recalled, "Brother [Steven] Wheelwright invited me to come up on the hill just off Route 2 where they were making arrangements to purchase a large tract of land. . . . We sat there together on the hillside looking down towards Boston, knowing that there would soon be a chapel there for the Belmont Ward. We were talking openly about our hope and prayer that there would be a temple there. It was right both because of the location and because of the beauty of the spot. . . . For twenty years we had been looking forward to the time that it would occur."[9]

The parcel obtained for the Belmont chapel was large, and, not long after its 1979 purchase, the stake presidency encountered pressure to sell the excess land. The stake presidency was unhappy with the request, convinced that the land should be preserved. In response they suggested the Church send someone east to look at the property, suggesting it was ideal for a temple. The idea that local Church leaders would be so presumptuous to propose a temple site was not greeted warmly. The stake presidency ultimately went through the motions of selling a few lots near the chapel to placate demands until the matter dropped.[10]

Bill Ence was a counselor in the stake presidency at the time and shared his unhappiness over the situation with his good friend, Ken Hutchins. "Hutch, you have to see this property," he said earnestly. "It will take your breath away. I know there's going to be a temple there someday."

"He couldn't contain himself when he talked about it," Ken Hutchins said, smiling. "That was my only exposure to the fact that there was a piece of ground there."

Brother Ence admitted he probably shouldn't have discussed the issue in such a context but had no lingering regrets about his remarks. After all, it was that casual exchange that Ken Hutchins drew upon over a decade later when, in a room full of stake presidents, President Hinckley asked where a temple could be built in New England.[11]

"My version of the story," said a subsequent stake president, "[is] this temple had been designated to be built on that site for a long time. . . . It's a series of what other people would say are random events, but clearly the Lord . . . put the temple up there." Ultimately, he smiled, it didn't matter what happened in zoning committee meetings. "The temple [was] going to get built. . . . This was decided a hundred years ago."[12]

## Preparations

One man with insight prior to the official announcement was Jerry Brown, whose childhood days spent visiting the grounds of the Logan Utah Temple led to his career as a landscape architect. Shortly after President Hinckley's visit, Brother Brown's firm was asked to take a look at the Belmont site to determine if a temple of specified dimensions could be built there. Working feverishly to meet Salt Lake City's tight deadline for the feasibility study, Jerry and his colleagues were able to report that the vacant land could accommodate such a structure.

"As I was trying to make things work," said Brother Brown of the intense assignment, "what was coming out of my pencil wasn't me. It just all seemed to fit. It didn't take me long to figure out how it all worked together. . . . The basic sketch that was developed [in the beginning] is not that different than what we have as a final plan now with modifications. The building has gotten smaller, but the basic configurations and the way we laid it out [remained the same]—'we' meaning 'me and the Lord,' I guess. It just all came together very quickly."

Notwithstanding this inspiring experience, following the temple's announcement, Jerry was overwhelmed by a heavy depression that made further work on the plans virtually impossible. The feeling was so dark and intense it seemed a tangible presence. "In that short period of time I went from having the closest experience of contact with the Lord guiding my hand to the darkest feeling of Satan trying to stop it," he said. "It was very difficult."

Jerry prayed and fasted with his wife, but the darkness persisted. He yearned to be taken off the task. Realizing they needed extra help, the Browns approached their bishop and knelt together with him, entreating the Lord for deliverance. Bishop Bennett called for a ward fast on behalf of all those working on the temple. Almost immediately the darkness departed.

"I have total faith and confidence that God lives and guides His work and temples are built under divine inspiration," said Brother Brown. "The things that are supposed to be done and built will be done and built. It won't be easy. None of the temples have been easy. They all have their opposition."[13]

Ground was broken for the temple in June 1997 once the necessary zoning permits were obtained. The event was kept very quiet, due to continuing controversy over the project. A small group of Saints joined Elder Richard G. Scott on the muddy hill following a morning downpour. A sister asked to photograph the gathering described the groundbreaking ceremony as one of most spiritual experiences of her life. "I felt like I was part of history," she said. "It was so sacred."[14]

When plans for the temple were announced, the Church had forty-six temples in operation. By its groundbreaking, there were fifty. Nine months later, in April 1998, President Hinckley announced his goal of having one hundred operating temples by the end of 2000. In an instant, the Boston Temple became one of over fifty sacred buildings simultaneously under construction.[15]

Don Mangum and Kent Bowen served as cochairs for the temple's open house and dedication. Initial timelines for construction and landscaping set plans for a June 2000 open house. As issues emerged and lingered, the completion date slipped to July and then August, requiring constant readjustment. "We were probably the most overplanned temple open house and dedication in Church history," Brother Bowen chuckled. "We planned and planned and planned. . . . All of our planning was for naught, except that we became very good at planning."[16]

Construction delays and community concerns had an impact on timing, but the most significant changes in direction and guidance came from the Church's drive to build so many temples in so short a time—a monumental effort, the likes of which had never before been undertaken.

When first announced, the anticipated Boston Temple District looked much like the original Atlantic District, serving the stakes of New England and those of the Canadian Maritime Provinces. Earlier completion of temples in Halifax, Nova Scotia, and Montreal, Quebec, however, met the needs of Saints in Canada and Vermont. A delay impacting a temple announced for Harrison, New York, resulted in ten stakes and districts from eastern New York being moved from the Washington D.C. Temple District to Boston just six weeks prior to its open house.

Unable to control details concerning schedules, the temple planning committee focused on preparing members for the temple dedication. Saints within the temple district were asked to come to the temple open house with friends and neighbors who would not otherwise come. They were also challenged to be worthy to attend the temple's dedication and participate in ordinance work thereafter. Special materials centered on these goals were prepared for use in sacrament meetings, Relief Society meetings, and priesthood quorums. Wards and branches throughout the district planned and held special events to help their Primary children, youth, and adults understand what it would mean to have a temple in their midst.[17]

Marci McPhee considered the unique blessings the temple dedication offered as she prepared to teach a combined priesthood and Relief Society lesson prior to the open house. "We can sit back and watch this happen," she said of the opportunities that members were free to partake or decline, "or we can jump on and invite our nonmember friends to the open house and work with the less-active [members] . . . to help them be temple worthy for the dedication."

Filled with a sense of urgency, Marci selected two china plates and set one on a plate stand in front of the class. She spoke of the sacrifices made by early Saints and recalled pioneer women who gave their dishes to be crushed and integrated into the outer walls of their temples. Without pausing, she withdrew a hammer and smashed the other plate sitting on the table, wrapped in paper. Marci carefully withdrew a shard that matched the plate on the stand and said quietly, "This time, the Lord doesn't want your china. He wants your heart."[18]

"At the beginning of that year, we were setting goals for ourselves," said one brother. "The number one goal in every category was to prepare for the Boston Temple open house and dedication. We wanted our family to be ready for it."[19]

Plans for the open house were in full swing, with the emphasis on bringing in as many people from the surrounding community as possible. To reduce public concerns around traffic and noise, those attending both the open house and dedication would need to be bused in from remote parking sites. A website was created for reservations and ticketing, a first for a temple open house, and a newspaper circular providing information about the temple and basic doctrines of the Church was distributed throughout Massachusetts, New Hampshire, and Rhode Island using donations from the twenty-two stakes and districts comprising the Boston Temple District.

Traditional open house tours were silent affairs in which visitors were led through specific rooms of the temple with signs explaining their purpose. General Authorities were the only individuals authorized to lead speaking tours, offered primarily to VIPs. The large volume of temple dedications in 1999 brought changes to this practice, and by the time of the Oklahoma City and Houston Texas temple dedications in 2000, stake presidents and bishops were being trained to provide these experiences for limited groups.

One week before the start of the Boston Temple open house, the planning committee learned there would be a week of speaking tours at the end of the open house period, in addition to the guided tours led by General Authorities for local dignitaries and prominent citizens on the opening day. Members were counseled to select special friends and individuals they wished to invite to that last week of tours, and approximately fifty area Church leaders were asked to attend a special training meeting so they could learn to lead those groups.

The date for the open house was rapidly approaching, but construction was still underway. The temple's interior was full of unfinished woodwork, the exterior was still being completed, and the front door of the temple was missing. None of the landscaping was in, the roads were not finished, and most of the parking areas were filled with crates of granite and other building materials. The day before the open house's scheduled commencement, visiting authorities from Utah suggested a postponement, concerned that the commotion and mess of ongoing construction would portray the Church in a negative light. Despite their own misgivings, local leaders pressed to go forward. "We were prepared," said Kent Bowen, "and somehow we would learn to work with the presence of the construction crews and the contractors."

The decision made, local leaders were quickly given new assignments. Prior temple open houses attracted thousands of visitors and generated valuable goodwill toward the Church, but Church leaders were sincerely concerned that this did not translate into increased missionary work. Based on lessons learned during the Oklahoma City and Houston open houses, the Boston leaders were instructed to offer every individual attending the open house a guided speaking tour. In addition, visitors needed a place to gather after going through the temple where they could share refreshments, speak to members, and have an opportunity to meet missionaries.

Less than twenty-four hours before the open house was to begin, this was a major change in direction for an event where logistics had been timed to the second. On two separate occasions, coordinators had rented buses to time runs between parking lots at different hours of the day and study how long it took to load and unload passengers. Using dozens of stopwatches and 150 volunteers, groups had been led through the temple over and over to determine the best route through the construction, the optimal size for tours, and how quickly people could be moved through the building. Based on their findings, the committee estimated that 800 people could be led through the temple each hour if they carefully coordinated how groups moved through each of the teaching stations. Because talking tours would take longer, they believed the maximum number of people who could be accommodated each hour would decrease to 300.

"We were quick to do the math in our heads, and we realized that there was absolutely no way that we could get enough [guides] to do talking tours," Brother Bowen recalled. "We couldn't imagine how we would handle the crowds . . . the very notion of having cookies and punch for 80,000 people! How could we get those arrangements? We imagined that it would destroy the logistics that were precisely timed . . . going up to 500, 600, 700, and 800 guests an hour, bringing them on buses, and feeding them cookies and punch. We didn't have space."

Notwithstanding the inconceivability of eleventh-hour request, tents outside the temple were rearranged to serve punch and cookies, to be provided by a quickly recruited local bakery. An urgent plea to stake presidents asked them to recommend additional brethren who could lead temple tours. Working all day Monday with the visiting authorities, a tour script was created, revised, and given to those who had been asked to serve as guides.[20]

Paul Anderson was one of many new recruits. At a bishops' council meeting, his stake president informed those gathered of the change in plans and asked the assembled bishops to submit names of members who could serve as guides. Paul's bishop turned to him and asked if he would like to participate. Although Paul had planned to dedicate the next week to his neglected Ph.D. dissertation, his reply was immediate: "Yes! Absolutely. Thank you for asking."

An orientation for the newly called guides was held at the Belmont chapel that evening with Elder Craig Zwick of the First Quorum of the Seventy and Kent Bowen. As Brother Bowen passed out detailed talking points for the tours, he tried to reassure his volunteer ranks. "This is what you say," he counseled. "If you don't want to do it word for word, just make sure that you don't step outside the bounds of the concepts. . . . Don't worry about reading it right now because you've got plenty of time to memorize it. You have until tomorrow morning."[21]

"Every time we turned around, all of these things changed on us, but we had gathered so much data that although it was painful, we could change quickly," Brother Bowen noted. By Tuesday morning, the committee had done everything they could. With the temple incomplete and construction ongoing, however, they still worried whether the timing was right.[22]

## Sharing Sacred Spaces

The first portion of opening day was reserved for media and special tours led by General Authorities, but the remainder had been specially set aside for members living in Belmont to invite town officials, neighbors, and even antagonists to see the temple for themselves. Confirmation that the open house would be well received came only at that time.

"We found that people rearranged their work to come in the middle of the day," Brother Bowen said with wonder. "All of the school board, all of the planning board, the zoning board, all of the school principals— they all came. . . . It was an incredible thing to see these people arrive.

"Here we were, not sure that anybody would come, with a construction site that was a mess. We didn't know whether we would have protesters. The first moment of truth occurred at 12:30 p.m. when all of these town officials were invited. They showed up, and all of them came dressed in their Sunday best. They had really caught the spirit that this was a sacred place for Mormons even though they were coming, essentially, to a construction site. . . . I was just struck by the reverence and respect that they had."

The volunteers felt a bit rickety as the first tours commenced, but as guests exited the temple and entered the refreshment tent—a simple canopy over temporary tables set on a rough asphalt floor—the coordinators found their visitors reluctant to leave. "They just hung around and talked," said Brother Bowen. "It was very clear from that moment on that there was something wonderful going on, both in the tours and . . . the temple itself, and in this opportunity after the tour to have some punch and cookies and talk. I timed some of them. Some of the selectmen were there for two hours. . . . That gave us the strong encouragement to try to do that better."[23]

Grant and Colleen Bennett had lived on the same street in Belmont for almost twenty years and had come to know their neighbors fairly well. In preparation for the open house, Colleen had gone up and down their street delivering invitations to each home, asking each family to join her on a 6:30 p.m. tour on the day set aside for town residents.

On the appointed evening, the Bennetts were astonished to find sixty-five people present for their tour. Every neighbor they'd invited had come with all their family members and, in some cases, extended family and friends in tow. Although the group vastly exceeded the recommended tour size, given the circumstances, they were kept together.

Standing in a sealing room after walking through the temple together, Grant cleared his throat. "Every now and then life hands you an experience that you just don't ever imagine is going to happen," he said with emotion. "I didn't think this temple would be here. It is here. I certainly didn't think that every one of my neighbors would be interested enough to simply come. But we are all here together, and I just want to say thank you."

As the group nodded in silent assent, a man in back replied, "You know, as a street we have never gotten together for anything before, and what a great reason to all be here together."

"I think they felt the Spirit," Grant stated. "I think through this idea, they know a lot more about what makes us tick than they did before. I think that we'll be closer for that reason."[24]

The Sunday after the open house commenced, the religion editor for *The Boston Globe*, the area's largest newspaper, ran a front-page article on the Church and the temple. Within hours, interest in the open house reached such a level that the server for the temple website crashed. Fortunately, it was back online by the end of the day. The website allowed every individual attending the open house to come with a reservation, eliminating long waits that had been common at other open houses. With everything documented and tracked, those in charge of buses, parking lots, and tours knew exactly what kind of crowd to anticipate each day.

Tours began outside with a video in which the prophet described the purpose of temples. Visitors were then divided into groups and assigned to guides to enter the temple. Over time the script the guides used was shortened. "One of the things we learned," Brother Bowen explained, "was that to shorten the number of words in the presentation was powerful. We kept hearing this from the brethren as they came out here. They would say, 'Let the Lord do the teaching in His house.' When we gave more abbreviated discussion . . . and then allowed for a quiet period, it allowed the guests to then think about what was said and to look and gaze about the temple and to allow the Spirit to work on them. Whenever we tried to talk all the time and fill the air with noise, our guests didn't have enough time to be reflective and feel and understand . . .

"The other thing we learned was to speak quietly. As soon as we began to speak very quietly, everyone in the tour groups quieted down, and they began to listen and be more reflective and listen to the Spirit."[25]

By the end of the open house, almost 83,000 people had visited the Boston Temple and a local National Public Radio station had aired a recorded version of the tour, posted to the Internet with photos. "One of the enduring images in my mind," said Bishop Grant Bennett, "is of . . . the buses pulling up and, almost continuously, . . . the door opening and people walking out of the bus. Just the image. Most of these people were nonmembers. . . . Who would have imagined that there would be busload after busload after busload of people coming respectfully, of their own free will and choice, to visit the temple?"[26]

Special tours were offered to congregations of other area churches on the first Sunday of the open house period. Over a hundred clergy members came through the temple over the course of the month, some several times. Many were struck by the sacred nature of the experience. "Some of my greatest moments were when rabbis came through," said Brother Bowen recalling conversations over shared symbolism found inside and outside the temple.[27]

Visiting over cookies after a tour, a Baptist minister asked Bishop Bennett his thoughts on New Testament allusions to marriage after death. One possible interpretation, the bishop suggested, was found in the sealing ordinances and proxy work described in the tour she'd just taken. Pausing for a moment, the minister responded, "You know, that interpretation, coupled with the statement in Corinthians talking about baptism for the dead—I am beginning to see how this belief ties together a series of things that are otherwise inexplicable."[28]

Kevin Schmidt was assisting with coordination efforts when he found himself talking to a tiny woman, not even five feet tall, outside the temple. She asked if he knew Bishop Bennett, and Brother Schmidt nodded. Happy, the woman exclaimed, "Well, you tell Bishop Bennett that our temple looks marvelous! We are so pleased—our prayers have been answered."

"Can I tell him who is giving me this message?" Brother Schmidt asked with a smile.

"You just tell him that Sister Mary told you," she answered. Seeing his confusion, she added, "I'm with the convent," referring to the Catholic convent next to a home commonly used by presidents of the Massachusetts Boston Mission.[29]

Shuttle drivers grew used to complaints about the lack of air conditioning as they circled parking lots to bring visitors to the temple in the August and September heat. They puzzled over the marked difference in the people after the tours, however, almost all of whom were peaceful and pleasant. The change was so noticeable that the drivers requested their own tour.[30]

It was Brother Bowen's habit to ask people about their tour after they came out of the temple. "People were extremely descriptive," he said, noting their comments revolved around four things. Guests always mentioned the building's beauty and their respect for the beliefs and testimonies that had been shared. Many complimented the volunteers assisting in the parking lots, buses, tents, and temple. Many also spoke of the peace and serenity they felt in the temple, although a number struggled to explain it. "My belief," said Kent, "is that they didn't know how to explain that it was the feeling of the Spirit that had impacted them."[31]

Linda Erickson of Hingham, Massachusetts, was leading a group out of a sealing room, when an older woman with a lovely Dutch accent said, "I feel like all the stress in my body has just melted away."

Linda smiled and told the woman what she was feeling was peace.

"That's it. It's peace," the visitor agreed, puzzling over its source.

Sister Erickson gently suggested the woman was feeling the influence of the Holy Ghost. After quietly considering this, the visitor told Sister Erickson that she had come to the United States as a young woman to attend college. During that time she had visited southern Utah, where she met and conversed with a returned missionary who recognized her accent from his mission in Belgium. She remembered being impressed by the young man, but she had not thought of Mormons again until she saw the notice for the temple open house in her newspaper.

Pausing a moment, she asked curiously, "Do you allow outsiders to join your church?"

Yes, Sister Erickson assured her, stating that missionaries would be happy to teach her more about the gospel in her home.

As they walked to the reception tent, the woman asked how long it took to be converted. That, Sister Erickson answered, was completely up to her, and she introduced the woman to a set of elders, starting them on a discussion about the restored gospel. "I will not forget her," Sister Erickson said of that experience, "and I will not stop hoping and praying that she finds herself back in that beautiful Boston Temple again someday!"[32]

"Bostonians are not easily impressed," said Brother Bowen frankly. "The intellectual community can be skeptical and cynical." Following the tours, however, "they spoke in superlatives." One university president who toured the building hesitated to leave when his tour ended. "Do you know what you have here?" he asked. "This is the most peaceful place I've ever been. I've visited all the religious places around the world and this is the most peaceful." [33]

That sense of peace touched even those who'd opposed the temple's construction, including those named as complainants in lawsuits against the Church. Grinning, Brother Bowen noted that several reluctantly admitted that they'd felt "this unusual peace" on their tours. "The impact of that [feeling] on people was tremendous," he said.[34]

A Jewish physician approached one guide at the conclusion of her tour to thank him and everyone affiliated with the open house. "You have done a very remarkable thing," she stated. "You have had the courage to let others see your sacred space. . . . It is an act of courage, in my mind, and an act of generosity. . . . This is a sacred space. Thank you for sharing that."[35]

As important as the tours were for the community, opined Brother Bowen, "the most significant impact was on the priesthood leaders who did the tours." After leading his first groups through the temple, one guide returned home and invited all his neighbors to visit the next time he was scheduled. He had lived in the area a long while but had never shared his testimony with his neighbors. The temple gave him an opportunity he was excited about.

"That happened to most of the tour leaders," Brother Bowen

remarked. They brought friends, colleagues and respected associates, and they shared sacred, intimate things about their faith within the temple's walls. Such experiences built the members themselves. When that occurs, he suggested, nonmembers will be nurtured as a natural consequence.[36]

"Instead of taking days off to work on my dissertation," said Paul Anderson of his end-of-summer plans, "I was [taking] days off and spend[ing] them at the temple. I signed up for double shifts every Saturday . . . I wanted to spend as much time doing [tours] as possible. . . . [T]he funny thing was that the tour guides were all just as excited as I was. . . . All we wanted to do was get another group of people to talk about this temple. It was so fun to take these people through."

While all the tours provided a spiritual high, "the best experiences for me were when I got to bring my own friends," Paul said. "The pinnacle of that whole period was when I brought my team from work to the temple one evening. . . .

"As we went through the temple that day, it was a wonderful experience. I felt like the words were just flowing out of my mouth . . . . When I got to the sealing room, the Spirit was so strong. I said, 'I can't tell you what a privilege it is to be here with you all. I'm glad to share this with you. I think this is just wonderful.' One of the people in the room who I didn't know . . . very quietly and very reverently said, 'Thank you.' He just said those two words, but he said them in a tone of voice that made me think, 'These people felt the same thing I did.'"[37]

"I think the temple open house carried this whole region for about a year," said Bishop Kerry Hopkin. "The Spirit that was there. . . . I was amazed at how much time people gave." Members took time off work to volunteer in the parking crew or serve as ushers. And in return, they experienced an infusion of testimony and the Spirit that lingered. "We were able to . . . bask in that Spirit and feed off of that experience," Bishop Hopkin continued. "We . . . all felt like we were sharing the gospel and giving people experiences with the Church in a way that was easy to do, so we did a lot of it. Every time you do that, you feel good. There was a wonderful feeling in the whole district and certainly in the Boston Stake."[38]

## The 100th Temple

By October 1, 2000, construction on the Boston Temple was complete, save for its steeple, which was enmeshed in litigation. Tall upon the granite hill, approximately twenty miles west of Boston, members gathered outside its walls early in the crystal blue morning. Over the course of four sessions, nearly 17,000 of the 68,000 members comprising the Boston Temple District attended the dedicatory services, either at the temple itself or at one of the many local meetinghouses where the proceedings were broadcast.

"This is a milestone in Church history," stated President Hinckley at a press conference prior to the dedication. "It's time we had a temple in Boston. We're so glad it's here." Acknowledging the lack of a steeple, he said simply, "We wish the steeple were on it. I regret that it isn't. But we can get along without it while awaiting the outcome of the legal action. In the meantime, we'll go forward performing the ordinance work of this sacred house."[39]

The dedicatory prayer included a reference to the building's unique status as the one hundredth operating temple. "We have looked forward to this occasion," the prophet stated. "We have prayed for this day. We extend our gratitude to all who have labored so faithfully and diligently, often in the face of serious opposition, to bring to pass the miracle of the completion of this temple. To us it is indeed a miracle. The ground on which it stands, the circumstances of its preservation for this use, and the decision to build it here—all are miracles unto those who have been a part of this process."

Despite the missing spire, the temple was dedicated as complete, with a petition to the Father that a way might be opened for the addition of a steeple crowned with a statue of the ancient prophet Moroni, who had trod the surrounding regions more than a millennium before.

Praying that the members of the temple district would be blessed in their righteous labors, the prophet closed the prayer with a reference to past events and a plea for the future. "In this area were enacted many of the historic events of the founding of our republic," he stated. "Bless Thy work in this nation and throughout the earth that it may grow and prosper, that none shall stay its progress, that the forces of evil shall fall before it, that righteousness may be its watch word, and faith its method."[40]

Elder Loren C. Dunn, an emeritus member of the First Quorum of the Seventy and the first president of the Boston Temple, spoke at general conference six days later and shared his thoughts on the dedication. "While every temple is important and offers the same ordinances necessary for eternal life, this dedication was, in many ways, historic," he offered. "This is the first temple in a city recognized as the birthplace of freedom in what was then the New World, and also it is recognized as the early home of many of the first leaders and members of the Church. The dedication seemed to represent the coming together of the great heritage of America and the sacred roots of the restored gospel of Jesus Christ."[41]

Within seven months of the temple's dedication, litigation against the Church ended when the Massachusetts Supreme Judicial Court overturned a lower court ruling against the steeple and the U.S. Supreme Court turned down a challenge to a Massachusetts law allowing the construction of religious buildings in residential neighborhoods.[42] On September 21, 2001, amidst a purposely small gathering, the steeple was set atop the Boston Temple, topped by a replica of the statue of the Angel Moroni created for the Salt Lake City Temple by sculptor Cyrus E. Dallin, a native of Arlington, Massachusetts—the next town over from Belmont.[43]

"How blessed we are to have in Belmont the Boston Temple about one hour away," said Earl Randall of Oxford, Massachusetts, recalling the cross-country train trip he and his wife took with their three children to be sealed as a family in Salt Lake City following their 1953 baptism.[44]

A sister who moved to Massachusetts with her husband in 1966 found that the closest temples were Salt Lake City and London. "So for ten or fifteen years we didn't go to the temple," she explained. "We had gone to the temple when we got married, and then we came back here and lived our life. I remember that when the Washington D.C. Temple was built and we were going down for the first time, I was scared. It was like I had forgotten everything."[45]

The Washington D.C. Temple made temple covenants more accessible, but attending the temple still entailed a drive of at least eight hours each way. Ward and stake temple trips provided opportunities to strengthen friendships, but time and distance created limits. "We liked it, but we just couldn't do it very often," one brother stated. "Now we go to the temple once a week."[46]

Simply assisting with the Belmont temple's cleaning prior to the open house impacted one family by increasing their children's desire to be in the temple. "Our youngest daughter is so excited to receive her endowments there," said the mother, "because it is her temple. . . . It holds special meaning to her."[47]

"The most significant event since the birth of the prophet Joseph Smith in New England is the Boston Temple," stated Elder Robert S. Wood. "The Boston temple is both a symbol of where we have come and the foundation for the Church in New England in the next century. I think, in fact, that it will be seen as the great turning point."[48]

Reflecting on the privilege of having a temple so close, Brother Randall uttered a personal plea: "Please help us to meet the challenge and the opportunities to serve and do the work for our ancestors. May we be blessed with the health, knowledge, and spirituality to be part of this great work in the last days, to be equal to the vision."[49]

## Fulfillment of Promise

When the Boston Massachusetts Stake was formed in 1962, there were more Roman Catholics in the diocese of Massachusetts than there were members of the Church in the world.[50] Mitt Romney recalled moving to Belmont ten years later to join a small handful of LDS families in the town. "Then people began moving in," he explained. "People started gathering to this area from all corners of the globe and began building the Church in a permanent way."[51]

Between 1994 and 2004, membership in the Church within Massachusetts increased 56 percent from just under 15,000 to over 23,000. In 1980 there were 15 wards and branches within the state. By 2004, there were 39 organized congregations, and over 400 members in Belmont.[52]

Speaking in April 2009 general conference, Elder David A. Bednar said, "The Prophet Joseph Smith declared that in all ages the divine purpose of gathering the people of God is to build temples so His children can receive the highest ordinances and thereby gain eternal life."[53]

"I always thought the temple should have been in the Boston area," said Elder Robert S. Wood, admitting his personal bias. "I've always thought the Lord really . . . intended it to be where it is. . . . It is a sign that the Church is here and it is becoming more firmly established. I just think it's a great moment of the history of the Church in New England."

The original work done in New England by men like Brigham Young and Wilford Woodruff was a preliminary phase that never got very far as a result of the gathering to the Salt Lake Valley, Elder Wood suggested. What we observe today, he continued, is the gathering back.

As evidence of this reverse gathering, Elder Wood shared an experience that took place soon after he had been called as a stake president. After discussing some routine business with Elder Joseph B. Wirthlin over the telephone, Elder Wirthlin asked the new stake president how he was doing. President Wood responded by mentioning some family history his brother had sent him. The records indicated one of his maternal great-great-grandmothers had been given a blessing by Joseph Smith, providing President Wood a personal link to the prophet.

Elder Wirthlin paused and asked if President Wood knew anything more about his ancestor, but Robert had little beyond her name, birthday, and date of death.

"We're looking through some of the journals and family history pertaining to blessings given by the Prophet," Elder Wirthlin explained, offering to look into it. "It's a long shot, but who knows? We might even have some of the words pertaining to that blessing."

A few weeks later, Elder Wirthlin called back. "We have a journal account of the blessing given by the Prophet Joseph Smith to your great-great-grandmother," he announced. Then, with some curiosity, he asked President Wood, "Do you know where her parents came from?"

The president of the Hingham Massachusetts Stake had to plead ignorance and was stunned when Elder Wirthlin stated, "They came from Hingham, Massachusetts." The short blessing was notable for one promise made to a young girl who had moved west with her parents to Illinois over 140 years earlier: "I bless you the time will come when your descendants will return to the land of your parents to more fully raise up Zion."

"At which point," Elder Wood said solemnly, "I realized that the decisions I had made, presumably on the basis of work, employment, were probably not the reason I was here. I also knew the reason why my brother was sent on a mission to this area and why he and his wife subsequently were called back when they went on a mission again. . . . I've had this strong feeling for some time that there is a gathering again taking place, but the gathering is taking place eastward rather than westward. . . . The fact of the matter is that the Westerners were actually sent back because they started out as Easterners."[54]

"We occasionally talk about those who would be interested in this temple," stated Don Mangum, cochair of the Boston Temple's steering committee. "I pull out the family history on my family and find that 25 percent of my ancestors over nine generations came from New England. Three of the first four presidents of the Church were born here as well as many other leaders. Large congregations of members were organized here and moved West with the Church.

"Considering the influence of New England members on the Church," he concluded, "we suppose interest in the temple is great on both sides of the veil."[55]

"I feel like there have been so many people that have been moved and influenced by the Lord over a period of years just to lay the groundwork for [the temple]," observed President Ken Hutchins. "I think what the Lord has done here . . . and this is just one small, tiny part of the world. . . . [It] is akin to creation." Referencing his own role in the meeting where President Hinckley asked where a temple could be built in New England, Ken continued, "I would be content to know that if the only reason I was called as a stake president was just so that at that opportune time I could raise my hand and say, 'I know, I know!'. . .

"I give the Lord full credit. He really does all the work. He orchestrated all of those things that came together in a million pieces in order to let the temple happen here in Boston. There's no doubt in my mind that the temple was [planned] hundreds of years ago. . . . But, look, a prophet of the Lord . . . had to struggle over a period of time to get that to the point where it happened. Why should it be any different for us? . . . I'm not anxious about the gospel. The gospel's true. . . . The issue should be what you do with it. It's got to change your life. It's got to drive who you are and what you do and how you treat people. When you become converted like that, then the joy flows into your life and it reinforces what you already know. . . . Life is good."[56]

❧

In the early 1900s, Damie Forrest and her family lived in Halifax, Nova Scotia. Although they were a God-fearing family, they did not have strong ties to any one religion. While undergoing a serious operation in 1909, Damie had an experience in which she saw her father, who had passed away, standing near a gate in front of a beautiful building with several spires. She noticed a few people headed toward the building, while large multitudes were headed in the opposite direction. She wondered why so many would choose darkness and ugliness in the presence of such beauty.

Damie Forrest had never seen such a building and did not know what it was. When she awoke, however, she knew she needed to guide her family to that structure. For the next several years, Damie and her husband, Herbert, took their children from one church to another, hoping one of the congregations would provide a link to her experience and help her understand what the distinctive six-spired building represented. Each time, she left disappointed and dissatisfied.

Persecution and strident opposition to the Church had caused missionaries to leave Nova Scotia around the turn of the century, but ten years after Damie's experience, the Canadian Mission was organized and the Church sent four young men to reopen the area. A set of elders arrived at the Forrests' home, and Damie took a pamphlet. After reading the tract, Herbert sought the young men out and invited them back to their home.

The first time the Forrest family attended church, they knew it was true. There on the podium were three books that Damie had seen in her dream. She didn't know what they were, but she recognized the writing—the Book of Mormon, the Doctrine and Covenants, and the Pearl of Great Price. Damie, Herbert, and all their children were baptized in 1921, the third family to join the Church in Nova Scotia. A year after their baptism, Damie shared her experience with a young elder, who listened carefully and then showed her a picture of the Salt Lake Temple. Damie immediately recognized the building and knew this was where her family belonged.[57]

"Temples are more than stone and mortar," stated President Thomas S. Monson. "They are filled with faith and fasting. They are built of trials and testimonies. They are sanctified by sacrifice and service.

"Some degree of sacrifice has ever been associated with temple building and with temple attendance. . . . Why are so many willing to give so much in order to receive the blessings of the temple? Those who understand the eternal blessings which come from the temple know that no sacrifice is too great, no price too heavy, no struggle too difficult in order to receive those blessings. . . . They understand that the saving ordinances received in the temple that permit us to someday return to our Heavenly Father in an eternal family relationship and to be endowed with blessings and power from on high are worth every sacrifice and every effort."[58]

Germaine Simon immigrated to the United States from Haiti in 1981. Twelve years later she was introduced to the Church by a pair of young missionaries and knew that she could not deny the Spirit she felt when they taught. Following baptism, Germaine learned she could go to the temple after a year if she was worthy. "I prepared myself and prayed," she said. "I paid my tithing. And I went. . . . It was a wonderful, wonderful feeling. The peace I found . . . I did not want to come out. . . . It was a feeling that I would like to share with everyone—to go and see for themselves."

In preparation for the dedication of the Boston Temple, Germaine helped members of her ward with family history work so that her stake would have 2,000 names ready for ordinances upon its opening. Said Germaine of ordinances she performed for her own family members, "It is a feeling of satisfaction—a feeling of happiness. A feeling that I have done something for my parents whom I love. It's a great feeling. That makes my testimony grow, my faith. . . It makes me feel happy."

Reflecting on the changes that have come to her through the gospel, Sister Simon wished everyone could find the same joy. "I hope one day everyone will know about the Church and join and be happy with their family. Not only here, but hereafter. . . . I know this Church is true. I know we have a prophet right now—a living prophet who teaches us about God. The prophet Joseph Smith, when I talk about him, I always have tears in my eyes. I know that he really did see God. There is nothing impossible to God. God did show himself, and Jesus Christ showed himself to Joseph as a young boy. . . . I know this Church is true with all my heart."[59]

# AFTERWORD

"IN THE YEARS since the dedication of the Boston Temple," observed temple president Robert Wood, "the House of the Lord has been an anchor in the lives of the faithful Saints and a beacon to all of New England." Non-members commonly regard the Boston Temple as the headquarters of the Church in the area, and each week the temple receives multiple requests for information regarding the Church and its members. Temple workers direct these inquiries to Church media representatives and stake and mission leaders, but it is remarkable, President Wood noted, how many people think first of the temple when they think of the Church.[1]

Three years after the First Vision, seventeen-year-old Joseph Smith sought assurance from the Father that he "might know of [his] state and standing" (Joseph Smith History 1:29). In answer to his supplication, the youth was visited by the Angel Moroni, who promised that God had a work for him to do, following which the heavenly messenger quoted the same verses from Malachi in each of four concurrent visits, including:

"And he shall plant in the hearts of the children the promises made to the fathers, and the hearts of the children shall turn to their fathers. If it were not so, the whole earth would be utterly wasted at his coming." (Joseph Smith—History 1:39)

Although the teenage prophet could not have comprehended it at the time, the building of temples and the restoration of temple covenants in fulfillment of Malachi's prophesies was to become one of the consuming tasks of his adult life.

"Those who understand the eternal nature of the gospel—planned before the foundation—understand clearly why all history seems to revolve around the building and use of temples," Elder John A. Widtsoe wrote. "The plan of salvation . . . involves the principle that God's work with respect to this work will not be complete until every soul . . . has been offered the privilege of accepting salvation and the accompanying great blessings which the Lord has in store for his children."[2]

As the spirit of the temple and promises of the gospel have penetrated the hearts and souls of the members in New England, said President Wood, they too have come to see the temple as the symbol of their faith and the ultimate focus of their discipleship.

Linda Erickson did not want to lose the spirit and camaraderie that she and her family had felt in the events surrounding the Boston Temple's open house and dedication in 2000. On the Wednesday following the dedication, she presented herself at the temple administration desk and asked if there was anything she could do, knowing her young children precluded her from serving as an ordinance worker. Offered the chance to answer the phone and later schedule appointments, Linda's "temple day" was Wednesday, and it became her spiritual midweek anchor.

For eleven years, much of Linda's temple work was spent sitting in a cubicle on the phone. "We often think that it will be in the celestial room of the temple where we will most commune with God to feel and hear answers to our prayers," Linda noted. But she felt the Spirit's influence as she helped a new convert make an appointment to receive his endowment and talked to a mother calling to schedule the sealing that would bind her to her children and newly reactivated husband. "It was a humbling experience for me to be a facilitator of information to fellow Saints with eternal goals for their families. For me, my cubicle became . . . a place where I would receive revelatory insights into the challenges of my life."[3]

Others share similar experiences. With a temple in their midst, young men and women are able to come to the temple to do proxy baptisms and experience personally the power of the temple in their lives. The demographics of the area result in many graduate and undergraduate students serving as ordinance workers, alongside fully-employed members and the more traditional retired couples. "[W]hat a blessing they have found it to be!" exclaimed President Wood of the number of individuals who have found ways to serve in the temple. "The business of their lives is shaped and animated by their opportunity to labor in the House of the Lord. Young returned missionaries 'continue' their mission in the work of the gospel through the redemptive ordinances of the temple, as do busy professional and business people," who find renewal, direction, and grounding in the teachings of the temple.[4]

In a general conference session held in 1902, President Joseph F. Smith voiced his hope that one day there would be "temples built in the various parts of the [world] where they are needed for the convenience of the people." With over 165 temples in operation or in progress, President Monson has remarked, "The goal of President Joseph F. Smith . . . is becoming a reality. Our desire is to make the temple as accessible as possible to our members."[5]

The seventeen acres that eventually came to house the Boston temple was owned by a Mrs. Rapoli in the late 1970s. After others had identified the parcel as a possible site for a meetinghouse and met with its owner, Steve Wheelwright visited Mrs. Rapoli. She began their conversation stating that she'd seen the temple in Washington, D.C., and loved it. Did the Church want to construct a building like that one? Told that the intent was to build a simple chapel, Mrs. Rapoli explained that her husband had been a devout Catholic who believed the world needed more churches. He had purchased a number of properties, upon which other denominations had built but had not found a suitable buyer for the seventeen acres before he passed away.

From the outset, Mrs. Rapoli was supportive of the Church's purchase, but she would not, under any circumstances, agree to divide the large parcel. Some twenty years later, Steve and Margaret Wheelwright returned to the site with the elderly Mrs. Rapoli and one of her sons to walk through the yet-to-be-completed temple. "My husband would be so happy with what you have done," she said joyously. "I'm sure he is here with us today."[6]

Now an ordinance worker with grown children, Linda Erickson said, "When I think back over the [years] . . . I can see the strength, the patience, and the hope of the Lord in me and in us as we have bathed in the blessings of the temple. What a privilege it has been to be a part of the Boston temple, the Lord's Holy House."[7]

"Every temple is a house of God, filling the same functions and with identical blessings and ordinances," President Monson has stated. "Each one stands as a beacon to the world, an expression of our testimony that

God, our Eternal Father, lives, that He desires to bless us and, indeed, to bless His sons and daughters of all generations."[8]

Today the Boston Temple is frequently visited by groups of Primary children. A member of the temple presidency and his wife make a point of meeting with each of these gatherings in the lobby of the temple distribution center. "The excitement for the temple [among] these youngsters is palpable," President Wood observed, reflecting on the efforts and sacrifices of the many Saints that led to such a blessing. Comparing the temple's presence and influence to the ripples that radiate from a stone cast into still water, he added, "The spirit of Elijah penetrates the lives and aspirations of future generations."[9]

# NOTES

INTRODUCTION

1. "New England Mission and Cambridge Branch Chapel Building—
   Church of Jesus Christ of Latter-Day Saints: Dedication September 23,
   1956," Cambridge Branch Church of Jesus Christ of Latter-day Saints,
   1956, 42. Published in conjunction with the dedication of the chapel at
   Longfellow Park in Cambridge, MA, hereafter referred to as "Cambridge
   Dedicatory Program."

CHAPTER 1 – THE PATHS THY SAINTS HAVE TROD

1. Jenson, *Latter-day Saint Biographical Encyclopedia,* 1:287.
2. Ibid.
3. Ibid.
4. Ibid.
5. Ibid.
6. Ibid., 1:287–88.
7. Ritchie, "Aurelia S. Rogers," *Sister Saints,* 225–26.
8. Ibid. 226, 228, and 232–33; Jenson, *Latter-day Saint Biographical
   Encyclopedia,* 1:288.
9. Watson, *The Orson Pratt Journals,* 12 and 16.
10. Scotland, "A History of the Boston Stake," 3; Journal History of the
    Church of Jesus Christ of Latter-day Saints, August 14, 1832. See also
    Himes, "An analysis of the Book of Mormon."
11. Journal History, December 22, 1832.
12. Dahl, "Vermont," in *Sacred Places,* 129.
13. Holzapfel and Cottle, *Old Mormon Palmyra,* 180–181, 185.
14. Cowley, *Wilford Woodruff,* 70–71; Donald Q. Cannon, "Wilford
    Woodruff's Mission to Maine," 83; Cannon, "Wilford Woodruff's
    Mission to the Fox Islands," 86.
15. Cowley, *Wilford Woodruff,* 75–77.
16. Ibid., 77–78.
17. Ibid.

18. Ibid., 78–79.
19. Ibid., 79.
20. Cannon, "Wilford Woodruff's Mission," 90.
21. Bitton, "A Church for All Lands."
22. Cowley, *Wilford Woodruff,* 94.
23. Hulbert, *Holliston,* 151–52.
24. Cannon, "Massachusetts with Selected Sites" in *Sacred Places,* 43.
25. Hulbert, *Holliston,* 154.
26. Ibid. 154; see also "The Havens of Massachusetts," 3–6.
27. "The Havens of Massachusetts," 7.
28. Hulbert, *Holliston,* 152–53.
29. Ibid., 151.
30. Ibid., 152.
31. Scotland, "History of the Boston Stake," 4–5.
32. May, "Boston's Mormon Landmark," 19.
33. Ibid.
34. Ibid.; Scotland, "History of the Boston Stake," 5.
35. Dahl, "Vermont," in *Sacred Places,* 125.
36. Larson, *Erastus Snow,* 67.
37. Cannon, "Massachusetts with Selected Sites," in *Sacred Places,* 24–25; Holzapfel and Cottle, *Old Mormon Palmyra,* 29
38. Larson, *Erastus Snow,* 67.
39. Ibid.; Journal History, February 4, 1842.
40. Larson, *Erastus Snow,* 68.
41. Journal History, February 4, 1842.
42. Ibid. See also Larson, *Erastus Snow,* 69.
43. Larson, *Erastus Snow,* 69.
44. Journal History, February 4, 1842.
45. Holzapfel and Cottle, *Old Mormon Palmyra,* 32.
46. Larson, *Erastus Snow,* 70-71.
47. Anderson, "New Hampshire with Selected Sites in Maine," in *Sacred Places,* 61.
48. Journal History, September 11, 1842.
49. Journal History, February 9, 1843.
50. Ibid.
51. Ibid.
52. Madsen, "Emmeline B. Wells," in *Supporting Saints,* 307–8, 313, 331.
53. Journal History, June 30, 1844.
54. "History of Brigham Young," *Millennial Star,* May 28, 1864, 343–44.
55. "History of Brigham Young," *Millennial Star,* June 4, 1864, 359.
56. Woodruff, "The Keys of the Kingdom," *Millennial Star,* September 2, 1889, 545–46.
57. Ibid., 546.
58. "History of Brigham Young," *Millennial Star,* June 4, 1864, 359.
59. Dahl, "Vermont," in *Sacred Places,* 94.

60. Journal History, October 9, 1844.

61. Journal History, July 12, 1845.

62. Scotland, "History of the Boston Stake," 9.

63. Journal History, June 2, 1847.

64. Ibid. See also, for example, Dahl, "Vermont," in *Sacred Places*, 89.

65. Scotland, "History of the Boston Stake," 9–10.

66. Cannon, "Massachusetts," in *Sacred Places*, 56–57.

67. Parrish, "Harvard and the Gospel, an Informal History," in *Regional Studies*, 122; Scotland, "History of the Boston Stake," 11.

68. Widtsoe, *In a Sunlit Land*, 31–32.

69. Ibid., 37.

70. Scotland, "History of the Boston Stake," 11; Cambridge Dedicatory Program, 12–13.

71. "Information Furnished by Mrs. Roy Bullen of Salt Lake City, Utah" (unpublished timeline covering 1845-1905), hereafter referred to as "Bullen timeline."

72. Cowan, "Yankee Saints," in *Regional Studies*, 102; Bullen timeline.

73. Bullen timeline.

74. "Dedicatory Services for the Director's Residence and Bureau of Information at the Joseph Smith Birthplace Memorial" (Boston, MA: University Press of Cambridge, Inc. 1961), hereafter referred to as "Joseph Smith Birthplace Memorial Program"; Gates, "Memorial Mount Dedication," *Improvement Era*, 308–9 and 312–13.

75. Joseph Smith Birthplace Memorial Program.

76. Scotland, "History of the Boston Stake," 12.

77. Cowan, "Yankee Saints," in *Regional Studies*, 105.

78. Cambridge Dedicatory Program, 13.

79. Cowan, "Yankee Saints," in *Regional Studies*, 105.

80. Cambridge Dedicatory Program, 23.

81. Ibid.

82. Mel and Eugenia Herlin, interview.

83. Cambridge Ward Relief Society, "Relief Society —126 Years," 2.

84. Cranney, interview.

85. Cambridge Ward Relief Society, "Relief Society—126 Years", 2.

86. Cranney, interview; *Naomi Remembers*, 73–74.

87. Cambridge Dedicatory Program, 32; *Naomi Remembers*, 73.

88. *Naomi Remembers*, 73.

89. Cambridge Dedicatory Program, 25 and 32.

90. Cowan, "Yankee Saints," in *Regional Studies*, 106.

91. Rolapp, "The Eastern States Mission," *Improvement Era*, 582–83.

92. Cranney, interview; *Naomi Remembers*, 76.

93. *Naomi Remembers*, 76.

94. Cowan, "Yankee Saints," in *Regional Studies*, 106–7.

95. Scotland, "History of the Boston Stake," 18.

96. Cranney, interview; *Naomi Remembers*, 77–78.

97. Madsen, interview; S. Dilworth Young, letter to Richard L. Bushman; Truman G. Madsen quoted in *Naomi Remembers*, 77–78. See also Cowan, "Yankee Saints," in *Regional Studies*, 108–9.

98. S. Dilworth Young, letter to Richard L. Bushman, March 31, 1976.

99. Cambridge Dedicatory Program, 17, 27, and 32–33; Parkinson and Barney, interview.

100. Cambridge Dedicatory Program, 27–28 and 33–34; Cranney Oral History, 41.

101. Hattie Maughan in *The New Englander* (prior publication of New England Mission), quoted in "Cambridge Dedicatory Program," 19–21; Tidd, interview. See also Cambridge Dedicatory Program, 33.

102. Cambridge Dedicatory Program, 30, 34–35, and 38; undated letter to former Cambridge Branch members regarding construction of new chapel.

103. Cambridge Dedicatory Program, 38; Gordon Williams, interview; Hartley, interview.

104. Tidd, "The Mormons Are Coming!" 118–122; Elsworth, email to Jeffrey Tidd. See also Tidd, interview.

105. Cowan, "Yankee Saints," in *Regional Studies*, 107–8.

106. Ibid.

107. Jacobsen, "The Awakening," in *The Oxford Ward Messenger*, March 1989 and April 1989.

108. Extracts from Documentary History of Church, 6:319, quoted in Cambridge Dedicatory Program, 42.

109. Scotland, "History of the Boston Stake," 19–21; Weston Ward and Boston Stake Dedication Program, October 6, 1968.

110. Cowan, "Yankee Saints," in *Regional Studies*, 110.

111. Cambridge Dedicatory Program, 42.

112. Joseph Smith Birthplace Memorial Program.

113. Porter, interview.

114. Eyring, interview.

## Chapter 2 – The Influence of the One

1. Finlayson, interview.

2. Hall, "Funeral Service," 3–4.

3. Robert Chipman Fletcher, unpublished manuscript.

4. Finlayson, interview.

5. Bennion, "Elizabeth Skolfield Hinckley," 6.

6. Truman G. Madsen, "Funeral Service," 12.

7. Bennion. "Elizabeth Skolfield Hinckley," 5–6; R. Hall, "Funeral Service," 5.

8. Truman G. Madsen, "Funeral Service," 12.

9. Nelson, *From Heart to Heart*, 85.

10. Eyring, interview.
11. Chase Peterson, interview.
12. Mulder, interview.
13. Salo, "Funeral Service," 9; Hall, "Funeral Service," 5.
14. Hall, "Funeral Service," 5.
15. Truman G. Madsen, interview.
16. Ibid.
17. Romish, letter to Clayton Christensen.
18. Romish, discussion with author.
19. Bennion, "Elizabeth Skolfield Hinckley."
20. Truman G. Madsen, "Funeral Service," 12.
21. Finlayson, interview.
22. Alan and Marcia Parrish, interview.
23. Lyon, interview.
24. Finlayson, interview.
25. Remarks by Clayton M. Christensen in Potvin, interview.
26. Kelleher, interview.
27. *Naomi Remembers*, 75.
28. Herlin, interview; Potvin, interview; Knecht, interview; *Naomi Remembers*, 76.
29. Knecht, interview.
30. Nielsen, interview.
31. Knecht, interview.
32. Robert Fletcher, unpublished manuscript; Rosemary Fletcher, interview.
33. Ann Madsen, interview.
34. Finlayson, interview.
35. Ibid.
36. Chase Peterson, interview.
37. Comments by Clayton Christensen in summary of William Knecht interview.
38. Vance Smith, interview.
39. Gordon Williams, interview.
40. Grethe Peterson, interview.
41. Tom and Pam Eagar, interview.
42. Parrish, interview.
43. Justin Lindsey, interview; see also Margaret and Steve Wheelwright, interview.
44. Dave Foster, interview.
45. Hutchins, interview.
46. Ibid.
47. Dave Foster, interview.
48. Grant Bennett, interview.
49. Helen and Ward Low, interview.
50. Ludwig, interview.
51. Ludwig, discussion with author.

52. Ludwig, interview; Ludwig, discussion with author.
53. Moorehead, "About Books & Basketball," 1.
54. Wyatt, "Excited to Learn," 4.
55. Ludwig, interview.
56. Hart, Books and Basketball newsletter, 1.
57. Ludwig, email to and discussion with author.
58. Morris, "Help and Hope in Washington, D.C.," 28–32; Ludwig, interview.
59. Goodliffe, Books and Basketball newsletter, 2.

## Chapter 3 – How Firm Is Your Foundation?

1. Cranney, interview; *Naomi Remembers*, 80–82.
2. Cranney, interview. See also Cranney Oral History, 36 and 53–55.
3. Berg, interview.
4. Ibid.
5. Dunn, interview.
6. Ibid.
7. Christensen, "Recollections," 7.
8. Ibid.
9. Gary Crittenden, interview.
10. Gary Crittenden, interview; Romney, interview.
11. Gary Crittenden, interview.
12. McKinnon, interview.
13. Ibid.
14. Horne, interview.
15. Clayton, interview.
16. Eddington, "Missed Opportunities."
17. Fresh, interview.
18. McPhee, interview.
19. Romney, interview.
20. Wright, interview.
21. Ibid.
22. Dunn, interview.
23. Romney, interview.
24. Knecht, interview.
25. Smith, *Lectures on Faith*, 69.
26. Schmidt, interview.
27. Lyon, interview.
28. Christensen, "Recollections," 1.
29. Chase Peterson, interview.
30. Baird, interview.
31. Kent and Kathy Bowen, interview.
32. Parrish, interview.
33. Cathy Crittenden, interview.

34. Christensen, "Recollections," 1.
35. Thibault, interview.
36. Maitland, interview.
37. Valerie Anderson, interview.
38. Conference Report, April 1947, 50.
39. Clark, interview.
40. Susan Bednar in Parkin et al., "Testimonies of the Restoration."
41. Lambert, interview.
42. Hutchins, interview.
43. Wheeler, interview.
44. Lee LaPierre, interview.
45. Hinckley, *Teachings of Gordon B. Hinckley*, 565.
46. Lee LaPierre, interview.
47. Jonathan Williams, interview.

CHAPTER 4 – BY WEAK AND SIMPLE THINGS

1. Wood, interview.
2. Quintera, interview.
3. Arias, interview. See also Christensen, "A Brief History of the Church in New England," 15–16; Christensen, "Jaime's Story."
4. Christensen, "An Unheralded Hero."
5. McLaughlin, interview; Christensen, "An Unheralded Hero."
6. Ballard, "The Essential Role of Member Missionary Work," 38–39.
7. Conference Report, October 1966, 86.
8. Christensen and Christensen, "Seven Lessons on Sharing the Gospel," 38.
9. Wood, interview.
10. Hutchins, interview.
11. Wood, interview.
12. Christensen, letter to author.
13. Forrest, interview.
14. Earnshaw, interview.
15. Gordon Williams, interview.
16. Eyring, interview.
17. Baird, interview.
18. Gaz, interview.
19. Chopelas, interview.
20. Dunn, "We Are Called of God," 43.
21. Truman G. Madsen, interview.
22. Ann Madsen, interview.
23. Low, interview.
24. Paredes, interview.
25. Romney, interview.
26. Paredes, interview.
27. Wheeler, interview.

28. Wood, interview.
29. McKinnon, interview.

## Chapter 5 – Bearing One Another's Burdens

1. Ann Madsen, interview.
2. Hales, interview. See also Lyon, interview.
3. Horne, interview.
4. Van Uitert, interview.
5. Gael Ulrich, interview.
6. Lyon, interview.
7. Cornwall, interview.
8. Clark, interview; Kim Clark, email to author.
9. Low, interview.
10. Brown, interview.
11. Lyon, interview.
12. Chandler, interview.
13. Rigby, interview.
14. Hafen and Hafen, *Handcarts to Zion*, 119–21.
15. Linda Hoffman Kimball, interview.
16. Einreinhofer, interview.
17. Holbrook, interview.
18. Gordon Williams, interview.
19. Judy Dushku, interview, August 13, 1997.
20. Judy Dushku, interview, September 11, 1997.
21. Kelleher, interview.
22. Hangen, interview.
23. Bowman, interview.
24. Elliott, interview.
25. Gael Ulrich, interview.
26. Kelleher, interview.
27. Porter, interview.
28. Coppins, interview.
29. Barnett, interview.
30. Coppins, interview.
31. McKinnon, interview.
32. Barnett, interview.
33. Lindsey, interview.
34. Benson, "Born of God," 6.
35. Lindsey, interview.
36. Sorenson, interview.
37. Romish, interview.
38. Rollins, interview.
39. Thibault, interview.
40. Nielsen, interview.

41. Coppins, interview.
42. Sorenson, interview.
43. Paul and Kristen Anderson, interview.
44. Lindsey, interview.
45. Hinckley, "Our Mission of Saving," 54.
46. Clark, interview.

## Chapter 6 – Taking the Leap of Faith

1. Neal, interview.
2. Bowman, interview.
3. Lavin, interview.
4. Christensen, letter to author.
5. Goldberg, interview.
6. Mark Johnson, interview.
7. McPhee, interview.
8. Goldberg, interview.
9. Knighton, interview.
10. Thibault, interview.
11. Cutler, interview.
12. "History of Thomas Baldwin Marsh," *Millennial Star*, June 11, 1864, 375.
13. Knighton, interview.
14. Munns, interview.
15. Ibid.
16. Berg, interview.
17. Camille Foster, interview.
18. Eagar, interview.
19. Mark Johnson, interview.
20. McLaughlin, interview.
21. Sloan, interview.
22. Thibault, interview.
23. Rivera, interview.
24. Peterson, "Taxi Talk," 68–69; Cortelyou, interview.
25. Schreck, interview.
26. Peterson, "Taxi Talk," 68–69.
27. Cutler, interview.
28. Dave Foster, interview.
29. Manderino, interview.
30. McPhee, interview.
31. Neal, interview.
32. Gordon Williams, interview.
33. Arias, interview.
34. Hinckley, "Inspirational Thoughts," 3.
35. Ibid., 4.
36. Camille Foster, interview.

37. Elliott, interview.
38. Garbutt, interview.
39. Ludlow, interview.
40. Bowman, interview.
41. Knighton, interview.
42. Elliott, interview.
43. Potvin, interview.
44. Bowman, interview.
45. Rivera, interview.
46. Hinckley, "Some Thoughts on Temples, Retention of Converts, and Missionary Service," 51.
47. Neal, interview.
48. Elbert and Elaine Johnson, interview.
49. Goldberg, interview.
50. Elbert and Elaine Johnson, interview.
51. Hinckley, "Every Convert Is Precious," 11.
52. Knighton, interview.
53. McLaughlin, interview.
54. Neal, interview.
55. Bowman, interview.
56. Elliott, interview.
57. Thibault, interview.
58. Bowman, interview.
59. Paul and Kristen Anderson, interview. See also Bennett, interview, February 1999.
60. Bennett, interview, February 1999.
61. Paredes, interview.
62. Neal, interview.
63. Mark Johnson, interview.
64. McLaughlin, interview.

## Chapter 7 – A Leader, a Disciple

1. Flake and Flake, "Wilbur W. Cox," 34–35; Ballantyne, "Recollections," 2; Nelson, *From Heart to Heart*, 86.
2. Finlayson, interview.
3. Flake and Flake, "Wilbur W. Cox," 37, quoting Martha Cox Ballantyne, untitled personal account in her possession.
4. Chase Peterson, interview.
5. Flake and Flake, "Wilbur W. Cox," 37, quoting Ballantyne.
6. Ibid., 37–38.
7. Flake and Flake, "Wilbur W. Cox," 41–42.
8. Church of Jesus Christ of Latter-day Saints, New England Mission. "Excerpts of addresses delivered at the organization of the Boston Stake in Cambridge, Mass., Sunday evening, May 20, 1962," BYU Special

Collections, Harold B. Lee Library, Provo, UT, quoted in Flake and Flake, "Wilbur W. Cox."

9. Fresh, interview.
10. Lambert, interview.
11. Romney, interview.
12. Rosemary Fletcher, interview.
13. McLaughlin, interview.
14. McKinnon, interview.
15. Gordon Williams, interview.
16. Gaz, interview.
17. Holton, interview.
18. Gordon Williams, interview.
19. Christensen, "Recollections," 2–3.
20. Finlayson, interview.
21. Lee LaPierre, interview.
22. Romney, interview.
23. Knighton, interview.
24. Richard Bushman, interview.
25. Romney, interview.
26. Hutchins, interview.
27. Gordon Williams, interview.
28. Camille Foster, interview.
29. Hangen, interview.
30. Gaz, interview.
31. Eagar, interview.
32. Romney, interview.
33. David Coppins quoting Kenneth Hutchins in Coppins, interview.
34. Coppins, interview.
35. Hoffmire, interview.
36. Gaz, interview.
37. Dottie LaPierre, interview.
38. Gordon Williams, interview.
39. Fresh, interview.
40. Lambert, interview.
41. Beck, "An Outpouring of Blessings," 13, quoting Boyd. K. Packer, "What Every Elder Should Know—and Every Sister as Well: A Primer on Principles of Priesthood Government," *Ensign*, Feb. 1993, 10.
42. Eyring, interview.
43. Lindsey, interview.
44. Simon, interview.
45. Lindsey, interview.

## Chapter 8 – We Gather Together

1. Johnson, "History of the Providence, R.I. Branch." See also Carter, "Brief

History of the Providence, Rhode Island Branch," 2 and 12–13. Carter quotes an article entitled "Branch Saints Enjoy Own Chapel: Activities in New England Mission Recounted" appearing in the March 31, 1945 Church News section of the *Deseret News* stating that the chapel was converted from a $68,000 private library that the church obtained for the "unusually low sum" of $6,000. Johnson states in his history that the amount was approximately $6,400.

2. Carter, "Brief History of the Providence, Rhode Island Branch," 2.
3 Ibid. 13, quoting article entitled "Branch Saints Enjoy Own Chapel: Activities in New England Mission Recounted" appearing in March 31, 1945 Church News section of the *Deseret News*.
4. Carter, "Brief History of the Providence, Rhode Island Branch," 4–5.
5. Van Uitert, interview. See also Laurel Thatcher Ulrich, interview, and Horne, interview.
6. Laurel Thatcher Ulrich, interview. See also Horne, interview and Gael Ulrich, interview.
7. Laurel Thatcher Ulrich, interview; Horne, interview; and Van Uitert, interview.
8. Horne, interview.
9. Ulrich, *A Beginner's Boston*, vii. See Horne, interview; Van Uitert, interview.
10. Horne, interview; Laurel Thatcher Ulrich, interview; and Van Uitert, interview.
11. Gordon Williams, interview; Laurel Thatcher Ulrich, interview; Horne, interview; Claudia L. Bushman, "Acknowledgements for the Revised Edition"; Ulrich, *A Beginner's Boston,* vi.
12. Horne, interview; Gael Ulrich, interview; Van Uitert, interview; Gordon Williams, interview.
13. Laurel Thatcher Ulrich, interview.
14. Gordon Williams, interview.
15. Christensen, "Recollections," 7.
16. McKinnon, interview.
17. Eagar, interview.
18. Brown, interview.
19. McKinnon, interview.
20. Carter, "Brief History of the Providence, Rhode Island Branch," 5.
21. Kelleher, interview.
22. Harper, interview.
23. Rollins, interview.
24. Randall, interview. See also *Worcester Daily Telegram*, Nov. 7, 1964; August 1962 Building Project Financial Statistics and letter to members (26 August 1962).
25. Harper, interview. See also Berg, interview.
26. Berg, interview.
27. Alexander, interview.

28. Van Uitert, interview. See also Brown, interview.
29. Brown, interview.
30. Murdock, interview.
31. McKinnon, interview.
32. Christensen, "Recollections," 13–14.
33. Christensen, "Recollections,"14–15. See also Atkinson, interview.
34. Atkinson, interview.
35. Murdock, interview; Gordon Williams, interview. See also Herlin, interview; Norma Chandler, interview.
36. Knecht, interview.
37. Rondina, interview.
38. Elliott, interview.
39. Anleu, interview.
40. Hoffmire, interview.
41. Ibid.
42. Laurel Thatcher Ulrich, interview.
43. See, for example, Laurel Thatcher Ulrich, interview; Low, interview.
44. Brown, interview.
45. Cornwall, interview.
46. Brown, interview.
47. Cornwall, interview. See also Kent and Kathy Bowen, interview.
48. Kent and Kathy Bowen, interview.
49. Cornwall, interview. See also Kent and Kathy Bowen, interview.
50. Barlow, interview.
51. Cornwall, interview. See also Kent and Kathy Bowen, interview.
52. "Leading in the Lord's Way," in *Teachings of Presidents of the Church: Joseph Smith*, 281–83.
53. Hoffmire, interview.
54. Rondina, interview.
55. Camille Foster, interview.
56. Barnett, interview. See also Clark, interview and Schreck, interview.
57. Schreck, interview.
58. Barnett, interview.
59. Coppins, interview.
60. Schreck, interview.
61. Christensen, letter to author.
62. Gaz, interview.
63. Elliott, interview.
64. Lee LaPierre, interview.
65. Nielsen, interview.
66. Dushku, interview, August 13, 1997; Dushku, interview, September 11, 1997.

## Chapter 9 – That Our Children May Know

1. See Gordon Williams, interview; Forrest, interview; John Hartley, interview; Randall, interview.
2. Gordon Williams, interview. See also Brown, interview.
3. Fresh, interview.
4. Perry, Perry, and Nelson, interview.
5. Barnett, interview.
6. Kathy Bowen, interview.
7. Christensen, "Recollections," 6.
8. Gordon Williams, interview.
9. Kathy Bowen, interview.
10. Ence, interview.
11. Holbrook, interview.
12. Clayton Christensen paraphrasing Kent Bowen in Lavin, interview.
13. Fish, interview.
14. Lindsey, interview.
15. Lavin, interview.
16. Fish, interview.
17. Butler, "Chain Reaction," 34–37. See also Letter from Clark Gilbert to Stephen Whyte, BYU School Relations, 2.
18. Butler, "Chain Reaction," 37.
19. Letter from Clark Gilbert to Stephen Whyte, BYU School Relations, 2.
20. Butler, "Chain Reaction," 39.
21. Potvin, interview.
22. David O. McKay, quoted in Backman, "Youth's Opportunity to Serve," 84.
23. Alexander, interview.
24. Perry, Perry, and Nelson, interview.
25. Laraine Wright, email to author.
26. Fish, interview.
27. Ibid.
28. Lindsey, interview.
29. Fish, interview.
30. Romney, interview.
31. Munns, interview.
32. Romney, interview.
33. Munns, interview. See also Hiller, "The Brotherhood-Sisterhood Thing," 21.
34. Wright, interview.
35. Kleekamp, "Never Too Young," 29–35.
36. Fish, interview.
37. Perry, Perry and Nelson, interview.
38. Bednar, "The Hearts of the Children Shall Turn," 26.
39. Christensen, "Recollections," 8.
40. Alexander, interview.

41. Kathy Bowen, interview.
42. Hopkin, interview.
43. Clark, interview.
44. "Love One Another," *Hymns*, no. 308.
45. Porter, interview. See also Porter, "Building the Kingdom," 80.

CHAPTER 10 – TENDING THE VINEYARD

1. Dunn, interview.
2. Rockwood, "Memories from Our Boston Years," 1–5.
3. Ibid., 2–6.
4. Ibid., 4–8.
5. Gaz, interview.
6. See Eagar, interview; Gordon Williams, interview.
7. Rockwood, 6–7.
8. Ibid., 10.
9. Gordon Williams, interview.
10. Ibid.
11. Rockwood, 8.
12. Ibid., 10.
13. Gaz, interview.
14. Joshua and Lillian Smith, interview.
15. Baird, interview.
16. Barnett, interview.
17. Romney, interview.
18. Knighton, interview.
19. Romney, interview; Hiers, interview.
20. Fish, interview.
21. Murdock, interview.
22. Holbrook, interview.
23. *Autobiography of Parley P. Pratt*, 145–46.
24. Romney, interview.
25. Bowman, interview.
26. Forrest, interview. See also Herlin, interview.
27. Hales, interview.
28. Rollins, interview.
29. Coppins, interview.
30. Hopkin, interview.
31. Paul and Kristen Anderson, interview.
32. Hopkin, interview.
33. Earnshaw, interview.
34. Gordon Williams, interview.
35. Romney, interview. See also Kent and Kathy Bowen, interview.
36. Romney, interview.
37. Kent and Kathy Bowen, interview.

38. Knighton, interview.
39. Arias, interview.
40. Evans, interview.
41. Romney, interview.
42. Baird, interview.
43. Romney, interview.
44. Wood, interview.
45. Cornwall, interview.
46. Gordon Williams, interview.
47. Romney, interview.
48. Hutchins, interview.
49. Wood, interview.
50. Gaz, interview.
51. Richard Bushman, interview.
52. Bennett, interview, February 1999.
53. Kent and Kathy Bowen, interview.
54. Richard Bushman, interview.
55. Remarks by Clayton M. Christensen in Horne, interview.
56. Fresh, interview.
57. Joshua and Lillian Smith, interview.
58. Gaz, interview.
59. Joshua and Lillian Smith, interview.
60. Sorenson, interview.

## CHAPTER 11 – ENLARGING THE BOUNDARIES

1. Tony Kimball, interview.
2. Ibid.
3. Wilson, "Tony Kimball."
4. Jim Jardine email to Clayton Christensen.
5. Kim and Sue Clark, interview.
6. Wilson, "Tony Kimball."
7. Cortelyou, interview.
8. Jim Jardine, email to Clayton Christensen.
9. Cooprider, interview.
10. Wilson, "Tony Kimball."
11. Cole Durham, email to Clayton Christensen.
12. Orton, interview.
13. Tony Kimball interview, 1998.
14. Richard Bushman, interview.
15. Dunn, interview.
16. "The Gospel Defined," in *Teachings of Presidents of the Church: Brigham Young*, 16.
17. Nielsen, interview.
18. Kelleher, interview.

19. Kent and Kathy Bowen, interview.
20. Hartiala-Sloan, interview.
21. Wood, interview.
22. Richard Bushman, interview.
23. Haglund, interview.
24. Robert Chipman Fletcher, unpublished manuscript.
25. Lyon, interview.
26. Dushku, interview, September 11, 1997.
27. Dushku, interview, August 13, 1997.
28. Tony Kimball, interview, 1998.
29. Grethe Peterson, interview. See also Laurel Thatcher Ulrich, interview.
30. Laurel Thatcher Ulrich, interview. See also Claudia Bushman, interview.
31. Hartiala-Sloan, interview.
32. Judy Dushku, interview, August 13, 1997.
33. Linda Hoffman Kimball, interview.
34. For example, see Judy Dushku, interview, August 13, 1997; see also Gordon Williams, interview.
35. Laurel Thatcher Ulrich, interview.
36. Romney, interview.
37. Atkinson, interview.
38. Laraine Wright, email to author.
39. Dredge, interview.
40. Chris Kimball, interview.
41. Lawrence A. Young, "Single Adults," 1317.
42. Christensen, "Recollections,"14.
43. Chris Kimball, interview.
44. Christensen, "Recollections," 14.
45. Christensen, "Recollections," 18.
46. Chris Kimball, interview.
47. Oaks and Wickman, "Same Gender Attraction."
48. Christensen, "Recollections," 18.
49. George McPhee in Wheeler, interview.
50. Lavin, interview.
51. Orton, interview.
52. George McPhee in Judy Dushku, interview, August 13, 1997.

## Chapter 12 – In the World

1. Peterson, "Belmont's Blessing," 28; Kent and Kathy Bowen, interview.
2. Romney, interview.
3. Peterson, "Belmont's Blessing," 27 and 30.
4. Christensen, "Recollections," 7–8; Peterson, "Belmont's Blessing," 26.
5. Peterson, "Belmont's Blessing," 26–27.
6. Stahle, "Boston temple to Become 100th edifice"; Letter from Jan McKinnon to Christine Christensen. See also Kent and Kathy Bowen, interview.

7. Kent and Kathy Bowen, interview; Baird, interview.
8. Romney, interview.
9. Kent and Kathy Bowen, interview. See also Christensen, "Recollections," 9; and Peterson, "Belmont's Blessing," 27.
10. Kent and Kathy Bowen, interview.
11. Peterson, "Belmont's Blessing," 28–29. See Romney, interview.
12. Romney, interview.
13. Peterson, "Belmont's Blessing," 29.
14. Cornwall, interview.
15. Romney, interview. See also Christensen, "Recollections," 8.
16. Peterson, "Belmont's Blessing," 26; see also Romney, interview.
17. Peterson, "Belmont's Blessing," 26; see also Christensen, "Recollections," 12.
18. Christensen, "Recollections," 9.
19. Bennett, interview, November 9, 2000.
20. Christensen, "Recollections," 9.
21. Ruth Ray Kelleher quoting Ira Terry in Kelleher, interview.
22. Brown, interview.
23. Wheelwright, interview.
24. Kathy Bowen, interview.
25. Chase Peterson, interview.
26. Christensen, "Recollections," 9-10.
27. Kathy Bowen, interview. See also Eagar, interview.
28. Hopkin, interview.
29. Hiers, interview.
30. Dee Dee Williams, interview.
31. Dottie LaPierre, interview.
32. Wheelwright, interview.
33. Bennett, interview, November 9, 2000.
34. Ibid.
35. Christensen, "Recollections," 9.
36. Bennett, interview, November 9, 2000. Also see Brown, interview.
37. Bennett, interview, November 9, 2000.
38. Brown, interview; Bennett, interview, November 9, 2000.
39. Cole, "Steeple Is at Center of Legal Battle"; Peggy Stack, "Mormon Milestone."
40. Bennett, interview, November 9, 2000.
41. Brown, interview.
42. Cole, "Steeple Is at Center of Legal Battle."
43. Stahle, "Boston Temple Dedicated as 100th Edifice."
44. Bennett, interview, November 9, 2000; Stahle, "Boston Temple Dedicated as 100th Edifice."
45. Bennett, interview, November 9, 2000.
46. Stahle, "Boston Temple Dedicated as 100th Edifice."
47. Stack, "Mormon Milestone."

48. Bennett, interview, November 9, 2000.
49. Mark Spencer in Brown, interview.
50. Bennett, interview, November 9, 2000.
51. Ibid.
52. Dee Dee Williams, interview.
53. Wheelwright, interview.
54. Kent Bowen, "John McArthur."
55. Perry, interview.
56. Sorenson, interview.
57. Hiers, interview.
58. Holbrook, interview.

## Chapter 13 – Promises to the Fathers

1. Oparowski, interview.
2. Hutchins, interview; Bennett, interview, November 9, 2000, 7–8; Tony Kimball, interview. See also Dew, *Gordon B. Hinckley*, 529–30.
3. Hutchins, interview; Bennett, interview, November 9, 2000, 7–8.
4. Gordon B. Hinckley journal, April 22, 1995, quoted in Dew, *Gordon B. Hinckley*, 530.
5. Hutchins, interview.
6. Brian Palmer in Hutchins, interview.
7. Cambridge Dedicatory Program, 42.
8. Clayton, interview.
9. Baliff, interview.
10. Ence, interview; Romney, interview; Kent and Kathy Bowen, interview.
11. Ence, interview; Hutchins, interview.
12. Baird, interview.
13. Brown, interview.
14. Alexander, interview.
15. Hinckley, "New Temples to Provide 'Crowning Blessings' of the Gospel," 87–88.
16. Kent Bowen, interview.
17. Ibid.
18. McPhee, interview.
19. Paul and Kristen Anderson, interview.
20. Kent Bowen, interview.
21. Paul and Kristen Anderson, interview.
22. Kent Bowen, interview.
23. Ibid.
24. Bennett, interview, November 9, 2000.
25. Kent Bowen, interview.
26. Bennett, interview, November 9, 2000.
27. Kent Bowen, interview.
28. Bennett, interview, November 9, 2000.

29. Schmidt, interview.

30. Stahle, "Boston Temple Dedicated as 100th Edifice."

31. Kent Bowen, interview.

32. Erickson, "A Guest at the Boston Temple Open House."

33. Stahle, "Boston Temple Dedicated as 100th Edifice."

34. Kent Bowen, interview.

35. Bennett, interview, November 9, 2000.

36. Kent Bowen, interview.

37. Paul and Kristen Anderson, interview.

38. Hopkin, interview.

39. Stahle, "Boston Temple Dedicated as 100th Edifice."

40. "Boston Massachusetts: 'We dedicate it as being complete,'" *Church News*, October 7, 2000.

41. Dunn, "Testimony," 13.

42. Stahle, "Court Upholds Boston Temple Zoning Case"; Pollock, "Steeple Placement Ends Legal Challenges to Boston Temple."

43. Pollock, "Steeple Placement Ends Legal Challenges."

44. Randall, interview.

45. Valerie Anderson, interview.

46. Hiers, interview.

47. Ibid.

48. Wood, interview.

49. Randall, interview.

50. Stack, "Mormon Milestone."

51. Romney, interview.

52. Lindsay, "Mormon Church Small But Expanding in Liberal Massachusetts."

53. Bednar, "Honorably Hold a Name and a Standing," 97, referencing *Teachings of Presidents of the Church: Joseph Smith*, 415–17.

54. Wood, interview.

55. Stahle, "Boston Temple Dedicated as 100th Edifice."

56. Hutchins, interview.

57. Forrest, interview and summary of Hugh and Muriel Forrest interview by Clayton Christensen. See also MacKinnon, "Saints in Halifax," 78.

58. Monson, "The Holy Temple," 92.

59. Simon, interview.

## Afterword

1. Wood, email to author.

2. Widtsoe, "Temple Worship," 54.

3. Erickson, email to author.

4. Robert Wood, email to author.

5. Monson, "The Holy Temple," quoting Joseph F. Smith in Conference Report, October 1902, 3.

6. Steven Wheelwright, email to Clayton M. Christensen.
7. Erickson, email to author.
8. Monson, "The Holy Temple," 93–94.
9. Wood, email to author.

# BIBLIOGRAPHY

Alexander, James and Marilee, interview by Clayton Christensen. October 3, 1999. Marlboro, MA: The Clayton M. Christensen collection of Boston Latter-day Saint Oral Histories, MSS 7770, L. Tom Perry Special Collections, Harold B. Lee Library, Brigham Young University, Provo, UT.

Anderson, Gary A. "New Hampshire with Selected Sites in Maine." In *Sacred Places: New England and Eastern Canada*, edited by LaMar C. Barratt. Salt Lake City, UT: Bookcraft, 1999.

Anderson, Paul and Kristen, interview by Elizabeth Young. January 19, 2003. Wellesley, MA: The Clayton M. Christensen collection of Boston Latter-day Saint Oral Histories, MSS 7770, L. Tom Perry Special Collections, Harold B. Lee Library, Brigham Young University, Provo, UT.

Anderson, Valerie, interview by Margaret Lazenby. May 11, 1998. Arlington, MA: The Clayton M. Christensen collection of Boston Latter-day Saint Oral Histories, MSS 7770, L. Tom Perry Special Collections, Harold B. Lee Library, Brigham Young University, Provo, UT.

Anleu, Francisco and Ana, interview by Nicole Stringham. February 21, 1999. Boston, MA: The Clayton M. Christensen collection of Boston Latter-day Saint Oral Histories, MSS 7770, L. Tom Perry Special

Collections, Harold B. Lee Library, Brigham Young University, Provo, UT.

Arias, Jim and Nancy, interview by Clayton Christensen. July 1998. Belmont, MA: The Clayton M. Christensen collection of Boston Latter-day Saint Oral Histories, MSS 7770, L. Tom Perry Special Collections, Harold B. Lee Library, Brigham Young University, Provo, UT.

Atkinson, Jennifer, interview by Clayton Christensen. June 7, 1998. Cambridge, MA: The Clayton M. Christensen collection of Boston Latter-day Saint Oral Histories, MSS 7770, L. Tom Perry Special Collections, Harold B. Lee Library, Brigham Young University, Provo, UT.

*Autobiography of Parley P. Pratt.* Salt Lake City, UT: Deseret Book, 1985.

Backman, Robert L. "Youth's Opportunity to Serve." *Ensign*, July 1973: 84–85.

Baird, Lloyd, interview by Karl H. Haglund. May 4, 1999. Belmont, MA: The Clayton M. Christensen collection of Boston Latter-day Saint Oral Histories, MSS 7770, L. Tom Perry Special Collections, Harold B. Lee Library, Brigham Young University, Provo, UT.

Baliff, Carma and Jae, interview by Nicole Stringham. January 13, 1999. Provo, UT: The Clayton M. Christensen collection of Boston Latter-day Saint Oral Histories, MSS 7770, L. Tom Perry Special Collections, Harold B. Lee Library, Brigham Young University, Provo, UT.

Ballantyne, J. M. "Recollections of my time in Boston 1959–1964." Unpublished manuscript. n.d.

Ballard, M. Russell. "The Essential Role of Member Missionary Work." *Ensign*, May 2003: 37.

Barlow, Philip, interview by Karl H. Haglund. January 18, 2000. Belmont, MA.

Barnett, Brent and Denise, interview by Clayton Christensen. February 25, 2001. Provo, UT: The Clayton M. Christensen collection of Boston Latter-day Saint Oral Histories, MSS 7770, L. Tom Perry Special Collections, Harold B. Lee Library, Brigham young University, Provo, UT.

Beck, Julie B. "An Outpouring of Blessings." *Ensign*, May 2006, 11–13.

Bednar, David A. "Honorably Hold a Name and a Standing." *Ensign*, May 2009, 97–100.

———. "The Hearts of the Children Shall Turn." *Ensign*, November 2011, 24–27.

Bennett, Grant, interview by Leon Elliott. February 1999, Belmont, MA: The Clayton M. Christensen collection of Boston Latter-day Saint Oral Histories, MSS 7770, L. Tom Perry Special Collections, Harold B. Lee Library, Brigham Young University, Provo, UT.

———. Interview by Leon Elliott. November 9, 2000. Belmont, MA: The Clayton M. Christensen collection of Boston Latter-day Saint Oral Histories, MSS 7770, L. Tom Perry Special Collections, Harold B. Lee Library, Brigham Young University, Provo, UT.

Bennion, Rachel. "Elizabeth Skolfield Hinckley." Unpublished manuscript. November 29, 2006.

Benson, Ezra Taft. "Born of God." *Ensign*, November 1985, 5–7.

Berg, Nephi Edward and Ruth Nielsen, interview by Clayton Christensen. November 14, 2004. Boston, MA: The Clayton M. Christensen collection of Boston Latter-day Saint Oral Histories, MSS 7770, L. Tom Perry Special Collections, Harold B. Lee Library, Brigham Young University, Provo, UT.

Bitton, Davis. "A Church for All Lands—Maine: A Momentous Letter." *Church News*, September 10, 1977.

"Boston Massachusetts: 'We Dedicate It as Being Complete'." *Church News*, October 7, 2000.

Bowen, Kathy, interview by Marti Elliott. February 19, 1999. Belmont, MA.

Bowen, Kent, interview by Karl H. Haglund. November 6, 2000. Belmont, MA.

———. "John McArthur: Learning about a Caring Institution." 1997.

Bowen, Kent and Kathy, interview by Clayton Christensen. November 1998. Belmont, MA.

Bowman, Fred, interview by Leon and Marti Elliott. January 31, 1999. Weston, MA: The Clayton M. Christensen collection of Boston Latter-day Saint Oral Histories, MSS 7770, L. Tom Perry Special Collections, Harold B. Lee Library, Brigham Young University, Provo, UT.

"Branch Saints Enjoy Own Chapel." *Deseret News*, March 31, 1945, 9.

Brown, Jerry and Peggy, interview by Mark Spencer. April 21, 1999. Belmont, MA: The Clayton M. Christensen collection of Boston Latter-day Saint Oral Histories, MSS 7770, L. Tom Perry Special Collections, Harold B. Lee Library, Brigham Young University, Provo, UT.

Bushman, Claudia, interview by Karen Haglund. June 3, 1999. New York, NY: The Clayton M. Christensen collection of Boston Latter-day Saint Oral Histories, MSS 7770, L. Tom Perry Special Collections, Harold B. Lee Library, Brigham Young University, Provo, UT.

Bushman, Richard, interview by Karl H. Haglund. June 4, 1998. New York, NY: The Clayton M. Christensen collection of Boston Latter-day Saint Oral Histories, MSS 7770, L. Tom Perry Special Collections, Harold B. Lee Library, Brigham Young University, Provo, UT.

Butler, Shanna. "Chain Reaction." *New Era*, June 2007, 34–39.

Cambridge Ward Relief Society. "Relief Society—126 Years." 1968.

Cannon, Donald Q. "Massachusetts with Selected Sites in Connecticut and Rhode Island." In *Sacred Places: New England and Eastern Canada*, edited by LaMar C. Barratt, 1–57. Salt Lake City, UT: Bookcraft, 1999.

———. "Wilford Woodruff's Mission to Maine." *The Improvement Era*, September 1970, 82–86.

———. "Wilford Woodruff's Mission to the Fox Islands." *Regional Studies in Latter-day Saint Church History: New England*, edited by Donald Q. Cannon, 85–99. Provo, UT: Brigham Young University, Department of Church History and Doctrine, 1988.

Carter, Richard Bert, Jr. "Brief History of the Providence, Rhode Island Branch of The Church of Jesus Christ of Latter-day Saints 1943–1945 by Richard Bert Carter, Jr., former Branch President." Unpublished manuscript. n.d.

Chandler, Bob, interview by Clayton Christensen. April 25, 1999. Medford, MA: The Clayton M. Christensen collection of Boston Latter-day Saint Oral Histories, MSS 7770, L. Tom Perry Special Collections, Harold B. Lee Library, Brigham Young University, Provo, UT.

Chandler, Norma, interview by Margaret Lazenby. April 19, 1998. Medford, MA.

Chopelas, Tim, interview by Ken Hafen. April 16, 1998. Melrose, MA: The Clayton M. Christensen collection of Boston Latter-day Saint Oral Histories, MSS 7770, L. Tom Perry Special Collections, Harold B. Lee Library, Brigham Young University, Provo, UT.

Christensen, Clayton M. "A Brief History of the Church in New England." Unpublished manuscript. 2000.

———. "An Unheralded Hero." The Clayton M. Christensen collection of Boston Latter-day Saint Oral Histories, MSS 7770, L. Tom Perry Special Collections, Harold B. Lee Library, Brigham Young Universitiy, Provo, UT, n.d.

———. "Jaime's Story." Unpublished manuscript. The Clayton M. Christensen collection of Boston Latter-day Saint Oral Histories, MSS 7770, L. Tom Perry Special Collections, Harold B. Lee Library, Brigham Young University, Provo, UT, n.d.

———. Letter to author. September 27, 2004.

———. "Recollections." Unpublished manuscript. The Clayton M. Christensen collection of Boston Latter-day Saint Oral Histories, MSS 7770, L. Tom Perry Special Collections, Harold B. Lee Library, Brigham Young University, Provo, UT, n.d.

Christensen, Elder Clayton M. and Christine Quinn. "Seven Lessons on Sharing the Gospel." *Ensign*, February 2005, 38.

Clark, Kim. Email to author. December 6, 2010.

Clark, Kim and Sue, interview by Elizabeth Young. January 26, 2003. Belmont, MA.

Clayton, Charles, interview by Leon Elliott. April 14, 1999. Natick, MA: The Clayton M. Christensen collection of Boston Latter-day Saint Oral Histories, MSS 7770, L. Tom Perry Special Collections, Harold B. Lee Library, Brigham Young University, Provo, UT.

Cole, Caroline Louise. "Steeple Is at Center of Legal Battle." *The Boston Globe*, August 27, 2000.

Conference Report. October 1966. 85–88.

Cooprider, Jay and Elizabeth, interview by Elizabeth Young. December 7, 2002. Acton, MA: The Clayton M. Christensen collection of Boston Latter-day Saint Oral Histories, MSS 7770, L. Tom Perry Special Collections, Harold B. Lee Library, Brigham Young University, Provo, UT.

Coppins, David and Carol, interview by Clayton Christensen. July 27, 2002. Boston, MA.

Cornwall, Carter, interview by Mark Spencer. April 14, 1999. Belmont, MA: The Clayton M. Christensen collection of Boston Latter-day Saint Oral Histories, MSS 7770, L. Tom Perry Special Collections, Harold B. Lee Library, Brigham Young University, Provo, UT.

Cortelyou, Bill, interview by Nicole Stringham. 1998. MA: The Clayton M. Christensen collection of Boston Latter-day Saint Oral Histories, MSS 7770, L. Tom Perry Special Collections, Harold B. Lee Library, Brigham Young University, Provo, UT.

Cowan, Richard O. "Yankee Saints: The Church in New England During the Twentieth Century." *Regional Studies in Latter-day Saint Church History: New England*, edited by Donald Q. Cannon, 101-118. Provo, UT: Brigham Young University, Department of Church History and Doctrine, 1988.

Cowley, Matthias F., ed. *Wilford Woodruff: History of His Life and Labors as Recorded in His Daily Journals.* Salt Lake City, UT: Deseret News, 1909.

Cranney, Naomi, interview by John Wright. 1998. Belmont, MA: The Clayton M. Christensen collection of Boston Latter-day Saint Oral Histories, MSS 7770, L. Tom Perry Special Collections, Harold B. Lee Library, Brigham Young University, Provo, UT.

Cranney, Naomi Broadhead and John William, interview by Matthew K. Heiss. 1999. *Naomi Broadhead and John William Cranney Oral History*, The James Moyle Oral History Program, Archives Division, Historical Department of The Church of Jesus Christ of Latter-day Saints, Salt Lake City, UT.

Crittenden, Cathy, interview by Karl H. Haglund. February 21, 2000. Belmont, MA: The Clayton M. Christensen collection of Boston Latter-day Saint Oral Histories, MSS 7770, L. Tom Perry Special Collections, Harold B. Lee Library, Brigham Young University, Provo, UT.

Crittenden, Gary, interview by Clayton Christensen. June 30, 2002. New Canaan, CT: The Clayton M. Christensen collection of Boston Latter-day Saint Oral Histories, MSS 7770, L. Tom Perry Special Collections, Harold B. Lee Library, Brigham Young University, Provo, UT.

Cutler, Ken and Helen, interview by Clayton and Christine Christensen. May 1, 1999. Belmont, MA: The Clayton M. Christensen collection of Boston Latter-day Saint Oral Histories, MSS 7770, L. Tom Perry Special Collections, Harold B. Lee Library, Brigham Young University, Provo, UT.

Dahl, Larry E. "Vermont." *Sacred Places: New England and Eastern Canada*, edited by LaMar C. Barratt, 87–132. Salt Lake City, UT: Bookcraft, 1999.

"Dedicatory Services for the Director's Residence and Bureau of Information at the Joseph Smith Birthplace Memorial." Boston, MA: University Press of Cambridge, 1961.

Dew, Sheri L. *Gordon B. Hinckley—Go Forward with Faith.* Salt Lake City, UT: Deseret Book, 1996.

Dredge, Nancy, interview by Karen Haglund. May 29, 1998. Arlington, MA: The Clayton M. Christensen collection of Boston Latter-day Saint Oral Histories, MSS 7770, L. Tom Perry Special Collections, Harold B. Lee Library, Brigham Young University, Provo, UT.

Dunn, Loren C., interview by Robert Fletcher. July 26, 1999. Salt Lake City, UT: The Clayton M. Christensen collection of Boston Latter-day Saint Oral Histories, MSS 7770, L. Tom Perry Special Collections, Harold B. Lee Library, Brigham Young University, Provo, UT.

———. "Testimony." *Ensign*, November 2000, 13–14.

———. "We Are Called of God." *Ensign*, July 1972, 43–44.

Durham, Cole. Email to Clayton Christensen. 2006.

Dushku, Judy, interview by George McPhee. August 13, 1997. Watertown,

MA: The Clayton M. Christensen collection of Boston Latter-day Saint Oral Histories, MSS 7770, L. Tom Perry Special Collections, Harold B. Lee Library, Brigham Young University, Provo, UT.

———. interview by George McPhee. September 11, 1997. Watertown, MA: The Clayton M. Christensen collection of Boston Latter-day Saint Oral Histories, MSS 7770, L. Tom Perry Special Collections, Harold B. Lee Library, Brigham Young University, Provo, UT.

Eagar, Tom and Pam, interview by Clayton Christensen. November 1998. Belmont, MA: The Clayton M. Christensen collection of Boston Latter-day Saint Oral Histories, MSS 7770, L. Tom Perry Special Collections, Harold B. Lee Library, Brigham Young University, Provo, UT.

Earnshaw, Lois and William, interview by Clayton Christensen. October 10, 2001. Arlington, MA: The Clayton M. Christensen collection of Boston Latter-day Saint Oral Histories, MSS 7770, L. Tom Perry Special Collections, Harold B. Lee Library, Brigham Young University, Provo, UT.

Eddington, Donald K. "Missed Opportunities." *A Time Such As This: Reflections on Life, Success, and the Gospel.* Essays collected for the Ivy League LDSSA Conference, Cambridge, MA, October 2005.

Einreinhofer, Roy and Jo-Ann, interview by Leon Elliott. May 2, 1999. Weston, MA: The Clayton M. Christensen collection of Boston Latter-day Saint Oral Histories, MSS 7770, L. Tom Perry Special Collections, Harold B. Lee Library, Brigham Young University, Provo, UT.

Elliott, Leon and Marti, interview by Clayton Christensen. November 22, 1998. Weston, MA: The Clayton M. Christensen collection of Boston Latter-day Saint Oral Histories, MSS 7770, L. Tom Perry Special Collections, Harold B. Lee Library, Brigham Young University, Provo, UT.

Ence, Bill and Lois, interview by Clayton Christensen. May 16, 1999. Weston, MA: The Clayton M. Christensen collection of Boston Latter-day Saint Oral Histories, MSS 7770, L. Tom Perry Special Collections, Harold B. Lee Library, Brigham Young University, Provo, UT.

Erickson, Linda. "A Guest at the Boston Temple Open House." n.d.

———. Email to author. February 23, 2012.

Evans, Steven, interview by Melvin Stanford. March 8, 1998.

Eyring, Henry B., interview by Karl H. Haglund. August 24, 1999. Salt Lake City, UT.

Finlayson, Mary and Norris, interview by Clayton Christensen. June 2, 1999. Palo Alto, CA: The Clayton M. Christensen collection of Boston Latter-day Saint Oral Histories, MSS 7770, L. Tom Perry Special Collections, Harold B. Lee Library, Brigham Young University, Provo, UT.

Fish, James Merlin, interview by James E. Curtis. September 15, 1999. Waltham, MA: The Clayton M. Christensen collection of Boston Latter-day Saint Oral Histories, MSS 7770, L. Tom Perry Special Collections, Harold B. Lee Library, Brigham Young University, Provo, UT.

Flake, Lawrence R. and Elaine M. "Wilbur W. Cox, First President of the Boston Massachussetts Stake." In *Regional Studies in Latter-day Saint Church History: The New England States*, edited by Arnold K. Garr, Donald Q. Cannon, and Bruce A. Van Orden. Provo, UT: Religious Studies Center, 2004.

Fletcher, Robert Chipman. Unpublished manuscript. January 19, 1998. The Clayton M. Christensen collection of Boston Latter-day Saint Oral Histories, MSS 7770, L. Tom Perry Special Collections, Harold B. Lee Library, Brigham Young University, Provo, UT.

Fletcher, Rosemary, interview by Marti Elliott. February 21, 1999. Belmont, MA: The Clayton M. Christensen collection of Boston Latter-day Saint Oral Histories, MSS 7770, L. Tom Perry Special Collections, Harold B. Lee Library, Brigham Young University, Provo, UT.

Forrest, Hugh A., Alice B. Ward and Muriel Grace Forrest, interview by Clayton Christensen. May 25, 1997. Wilmington, MA: The Clayton M. Christensen collection of Boston Latter-day Saint Oral Histories, MSS 7770, L. Tom Perry Special Collections, Harold B. Lee Library, Brigham Young University, Provo, UT.

Foster, Camille, interview by Clayton Christensen. September 26, 1999. Marlboro, MA: The Clayton M. Christensen collection of Boston Latter-day Saint Oral Histories, MSS 7770, L. Tom Perry Special Collections, Harold B. Lee Library, Brigham Young University, Provo, UT.

Foster, Dave, interview by Clayton Christensen. April 30, 1999. Marlborogh, MA: The Clayton M. Christensen collection of Boston Latter-day Saint Oral Histories, MSS 7770, L. Tom Perry Special Collections, Harold B. Lee Library, Brigham Young University, Provo, UT.

Fresh, William A., interview by Clayton Christensen. April 26, 1999. St. George, UT: The Clayton M. Christensen collection of Boston Latter-day Saint Oral Histories, MSS 7770, L. Tom Perry Special Collections, Harold B. Lee Library, Brigham Young University, Provo, UT.

Garbutt, Ralph and Roberta, interview by Clayton Christensen. December 13, 1998. Nashua, NH: The Clayton M. Christensen collection of Boston Latter-day Saint Oral Histories, MSS 7770, L. Tom Perry Special Collections, Harold B. Lee Library, Brigham Young University, Provo, UT.

Gates, Susa Young. "Memorial Mount Dedication." *Improvement Era*, February 1906, 308–19.

Gaz, Randy and Jeanne, interview by Mark Spencer. May 23, 1999. Belmont, MA: The Clayton M. Christensen collection of Boston Latter-day Saint Oral Histories, MSS 7770, L. Tom Perry Special Collections, Harold B. Lee Library, Brigham Young University, Provo, UT.

Goldberg, Hannah, interview by Robert C. Fletcher. December 16, 1998. Watertown, MA: The Clayton M. Christensen collection of Boston Latter-day Saint Oral Histories, MSS 7770, L. Tom Perry Special Collections, Harold B. Lee Library, Brigham Young University, Provo, UT.

Goodliffe, Bryan. Books and Basketball newsletter, May 2004: 2.

"The Gospel Defined." *Teachings of the Presidents of the Church: Brigham Young*, 15–20. Salt Lake City: The Church of Jesus Christ of Latter-day Saints, 1997.

Hafen, LeRoy R., and Ann W. Hafen. *Handcarts to Zion: The Story of a Unique Western Migration, 1856–1860*. Lincoln, NE: University of Nebraska Press, 1992.

Haglund, Karl, interview by Chris Kimball. May 25, 1997. Belmont, MA: The Clayton M. Christensen collection of Boston Latter-day Saint Oral

Histories, MSS 7770, L. Tom Perry Special Collections, Harold B. Lee Library, Brigham Young University, Provo, UT.

Hales, Robert D., interview by Robert C. Fletcher. February 7, 2000. Salt Lake City, UT: The Clayton M. Christensen collection of Boston Latter-day Saint Oral Histories, MSS 7770, L. Tom Perry Special Collections, Harold B. Lee Library, Brigham Young University, Provo, UT.

Hall, R. Stanley. "The Funeral Service for Elizabeth Skolfield Hinckley." January 1979.

Hangen, Don and Tona, interview by Elizabeth Young. January 26, 2003. Stow, MA: The Clayton M. Christensen collection of Boston Latter-day Saint Oral Histories, MSS 7770, L. Tom Perry Special Collections, Harold B. Lee Library, Brigham Young University, Provo, UT.

Harper, Louise, interview by Clayton Christensen. November 29, 1998. Lynnfield, MA: The Clayton M. Christensen collection of Boston Latter-day Saint Oral Histories, MSS 7770, L. Tom Perry Special Collections, Harold B. Lee Library, Brigham Young University, Provo, UT.

Hart, Katie. Books and Basketball newsletter, May 2004: 1.

Hartiala-Sloan, Mimmu, interview by Karen Haglund. March 19, 2000. Harvard, MA: The Clayton M. Christensen collection of Boston Latter-day Saint Oral Histories, MSS 7770, L. Tom Perry Special Collections, Harold B. Lee Library, Brigham Young University, Provo, UT.

Hartley, John, interview by Robert C. Fletcher. May 8, 1997. Waltham, MA: The Clayton M. Christensen collection of Boston Latter-day Saint Oral Histories, MSS 7770, L. Tom Perry Special Collections, Harold B. Lee Library, Brigham Young University, Provo, UT.

"The Havens of Massachusetts." n.d. http://freepages.genealogy.rootsweb. ancestry.com/~socrateselder/Westover/CHapter%2003%Havens%20 of%20Massachussetts%20and%20Notes.pdf (accessed November 6, 2011).

Herlin, Mel and Eugenia, interview by Karl Haglund. March 10, 2000. Laguna Nigel, CA: The Clayton M. Christensen collection of Boston Latter-day Saint Oral Histories, MSS 7770, L. Tom Perry Special

Collections, Harold B. Lee Library, Brigham Young University, Provo, UT.

Hiers, Maurice and Charlene, interview by Jenny Shafer. May 14, 2003. Northborough, MA: The Clayton M. Christensen collection of Boston Latter-day Saint Oral Histories, MSS 7770, L. Tom Perry Special Collections, Harold B. Lee Library, Brigham Young University, Provo, UT.

Hiller, Larry A. "The Brotherhood-Sisterhood Thing." *New Era*, June 1992, 20–25.

Himes, Alexander Campbell with prefatory remarks by Joshua V. "An analysis of the Book of Mormon with an examination of its internal and external evidences, and a refutation of its pretenses to divine authority." August 14, 1832. htttp://www.saintsalive.com/media-library/online-books/the-mormon-church-an-1832-essay (accessed November 6, 2011).

Hinckley, Gordon B. "Inspirational Thoughts." *Ensign*, October 2003, 3–5.

———. "New Temples to Provide 'Crowning Blessings' of the Gospel." *Ensign*, May 1998, 87–88.

———. "Our Mission of Saving." *Ensign*, November 1991, 52–59.

———. "Some Thoughts on Temples, Retention of Converts, and Missionary Service." *Ensign*, 1997, 49–52.

———. "Every Convert is Precious." *Liahona*, February 1999, 9–13.

———. *Teachings of Gordon B. Hinckley.* Salt Lake City, UT: Deseret Book, 1997.

"History of Brigham Young." *The Latter-day Saints' Millennial Star.* June 4, 1864, 359.

"History of Brigham Young." *The Latter-day Saints' Millennial Star.* May 28, 1864, 342–44.

"History of Thomas Baldwin Marsh." *The Latter-day Saints' Millennial Star.* June 11, 1864, 375–76.

Hoffmire, John and Shelley, interview by Clayton Christensen. July 30, 1998. Lexington, MA.

Holbrook, Jay and DeLene, interview by Clayton Christensen. May 16, 1999. Oxford, MA: The Clayton M. Christensen collection of Boston Latter-day Saint Oral Histories, MSS 7770, L. Tom Perry Special Collections, Harold B. Lee Library, Brigham Young University, Provo, UT.

Holton, Fred and Penny, interview by Robert C. Fletcher. January 12, 1999. Newton, MA: The Clayton M. Christensen collection of Boston Latter-day Saint Oral Histories, MSS 7770, L. Tom Perry Special Collections, Harold B. Lee Library, Brigham Young University, Provo, UT.

Holzapfel, Richard Neitzel, and T. Jeffrey Cottle. *Old Mormon Palmyra: Historic Photographs and Guide.* Santa Ana, CA: Fieldbrook Productions, 1991.

Hopkin, Kerry and Marianne, interview by Elizabeth Young. November 8, 2002. Needham, MA: The Clayton M. Christensen collection of Boston Latter-day Saint Oral Histories, MSS 7770, L. Tom Perry Special Collections, Harold B. Lee Library, Brigham Young University, Provo, UT.

Horne, Bonnie, interview by Clayton Christensen. July 4, 1999. Watertown, MA.

Hulbert, Joanne. *Holliston: A Good Town.* Holliston, MA: Joanne Hulbert, 2000.

Hutchins, Ken and Priscilla, interview by Brian Palmer. May 25, 1999. Northborough, MA: The Clayton M. Christensen collection of Boston Latter-day Saint Oral Histories, MSS 7770, L. Tom Perry Special Collections, Harold B. Lee Library, Brigham Young University, Provo, UT.

"Information Furnished by Mrs. Roy Bullen of Salt Lake City, Utah." Unpublished timeline covering 1845–1905. n.d.

Jacobsen, Isabelle. "The Awakening." The Oxford Ward Messenger, March 1989.

———. "The Awakening." The Oxford Ward Messenger, April 1989.

Jardine, Jim. Email to Clayton Christensen. May 10, 2006.

Jensen, Andrew. *Latter-day Saint Biographical Encyclopedia 1901–36.* Reprint. 4 vols. Salt Lake City: Western Epics, 1971.

Johnson, Elbert and Elaine, interview by Clayton Christensen. November 8, 2003. Glendale, AZ: The Clayton M. Christensen collection of Boston Latter-day Saint Oral Histories, MSS 7770, L. Tom Perry Special Collections, Harold B. Lee Library, Brigham Young University, Provo, UT.

Johnson, Mark, interview by Elizabeth Young. November 8, 2002. Belmont, MA: The Clayton M. Christensen collection of Boston Latter-day Saint Oral Histories, MSS 7770, L. Tom Perry Special Collections, Harold B. Lee Library, Brigham Young University, Provo, UT.

Johnson, Oscar E. "History of the Providence, R.I. Branch from February 1937 to February 28, 1943." Unpublished manuscript. n.d.

Journal History of the Church of Jesus Christ of Latter-day Saints. Church History Library, Salt Lake City, UT.

Kelleher, Ruth Ray, interview by Marti Elliott. April 2, 1999. Weston, MA: The Clayton M. Christensen collection of Boston Latter-day Saint Oral Histories, MSS 7770, L. Tom Perry Special Collections, Harold B. Lee Library, Brigham Young University, Provo, UT.

Kimball, Chris, interview by Karl H. Haglund. July 3, 1999. Evanston, IL: The Clayton M. Christensen collection of Boston Latter-day Saint Oral Histories, MSS 7770, L. Tom Perry Special Collections, Harold B. Lee Library, Brigham Young University, Provo, UT.

Kimball, Linda Hoffman, interview by Karen Haglund. July 3, 1999. Evanston, IL: The Clayton M. Christensen collection of Boston Latter-day Saint Oral Histories, MSS 7770, L. Tom Perry Special Collections, Harold B. Lee Library, Brigham Young University, Provo, UT.

Kimball, Tony, interview by Karl H. Haglund. July 5, 1998. Belmont, MA: The Clayton M. Christensen collection of Boston Latter-day Saint Oral Histories, MSS 7770, L. Tom Perry Special Collections, Harold B. Lee Library, Brigham Young University, Provo, UT.

———. Interview by Karl H. Haglund. July 23, 2000. Belmont, MA: The Clayton M. Christensen collection of Boston Latter-day Saint Oral Histories, MSS 7770, L. Tom Perry Special Collections, Harold B. Lee Library, Brigham Young University, Provo, UT.

Kleekamp, Kathy. "Never Too Young." *New Era*, June 1989, 29–35.

Knecht, William, interview by Clayton Christensen. July 8, 1999. Sandy, UT: The Clayton M. Christensen collection of Boston Latter-day Saint Oral Histories, MSS 7770, L. Tom Perry Special Collections, Harold B. Lee Library, Brigham Young University, Provo, UT.

Knighton, Keith, interview by Mark Spencer. June 21, 1999. Needham, MA.

Lambert, Brent, interview by Robert Fletcher. October 3, 1999. Hingham, MA: The Clayton M. Christensen collection of Boston Latter-day Saint Oral Histories, MSS 7770, L. Tom Perry Special Collections, Harold B. Lee Library, Brigham Young University, Provo, UT.

LaPierre, Dottie, interview by Margaret Lazenby. June 10, 1998. Woburn, MA: The Clayton M. Christensen collection of Boston Latter-day Saint Oral Histories, MSS 7770, L. Tom Perry Special Collections, Harold B. Lee Library, Brigham Young University, Provo, UT.

LaPierre, Lee, interview by Leon Elliott. February 2, 1999. Woburn, MA: The Clayton M. Christensen collection of Boston Latter-day Saint Oral Histories, MSS 7770, L. Tom Perry Special Collections, Harold B. Lee Library, Brigham Young University, Provo, UT.

Larson, Andrew Karl. *Erastus Snow: The Life of a Missionary and Pioneer for the Early Mormon Church.* Salt Lake City, UT: The University of Utah Press, 1971.

Lavin, Dick and Marsha, interview by Clayton Christensen. November 8, 1998. Waltham, MA: The Clayton M. Christensen collection of Boston Latter-day Saint Oral Histories, MSS 7770, L. Tom Perry Special Collections, Harold B. Lee Library, Brigham Young University, Provo, UT.

"Leading in the Lord's Way." *Teachings of Presidents of the Church: Joseph Smith*, 281–91. Salt Lake City, UT: The Church of Jesus Christ of Latter-day Saints, 2007.

Lindsay, Jay. "Mormon Church Small But Expanding in Liberal Massachusetts." *The Associated Press*, February 12, 2006.

Lindsey, Justin, interview by Clayton Christensen. October 13, 2005. Boston, MA: The Clayton M. Christensen collection of Boston Latter-day Saint Oral Histories, MSS 7770, L. Tom Perry Special Collections, Harold B. Lee Library, Brigham Young University, Provo, UT.

Low, Helen and Ward, interview by Clayton Christensen. June 1, 1999. Palo Alto, CA: The Clayton M. Christensen collection of Boston Latter-day Saint Oral Histories, MSS 7770, L. Tom Perry Special Collections, Harold B. Lee Library, Brigham Young University, Provo, UT.

Ludlow, Victor and Virginia Ann, interview by Clayton and Christine Christensen. April 5, 2005. Midway, UT: The Clayton M. Christensen collection of Boston Latter-day Saint Oral Histories, MSS 7770, L. Tom Perry Special Collections, Harold B. Lee Library, Brigham Young University, Provo, UT.

Ludwig, Kristy, interview by JaNeece Watkins. June 27, 2005. Boston, MA: The Clayton M. Christensen collection of Boston Latter-day Saint Oral Histories, MSS 7770, L. Tom Perry Special Collections, Harold B. Lee Library, Brigham Young University, Provo, UT.

———. Discussion with author. December 2006.

———. Email to author. March 10, 2011.

Lyon, James and Dorothy, interview by Clayton Christensen. May 10, 1998. Provo, UT: The Clayton M. Christensen collection of Boston Latter-day Saint Oral Histories, MSS 7770, L. Tom Perry Special Collections, Harold B. Lee Library, Brigham Young University, Provo, UT.

MacKinnon, Jane Anne. "Saints in Halifax." *Ensign*, April 1991: 78–79.

Madsen, Ann, interview by Karl H. Haglund. August 23, 1999. Provo, UT.

Madsen, Carol Cornwall. "Emmeline B. Wells: Romantic Rebel." In *Supporting Saints: Life Stories of Nineteenth-Century Mormons*, edited by Donald Q. Cannon and David J. Whittaker, 305–41. Provo, UT: Brigham Young University, Religious Studies Center, 1985.

Madsen, Truman G., interview by Karl H. Haglund. April 23, 1999. Provo, UT.

———. "The Funeral Service for Elizabeth Skolfield Hinckley." January 1979.

Maitland, Bill and Jo, interview by Harriet and Warren Rapson. November 16, 1999. Arlington, MA: The Clayton M. Christensen collection of Boston Latter-day Saint Oral Histories, MSS 7770, L. Tom Perry

Special Collections, Harold B. Lee Library, Brigham Young University, Provo, UT.

Manderino, Gus and Betty, interview by Leon and Marti Elliott. April 11, 1999. Arlington, MA: The Clayton M. Christensen collection of Boston Latter-day Saint Oral Histories, MSS 7770, L. Tom Perry Special Collections, Harold B. Lee Library, Brigham Young University, Provo, UT.

May, Dean. "Boston's Mormon Landmark: Abijah Tewkesbury's Office." *Ensign*, November 1973, 17–19.

McKinnon, Jan. Letter to Christine Christensen. February 4, 1997.

McKinnon, Paul and Jan, interview by Clayton Christensen. May 2, 1998. Provo, UT: The Clayton M. Christensen collection of Boston Latter-day Saint Oral Histories, MSS 7770, L. Tom Perry Special Collections, Harold B. Lee Library, Brigham Young University, Provo, UT.

McLaughlin, George and Karline, interview by Clayton Christensen. December 4, 2002. Gardiner, ME: The Clayton M. Christensen collection of Boston Latter-day Saint Oral Histories, MSS 7770, L. Tom Perry Special Collections, Harold B. Lee Library, Brigham Young University, Provo, UT.

McPhee, George and Marci, interview by Clayton Christensen. January 23, 2000. Natick, MA: The Clayton M. Christensen collection of Boston Latter-day Saint Oral Histories, MSS 7770, L. Tom Perry Special Collections, Harold B. Lee Library, Brigham Young University, Provo, UT.

Monson, Thomas S. "The Holy Temple—A Beacon to the World." *Ensign*, May 2011, 90–93.

Moorehead, Lisa. "About Books and Basketball." Books and Basketball newsletter. May 2004.

Morris, Michael R. "Help and Hope in Washington, D.C." *Ensign*, April 2008, 28–32.

Mulder, William, interview by Karl H. Haglund. June 20, 1999. Salt Lake City, UT: The Clayton M. Christensen collection of Boston Latter-day Saint Oral Histories, MSS 7770, L. Tom Perry Special Collections, Harold B. Lee Library, Brigham Young University, Provo, UT.

Munns, April, interview by Clayton Christensen. January 23, 1998.
Orlando, FL.

Murdock, Bill and Addis, interview by Leon Elliott. April 25, 1999. UT.

*Naomi Remembers: One Hundred Years of Living.* Belmont, MA: The
Cranney Family, 2007.

Neal, Jim and Jo Anne, interview by Leon and Marti Elliott. January 23,
1999. Weston, MA: The Clayton M. Christensen collection of Boston
Latter-day Saint Oral Histories, MSS 7770, L. Tom Perry Special
Collections, Harold B. Lee Library, Brigham Young University, Provo,
UT.

Nelson, Russell Marion. *From Heart to Heart.* Quality Press, Inc., 1979.

"New England Mission and Cambridge Branch Chapel Building—Church
of Jesus Christ of Latter-Day Saints: Dedication September 23, 1956."
Cambridge Branch, The Church of Jesus Christ of Latter-day Saints,
1956.

Nielsen, Dorothy and Talmage, interview by Karl H. Haglund. June 21,
1999. Salt Lake City, UT: The Clayton M. Christensen collection
of Boston Latter-day Saint Oral Histories, MSS 7770, L. Tom Perry
Special Collections, Harold B. Lee Library, Brigham Young University,
Provo, UT.

Oaks, Dallin H. and Lance B. Wickman. 2006. http://newsroom.lds.org/
official-statement/same-gender-attraction (accessed December 4, 2011).

Oparowski, Ted and Pat, interview by JaNeece Thacker. November 9, 1999.
South Royalton, VT: The Clayton M. Christensen collection of Boston
Latter-day Saint Oral Histories, MSS 7770, L. Tom Perry Special
Collections, Harold B. Lee Library, Brigham Young University, Provo,
UT.

Orton, Doug, interview by Clayton Christensen. November 29, 1998.
Boston, MA: The Clayton M. Christensen collection of Boston Latter-
day Saint Oral Histories, MSS 7770, L. Tom Perry Special Collections,
Harold B. Lee Library, Brigham Young University, Provo, UT.

Paredes, Mauricio, interview by Nicole Stringham. December 9, 1998.
Brighton, MA: The Clayton M. Christensen collection of Boston Latter-
day Saint Oral Histories, MSS 7770, L. Tom Perry Special Collections,
Harold B. Lee Library, Brigham Young University, Provo, UT.

Parkin, Bonnie D., Kristen Oaks, Susan Bednar, and Jean S. Groberg. "Testimonies of the Restoration, panel discussion at BYU Women's Conference, Brigham Young University, Provo, UT." April 29, 2005. http://ce.byu.edu/cw/womensconference/archive/2005/pdf/2005-GApanel.pdf.

Parkinson, Blaine and Lenore and Martha Barney, interview by Margaret Lazenby. n.d. Ogden, UT.

Parrish, Alan and Marcia, interview by Clayton Christensen. May 10, 1998. Provo, UT: The Clayton M. Christensen collection of Boston Latter-day Saint Oral Histories, MSS 7770, L. Tom Perry Special Collections, Harold B. Lee Library, Brigham Young University, Provo, UT.

Parrish, Alan K. "Harvard and the Gospel, an Informal History." In *Regional Studies in Latter-day Saint Church History: New England*, edited by Donald Q. Cannon. Provo, UT: Brigham Young University, Department of Church History and Doctrine, 1988.

Perry, L. Tom, interview by Karl H. Haglund. August 24, 1999. Salt Lake City, UT: The Clayton M. Christensen collection of Boston Latter-day Saint Oral Histories, MSS 7770, L. Tom Perry Special Collections, Harold B. Lee Library, Brigham Young University, Provo, UT.

Perry, L. Tom, Tom Perry, and Linda Perry Nelson, interview by Clayton Christensen. July 7, 2004. Weston, MA: The Clayton M. Christensen collection of Boston Latter-day Saint Oral Histories, MSS 7770, L. Tom Perry Special Collections, Harold B. Lee Library, Brigham Young University, Provo, UT.

Peterson, Chase, interview by Karl H. Haglund. August 30, 1998. Park City, UT.

Peterson, Grethe, interview by Karen Haglund. August 30, 1998. Park City, UT.

Peterson, Janet. "Belmont's Blessing in Disguise." *Ensign*, April 1987, 26–30.

———. "Taxi Talk." *Ensign*, January 1998, 68–69.

Pollock, Rosemary. "Steeple Placement Ends Legal Challenges to Boston Temple." *Mormon News.* October 5, 2001. http://www.mormonnews.com/011005/N1BostonTemple01.shtml.

Porter, Bruce, interview by Clayton Christensen. February 17, 1999. Boston, MA: The Clayton M. Christensen collection of Boston Latter-day Saint Oral Histories, MSS 7770, L. Tom Perry Special Collections, Harold B. Lee Library, Brigham Young University, Provo, UT.

———. "Building the Kingdom." *Ensign*, May 2001, 80–81.

Potvin, Phil and Jackie, interview by Clayton Christensen. May 1, 1999. Lynnfield, MA: The Clayton M. Christensen collection of Boston Latter-day Saint Oral Histories, MSS 7770, L. Tom Perry Special Collections, Harold B. Lee Library, Brigham Young University, Provo, UT.

Quintera, Carmen Francisco, interview by Clayton Christensen. May 16, 2007. San Diego, CA.

Randall, Earl and Mary, interview by Clayton Christensen. July 11, 1999. Oxford, MA: The Clayton M. Christensen collection of Boston Latter-day Saint Oral Histories, MSS 7770, L. Tom Perry Special Collections, Harold B. Lee Library, Brigham Young University, Provo, UT.

Rigby, Darrell, interview by Bret Wuderli. May 25, 1997. Belmont, MA.

Ritchie, Elizabeth K. "Aurelia S. Rogers." *Sister Saints*, edited by Vicky Burgess-Olson, 225–40. Provo, UT: Brigham Young University Press, 1978.

Rivera, Carmen, interview by John Hoffmire. September 7, 1999. Lynn, MA.

Rockwood, Jolene E. "Memories from our Boston Years 1972–1977." Unpublished manuscript. May 2006.

Rolapp, Henry H. "The Eastern States Mission." *Improvement Era*, May 1928, 582–84.

Rollins, James and Norma, interview by Clayton Christensen. October 22, 1998. Lincoln, MA: The Clayton M. Christensen collection of Boston Latter-day Saint Oral Histories, MSS 7770, L. Tom Perry Special Collections, Harold B. Lee Library, Brigham Young University, Provo, UT.

Romish, Ann Hinckley, interview by Clayton Christensen. April 10, 1999. Seattle, WA: The Clayton M. Christensen collection of Boston Latter-day Saint Oral Histories, MSS 7770, L. Tom Perry Special Collections,

Harold B. Lee Library, Brigham Young University, Provo, UT

———. Discussion with author. November 15, 2011.

———. Letter to Clayton Christensen. April 28, 1999.

Romney, Mitt, interview by Clayton Christensen. February 7, 1999. Belmont, MA.

Rondina, Carole and Paul, interview by Leon and Marti Elliott. March 28, 1999. Hudson, MA: The Clayton M. Christensen collection of Boston Latter-day Saint Oral Histories, MSS 7770, L. Tom Perry Special Collections, Harold B. Lee Library, Brigham Young University, Provo, UT.

Salo, Ronald R. "The Funeral Service for Elizabeth Skolfield Hinckley." January 1979.

Schmidt, Kevin and Sue, interview by Elizabeth Young. January 12, 2003. Shrewsbury, MA: The Clayton M. Christensen collection of Boston Latter-day Saint Oral Histories, MSS 7770, L. Tom Perry Special Collections, Harold B. Lee Library, Brigham Young University, Provo, UT.

Schreck, Michael and Cari, interview by Clayton Christensen. May 2, 2002. Belmont, MA: The Clayton M. Christensen collection of Boston Latter-day Saint Oral Histories, MSS 7770, L. Tom Perry Special Collections, Harold B. Lee Library, Brigham Young University, Provo, UT.

Scotland, Robert H. "A History of the Boston Stake." n.d.

Simon, Germaine, interview by James E. Curtis. May 30, 1999. Boston, MA: The Clayton M. Christensen collection of Boston Latter-day Saint Oral Histories, MSS 7770, L. Tom Perry Special Collections, Harold B. Lee Library, Brigham Young University, Provo, UT.

Sloan, Jim, interview by Karl H. Haglund. March 16, 2000. Harvard, MA: The Clayton M. Christensen collection of Boston Latter-day Saint Oral Histories, MSS 7770, L. Tom Perry Special Collections, Harold B. Lee Library, Brigham Young University, Provo, UT.

Smith, Joseph. *Lectures on Faith*. Salt Lake City, UT: Deseret Book, 1985.

Smith, Joshua and Lillian, interview by James E. Curtis. June 13, 1999.

Boston, MA: The Clayton M. Christensen collection of Boston Latter-day Saint Oral Histories, MSS 7770, L. Tom Perry Special Collections, Harold B. Lee Library, Brigham Young University, Provo, UT.

Smith, Vance, interview by Clayton Christensen. September 19, 1999. Belmont, MA: The Clayton M. Christensen collection of Boston Latter-day Saint Oral Histories, MSS 7770, L. Tom Perry Special Collections, Harold B. Lee Library, Brigham Young University, Provo, UT.

Sorenson, Gregory, interview by Nicole Stringham. March 14, 1999. Lexington, MA: The Clayton M. Christensen collection of Boston Latter-day Saint Oral Histories, MSS 7770, L. Tom Perry Special Collections, Harold B. Lee Library, Brigham Young University, Provo, UT.

Stack, Peggy. "Mormon Milestone: 100th Temple Dedicated in Boston, but Rancor Remains." *The Salt Lake Tribune*, September 30, 2000.

Stahle, Shaun D. "Boston Temple Dedicated as 100th Edifice." *Church News*, October 7, 2000.

———. "Boston Temple to Become 100th Edifice." *Church News*, July 22, 2000.

———. "Court Upholds Boston Temple Zoning Case." *Church News*, January 13, 2001.

Thibault, Edna and Tom, interview by Clayton Christensen. October 3, 1999. Marlborough, MA: The Clayton M. Christensen collection of Boston Latter-day Saint Oral Histories, MSS 7770, L. Tom Perry Special Collections, Harold B. Lee Library, Brigham Young University, Provo, UT.

Tidd, Ellsworth, interview by Clayton Christensen. November 2006.

———. Email to Jeffrey Tidd. December 7, 2005.

———. "The Mormons Are Coming! The Mormons Are Coming!" Unpublished manuscript. n.d.

Ulrich, Gael, interview by Karl H. Haglund. July 25, 1999. Durham, NH: The Clayton M. Christensen collection of Boston Latter-day Saint Oral Histories, MSS 7770, L. Tom Perry Special Collections, Harold B. Lee Library, Brigham Young University, Provo, UT.

Ulrich, Laurel Thatcher. *A Beginner's Boston.* rev. Edited by Claudia L. Bushman. Cambridge Ward, 1973.

———. Interview by Karen Haglund. July 25, 1999. Durham, NH: The Clayton M. Christensen collection of Boston Latter-day Saint Oral Histories, MSS 7770, L. Tom Perry Special Collections, Harold B. Lee Library, Brigham Young University, Provo, UT.

Van Uitert, Bert and Luanne, interview by Robert C. Fletcher. July 31, 1997. Salt Lake City, UT: The Clayton M. Christensen collection of Boston Latter-day Saint Oral Histories, MSS 7770, L. Tom Perry Special Collections, Harold B. Lee Library, Brigham Young University, Provo, UT.

Watson, Elden Jay, ed. *The Orson Pratt Journals.* Salt Lake City, UT: Elden J. Watson, 1975.

*Weston Ward and Boston Stake Dedication Program.* October 6, 1968.

Wheeler, Ned, interview by George McPhee. October 27, 1999. Belmont, MA: The Clayton M. Christensen collection of Boston Latter-day Saint Oral Histories, MSS 7770, L. Tom Perry Special Collections, Harold B. Lee Library, Brigham Young University, Provo, UT.

Wheelwright, Steven. Email to Clayton Christensen. February 12, 2012.

Wheelwright, Steven and Margaret, interview by Clayton Christensen. November 14, 1998. Belmont, MA: The Clayton M. Christensen collection of Boston Latter-day Saint Oral Histories, MSS 7770, L. Tom Perry Special Collections, Harold B. Lee Library, Brigham Young University, Provo, UT.

Widtsoe, John A. *In a Sunlit Land.* Salt Lake City, UT: Deseret News Press, 1952.

———. "Temple Worship." *Utah Genealogical and Historical Magazine,* Volume 12, April 1921, 49.

Williams, Dee Dee, interview by Marti Elliott. January 29, 1999. Belmont, MA: The Clayton M. Christensen collection of Boston Latter-day Saint Oral Histories, MSS 7770, L. Tom Perry Special Collections, Harold B. Lee Library, Brigham Young University, Provo, UT.

Williams, Gordon, interview by Clayton Christensen. July 12, 1998. Belmont, MA: The Clayton M. Christensen collection of Boston

Latter-day Saint Oral Histories, MSS 7770, L. Tom Perry Special Collections, Harold B. Lee Library, Brigham Young University, Provo, UT.

Williams, Jonathan, interview by Mark Spencer. May 17, 1999. Ashland, MA: The Clayton M. Christensen collection of Boston Latter-day Saint Oral Histories, MSS 7770, L. Tom Perry Special Collections, Harold B. Lee Library, Brigham Young University, Provo, UT.

Wilson, Larry Y. "Tony Kimball: Guardian Angel of LDS Freshman at Harvard." April 2006.

Wood, Robert. Email to author. January 25, 2012.

Wood, Robert and Dixie, interview by Robert Fletcher. January 17, 1999. Belmont, MA: The Clayton M. Christensen collection of Boston Latter-day Saint Oral Histories, MSS 7770, L. Tom Perry Special Collections, Harold B. Lee Library, Brigham Young University, Provo, UT.

Woodruff, Wilford. "The Keys of the Kingdom." *The Latter-day Saints' Millennial Star*, September 2, 1889, 545–49.

Wright, John and Laraine, interview by Clayton Christensen. April 25, 1999. Belmont, MA: The Clayton M. Christensen collection of Boston Latter-day Saint Oral Histories, MSS 7770, L. Tom Perry Special Collections, Harold B. Lee Library, Brigham Young University, Provo, UT.

Wright, Laraine. Email to author. February 27, 2011.

Wyatt, Jamie. "Excited to Learn." Books and Basketball newsletter, May 2004: 4.

Young, Lawrence A. "Single Adults." *Encyclopedia of Mormonism*, ed. Daniel H. Ludlow, 1316–19. New York: Macmillan Publishing Company, 1992.

Young, S. Dilworth. Letter to Richard L. Bushman. March 31, 1976.

# INDEX

# G

Gaz
  Jeanne  189, 204
  Randy  84–86, 144, 146, 189,
    191, 206
Georgetown, Massachusetts.
    *See* Massachusetts,
    Georgetown
Goldberg, Hannah  114, 116, 126

# H

Haglund, Karl  214
Haitian  44, 148, 158, 172, 193,
    206
Hales, Robert D.  29, 82, 92, 196
Hangen
  Don  144
  Tona  99
Harper, Louise  155
Harris, Martin  117
Hartley, John  105
Harvard Business School  20–21,
    39, 237, 247–48
Harvard University  17, 42, 64,
    184, 207
Haven, John  9
Hiers, Charlene  234
Hinckley  142
  Elizabeth (Betty)  33–38, 40,
    44
  Gordon B.  1, 28, 68, 70, 109,
    124, 126–27, 143, 251–
    53, 255–56, 266, 270
  John  30, 33
Hingham, Massachusetts. *See*
    Massachusetts, Hingham

Hoffmire
  John  161
  Shelley  145
Holbrook
  DeLene  194
  Jay  194, 248
Holliston, Massachusetts.
    *See* Massachusetts,
    Holliston
Holton, Penny  139
home teaching/teacher  45, 46,
    94, 97–99, 101, 125, 132,
    155, 189, 198, 237
Hopkin
  Kerry  197, 265
  Marianne  234
  Megan  182
Hopkinton, Massachusetts.
    *See* Massachusetts,
    Hopkinton
Horne, Bonnie  92, 152
Hutchins, Kenneth (Ken)  45,
    69, 80–82, 86, 142, 145,
    202–3, 251–55, 270
Hyde, Orson  6, 7

# I

Illinois
  Nauvoo  6, 12, 15–16, 28

# J

Jacobson
  Isabelle  27
  John  27, 28
Jardine, Jim  208

# R

# S